# Why Do You Need this New Edition?

**If you're wondering why you should buy this new edition of *What Matters in America*, here are 5 good reasons!**

**1** Four new chapters present multiple perspectives on **social networking, immigration, climate change,** and the tensions (and accords) between **religion and science.** In addition, the most popular and frequently taught chapters from the first edition have been updated with new readings offering fresh voices.

**2** This new edition features a **cross-section of blogs** demonstrating the breadth and depth of information, and how people are sharing information and viewpoints online. Students are encouraged to "post" their own response to the blog discussion.

**3** The Introduction now includes **enhanced writing instruction** that models strategies for critical writing.

**4** *Words in Context* now includes **additional support for critical reading** by providing a paragraph number and a part-of-speech identifier for each word, to help reinforce how new vocabulary is used in context.

**5** And now—use *What Matters in America* alongside Pearson's unique MyCompLab and find a world of resources developed especially for you!

PEARSON
Longman

# What Matters in America

## Reading and Writing About Contemporary Culture

### Second Edition

*Gary Goshgarian*

NORTHEASTERN UNIVERSITY

with

*Kathryn Goodfellow*

NORTHEASTERN UNIVERSITY

**Longman**

New York   San Francisco   Boston

London   Toronto   Sydney   Tokyo   Singapore   Madrid

Mexico City   Munich   Paris   Cape Town   Hong Kong   Montreal

**Executive Editor:** Suzanne Phelps Chambers

**Senior Development Editor:** Meg Botteon

**Senior Marketing Manager:** Sandra McGuire

**Editorial Assistant:** Erica Schweitzer

**Production Manager:** Stacey Kulig

**Project Coordination, Text Design, and Electronic Page Makeup:** Pre-Press PMG

**Cover Design Manager:** John Callahan

**Cover Designer:** Maria Ilardi

**Cover Image:** Courtesy of Getty Images

**Photo Researcher:** Julie Tesser

**Senior Manufacturing Buyer:** Dennis J. Para

**Printer and Binder:** RR Donnelley and Sons

**Cover Printer:** R.R. Donnelley and Sons

For permission to use copyrighted material, grateful acknowledgment is made to the copyright holders on pp. 425–429, which are hereby made part of this copyright page.

**Library of Congress Cataloging-in-Publication Data**
Goshgarian, Gary.
  What matters in America : reading and writing about contemporary culture /
Gary Goshgarian with Kathryn Goodfellow. — 2nd ed.
      p. cm.
  Includes bibliographical references and index.
  ISBN 978-0-205-66922-6
  1.  Readers—Popular culture.  2.  English language—Rhetoric—Problems,
exercises, etc.  3.  Report writing—Problems, exercises, etc.  4.  Critical
thinking—Problems, exercises, etc.  5.  Popular culture—Problems,
exercises, etc.  I. Goodfellow, Kathryn.  II. Title.
  PE1127.P6G67 2010
  808'.0427--dc22

                                                    2008052904

2 3 4 5 6 7 8 9 10—DOC—12 11 10 09

**Longman**
is an imprint of

www.pearsonhighered.com

ISBN 13:  978-0-205-66922-
ISBN 10:      0-205-66922-

# Contents

## 4 Do the Media Promote a Culture of Fear? 142

### Extreme Reality: How Media Coverage Exaggerates Risks and Dangers 144
*John Stossel*

"If you watch television news regularly, you can't help but think that the world is a very scary place."

## 5 What Does Freedom of Speech Really Mean? 182

# 6   What's the Big Deal About Immigration?   222

## VISUAL CONNECTIONS

## VISUAL CONNECTIONS

# 8    Is Fast Food Responsible for a Crisis in Public Health?    306

Compare that with 1960, when only 45 percent of Americans fell into those categories and proportionally far fewer were obese."

*Richard Daynard*

"The more I learned about the food industry's operations—the massive marketing budgets; the deceptive health and low-fat claims; the rush to supersize—the more I became convinced that changing the industry's behavior is the key to stopping the obesity epidemic."

*Emily Wierenga*

*R. A. Ames*

"The truth is that it is a whole lot easier to get fat than to stay thin. And because of this, it is much more appealing to try and make yourself believe that cultural attitudes against obesity are the fault of advertisers, the fashion industry, society, you name it. The only one you don't want to blame is yourself."

*National Institutes of Health*

*Rahul K. Parikh*

"Dear Mr. Lucas and Mr. Spielberg: You tied 'Star Wars' to Pepsi and Frito-Lay, plastering Yoda and Obi-Wan over 2-liter bottles and Doritos bags . . . I wonder, would Lord Vader chug down a Pepsi before he wielded his light saber?"

*Paul King*

"In all truthfulness I think that the 'food police' have a very valid point: Most Americans, given several nutritional paths, will choose the tastiest road. But does our already litigious society need to clog the courts with nutrition lawsuits faster than our eating habits can harden our blood vessels? I don't think so."

*Rosie Mestel*

"Writing the dietary guidelines is honor, toil, aggravation and tedium—in unequal measure. The results are bland and seemingly obvious bits of advice that most Americans have never read."

# 9 Can Religion and Science Coexist? 350

# 10 Why Do We Work?   386

# Rhetorical Contents

## Persuasion and Argument: Appealing to Reason and Emotion

## Illustration: Explaining with Examples and Statistics

# Preface

Like its inspiration text, *The Contemporary Reader* (now in its ninth edition), *What Matters in America* is designed to stimulate critical thinking skills in introductory writing students through a variety of contemporary subjects connected to popular culture, media, and society.

The book provides a collection of well-written, thought-provoking, thematically organized readings that students can relate to—readings that stimulate classroom discussion, critical thinking, and writing. The text's study apparatus aims to elicit thoughtful response while providing students with the tools they need to approach each reading as informed, critical thinkers.

Preceding each reading is an author headnote and a short paragraph, *Connecting to the Topic*, that orients students to the subject matter. *Words in Context* provides students with the vocabulary support they may need to understand the material.

Directly following each reading are four areas of inquiry designed to help students think about the reading and the issue within a broader framework. *Considering the Issues* questions encourage students to think about issues raised by the readings in a thematic context. *Craft and Content* questions ask students to consider rhetorical issues connected to the reading itself. *Critical Thinking* and *Writing About the Issues* questions promote analytical approaches to the readings and support thoughtful writing projects.

Visuals are interspersed throughout the text, and many include *Visual Connections* exercises designed to help students think about the ways images, photographs, and cartoons present ideas and concepts visually. Another visual element of *What Matters in America* is the editorial cartoon on the title page of each unit followed by critical thinking questions designed to elicit thoughtful consideration of each image. Instructions on how to view editorial cartoons are included in the book's introductory material.

Each unit closes with a *Topical Considerations* section that encourages students to make broad thematic associations related to the unit's overarching subject matter. Included in this section are group projects, research topics, and web exercises.

# New to this Edition

- **Enhanced writing instruction.** In response to reviewer requests, the Introduction now discusses and models strategies for critical writing. The apparatus for each reading reflects the latest and most effective rhetorical theory and practice.
- **Additional support for critical reading.** *Words in Context* now includes a paragraph number and a part-of-speech identifier to help reinforce how new vocabulary is used in context
- *Blog Matters.* Current data suggests that there are more than one hundred million blogs online with hundreds more being added daily. Blogs are becoming increasingly influential as people use them to share ideas, convey information, and spread opinion. Many reputable journals such as *Scientific American*, the *New Republic*, and *Slate* magazine feature regular blogs run by journalists and topic experts. Blogs can link to other blogs, news articles and essays of interest, and government sites providing data. They can also simply serve as online diaries. *What Matters in America*, Second Edition, features a cross-section of blogs demonstrating the breadth and depth of information available and illustrating how people are sharing information and viewpoints online. *Blog Matters* presents the perspective of the "blogger" on the section's subject matter. Students are encouraged to "post" their own response to the blog discussion.
- **Timely new topics.** Four *new* chapters present multiple perspectives on social networking, immigration, climate change, and the tensions (and accords) between religion and science. In addition, the most popular and frequently taught chapters from the first edition have been updated with new readings offering fresh voices.

# Unit Topics

Most of the book's material comes from essays and articles written within the last five years, and more than half were written in the last two years. With more than 60 short essays and visuals from over 35 periodicals, journals, newspapers, and recently released books, the text's readings are organized into 10 thematic areas, framed as questions:

1. Is the Internet Changing Our Social Lives?
2. Does Personal Privacy Have Limits?
3. How Does Advertising Influence Us?
4. Do the Media Promote a Culture of Fear?
5. What Does Freedom of Speech Really Mean?
6. What's the Big Deal About Immigration?
7. Is Climate Change a Pressing Problem or Pumped-up Propaganda?
8. Is Fast Food Responsible for a Crisis in Public Health?
9. Can Religion and Science Coexist?
10. Why Do We Work?

These themes were chosen to reflect a wide spectrum of issues that affect all of us. Most importantly, they capture some of the conflicts and paradoxes that make our culture unique, for ours is a culture caught in conflicts. From fashion and advertising to television and privacy, we are a people that crave the modern, yet long for nostalgia. We are as much a society steeped in traditional values and identities as a culture that redefines itself in response to trends and new ideas.

# Variety of Readings

Expository communication comes in all shapes and models. This book includes newspaper stories, editorials, political cartoons, advertisements, academic essays, magazine articles, television interviews, Internet articles from "e-zines," student essays, humor columns, and much more. Students will read personal narratives, objective essays, position papers, political and social arguments, and research reports. Readings come from a wide variety of sources expressing many different points of view, including *Mother Jones*, the *Nation*, *Science and Spirit*, the *Wall Street Journal*, the *New York Times*, the *National Review*, the *Boston Globe*, the *Atlantic City Journal*, *New Black Magazine*, *Newsweek*, and *TIME*. We have also included readings from student newspapers and campus magazines, as well as online articles from *Slate* and *Salon*. And of course, blog entries provide diversity of voice as well as opinion.

# Instructor's Manual

The Instructor's Manual includes suggested responses to the Craft and Content and Critical Thinking questions in the text while offering ideas for directing class discussion and eliciting student response.

# The New MyCompLab Website

The new MyCompLab integrates the market-leading instruction, multimedia tutorials, and exercises for writing, grammar, and research that users have come to identify with the program with a new online composing space and new assessment tools. The result is a revolutionary application that offers a seamless and flexible teaching and learning environment built specifically for writers. Created after years of extensive research and in partnership with composition faculty and students across the country, the new MyCompLab provides help for writers in the context of their writing, with instructor and peer commenting functionality; proven tutorials and exercises for writing, grammar, and research; an e-portfolio; an assignment-builder; a bibliography tool; tutoring services; and a gradebook and course management organization created specifically for writing classes. Visit www.mycomplab.com for more information.

# Acknowledgments

Many people behind the scenes deserve gratitude for bringing this second edition of *What Matters in America* to publication. It would be impossible to thank all of them, but there are some for whose help I am particularly grateful. I would like to thank those instructors who provided their input and advice by answering lengthy questionnaires on the effectiveness of the essays in the prototype chapters of the text. Their helpful comments and suggestions have been incorporated into this finished volume.

Noreen Lace, California State University, Northridge
James E. Porter, Michigan State University
Ken Holliday, Southern State Community College

Mahli Xuan Mechenbier, Kent State University
Benjamin Erickson, Bridgewater College
Michael K. Yetter, Waubonsee Community College
Carol Myers, Athens Technical College

Special thanks go to Kathryn Goodfellow for her assistance in developing the content, locating articles, and writing the study apparatus. This book would not have been possible without her thoughtful contributions, enthusiasm, and unwavering work ethic. I would also like to thank Amy Trumbull for her help in securing permissions for the readings featured in this volume, and to Kristine Perlmutter for her valuable assistance formulating some of the study questions for this edition. I would also like to extend my thinks to those students who allowed us to reprint their essays in this text.

Finally, my thanks to the people of Longman Publishers, especially Executive Editor Suzanne Phelps Chambers and her assistant Erica Schweitzer, and to Senior Development Editor Meg Botteon who helped conceptualize this edition.

*Gary Goshgarian*

# Introduction
## Critical Thinking, Reading, and Writing

## What Is Critical Thinking?

Whenever you question the message or implications of what you see and read, you are exercising critical thinking. You look beneath the surface of words and images and debate their meaning and significance. You ask for definitions, weigh claims, evaluate information, look for proof, question assumptions, and make judgments.

## Critical Thinking and Reading Critically

When you read critically, you think critically. Instead of passively accepting what's written, you actively decide for yourself what is or is not important or logical or correct. And you do so because you bring to your reading your own perspective, experience, education, and personal values, as well as your powers of comprehension and analysis. Such skills apply to every facet of your life.

### Critical Reading Is a Process of Discovery

Critical reading initiates a dialogue between you and an author. You discover an author's view on a subject; you discover the strengths and weaknesses of the author's thesis or argument, and you decide if you agree or disagree with the author's views. At the same time, critical reading encourages you to question accepted norms, views, and beliefs. You will find yourself asking tough questions about your own experiences and views—and by so doing, you develop the skills you need to be an active participant in today's global society.

## Critical Reading Is the Key to Good Writing

Critical reading also helps you become a better writer, because critical reading is the first step to good writing. Good readers look at another author's writing the way an architect looks at a house: They study the fine details and how those details connect and create the whole. Likewise, good readers consider the particular slants and strategies of appeal. Good writers always have a clear sense of their audience—their readers' racial makeup, gender, and educational background; their political and/or religious persuasions; their values, prejudices, and assumptions about life; and so forth.

Critical reading helps you evaluate your own writing. The more you analyze and react to another's written work, the better you will analyze and react to your own. You will learn to ask yourself: Is my argument logical? Do my points come across clearly? Are my examples solid enough? Is this the best wording? Is my conclusion persuasive? Do I have a clear sense of my audience? What appeal strategy did I take—to logic, emotions, or ethics?

## How to Read Critically

To help you read critically, use these six basic steps:

- Keep a journal about what you read.
- Annotate what you read.
- Outline what you read.
- Summarize what you read.
- Question what you read.
- Analyze what you read.

## Keep a Journal About What You Read

Unlike writing an essay or a paper, keeping a journal is a personal exploration in which you develop your own ideas without set rules. It is an opportunity to write without restrictions and without judgment.

What do you include in your journal? Although it may serve as a means to understand an essay you're assigned, you are not required to write only about the essay itself. Perhaps the piece reminds you of something in your personal experience. Maybe it triggers an opinion you didn't know you had. Or perhaps you wish to explore a particular phrase or idea presented by the author. Date your entries and include the titles of the articles to which you are responding. Eventually, you should have a substantial number of pages to review so you can see how your ideas and writing style are developing over time.

## Annotate What You Read

It's a good idea to underline (or highlight) key passages and to make marginal notes when reading an essay. In annotating a piece of writing, you are engaging in a dialogue with the author. As in any meaningful dialogue, you may hear things you may not have known, things that may be interesting and exciting to you, things that you may agree or disagree with, or things that give you cause to ponder. The other side of the dialogue, of course, is your response. In annotating a piece of writing, that response takes the form of underlining (or highlighting) key passages and jotting down comments in the margin. Such comments can take the form of brief sentences like the following:

- That's not true.
- You're contradicting yourself.
- I see your point, but I don't agree.
- That's not a good choice of words.
- You're jumping to conclusions.
- Good point. I never thought of that.
- That was nicely stated.
- This is an extreme view.

Annotating can also help you become a stronger reader. Underline or circle unfamiliar words and references, and look them up. Highlight or underline the main thesis statement or claim and jot down "Claim" or "Thesis" in the margin.

Here is an excerpt from "Hate Violence? Turn it off!" by Tim Goodman. (You can read the entire essay beginning on page 165.)

1   **P**erhaps it's a sign of progress that Americans are becoming just as concerned about violence on television as they are about sex. <u>For years, a barely concealed nipple or a tame bed scene was deemed worse than hundreds of people being brutally shot down on cop shows and the like.</u>  } Sarcastic tone

2    Now you can't pick up the paper without some watchdog group denouncing Hollywood for ruining their children's lives with a plethora of violent images nightly. Some kid goes postal at his high school and "Starsky and Hutch" is the root cause.

*What watchdog group?*

*Look up reference*

3    We're getting our priorities right and wrong simultaneously. If sexuality is now not the enemy, great. But to continue to demonize Hollywood for its portrayals of violence is to put our heads in the sand about the world we live in.

*Main point*

4    Worse, it's just plain wrong, reeks of censorship and, in the context of parents worried about their children, it's looking for a scapegoat when lax parenting skills are more to blame.

*Look up "scapegoat"*

5    For example, parents have put pressure on their elected officials to "do something" about violence, and the result has been a ratings system that surveys suggest most parents never use. And then there's the vaunted "V-chip," which effectively shifted parental responsibility to the government and doesn't consider the simplest way for everyone to solve this problem: Vote with your remote.

*Check out rating system*
*Research how V-chip works*

*Catchy slogan*

6    Some of us like violence. Some of us like shows that have a gritty realism to them, rather than the glossy pap offered up by most networks. And think of all the people without children who, as grown-ups, choose to watch programming clearly geared to adults. Just because you've given little Jimmy his own TV set upstairs and now you can't stop him from watching "Jackass" on MTV or "Oz" on HBO, don't cry foul and ruin it for the rest of us.

*What kind or degree of violence is he thinking about?*

*Should parents bear sole responsibility?*

7    This is an old and now increasingly tired defense of art, anti-censorship and the need for parents to take more responsibility for what their children are watching. Don't like it? Don't watch it. There are enough elements in place now—blocking devices, ratings, V-chips, etc.—that to whine about how Hollywood should tone it down (as you allow the blood-and-guts nightly news to waft over dinner) completely misses the point about whose kid it is.

8    Then again, many adults also dislike violence. Fine. Vote with the remote. Go to PBS, the History Channel, Disney—whatever—just stop writing letters to politicians who have already had a chilling effect

*Slogan again*

*Give example*

(thus a watering- and dumbing-down of content) on what we already see.

<table>
<tr><td>}</td><td>Give example</td></tr>
</table>

9    Most recently, there has been a backlash against "The Sopranos," with many people thinking there's been an amping up of the violence and at least two very disturbing episodes filled with violence toward women.

## Outline What You Read

Briefly outlining an essay is a good way to see how writers structure their ideas. When you diagram the thesis statement, claims, and the supporting evidence, you can better assess the quality of the writing and decide how convincing it is. You may already be familiar with detailed, formal essay outlines where structure is broken down into main ideas and subsections. However, for our purposes here, I suggest simply jotting down a one-sentence summary of each paragraph to create a concise outline of an essay's components.

## Summarize What You Read

Summarizing is perhaps the most important technique to develop for understanding and evaluating what you read. For a summary, write a brief (about 100 words) synopsis of the reading in your own words. Note the claim or thesis of the discussion (or argument) and the chief supporting points. It is important to write these points down, rather than highlight them with a pen or pencil, because the act of jotting down a summary helps you absorb the argument. At times, it may be impossible to avoid using the author's own words in a summary. But if you do, remember to use quotation marks.

## Question What You Read

The separate steps of critical reading naturally overlap as you read. While reading an essay, you will simultaneously summarize and evaluate the writer's points in your head, perhaps adding your own ideas and arguments. If something strikes you as particularly interesting or insightful, make a mental note. Likewise, if something rubs you the wrong way, argue back. For beginning writers, a good strategy is to convert that automatic mental response into actual note taking.

In your journal or in the margins of the text, question and challenge the writer. Questions to ask include:

- What did you mean by that?
- Can you back up that statement?
- How do you define that term?
- How did you draw that conclusion?
- Do all the experts agree?
- Is this evidence dated?
- So what? Why does it matter?
- What is your point?
- Why do we need to know this?

Even if you do not feel personally qualified to pass judgment on an author's views, get into the habit of thinking of other views on the issue. If you've read or heard of experiences different from the author's or arguments based on opposing views, jot them down.

## Analyze What You Read

To analyze something means breaking it down into its components, examining those components closely to evaluate their significance, and determining how they relate as a whole. You do this when you outline an essay. But analyzing what you read also requires interpreting and evaluating the points of a discussion or argument as well as its language and structure.

Analyzing an essay after establishing its main idea will help you understand what may not be evident at first. A closer examination of the author's words takes you beneath the surface and sharpens your understanding of the issue.

Although there is no set procedure for analyzing a piece of prose, here are some specific questions you should raise when reading an essay, especially one that is trying to influence or change your opinion:

- Who is the audience the author is addressing?
- What are the author's assumptions?
- What are the author's purposes and intentions?
- How well does the author accomplish those purposes?
- How convincing is the evidence presented? Is it sufficient and specific? Relevant? Reliable and not dated? Slanted?

- How good are the sources of the evidence used? Were they based on personal experience, scientific data, or outside authorities?
- Did the author address opposing views on the issue?
- Is the author's perspective persuasive?

## What Is Critical Writing?

Critical writing is a systematic process. Experienced writers do not plan, write, edit, and proofread all at the same time. Rather, critical writing occurs one thoughtful step at a time.

Some writing assignments may require more steps than others. An in-class freewriting exercise may take only one or two steps—light planning and writing. An essay question on a midterm examination may permit enough time for only three steps—planning, writing, and proofreading. A simple plan for such an assignment needs to answer only two questions: "What am I going to say?" and "How am I going to develop my idea convincingly?"

## Developing Ideas

Even the most experienced writers sometimes have trouble getting started. Common problems you may encounter include focusing your ideas, knowing where to begin, having too much or too little to say, and determining your position on an issue. But there are strategies that can help promote the free expression of your ideas and make you more comfortable with writing. Two of the most common are brainstorming and freewriting.

### Brainstorming

The goal of brainstorming is to generate and focus ideas. Brainstorming can be a personal exercise or a group project. You begin with a blank sheet of paper (or a blackboard) and, without paying attention to spelling, order, or grammar, simply list ideas about the topic as they come to you. You should spend at least 10 minutes brainstorming, building on the ideas you write down. There are no "dumb" ideas in brainstorming—the smallest detail may turn into a great essay.

Let us assume, for example, that you decide to write a paper supporting Tim Goodman's assertion in "Hate Violence? Turn it off!" Brainstorming for a few minutes may provide something like this:

> Goodman's main idea is captured in the title, but the essay's tone is very sarcastic. Is essay more or less persuasive? Will reader find tone condescending? Insulting? Does this weaken his argument?
>
> What watchdog groups denounce Hollywood for violent images? Find examples online. Are the claims of these groups reasonable or not?
>
> Who is to blame for children watching violent TV or movies? Is it Hollywood or lax parents?
>
> Check out how the "V-chip" works.
>
> List occasions when I've seen young kids watching inappropriately violent films or TV shows. Who's responsible for this? What could be done to change it?
>
> The phrase "Vote with your remote" is catchy and seems sensible. But is it a realistic solution?
>
> It's easy to control what young kids watch, but what about tweens? Is it solely the responsibility of parents to control their viewing? Is it possible for parents to control what tweens view?
>
> Is censorship the only way to protect young teens from viewing violence? Is censorship too high a price to pay?
>
> Interview parents of young children to get their views on this issue. Interview parents of teenagers. Interview teenagers. How do their opinions compare?
>
> Research the movie rating system. Does it seem to have an impact on what young children watch? On what teens watch?

You may notice that this brainstorming example is more like a list with little structure, no apparent order, and even spelling errors. Its purpose is to elicit all the ideas you have about a subject so you can read your ideas and identify an interesting topic to develop.

### Freewriting

As you can see from the above, brainstorming is the listing or bulleting of ideas, reactions, writing strategies, and research possibilities as they occur to you. The next step is freewriting, which is a more focused preliminary step to the actual formal writing process. In freewriting, you write down your free flow of ideas on the topic without regard to spelling, grammar, or punctuation. To help keep your focus, note your topic at the top of your paper, then spend 10 or 15 minutes writing down the free flow of ideas on the topic as they occur to you. And above all, don't stop writing—even if you feel that what you are writing is silly or irrelevant or digressing. Any one, or a combination, of the ideas expressed in a freewrite can be developed into a thoughtful essay.

Here is an example of a freewriting exercise:

At first, I was put off by Goodman's piece. I found the tone angry and condescending—especially with remarks like "Now you can't pick up a paper without some watchdog group denouncing Hollywood for ruining their children's lives with a plethora of violent images nightly." (I didn't even know what 'plethora' meant.) Goodman seemed to think that violence on television is a boring, unimportant concern. But as I read on, Goodman got me interested in the topic. Especially when he talked about Hollywood as a scapegoat for lazy parents. That made me wonder who really is responsible for what children and young people watch. Should Hollywood be blamed if kids watch films made for adults? Goodman mentioned several options available to protect young viewers from violent shows and movies—"V-chips," rating systems, and the simple act of changing the channel. For young children, these can work. But then I got to thinking about tweens and adolescents. Every child over 10 can get around their parent's efforts to control what they watch. With so many channels on cable TV and lots of unsupervised time, they can view almost anything they want including pornography and explicit violence. But does it make sense to resort to censorship? And with a V-chip? Goodman feels this shifts parental responsibility to the government. Do we want a society where the government restricts what people watch? Is Hollywood a scapegoat for lax parenting as Goodman claims? I am a little confused. Perhaps I'll write a paper focusing specifically on young adolescents and violence in television. If channel blocking and ratings systems fail, what alternatives exist? Maybe I could interview some teenagers to see what they think. Do they really watch a lot of violence on TV? Or do they use common sense? If they do watch violence, does it influence their behavior? Do they really change the channel? Maybe I could write a paper about these ideas and come up with suggestions as to how to help teens make good choices.

## Narrowing Your Topic and Developing Your Thesis

Although brainstorming and freewriting help generate ideas, you still need to narrow down one idea to something more manageable. But this can be quite a challenge since you might like more than one idea, or you may be afraid of limiting yourself to only one concept. Choose an idea that will interest you and your audience. Remember that if you do not like the way one idea begins to develop, you can always go back to your brainstorming list and choose another to develop instead. Once you identify your topic, you are ready to develop the thesis statement for your essay.

Based on the freewriting exercise described earlier, we will follow a student who has decided to write his paper on the idea that educating adolescents on the potentially harmful effects of television violence might be a better solution than government regulation. The idea stems from a response to Goodman's essay, but it will develop into a thesis that uniquely belongs to the student.

## Developing a Thesis

The **thesis** is a form of contract between the writer and reader. It makes a claim or declaration—telling your audience exactly what you are going to discuss. It should be stated in the opening paragraph, with the rest of the essay developing and supporting it.

Your thesis should guide the development of your essay. Don't be constrained by your first thesis. If your paper is changing as you write, your thesis may evolve as well. Remember to go back and revise the thesis so that it matches the points made in your essay.

Although the thesis represents the last step in developing the topic for your essay, it is only the beginning of the actual writing process. For his paper, our student worked out the following opening paragraph to help develop his thesis:

It is widely assumed that violence, whether in film or on television, negatively affects teenagers and that regulations are necessary to protect them. These regulations include V-chips, ratings systems, and even artistic censorship. However, it is clear that these regulations are ineffective. We are better off as a society if teenagers are educated in visual literacy, learn early on to "vote with the remote," and make independent decisions about their viewing choices [thesis statement].

## Identifying Your Audience

Knowing what your audience needs and expects from your essay will help you compose a convincing, effective paper. The following questions can help you identify the expectations of your audience:

- Who is my audience?
- What do they already know about my topic?
- What question do they have about my topic?
- What do they need to know to understand my point?
- What is the best order to present the information they need to know?
- How do they feel about this topic?
- Why would they want to read my essay?

Based on these questions, our student determined that his audience would be his teacher and expository writing classmates. All of them would be familiar with Goodman's article and would have discussed it to some extent in class. They might have different opinions on the issue, so supporting evidence (from both Goodman's article and some outside research) would be necessary to effectively make his point. Because the essay would be about an issue directly concerning teachers, parents, and students, it should generate some level of personal interest, and, thus, engage his readers.

## Organizing and Drafting Your Essay

There are many ways to organize your paper. Some students prefer to use the standard outline technique, complete with roman numerals and indented subpoints. Other students prefer more flexible flowcharts. The key to organizing is to define your focus and plan how to support your thesis statement from point to point in a logical order.

When writing your essay, think of your draft as a work in progress. Your objective should be to present your ideas in a logical order. You can address spelling, grammar, and sentence structure later. If you get stuck writing one paragraph or section, move on to another. You may choose to write your draft sequentially, or you may choose to move from your thesis to your body paragraphs, leaving your introduction and conclusion for last. Feel free to leave gaps or write notes to yourself in brackets to indicate areas to develop later when revising. Do not make the mistake of thinking that your first draft has to be your final draft. Remember that writing is a process of revision—you can always go back and fix things later.

## Developing Paragraphs and Making Transitions

A paragraph is a group of sentences that supports and develops a central idea. The central idea serves as the core point of the paragraph, and the surrounding sentences support it.

Three primary types of sentences compose a paragraph: the topic sentence, supporting sentences, and transitional sentences.

The core point, or the **topic sentence,** is usually the first or second sentence in the paragraph. It is the controlling idea of the paragraph. Placing the topic sentence first lets the reader immediately know what the paragraph is about. However, sometimes a transition sentence or some supporting material needs to precede the topic sentence, in which case the topic sentence may appear as the second or third sentence in the paragraph. The topic sentence should connect logically to the topic sentences in the paragraphs before and after it.

**Supporting sentences** do just that; they support the topic sentence. This support may be from outside sources in the form of quotations or paraphrased material, or it may be from your own ideas. Think of the support sentences as "proving" the validity of your topic sentence.

**Transitional sentences** link paragraphs together, making the essay cohesive and readable. Transitional sentences are usually the first and last sentences of the paragraph. When they appear at the end of the paragraph, they foreshadow the topic to come. Words such as *in addition, yet, moreover, furthermore, meanwhile, likewise, also, since, before, hence, on the other hand, as well,* and *thus* are often used in transitional sentences. There words can also be used within the body of the paragraph to clarify and smooth the progression from idea to idea. For example, the last sentence in our student's introductory paragraph sets up the reader's expectations that the paragraphs that follow will explain why V-chips and other viewing regulations are ineffective and why society would be better off it teenagers learned to make educated decisions about what they view.

Paragraphs have no required length. Remember, however, that an essay comprising long, detailed paragraphs might prove tiresome and confusing to the reader. Likewise, short, choppy paragraphs may sacrifice clarity and leave the reader with unanswered questions. Remember that a paragraph presents a single unified idea. It should be just long enough to effectively support its subject. Begin a new paragraph when your subject changes.

Use this list to help keep your paragraphs organized and coherent:

- Organize material logically—present your core idea early in the paragraph.
- Include a topic sentence that expresses the core point of the paragraph.
- Support and explain the core point.
- Use transitional sentences to indicate where you are going and where you have been.

Let us see how our student applies these ideas to the second paragraph of his essay.

In his piece, "Hate Violence? Turn it off!" Goodman discounts the value of currently available measures designed to control violence on TV or in film. To understand his position, we should first be familiar with these measures and understand how a teenager views them [*topic sentence*]. The first is the V-chip, a technology which lets parents block television programming they don't want their children to watch [*supporting sentence*]. Television shows are rated according to a system created by the broadcasting industry, and a parent can program the V-chip to block shows with particular ratings [*supporting sentence*]. The problem is that any clever teen can easily deprogram and reprogram this chip, and Mom and Dad are none the wiser [*supporting sentence*]. A second measure is the familiar film rating system of the Motion Picture Association of America: G, PG, PG-13, N-17 ratings [*supporting sentence*]. But even if an N-17 rating prohibits young teens from seeing a film in a theater, they can always see it when it's available on DVD. The third attempt is artistic censorship [*supporting sentence*]. As Goodman says, censoring a show like the wildly successful and artistically acclaimed HBO series *The Sopranos* poses more risks than benefits for society [*supporting sentence*]. Do we really want our teens living in a world where a panel of parents, special interest groups, or a religious institution makes decisions as to what an artist can or cannot create [*transitional sentence*]? No, and that's why visual literacy may be the best strategy to protect teens from excessive violence in film and on television.

## Editing and Revising

Once you have drafted a paper and, if possible, spent some time away form it, you should begin editing and revising it. To edit your paper, read it closely, marking the words, phrases, and sections you want to change. Have a grammar handbook nearby to quickly reference any grammatical questions that may arise. Look for things that seem out of place or sound awkward, passages that lack adequate support and detail, and sentences that seem wordy or unclear. Many students find that reading the essay aloud helps them to recognize awkward sentences and ambiguous wording.

As you read, you should always ask if what you have written refers back to your thesis:

- Does this paragraph support my thesis?
- What does my reader need to know?
- Do my paragraphs flow in a logical order?
- Have I deviated from my point?

As you revise your paper, think about the voice and style you are using to present your material. Is your style smooth and confident? How much of yourself is in the essay, and is this level appropriate for the type of paper you are writing? Some writers, for example, overuse the pronoun "I." If you find that this is the case, try to rework your sentences to decrease the use of this pronoun.

## Proofreading Effectively

To proofread correctly, you must read slowly and critically. Look for and mark errors in spelling and usage, sentence fragments and comma splices, inconsistencies in number between nouns and pronouns and between subjects and verbs, faulty parallelism, other grammatical errors, unintentional repetitions, and omissions.

After you have identified the errors, go back and correct them. When you have finished, proofread the paper again to make sure you have caught everything. As you proofread for grammar and style, ask yourself the questions listed above and make corrections on your paper. Be prepared to re-read your essay multiple times. Having only one or two small grammatical corrections is a good indication that you are done revising.

If your schedule permits, you might want to show your paper to a friend or instructor for review. Obtaining feedback from your audience is another way you can test the effectiveness of your paper. An outside reviewer will probably think of questions you have not thought of, and if you revise to answer those questions, you will make your paper stronger.

# Critically Reading a Visual World

Our culture bombards us with images competing for our attention. Some want to sell us something, others want to sway our opinion or tell a story. It is easy to allow our gut emotions to serve as our guide in a visual world, but critically approaching this world gives us an edge. When we read critically the ads and appeals around us, we are better able to make informed decisions about them. As you review the various visual presentations throughout the text, consider the ways symbolism, brand recognition, stereotyping, and cultural expectations contribute to how such illustrations communicate their ideas.

To understand how visuals work and to analyze the way visuals persuade and influence us, we must also ask questions about specific aspects of form and design. Some questions to ask about print images such as those in newspaper and magazine ads include the following:

- What element within the frame catches your attention immediately?
- What is the central image? What is the background image? Foreground images? What are the surrounding images? What is significant in the placement of these images? Their relationship to one another?
- What verbal information is included? How is it made prominent? How is it related to the other graphics or images?
- What specific details (people, objects, locale) are emphasized? Which are exaggerated or idealized?
- What is the effect of color and lighting?
- What emotional effect is created by the images—pleasure? longing? anxiety? nostalgia?
- Do the graphics and images make you want to know more about the subject or product?
- What special significance might objects in the image have?
- Is there any symbolism imbedded in the images?

Considering these questions helps us to critically survey a visual argument and enables us to formulate reasoned assessments of its message and intent.

You will notice that the title page of each unit in this book features an editorial cartoon addressing the thematic focus of the unit. The editorial cartoon presents a moment in the flow of familiar current events. For the cartoon to be effective, it must make the issue clear at a glance and it must establish where it stands on the argument.

To convey less-obvious issues and figures at a glance, cartoonists resort to images that are instantly recognizable—called visual clichés—that we don't have to work hard to grasp. The cartoonist is also likely to employ stock figures, which are images instantly recognizable from cultural stereotypes: the fat-cat tycoon, the mobster thug, the sexy female movie star. And these come to us in familiar outfits and props that give away their identities and professions. These are visual clichés known by the culture at large, and we recognize them immediately.

As you view each of the editorial cartoons in this book, consider the visual clichés the cartoonist uses. What information is important for the viewer to know? What assumptions does the cartoonist make? What issue is the cartoonist holding up for public scrutiny, and why?

# Discussing What You Read, In Class and Online

We all have the yearning to express ourselves freely and clearly—to contribute to open discussion and debate, to be an active participant in the group. Ideally, the classroom is the perfect venue for students to practice communication skills—to exchange ideas and explore differences of opinions. With the guidance of an instructor and with the mutual support and respect of classmates, an environment can exist where each student feels comfortable exercising his or her discussion skills and feedback is encouraged. The result is a class that's fun, engaging, and informative—a class that enjoys a group spirit of mutual respect and attentiveness. Toward that end, we offer the following guidelines for discussion.

## Guidelines for Discussion in Class and Online

1. Take time to process the questions your instructor or classmates have posed. Be sure you understand what is being asked before you respond.
2. If the question is unclear, ask for clarification or restate what you understood the question to be.
3. When you offer your answer, speak in an audible, clear voice. Online, quickly proofread your response before posting.

4. In class, listen carefully to answers or comments made by your classmates. Online, read every contribution to a conversation before jumping in.

5. Take notes during the discussion so that you can refer to specific remarks. Also, jot down ideas that will help you express yourself as you give feedback.

6. Refer to comments made by other classmates in your response. Then elaborate on how your ideas agree or disagree with statements made by classmates.

7. In an online or synchronous class discussion, resist the temptation to IM friends or visit other websites.

8. Do not interrupt a classmate when he or she is speaking. Give the speaker a chance to finish a thought. Some people need more time than others to articulate their ideas.

9. In an online class discussion, try not to use common IM abbreviations such as "srsly" or "LOL." Your language choices should be thoughtful and engaging.

10. Use context to connect your thoughts to the larger conversation. You may begin your response by saying, "I disagree with Tom's view that . . . because . . .," or "I agree with what Mary just said and can offer an example . . ." or "In the piece we read by David Plotz, this idea was discussed."

11. Make sure your response addresses the topic being discussed and does not go off on a tangent.

12. Rely on the moderator of the discussion for prompting and direction. It might naturally be your instructor or another student in the class. The moderator's job is to call on individuals to speak, ask new questions, or prompt students to explore new ideas.

13. Regard every speaker with respect—just as you would like to be treated with respect.

14. A spirited answer is acceptable, but not an aggressive, loud, or rude one.

15. If you know the topic your class will be discussing on a given day, jot down your ideas or opinions beforehand. You might want to look up an article on the topic online before your class.

# 1 Is the Internet Changing Our Social Lives?

## Is the Internet Changing Our Social Lives?

The phrase "social networking," while understood in concept offline, is really a phenomenon of the Internet that has evolved over the last 10 years. While web communities have changed the way many of us think about meeting people and sharing information, social networking sites such as MySpace and Facebook have revolutionized the way we communicate with friends and share information about ourselves.

While there are many social networking sites worldwide, the clear leaders in the industry are MySpace and Facebook. These two are the most popular sites in North America, and Bebo, Skyrock Blog, StudiVZ, and Hi5 lead in different parts of Europe. Orkut and Hi5 tend to dominate South America and Central America, and Friendster, once very popular in the United States, still has a strong following in Asia and the Pacific Islands. With over 120 million active users and an average of 250,000 new registrations daily, Facebook now leads the social networking sites in popularity. MySpace is a close second with over 110 million active users.

Within these vast numbers, user demographic profiles have emerged. MySpace users tend to be younger and to use the site to network with friends and share music. Facebook users tend to be college-educated, with a large membership over 25 years of age. Facebook users prepare carefully constructed pages that highlight their favorite books and movies, and even encourage giving to certain charitable causes. Both sites allow their users to present an image of how registrants view themselves and how they wish to be seen by others.

This unit explores how social networking sites influence our relationships with each other and the ways we relate to the world around us. Is the

## CRITICAL THINKING

1. What is the woman's "threat"? Why would her kids be concerned if she followed through with this threat?
2. What do you need to know in order to understand the point of this cartoon? Explain.
3. Would this cartoon have made sense 10 years ago? Why or why not?

Internet redefining friendships and what it means to be a "friend"? How is it changing the way we think and speak? Will Facebook, MySpace, or some new web-based network continue to hold such sway over us? Or is it merely a passing fad?

"When my kids get out of line, I threaten to
start a 'My Space' page and invite their friends."

www.cartoonstock.com

# MySpace, Facebook, and Other Social Networking Sites: Hot Today, Gone Tomorrow?

This review of popular online social networking sites was published on May 3, 2006, by Knowledge@Wharton, the online business journal of the Wharton School of the University of Pennsylvania. It draws upon the knowledge and expertise of many marketing and business professors at the Wharton School, including David Bell, Peter Fader, Leonard Lodish, and Eric K. Clemons.

## CONNECTING TO THE TOPIC

Members of the next generation use the Internet to network for business, friendships, and dating. It is inextricably connected to daily life and social experience. What is still unclear is the sustainability of social networking sites such as Facebook and MySpace. While popular now, will such sites remain a fixture in the lives of the next generation? This essay explores current trends and the future of social networking sites. Will children born today use My-Space and Facebook as teens and young adults, or will such sites be long-distant memories?

## WORDS IN CONTEXT

**serendipitous** (3)   random (adj.)
**mercurial** (4)   fluid, moving (adj.)
**touted** (4)   highly praised (v.)
**domiciled** (5)   housed (adj.)

1   **P**opular social networking sites, including MySpace and Facebook, are changing the human fabric of the Internet and have the potential to pay off big for investors, but—given their youthful user base—they are unusually vulnerable to the next "new new" thing. As quickly as users flock to one trendy Internet site, they can just as quickly move on to another, with no advance warning, according to Wharton faculty and Internet analysts.

2      MySpace, with 70 million visitors, has become the digital equivalent of hanging out at the mall for today's teens, who load the site with photos, news about music groups and detailed profiles of their likes and dislikes. Other social network sites include Facebook, geared to college students, LinkedIn, aimed at professionals, and Xanga, a blog-based community site. In all, an estimated 300 sites, including smaller ones such as Study-Breakers for high schoolers and Photobucket, a site for posting images, make up the social network universe.

3      Wharton marketing professor David Bell says the long-term success of these sites will depend on their ability to retain the interest of their members. "There is a fad or a fashion component to all these networks. Some will come and go," says Bell. The classic example, he suggests, is Friendster, which burst onto the Internet in 2003 and soon had 20 million visitors. Late last year, it slipped below a million after MySpace and other sites with better music and video capability lured Friendster users away. "A lot of the [success] is **serendipitous**. These things can have exponential growth. Then, if another community shows up that has better functionality in some way, there can be a mass migration."

4      Wharton marketing professor Peter Fader agrees that social network sites are powerful, but **mercurial**, particularly since most are aimed at teenagers and young adults. "It's a complete crapshoot. Look how many of these have come along and how many were **touted** as the next big thing. How many have disappeared completely or find themselves in some strange little unexplainable niche?"

5      He points to Orkut, an invitation-only service introduced by Google in 2004 that is little known in the United States, but wildly popular in Brazil, where more than 70% of its users are based. Indeed, Orkut has made Portuguese a second language in its interface. "In Brazil it's gold, but in the U.S., where the service is **domiciled**, nobody's even heard of Orkut. And there's no good reason why." While MySpace and Facebook currently rule the popular crowd on the Internet social scene, Fader says the forces that make a hot site are difficult to quantify; any site could become the next outcast. "There is no reason to believe that these, or future ones that are emerging on the radar screen, will be any different. I don't think anyone can come up with a genuine reason why they have become so popular, outside of 20-20 hindsight." Echoing that point, an article in the April 30 *New York Times* reports that AOL plans to launch a social networking site to be called AIM Pages as a competitor to MySpace, Yahoo360 and other such services.

6     One way for investors to benefit from the rise of social networks would be to develop a highly diverse portfolio, Fader adds. "I have no problem with betting on a crapshoot, but you want to hedge your bets carefully and accept the downside in exchange for what could be an incredible upside. You can't control your destiny with these nearly as much as any other web site or portal."

## Next Target: Cell Phones

7  For the moment, MySpace and Facebook are hot. News Corp. paid $580 million last year for MySpace as part of a $1.3 billion Internet acquisition spree. Facebook just received an additional $25 million in venture capital. Both companies are planning to extend their reach beyond the computer screen to cell phones. Cingular Wireless, Sprint Nextel and Verizon Wireless are starting a service that will allow users to post messages on Facebook's home pages or search for other users' phone numbers and email addresses from a cell phone. MySpace has a pact with Helio, a wireless joint venture between SK Telecom and Earthlink, that will allow users to send photos and update their blogs or profiles by cell phone.

8     According to ComScore Media Metrix, MySpace, with its 70 million users, ranks second behind Yahoo in pages viewed and time spent on the site. Facebook, founded by a 21-year-old student on leave from Harvard and backed by Silicon Valley venture capitalists, has 7.3 million registered users. Chris Hughes, a spokesperson for Facebook, says the company thinks of itself more as a directory grounded in real life rather than a social network creating connections between strangers. "We model people's real lives at their individual schools in a virtual space that enables them to exchange information about themselves. We are not focused on meeting new people, dating or anything like that. Instead, we want to manage information efficiently so that we can provide our users the information that matters most to them."

9     Social networking sites in general rely mainly on a simple advertising model—selling banner and text ads (although they ban uncool pop-up ads). Facebook also permits sponsored groups in which a marketer can build communities within the site. BusinessWeek recently reported that Facebook had rejected a $750 million buyout offer and was holding out for $2 billion. "That number is nothing but rumor," Hughes says.

10     When it comes to placing a valuation on the social network sites, Wharton marketing professor Leonard Lodish says traditional tools, such

as the discounted present value of the profit stream, apply to these new Internet networks as much as they do to any other business. He recalls an argument he had with marketing students during the Internet boom of 2000 about Internet music seller CDNow. Lodish said the firm would never be able to justify costs of $70 to attain each customer. The following year the firm declared bankruptcy.

11    In the case of MySpace and Facebook, Lodish points out, the cost of gaining new customers is practically nothing because users join voluntarily and provide their own content through their profiles. In addition, the cost of running the sites' web servers is relatively low. If a classic advertising or subscription revenue model is used, he says, low-cost social network sites could be highly profitable. Yahoo must buy or develop content for its site to attract advertisers and Google has to invest in its search capabilities, Lodish notes. "Yahoo makes a lot of money selling ads on its sites. Why can't Facebook and MySpace do the same thing?"

12    Nitin Gupta, an analyst with The Yankee Group in Boston, says MySpace is rooted in linking emerging bands to new fans, which makes it a logical partner for a media company, such as News Corp. The company can use the site to test or build buzz around its products. "These have become almost living systems, as the social network has begun to expand beyond a place for people with certain musical tastes and become popular for dating and all sorts of things."

13    While the MySpace population has grown, the site's roots remain in media, Gupta adds. "Today, it continues to be used to identify individuals interested in, not just music, but television and radio as well." Before News Corp. bought MySpace, NBC used it to show clips of "The Office" before the show was aired on the network. While media companies may be a more logical fit with a social networking site, other businesses might mesh too, according to Gupta. "It's a little more difficult to build a community around a Norelco razor, but it's possible."

14    Meanwhile, Gupta says, social networks have power beyond ad revenue to act as a customer relationship management (CRM) tool for companies selling products or services. "There's a lot of focus on advertising and banner ads and the amount of traffic. But it's important to look beyond traditional forms of web adverting to see the real potential—which is leveraging the connectivity of the sites and using them to form communities around products, media or services to really be in contact with your users." Still, he acknowledges, it will not be easy to convert those relationships to new revenue sources. "The future is in finding ways to monetize the

online community beyond just traditional web advertising, although it's going to be difficult for online communities, even those behemoths like MySpace."

15    According to Wharton professor of operations and information management Eric K. Clemons, connectivity is nice, but the Internet bust of 2000 showed that revenue is what matters. "As we learned from the first dot-com silliness, value is not in click-through or eyeballs. Value comes from revenues. . . . Can you sell subscriptions to your data or your service? Can you charge for referrals or for purchases that result from referrals? Can you sell stuff? If not, your revenue is zero and your market value is zero."

## Safety and Privacy Concerns

16    As MySpace and other social networking sites have grown, so, too, have concerns about Internet safety and privacy. The Center for Missing and Exploited Children reported more than 2,600 incidents of adults using the web to target children online in order to engage in sexual activity. In March, federal prosecutors in Connecticut charged two men with using MySpace to contact youths with whom they later had sexual contact. Following Congressional hearings about online sexual predators, MySpace hired a safety czar to improve the site's protections for young users.

17    The popularity of social networking sites may also have unexpected consequences for users. A gay student attending a Christian college was expelled after administration officials viewed photos of the student in drag on Facebook. Twenty middle school students in California were suspended after participating in a MySpace group where one student allegedly threatened to kill another and made anti-Semitic remarks. In Kansas, authorities arrested five teenagers after one of the suspects used MySpace to outline plans for a Columbine-like attack on the boys' school.

18    Gary Arlen, president of Arlen Communications, a Bethesda, Md., research and consulting firm, says MySpace users may also begin to shy away as they grasp the long-term consequences of putting up photos of wild parties or tales of sexual bravado. "This stuff may come back to haunt you 20 years from now. MySpace runs the risk of a social reaction, but that is part of being the pioneer." Despite those obstacles, he is enthusiastic about social networks' promise, although he says the sites' ultimate value is less clear-cut than other Internet successes, such as eBay and Amazon. "It may be that this is a very slow play because the existing sites, Friendster and now MySpace and Facebook, are building a habit among

young users. It will become a part of how they operate in their 20s and 30s. This service will be part of the landscape."

19    According to Bell, there are strategies that social network sites can use to avoid becoming tomorrow's abandoned property. One way to retain a site's aura is to limit membership. For example, Bell notes that when Diesel jeans faced the problem of losing marketing cachet by becoming too popular, the brand cut back on the number of outlets it would sell to. Facebook tries to limit itself to college students. Social networks seem to operate best when they strike a balance between heterogeneity, which provides large numbers of members, and selectivity, which keeps the hordes focused and engaged in the site, he says, adding that social networking sites also must keep pace with technology and provide new features—for example, fast downloads. "To create stickiness you must have functional value and also community value. If either of those becomes diluted, you give people a reason to start looking elsewhere."

20    As a web-based business, social networks do have some advantages over traditional companies in tracking user behavior in order to detect problems early. "If you are sophisticated, you can measure and monitor the rate at which users join and you can detect early warning signs, such as a drop-off in the number of people interacting," says Bell. "There would be metrics to monitor if you are headed in the wrong direction." Bell also cautions that sites will need to remain subtle in their approach to marketing if they are to build on their current success. While they provide banner and text ads, even more valuable word-of-mouth promotion lurks in the buzz within user profile pages. "Part of the popularity of these things is that they are more credible and not explicitly commercial," he says. "If somebody on the Mac fanatic site tells me about iPod, it's more credible than Mac advertising. If people feel the networks are too corporate, that's a turnoff."

21    Still, no matter how their future takes shape, Bell says these types of networks are ingrained in Internet society. "They're here to stay. Like eBay, they are embedded now. The idea of joining online communities and being able to participate in them is not going to disappear." ◆

## CONSIDERING THE ISSUES

1. Which social networking sites do you currently use? Have you ever switched from one site to another? If so, what were the reasons behind the switch? If not, why have you remained loyal to your original site?

2. Wharton marketing professor Leonard Lodish notes, "Yahoo makes a lot of money selling ads on its sites. Why can't Facebook and MySpace do the same thing?" Do you think social networking sites should sell ads? Explain the consequences of doing so.

### CRAFT AND CONTENT

1. Review the section on "Safety and Privacy Concerns." How have social networking sites been abused? Should these sites be shut down or does the responsibility lie elsewhere?
2. The essay provides several examples of traditional forms of web advertising and discusses additional ways advertisers can survive in the age of the Internet. Evaluate these examples. Do you have any experience with them? Can you think of other methods to reach consumers online?

### CRITICAL THINKING

1. Do you agree with the spokesperson for Facebook who surmises that Facebook is "a directory grounded in real life rather than a social network creating connections between strangers"? On what evidence is this based? Do you agree? Why or why not?
2. In this essay, Wharton marketing professor David Bell observes, "If somebody on the Mac fanatic site tells me about iPod, it's more credible than Mac advertising. If people feel the networks are too corporate, that's a turnoff." Do you agree with this statement? Explain.

### WRITING ABOUT THE ISSUES

1. This essay describes the transitory nature of social networking sites (note that Friendster in the United States has dramatically declined in popularity). What other Internet phenomena have experienced "hot today, gone tomorrow" lifespans? Based on your own experiences with the Internet and with social networking sites, do you believe Facebook and MySpace will remain fixtures online, or is social networking likely to be replaced by something else in the near future?

2. Have you ever put anything on MySpace or Facebook that could potentially embarrass you in five, 10, or even 20 years? Write a brief essay in which you describe the information you have personally shared online (include e-mails) and the ramifications of having a record of your online activity possibly accessible in the future.

# Someone to Watch Over Me
*Theodora Stites*

Theodora Stites lives in New York where she works in market research. This essay, which appeared in the July 9, 2006, edition of the *New York Times*, is adapted from *Twentysomething Essays by Twentysomething Writers* (2006).

## CONNECTING TO THE TOPIC

Can social networking fulfill the need to connect with others in the same way face-to-face relationships do? Can friendships on Facebook be even better than sitting down to chat with a friend in a coffee shop? Would you rather be "poked" or "pinged" than get a call on your cell phone? The next piece describes a truly wired life. Can you have too much of a good thing?

1     I'm 24 years old, have a good job, friends. But like many of my generation, I consistently trade actual human contact for the more reliable emotional high of smiles on MySpace, winks on Match.com and pokes on Facebook. I live for Friendster views, profile comments and the Dodgeball messages that clog my cellphone every night.

2     I prefer, in short, a world cloaked in virtual intimacy. It may be electronic, but it is intimacy nevertheless. Besides, eye contact isn't all it's cracked up to be and facial expressions can be so hard to control. My life goes like this: Every morning, before I brush my teeth, I sign in to my Instant Messenger to let everyone know I'm awake. I check for new e-mail, messages or views, bulletins, invitations, friend requests, comments on my blog or mentions of me or my blog on my friends' blogs.

3    Next I flip open my phone and check for last night's Dodgeball messages. Dodgeball is the most intimate and invasive network I belong to. It links my online community to my cellphone, so when I send a text message to 36343 (Dodge), the program pings out a message with my location to all the people in my Dodgeball network. Acceptance into another person's Dodgeball network is a very personal way to say you want to hang out.

4    I scroll through the messages to see where my friends went last night, and when, tracking their progress through various bars and noting the crossed paths. I check the Google map that displays their locations and proximity to one another. I note how close Christopher and Tom were last night, only a block away, but see that they never met up.

5    I log on to my Friendster, Facebook, MySpace and Nerve accounts to make sure the mail bars are rising with new friend requests, messages and testimonials.

6    I am obsessed with testimonials and solicit them incessantly. They are the ultimate social currency, public declarations of the intimacy status of a relationship. "I miss running around like crazy w/you in the AM and sneaking away to grab caffeine and gossip," Kathleen commented on my MySpace for all to see. Often someone will write, "I just posted to say I love you."

7    I click through the profiles of my friends to the profiles of their friends (and their friends of friends, and so on), always aware of the little bar at the top of each profile indicating my multiple connections. A girl I know from college is friends with my friend from college's best friend from Minnesota. They met at camp in seventh grade. The boyfriend of my friend from work is friends with one of my friends from high school. I note the connections and remind myself to IM them later. On Facebook, I skip from profile to profile by clicking on the faces of posted pictures. I find a picture of my sister and her boyfriend, click on his face and jump right to his page.

8    Pictures are extremely necessary for enticing new friends—the more pictures the better. I change my pictures at least once a week.

9    There are hidden social codes in every image. Shadows and prominent eyes: not confident about their looks. Far away and seated in beautiful scenery: want you to know they're adventurous. Half in the picture: good looking but want you to know they're artistic, too.

10    Every profile is a carefully planned media campaign. I click on the Friendster "Who's Viewed Me" tab to see who has stumbled upon my profile

recently, and if people I don't know have checked me out, I immediately check them back. I get an adrenaline rush when I find out that a friend of a friend I was always interested in is evidently interested in me, too.

11    Just imagine if we could be this good in person. Online, everyone has bulletproof social armor.

12    Finding the perfect online community is not as easy as it looks. Some are too small. Dodgeball is so tiny it's almost too personal and requires constant attention. Not only does my online profile need to be updated regularly but the text messages demand prompt responses. To stay in the loop, it is even occasionally necessary to meet up with the members of my Dodgeball network in person.

13    Meanwhile, MySpace is so big that I can't even seem to find a place to start my own mini-network and branch out. I have 10 profiles, but not nearly enough friends.

14    I am constantly searching the Internet for new communities. Are there enough people on Plazes.com yet? Am I hip enough for Nerve? Can I be a part of Geocaching.com without having a GPS? Are the people on Fark.com my kind of people?

15    Fark.com members apparently opened their homes to other Fark.com members who were stranded after Hurricane Katrina. This makes their community seem beautiful and touching. Definitely worth starting a pro-file. Plazes.com is based on posting your GPS address on Google maps and finding people not just through interests but exact location. I, of course, have a profile and log in every day. But I don't know anyone else on it yet, so I'm not really ready to tell my friends.

16    WHY, you ask, do I have to be a part of so many online communities? Isn't it hard to keep track? I need to belong to all of them because each one enables me to connect to people with different levels of social intimacy.

17    Don't know you but think I may want you to be part of my network? I'll contact you through Match.com or Nerve. Just met? I'll look you up on MySpace. Known each other for a while, but haven't been in touch re-cently? Friendster message. Friends with my friends and want to get to know you better? Dodgeball or MySpace. Good friends and want to con-nect more often? Dodgeball. Really good friends? Instant Message.

18    I now think of most people by their screen names. Even when I see them in person.

19    Through IM, I talk to my friends in Japan and Jamaica as much as the friends I see every weekend. Likewise, I have friends on my buddy list

who live in my neighborhood, but we only talk on IM. We would never dream of hanging out in person. We have enough connection online for our degree of closeness and don't need to enhance our relationship by spending time together offline. As Friendster puts it, some people are just second- or third-degree friends.

20      I also use IM as a tool for keeping track of my exes. I know when they sign on and I read their away messages. I can keep track of what's happening in their lives without their ever knowing I still care. Good or bad day, sick or asleep, I see what they're doing. I know if and when they're on the Internet. Sometimes they get smart, though, and click the little eye on the AIM Buddy List that makes them "invisible." It's a much less aggressive move than simply not responding to a message.

21      After I have checked the status of my communities I move along to the blogs. Blog content is so niche; if you like a blog, then the other people reading it must be just like you. Every site wants to feel like a community. More and more, the popular blogs and sites are going in the opposite direction of everything else and trying to extend into the offline world. Sites such as Flavorpill, Meetup and GeoCaching actually encourage and facilitate real interactions between their respective members. Flavorpill throws monthly parties for their subscribers.

22      Attending these parties, I found myself in awkward social situations I couldn't log out of, so I joined SecondLife. Every member of SecondLife is given an avatar—a three-dimensional body with a choice of clothing, hairstyle, body type and gender. Members of SecondLife have SecondLife jobs, families and friends. The population is over 200,000.

23      The virtual people in SecondLife talk to each other in intimate gatherings. They spend the day gossiping, shopping, fighting, giving each other tattoos, kissing, marrying, even engaging in prostitution and filing complaints of sexual abuse. I recently enlarged the breasts of my avatar, and men immediately started grabbing me. I could have filed abuse complaints about this if I'd wanted to, but I didn't. For a while I had a virtual boyfriend, Darren, but he hasn't contacted me recently.

24      Ostensibly, there are no flaws in this world. You don't have to eat, and no one gets sick. All the members choose their body type, so no one is unattractive. You may think you'd act differently on SecondLife, in your perfect body and specially created persona. But I've found that I act much as I do in real life, and my SecondLife relationships tend to fail the same way my real-life relationships do. Virtual love is still complicated.

25    For now I've been placed on a lush tropical island to learn how to maneuver. Once I improve at virtually picking things up and moving them, sitting, walking and jumping, I'll be moved to the main city. But I've been called a newborn enough times to know I'm not ready yet.

26    I can't wait to log back in.

27    Hanging out in the real world one weekend, I went to a Flavorpill party. I was sucking down a cigarette with the head of Flavorpill when our cellphones rang at the same time. We flipped them open to see who was contacting us. He turned to me and said, "Dennis? He's really got to go someplace new."

28    I looked down at my screen and noticed that Dennis had sent out a Dodgeball message that he was at a bar on the Lower East Side—the fourth such message that week. I turned to the Flavorpill guy and said, "I didn't know you were in Dennis's network."

29    He nodded. We laughed. I exclaimed: "You aren't in my network. Why aren't you in my network?" I couldn't believe it. Here we were in person and both in Dennis's network, but not in each other's. That almost never happens.

30    Without looking at me, he responded, "Rock it."

31    "Rock what?"

32    "Rock my network." ◆

## CONSIDERING THE ISSUES

1. How many online networks and services do you subscribe to? In what ways do these services (e-mail, networking sites, etc.) enhance and enrich your life? In what ways do they complicate it? Explain.

2. In this essay, a young woman describes her virtual connectivity throughout the day. Track your own online/virtual activity in a short diary. Note how your life would be different without the Internet and other mobile connections. Do you think online networking commands too much of our time, or is it an essential form of communication? How would your life be affected if you had no access to the Internet for an extended period of time? Explain.

## CRAFT AND CONTENT

1. Stites provides an outline of her online activity during the course of a day. What does this activity reveal about her to her reader?

2. Evaluate Stite's tone and style in her essay. Does it engage the reader? Why or why not?

## CRITICAL THINKING

1. Stites notes that she prefers online communication to face-to-face meetings, although her essay reveals that she engages in personal connections at bars and parties. Why does she prefer online communication? What does she feel it affords her that face-to-face interaction does not? What is your view of this preference?

2. Evaluate your own Internet relationships and friendships. Are you a different person online from the way you are in "real" life? Have you, like Stites, ever experienced the feeling that you could be a different person online? Do you feel more in control? Explain.

## WRITING ABOUT THE ISSUES

1. Evaluate your online communication style. Are you brief and to the point, or do you compose in more detail? What do you think your style says about you? What does it communicate to others? Do you have different styles for different situations? Explain.

2. Write about a relationship, romantic or merely friendship, in which online networking was an essential component of the connection you had with the other person. Cite examples of how social networking contributed to your relationship and how it enriched its quality.

# Blog Matters

A blog ("web log") is an online diary or commentary site that features regular entries that describe events, impressions, and viewpoints. Blogs may contain text, images, video, and often link to other websites, blogs, and online media. Most blogs allow readers to comment on the content of the post and respond to each other. As of 2007, the blog search engine estimated there were over 112 million blogs. While many blogs are maintained by individuals, some are run by journals, newspapers, and other media outlets. Remember that most blogs are not monitored for factual accuracy, and often express the opinion and views of the "blogger" writing the content.

The following blog is by British comedian, writer, and actor Stephen Fry, published by the *Guardian's* column "Dork Talk" on January 12, 2008. In this entry, Fry observes that there is some sort of deep human instinct that compels us to take a wild and open territory and divide it into citadels, independent city-states, MySpaces and Facebooks. Social networking sites, rather than being the next new thing, are subject to the same compartmentalization, rules, and social constructs of more traditional communities.

# Social Networking Through the Ages

*Stephen Fry*
*January 12, 2008*

1  **M**uch ink, electronic and atomic, has been expended on the subject of social networking and web 2.0. First, let's decide on how this last is pronounced. "Web two" won't do. "Web two point oh" is common, but I heard it as "web two dot oh."

2  These days web 2.0 refers both to user-generated content and to social networking sites. Rather than passively searching, browsing and eyeballing the billions of pages of the web, millions now contribute their videos, their journals, their music, their photos, their lives.

## The Big New Thing

3  Social networking (Facebook, MySpace, Bebo, etc.) has been identified as the Big New Thing. In other words, people who watch My Family have now heard of it and are at last aware of the difference between downloading and uploading. A sure sign, perhaps, that the phenomenon is on the way out. MySpace is already as seriously uncool (and as hideously girlie, pink and spangly) as My Little Pony; Facebook is taking its advantage (openness to having applications written for it) to such extremes that it's in danger of losing the original virtues of elegance, intelligence and simplicity that established it as a classy, upmarket place in which to live a digital life in the first place.

4  I am old enough to remember Prestel and the original bulletin boards and "commercial online services" Prodigy, CompuServe and America Online. These were closed communities. You paid a subscription, dialed in and connected. You made new friends and you chatted in "rooms" designated for the purpose according to special interests, hobbies and propensities. CompuServe and AOL were shockingly late to add what was called an "internet ramp" in the 90s. This allowed those who dialled up to go beyond the confines of the provider's area and explore the strange new world of the internet unsupervised. AOL offered its members a hopeless browser and various front ends that it hoped would keep people loyal to its squeaky-clean, closed world. This lasted through the 90s as it covered the planet in CDs in an attempt to recruit subscribers. A lost cause, naturally, and the company ended up as little more than an ordinary ISP. Made millions for Steve Case on the way as AOL merged with Time Warner, but that's another story.

## Opening and Closing Like a Flower

5   My point is this: what an irony! For what is this much-trumpeted social networking but an escape back into that world of the closed online service of 15 or 20 years ago? Is it part of some deep human instinct that we take an organism as open and wild and free as the internet, and wish then to divide it into citadels, into closed-border republics and independent city states? The systole and diastole of history has us opening and closing like a flower: escaping our fortresses and enclosures into the open fields, and then building hedges, villages and cities in which to imprison ourselves again before repeating the process once more. The internet seems to be following this pattern.

6   How does this help us predict the Next Big Thing? That's what everyone wants to know, if only because they want to make heaps of money from it. In 1999 Douglas Adams said: "Computer people are the last to guess what's coming next. I mean, come on, they're so astonished by the fact that the year 1999 is going to be followed by the year 2000 that it's costing us billions to prepare for it."

7   But let the rise of social networking alert you to the possibility that, even in the futuristic world of the net, the next big thing might just be a return to a made-over old thing.

**RESPOND TO THE BLOG:**

What do you think? Do you participate in online social networks? Do you think they represent a new way of connecting with people, or are they really just a "return to a made-over old thing"?

# Living Online: I'll Have to Ask My Friends

*Sherry Turkle*

Sherry Turkle is the Abby Rockefeller Mauzé Professor of the Social Studies of Science and Technology at the Massachusetts Institute of Technology in Boston, MA. She has written extensively on psychoanalysis, culture, and the relationship humans have with technology, especially computers. Her books include *Evocative Objects: Things We Think With* (2007), *The Second Self: Computers and the Human Spirit* (2005), and *Life on the Screen: Identity in the Age of the Internet* (1997). This interview appeared in the September 2006 issue of *New Scientist*.

## CONNECTING TO THE TOPIC

In this interview with Liz Else from *New Scientist* magazine, Sherry Turkle discusses how social networking sites influence how we think, speak, and interact with each other. Is the immediate satisfaction of "venting" online, of communicating at any hour to almost anyone, inhibiting our ability to cope with our emotions? With the Internet, explains Turkle, you are never really ever alone. While this may seem like a comforting thought, she wonders if it may also harm our ability to handle our emotions, affecting how we define ourselves.

## WORDS IN CONTEXT

**autonomy** (3)    independence (n.)
**polarized** (6)    divided into opposing groups (adj.)
**enmeshed** (7)    tangled up together (adj.)
**paradoxical** (7)    contradictory (adj.)
**parochially** (7)    locally, in a very limited fashion (adv.)

## Is Social Networking Changing the Way People Relate to Each Other?

1   For some people, things move from "I have a feeling, I want to call a friend" to "I want to feel something, I need to make a call." In either case, what is not being cultivated is the ability to be alone and to manage and contain one's emotions. When technology brings us to the point where we're used to sharing our thoughts and feelings instantaneously, it can lead to a new dependence, sometimes to the extent that we need others in order to feel our feelings in the first place.

2       Our new intimacies with our machines create a world where it makes sense to speak of a new state of the self. When someone says "I am on my cell," "online," "on instant messaging" or "on the web," these phrases suggest a new placement of the subject, a subject wired into social existence through technology, a tethered self. I think of tethering as the way we connect to always-on communication devices and to the people and things we reach through them.

## How Is It Affecting Families?

3 Let me take a simple example. Tethered adolescents are given a cellphone by their parents. In return, they are expected to answer their parents' calls. On the one hand, this arrangement gives the adolescent new freedoms. On the other, the adolescent does not have the experience of being alone, of having only him or herself to count on: there is always a parent on speed dial. This provides comfort in a dangerous world, yet there is a price to pay in the development of **autonomy**. There used to be a moment in the life of an urban child, usually between the ages of 12 and 14, when there was a first time to navigate the city alone. It was a rite of passage that communicated, "You are on your own and responsible." Tethering via a cellphone buffers this moment; tethered children think differently about themselves. They are not quite alone.

## Does It Worry You?

4 Our society tends toward a breathless techno-enthusiasm: "We are more connected; we are global; we are more informed." But just as not all information put on the web is true, not all aspects of the new sociality should be celebrated. We communicate with quick instant messages, "check-in" cell calls and emoticon graphics. All of these are meant to quickly communicate a state. They are not meant to open a dialogue about complexity of feeling. Although the culture that grows up around the cellphone is a "talk culture," it is not necessarily a culture that contributes to self-reflection. Self-reflection depends on having an emotion, experiencing it, taking one's time to think it through and understand it, but only sometimes electing to share it.

## Is This a Bad Thing?

5 The self that grows up with multitasking and rapid response measures success by calls made, emails answered, messages responded to. In this buzz of activity, there may be losses that we are not ready to sustain. We insist that our world is increasingly complex, yet we have created a communications culture that has decreased the time available for us to sit and think, uninterrupted. Teens growing up with always-on communication are primed to receive a quick message to which they are expected to give a rapid response. They may never know another way. Their experience raises a question for us all: are we leaving enough time to take one's time?

## Are You Talking About a Permanent Change?

6   It seems to be part of a larger trend in media culture for people not to know what they think until they get a sense of what everyone else thinks. But we learn about what everyone else thinks by reading highly **polarized** opinions that encourage choosing sides rather than thinking things through. You can give media culture a positive spin and say that people are more socially **enmeshed**, but it has a darker side: as a feeling emerges, people share the feeling to see if they have the feeling. And sometimes they don't have the feeling until they check if other people have it too. This kind of behavior used to be associated with early adolescents, with their need for validation. Now always-on technology is turning it into a norm.

## Surely Being Socially Enmeshed Can Also Have a Positive Side?

7   The challenge for this generation is to think of sociality as more than the cyber-intimacy of sharing gossip and photographs and profiles. This is a **paradoxical** time. We have more information but take less time to think it through in its complexity. We're connecting globally but talking **parochially**.

## Are You Saying That People Are Missing the Broader Picture?

8   People are connecting one-on-one—they have their online social network or their cellphone with 250 people on speed dial—but do they feel part of a community? Do they feel responsibility to a set of shared political commitments? Do they feel a need to take responsibility for issues that would require that they act in concert rather than just connect? Recently, connectivity and statements of identity on places such as Facebook or MySpace have themselves become values. It is a concern when self-expression becomes more important than social action.

## What Kind of Responsibility Are They Ducking?

9   The world [is] enmeshed in multiple wars and genocidal campaigns. It finds the world incapable of calling a halt to environmental destruction. Yet, with all of this, people seem above all to be fascinated by novel technologies. On college campuses there is less interest in asking questions about the state of the world than in refining one's presence on Facebook or MySpace. Technology pundits may talk in glowing terms about new forms of social life, but the jury is out on whether virtual self-expression will translate into collective action.  ◆

## CONSIDERING THE ISSUES

1. Think about your life online. How often do you use e-mail, and to what extent? Do you maintain a page on a social networking site? How long do you wait before responding to a text message, an e-mail, or a posting online? What expectations do you have in return from people with whom you communicate online?

2. When you are upset, happy, angry, or anxious, what do you do to handle your emotions? Do you sit quietly and think about how you feel? Do you call a friend or family member? Do you state your feelings online? If so, do you simply want to express your view, or do you hope others will discuss your feelings? Explain.

## CRAFT AND CONTENT

1. What evidence does Turkle provide that the Internet is changing the way we perceive ourselves and others? Does she supply enough examples that convince you that she makes a valid point? Why or why not?

2. Consider Turkle's closing statements. Why does she juxtapose genocide, war, and global warming with the current popularity of Facebook and MySpace? What point is she trying to make?

## CRITICAL THINKING

1. Turkle asserts that social networking sites and online life hinders our ability to "be alone" and "manage emotions." Why does she think this situation can be harmful? Do you agree? Explain.

2. How might the Internet rewire our brains and how we think about ourselves and the world?

## WRITING ABOUT THE ISSUES

1. Review a few social networking websites of friends (you may wish to include yourself) and compare the points made in Turkle's interview to what you find online. How are emotions conveyed online? Do you see any emoticons? What happens when someone expresses an emotion? What do you think they expected from sharing their feelings? Explain.

2. How are web-based relationships different from face-to-face ones? How would your life—and the relationships that enrich it—be different without the Internet and social networking sites?

# Faceless on Facebook
*Kate Beals*

Kate Beals is a writing instructor in Boston, Massachusetts.

## CONNECTING TO THE TOPIC

While social networking sites help people network, connect, and meet new friends, they also project an image of their users online. For people who network or meet online, a user's profile page is their online self—the first impression they present to others. Have you ever thought about what your Facebook profile says about you? What image do you project? What do you hope people will learn about you from what you share? Do you carefully consider what messages you are conveying online about who you are and what you want people to think about you? In this next essay, a newcomer to Facebook describes how the experience forces her to question every word she puts online.

## WORDS IN CONTEXT

**Epicurious** (2)   Website that contains recipes from *Gourmet* and *Bon Appetit* magazines and cooking information (www.epicurious.com)
**fraught** (7)   filled with something, charged (n.)
**covet** (9)   to desire or want something to the point of envy (v.)
**Xanax** (10)   the trade name for a drug of the benzodiazepine class used to treat moderate to severe anxiety and/or panic attacks (n.)

1   **A**fter great urging from my younger, hipper friends, I gave into pressure and registered on Facebook. As I am on the other side of 30, they told me to network on Facebook, and leave MySpace to the kids.

2   I consider myself to be quite Internet savvy. I used a blog site to connect my graduating class in order to organize my 20th high school reunion. I read Salon.com and Slate.msn weekly. I prefer email to the telephone, and even text message my twenty-something cousin fairly regularly (but I admittedly spell out all the words). I cannot imagine living without Google, Mapquest, or eBay. I regularly look up recipes

on **Epicurious**, and do at least 90 percent of my merchandise shopping online. I suppose you could say that I am young enough to handle technology, but still old enough to be impressed by it and how it has changed my life.

3    So why the holdout on social networking sites? I had poked around on Facebook before, but without registering, you can't see that much. Thus, I didn't see a need. But with my friends raving about how connected it made them feel and how they used it for everything from sharing photographs to blogging, I decided to give it a whirl.

4    I had no idea what I was getting myself into.

5    After registering, I was encouraged to add my friends (or at least try to find them). Right from the get-go I started feeling anxious. What if I didn't have many friends? At least on MySpace, I hear everyone gets Tom. Without friends, would I look like a loser? What if I couldn't get enough? Suddenly, I felt like I was back in eighth grade vying for a place in the popular group (or at least in the "not total geek" group).

6    I am supposed to select and post a photo that represents "me." Do I use a real photo? Taken recently? Should I use some abstract piece of art that conveys "me" in a more cerebral artistic way? After deciding that my photos looked more like mug shots (and bloated mug shots at that), and waffling over the copyright issues that may be connected to posting a piece of art, I decided to leave this blank (at least for now).

7    Then I needed to fill out a "profile." This is my opportunity to tell the world more about me (presumably one's favorite subject). I found the profile page a bit confusing because I presume that the people I invite to connect on Facebook would already have a handle on this sort of information. The "Personal" area I discovered, however, is less about the real you, and more about what you want people to think about you. And each field is **fraught** with peril.

8    It didn't start off very promising. My first few fields made me look like an insufferable bore. **Activities**: golf, reading and toddler time; **Interests**: sociology, culture, medicine, child psychology; **Music**: classical and 80s punk rock (well, maybe that was a little interesting); **TV**: *House Hunters*; **Movies**: They still make those?; **Books**. . . .

9    Now a book list I can handle, I thought perking up. I love books. I usually have at least three going at one time, so I thought this field would be easy. But wait, umm—should I share that the last thing I read was a trashy regency romance (left in the room of a historic hotel in New Hampshire, and gratefully pounced upon instead of the academic fare I had brought with me). Or should I instead say the *The Rachel Papers,* which conveyed

the image of the sophisticated, well-read woman I imagine myself to be in daydreams? If I owned up to reading *Snoop*—a sociology book about what your stuff says about you, will people think I read it because I am shallow? I just read a great book by Stephen Pinker, but the book hardly projects the persona I **covet**—you know, smart, sexy and quirky in an intriguing way (as opposed to nerdy, dependable, and quirky in a weird way).

10     So I stopped at the book list. In fact, I stopped altogether. My life is too busy to think so much about myself—or worry about what I am saying about myself. I know that I probably was over-thinking this. Most people, I suspect, are able to fill out these fields without looking for a bottle of **Xanax.** But there is my page, woefully barren. No friends. No interests. The question "What are you doing right now" hangs unanswered—for an honest "looking at my empty page" would be hardly inspirational.

11     Let people make their own judgments in person. Let someone find out about that trashy book when *they* admit to a great bodice ripper. I'll jump right in and share. When cocktail conversation turns to linguistics (and it very well may at the parties I attend), I will turn to my companions and explore brain science with some like-minded nerdy types.

12     But at least for now, I've decided to let this area of the Internet remain "Kate free." ◆

## CONSIDERING THE ISSUES

1. You have probably heard the expression, "Don't judge a book by its cover." The truth is, however, that most of us do make snap judgments based on what we see. How do Facebook and MySpace (and other social networking pages) serve as our on-line selves? How do they make that "first impression?"

2. The author of this essay reveals that she is nearing 40 years of age. Do you think older adults should use social networking sites? Based on what you know about such places, would older adults be comfortable networking on pages that have tradition-ally been dominated by teens and twenty-somethings? Explain.

## CRAFT AND CONTENT

1. What is the author's tone in this essay? What sort of person do you think she is? How would you describe her based on the in-formation she provides?

2. How does the author use humor to connect with her audience? As a reader, can you relate to her points better? Do you think she really takes the issue of Facebook seriously, or is she just having some fun with her audience?

### CRITICAL THINKING

1. Why is the author "anxious" about what she posts about herself in her Facebook profile?
2. The author is conflicted about the image she wishes to convey, and the person she really is. In what ways do we grapple with such issues every day? Why is image so important? Should it be?

### WRITING ABOUT THE ISSUES

1. The author argues that the "Profile" section of Facebook is "less about the real you, and more about what you want people to think about you." Does she have a point? If you have a Facebook or MySpace account, share your own perspective on this observation.
2. Go to Facebook or MySpace and visit some random pages. Based on what you see, what conclusions, if any, can you draw about the users? Would you like to get to know them better? Why or why not? What "hooks" do they use to draw you into their page? How do they engage you? Based on your research and personal experience, write a short essay about what you think makes an effective Facebook or MySpace page.

# Virtual Friendship and the New Narcissism

*Christine Rosen*

Christine Rosen is a senior editor of *The New Atlantis* and resident fellow at the Ethics and Public Policy Center in Washington, DC. She writes about the history of genetics, bioethics, the fertility industry, and the social impact of technology. She is the author of *Preaching Eugenics: Religious Leaders and the American Eugenics Movement* (2004). She is widely published in many journals and newspapers including the *New York Times Magazine*, the *Wall Street Journal*, the *Washington Post*, *New Republic*, *National Review*, the *Weekly Standard*, *Commentary*, and the *New England Journal of Medicine*. This essay, abridged for space, appeared in the Summer 2007 issue of *The New Atlantis*, where it can be viewed online in its entirety.

## CONNECTING TO THE TOPIC

How are Facebook pages like a self-portrait? What do they reveal about subjects and how they view themselves? More than simply connecting us with each other, social networking sites allow us to present a persona to the world—publicly sharing who we know, what we think, what we do, and even what we own. Are social networking sites raising the bar on our level of self-absorption?

## WORDS IN CONTEXT

**narcissism** (title)   excessive love for or admiration of oneself (n.)

**ephemeral** (3)   fleeting; brief (adj.)

**ubiquity** (10)   being everywhere at once (n.)

**bureaucratize** (16)   placed under formal control, usually government control (v.)

**philately** (16)   stamp collecting (n.)

**debasement** (19)   lowered in quality or value (n.)

**parochial** (19)   limited in scope, restricted (adj.)

1   **F**or centuries, the rich and the powerful documented their existence and their status through painted portraits. A marker of wealth and a bid for immortality, portraits offer intriguing hints about the daily life of their subjects—professions, ambitions, attitudes, and, most importantly, social standing. Such portraits, as German art historian Hans Belting has argued, can be understood as "painted anthropology," with much to teach us, both intentionally and unintentionally, about the culture in which they were created.

2   Self-portraits can be especially instructive. By showing the artist both as he sees his true self and as he wishes to be seen, self-portraits can at once expose and obscure, clarify and distort. They offer opportunities for

both self-expression and self-seeking. They can display egotism and modesty, self-aggrandizement and self-mockery.

3    Today, our self-portraits are democratic and digital; they are crafted from pixels rather than paints. On social networking websites like MySpace and Facebook, our modern self-portraits feature background music, carefully manipulated photographs, stream-of-consciousness musings, and lists of our hobbies and friends. They are interactive, inviting viewers not merely to look at, but also to respond to, the life portrayed online. We create them to find friendship, love, and that ambiguous modern thing called connection. Like painters constantly retouching their work, we alter, update, and tweak our online self-portraits; but as digital objects they are far more **ephemeral** than oil on canvas. Vital statistics, glimpses of bare flesh, lists of favorite bands and favorite poems all clamor for our attention—and it is the timeless human desire for attention that emerges as the dominant theme of these vast virtual galleries.

4    Although social networking sites are in their infancy, we are seeing their impact culturally: in language (where to *friend* is now a verb), in politics (where it is de rigueur for presidential aspirants to catalogue their virtues on MySpace), and on college campuses (where not using Facebook can be a social handicap). But we are only beginning to come to grips with the consequences of our use of these sites: for friendship, and for our notions of privacy, authenticity, community, and identity.

## Making Connections

5    The earliest online social networks were arguably the Bulletin Board Systems of the 1980s that let users post public messages, send and receive private messages, play games, and exchange software. Some of those BBSs, like The WELL (Whole Earth 'Lectronic Link) that technologist Larry Brilliant and futurist Stewart Brand started in 1985, made the transition to the World Wide Web in the mid-1990s. (Now owned by Salon.com, The WELL boasts that it was "the primordial ooze where the online community movement was born.") Other websites for community and connection emerged in the 1990s, including Classmates.com (1995), where users register by high school and year of graduation; Company of Friends, a business-oriented site founded in 1997; and Epinions, founded in 1999 to allow users to give their opinions about various consumer products.

6    A new generation of social networking websites appeared in 2002 with the launch of Friendster, whose founder, Jonathan Abrams, admitted

that his main motivation for creating the site was to meet attractive women. Unlike previous online communities, which brought together anonymous strangers with shared interests, Friendster uses a model of social networking known as the "Circle of Friends" (developed by British computer scientist Jonathan Bishop), in which users invite friends and acquaintances—that is, people they already know and like—to join their network.

7     Friendster was an immediate success, with millions of registered users by mid-2003. But technological glitches and poor management at the company allowed a new social networking site, MySpace, launched in 2003, quickly to surpass it. Originally started by musicians, MySpace has become a major venue for sharing music as well as videos and photos. It is now the behemoth of online social networking, with over 100 million registered users. Connection has become big business: In 2005, Rupert Murdoch's News Corporation bought MySpace for $580 million.

8     Besides MySpace and Friendster, the best-known social networking site is Facebook, launched in 2004. Originally restricted to college students, Facebook—which takes its name from the small photo albums that colleges once gave to incoming freshmen and faculty to help them cope with meeting so many new people—soon extended membership to high schoolers and is now open to anyone. Still, it is most popular among college students and recent college graduates, many of whom use the site as their primary method of communicating with one another. Millions of college students check their Facebook pages several times every day and spend hours sending and receiving messages, making appointments, getting updates on their friends' activities, and learning about people they might recently have met or heard about.

9     There are dozens of other social networking sites, including Orkut, Bebo, and Yahoo 360°. Microsoft recently announced its own plans for a social networking site called Wallop; the company boasts that the site will offer "an entirely new way for consumers to express their individuality online." (It is noteworthy that Microsoft refers to social networkers as "consumers" rather than merely "users" or, say, "people.") Niche social networking sites are also flourishing: there are sites offering forums and fellowship for photographers, music lovers, and sports fans. There are professional networking sites, such as LinkedIn, that keep people connected with present and former colleagues and other business acquaintances.

10     Despite the increasingly diverse range of social networking sites, the most popular sites share certain features. On MySpace and Facebook, for

example, the process of setting up one's online identity is relatively simple: Provide your name, address, e-mail address, and a few other pieces of information and you're up and running and ready to create your online persona. MySpace includes a section, "About Me," where you can post your name, age, where you live, and other personal details such as your zodiac sign, religion, sexual orientation, and relationship status. There is also a "Who I'd Like to Meet" section, which on most MySpace profiles is filled with images of celebrities. Users can also list their favorite music, movies, and television shows, as well as their personal heroes; MySpace users can also blog on their pages. A user "friends" people—that is, invites them by e-mail to appear on the user's "Friend Space," where they are listed, linked, and ranked. Below the Friends space is a Comments section where friends can post notes. MySpace allows users to personalize their pages by uploading images and music and videos; indeed, one of the defining features of most MySpace pages is the **ubiquity** of visual and audio clutter. With silly, hyper flashing graphics in neon colors and clip-art style images of kittens and cartoons, MySpace pages often resemble an overdecorated high school yearbook.

11      By contrast, Facebook limits what its users can do to their profiles. Besides general personal information, Facebook users have a "Wall" where people can leave them brief notes, as well as a Messages feature that functions like an in-house Facebook e-mail account. You list your friends on Facebook as well, but in general, unlike MySpace friends, which are often complete strangers (or spammers) Facebook friends tend to be part of one's offline social circle. (This might change, however, now that Facebook has opened its site to anyone rather than restricting it to college and high school students.) Facebook (and MySpace) allow users to form groups based on mutual interests. Facebook users can also send "pokes" to friends; these little digital nudges are meant to let someone know you are thinking about him or her. But they can also be interpreted as not-so-subtle come-ons; one Facebook group with over 200,000 members is called "Enough with the Poking, Let's Just Have Sex."

## Won't You Be My Digital Neighbor?

12  According to a survey recently conducted by the Pew Internet and American Life Project, more than half of all Americans between the ages of twelve and seventeen use some online social networking site. Indeed, media coverage of social networking sites usually describes them as vast

teenage playgrounds—or wastelands, depending on one's perspective. Central to this narrative is a nearly unbridgeable generational divide, with tech-savvy youngsters redefining friendship while their doddering elders look on with bafflement and increasing anxiety. This seems anecdotally correct; I can't count how many times I have mentioned social networking websites to someone over the age of forty and received the reply, "Oh yes, I've heard about that MyFace! All the kids are doing that these days. Very interesting!"

13      Numerous articles have chronicled adults' attempts to navigate the world of social networking, such as the recent New York Times essay in which columnist Michelle Slatalla described the incredible embarrassment she caused her teenage daughter when she joined Facebook: "everyone in the whole world thinks its super creepy when adults have facebooks," her daughter instant-messaged her. "unfriend paige right now. im serious. . . . i will be soo mad if you dont unfriend paige right now. actually." In fact, social networking sites are not only for the young. More than half of the visitors to MySpace claim to be over the age of 35. And now that the first generation of college Facebook users have graduated, and the site is open to all, more than half of Facebook users are no longer students. What's more, the proliferation of niche social networking sites, including those aimed at adults, suggests that it is not only teenagers who will nurture relationships in virtual space for the foreseeable future.

## The New Taxonomy of Friendship

14      There is a Spanish proverb that warns, "Life without a friend is death without a witness." In the world of online social networking, the warning might be simpler: "Life without hundreds of online 'friends' is virtual death." On these sites, friendship is the stated raison d'être. "A place for friends," is the slogan of MySpace. Facebook is a "social utility that connects people with friends." Orkut describes itself as "an online community that connects people through a network of trusted friends." Friendster's name speaks for itself.

15      But "friendship" in these virtual spaces is thoroughly different from real-world friendship. In its traditional sense, friendship is a relationship which, broadly speaking, involves the sharing of mutual interests, reciprocity, trust, and the revelation of intimate details over time and within specific social (and cultural) contexts. Because friendship depends on mutual revelations that are concealed from the rest of the world, it can only

flourish within the boundaries of privacy; the idea of public friendship is an oxymoron.

16     The hypertext link called "friendship" on social networking sites is very different: public, fluid, and promiscuous, yet oddly **bureaucratized**. Friendship on these sites focuses a great deal on collecting, managing, and ranking the people you know. Everything about MySpace, for example, is designed to encourage users to gather as many friends as possible, as though friendship were **philately**. If you are so unfortunate as to have but one MySpace friend, for example, your page reads: "You have 1 friends," along with a stretch of sad empty space where dozens of thumbnail photos of your acquaintances should appear.

17     The structure of social networking sites also encourages the bureaucratization of friendship. Each site has its own terminology, but among the words that users employ most often is "managing." The Pew survey mentioned earlier found that "teens say social networking sites help them manage their friendships." There is something Orwellian about the management-speak on social networking sites: "Change My Top Friends," "View All of My Friends" and, for those times when our inner Stalins sense the need for a virtual purge, "Edit Friends." With a few mouse clicks one can elevate or downgrade (or entirely eliminate) a relationship.

18     To be sure, we all rank our friends, albeit in unspoken and intuitive ways. One friend might be a good companion for outings to movies or concerts; another might be someone with whom you socialize in professional settings; another might be the kind of person for whom you would drop everything if he needed help. But social networking sites allow us to rank our friends publicly. And not only can we publicize our own preferences in people, but we can also peruse the favorites among our other acquaintances. We can learn all about the friends of our friends—often without having ever met them in person.

## Status-Seekers

19     Of course, it would be foolish to suggest that people are incapable of making distinctions between social networking "friends" and friends they see in the flesh. The use of the word "friend" on social networking sites is a dilution and a **debasement**, and surely no one with hundreds of MySpace or Facebook "friends" is so confused as to believe those are all real friendships. The impulse to collect as many "friends" as possible on a MySpace page is not an expression of the human need for companionship, but of a

different need no less profound and pressing: the need for status. Unlike the painted portraits that members of the middle class in a bygone era would commission to signal their elite status once they rose in society, social networking websites allow us to create status—not merely to commemorate the achievement of it. There is a reason that most of the MySpace profiles of famous people are fakes, often created by fans: Celebrities don't need legions of MySpace friends to prove their importance. It's the rest of the population, seeking a form of **parochial** celebrity, that does.

20    But status-seeking has an ever-present partner: anxiety. Unlike a portrait, which, once finished and framed, hung tamely on the wall signaling one's status, maintaining status on MySpace or Facebook requires constant vigilance. As one 24-year-old wrote in a *New York Times* essay, "I am obsessed with testimonials and solicit them incessantly. They are the ultimate social currency, public declarations of the intimacy status of a relationship. . . . Every profile is a carefully planned media campaign."

21    The sites themselves were designed to encourage this. Describing the work of B.J. Fogg of Stanford University, who studies "persuasion strategies" used by social networking sites to increase participation, *The New Scientist* noted, "The secret is to tie the acquisition of friends, compliments and status—spoils that humans will work hard for—to activities that enhance the site." As Fogg told the magazine, "You offer someone a context for gaining status, and they are going to work for that status." Network theorist Albert-László Barabási notes that online connection follows the rule of "preferential attachment"—that is, "when choosing between two pages, one with twice as many links as the other, about twice as many people link to the more connected page." As a result, "while our individual choices are highly unpredictable, as a group we follow strict patterns." Our lemming-like pursuit of online status via the collection of hundreds of "friends" clearly follows this rule.

22    What, in the end, does this pursuit of virtual status mean for community and friendship? Writing in the 1980s in *Habits of the Heart,* sociologist Robert Bellah and his colleagues documented the movement away from close-knit, traditional communities, to "lifestyle enclaves" which were defined largely by "leisure and consumption." Perhaps today we have moved beyond lifestyle enclaves and into "personality enclaves" or "identity enclaves"—discrete virtual places in which we can be different (and sometimes contradictory) people, with different groups of like-minded, though ever-shifting, friends.

## Beyond Networking

23 This past spring, Len Harmon, the director of the Fischer Policy and Cultural Institute at Nichols College in Dudley, Massachusetts, offered a new course about social networking. Nichols is a small school whose students come largely from Connecticut and Massachusetts; many of them are the first members of their families to attend college. "I noticed a lot of issues involved with social networking sites," Harmon told me when I asked him why he created the class. How have these sites been useful to Nichols students? "It has relieved some of the stress of transitions for them," he said. "When abrupt departures occur—their family moves or they have to leave friends behind—they can cope by keeping in touch more easily."

24 So perhaps we should praise social networking websites for streamlining friendship the way e-mail streamlined correspondence. In the nineteenth century, Emerson observed that "friendship requires more time than poor busy men can usually command." Now, technology has given us the freedom to tap into our network of friends when it is convenient for us. "It's a way of maintaining a friendship without having to make any effort whatsoever," as a recent graduate of Harvard explained to *The New Yorker*. And that ease admittedly makes it possible to stay in contact with a wider circle of offline acquaintances than might have been possible in the era before Facebook. Friends you haven't heard from in years, old buddies from elementary school, people you might have (should have?) fallen out of touch with—it is now easier than ever to reconnect to those people.

25 But what kind of connections are these? In his excellent book *Friendship: An Exposé,* Joseph Epstein praises the telephone and e-mail as technologies that have greatly facilitated friendship. He writes, "Proust once said he didn't much care for the analogy of a book to a friend. He thought a book was better than a friend, because you could shut it—and be shut of it—when you wished, which one can't always do with a friend." With e-mail and caller ID, Epstein enthuses, you can. But social networking sites (which Epstein says "speak to the vast loneliness in the world") have a different effect: they discourage "being shut of" people. On the contrary, they encourage users to check in frequently, "poke" friends, and post comments on others' pages. They favor interaction of greater quantity but less quality.

26 This constant connectivity concerns Len Harmon. "There is a sense of, 'if I'm not online or constantly texting or posting, then I'm missing something,'" he said of his students. "This is where I find the generational impact the greatest—not the use of the technology, but the overuse of the technology." It is unclear how the regular use of these sites will affect behavior over

the long run—especially the behavior of children and young adults who are growing up with these tools. Almost no research has explored how virtual socializing affects children's development. What does a child weaned on Club Penguin learn about social interaction? How is an adolescent who spends her evenings managing her MySpace page different from a teenager who spends her night gossiping on the telephone to friends? Given that "people want to live their lives online," as the founder of one social net-working site recently told *Fast Company* magazine, and they are beginning to do so at ever-younger ages, these questions are worth exploring.

27      The few studies that have emerged do not inspire confidence. Re-searcher Rob Nyland at Brigham Young University recently surveyed 184 users of social networking sites and found that heavy users "feel less socially involved with the community around them." He also found that "as individu-als use social networking more for entertainment, their level of social in-volvement decreases." Another recent study conducted by communications professor Qingwen Dong and colleagues at the University of the Pacific found that "those who engaged in romantic communication over MySpace tend to have low levels of both emotional intelligence and self-esteem."

28      The implications of the narcissistic and exhibitionistic tendencies of social networkers also cry out for further consideration. There are oppor-tunity costs when we spend so much time carefully grooming ourselves online. Given how much time we already devote to entertaining ourselves with technology, it is at least worth asking if the time we spend on social networking sites is well spent. In investing so much energy into improving how we present ourselves online, are we missing chances to genuinely im-prove ourselves?

29      We should also take note of the trend toward giving up face-to-face for virtual contact—and, in some cases, a preference for the latter. Today, many of our cultural, social, and political interactions take place through eminently convenient technological surrogates—Why go to the bank if you can use the ATM? Why browse in a bookstore when you can simply peruse the personalized selections Amazon.com has made for you? In the same vein, social networking sites are often convenient surrogates for off-line friendship and community. In this context it is worth considering an observation that Stanley Milgram made in 1974, regarding his experi-ments with obedience: "The social psychology of this century reveals a major lesson," he wrote. "Often it is not so much the kind of person a man is as the kind of situation in which he finds himself that determines how he will act." To an increasing degree, we find and form our friendships and

communities in the virtual world as well as the real world. These virtual networks greatly expand our opportunities to meet others, but they might also result in our valuing less the capacity for genuine connection. As the young woman writing in the *Times* admitted, "I consistently trade actual human contact for the more reliable high of smiles on MySpace, winks on Match.com, and pokes on Facebook." That she finds these online relationships more reliable is telling: it shows a desire to avoid the vulnerability and uncertainty that true friendship entails. Real intimacy requires risk—the risk of disapproval, of heartache, of being thought a fool. Social networking websites may make relationships more reliable, but whether those relationships can be humanly satisfying remains to be seen.

### CONSIDERING THE ISSUES

1. This article makes the bold statement: "public friendship is an oxymoron." From your point of view, discuss the meaning of friendship and decide whether social networking sites are using the term "friend" properly.
2. Rosen compares online networking pages to "self-portraits." Explore this concept in more depth. In what ways is this true? If you have a personal page, discuss what that page says about you and in what ways it is indeed a "self-portrait." How are painted portraits and websites similar, and how are they different?

### CRAFT AND CONTENT

1. What does Rosen mean when she uses the term "Orwellian" and the phrase "our inner Stalins" when referring to social networking sites? To what/whom is she referring, and how do these references connect to her point?
2. What does Rosen think of online networking sites? Identify areas in her essay in which she reveals her viewpoint.

### CRITICAL THINKING

1. Rosen comments in an aside, "It is noteworthy that Microsoft refers to social networkers as 'consumers' rather than merely 'users' or, say, 'people.'" Why do you think Microsoft uses the term "consumers"? Do you see this as negative or positive? Explain.

2. The author comments, "tech-savvy youngsters [are] redefining friendship while their doddering elders look on with bafflement and increasing anxiety." Do you find this to be true? How do your older family members view social networking sites—do any of them have MySpace or Facebook pages? Why or why not?

### WRITING ABOUT THE ISSUES

1. Write an essay exploring the consequences of social networking sites on the future of friendship and community.
2. This article traces the evolution of social networking sites: outline this evolution showing how these sites have evolved from "the primordial ooze" of the 1980s to the newest site being planned by Microsoft.

## TOPICAL CONNECTIONS

### GROUP PROJECTS

1. Track all of your online correspondence—received and sent—for a period of one week. This should include e-mail, IM, text messaging, and posting on social networking sites. Develop categories for the communication (social, family, work, school, junk, etc.) and chart how many of each you receive and send in each category. Keep track of how much time you spend online. Discuss your personal results with the group. Discuss as a group how the Internet both enhances and complicates life, and whether it is indeed changing your personal relationships for better or for worse.
2. Several of the writers in this unit are critical of social networking sites, noting that they promote self-centeredness, reduce our ability to cope with emotions, and cheapen what it means to be "a friend." Interview at least 10 people of different age groups about how they use online communication and their views of social networking sites. Create simple questions, but make them broad enough to allow for the expression of detailed viewpoints and options. Discuss the interviews as a group, and write a short essay evaluating the role of social networking in the lives of people today. Include any differences or similarities you noticed between age groups, professions, and/or social backgrounds.

Based on your surveys, can you predict the role social network-ing will have in our lives in the next decade?

### WEB PROJECTS

3. Is there a connection between how we communicate and relate to others online and how we develop our own sense of identity? How others perceive us? Print the profiles of at least 10 people you know (you may need to ask for permission if you are not part of a social network) and compare the profiles they present to the people you know in "real life." Alternatively, you could ask an acquaintance to share five profiles of people you don't know for analysis.
4. Research the pages of at least four different social networking sites (many are named in this unit). Describe how they are simi-lar and how they are different. Do they attract different groups? Are some, as Stites states in her essay, cooler than others? What groups do they attract and how do they promote a sense of be-longing and community? Explain.

### FOR FURTHER INQUIRY

5. What might the erosion of the real and virtual boundaries that social networking promotes eventually do to the way we com-municate with each other? Will the way people define them-selves now be different in 20 years as a result of blending online and offline relationships? Explain.
6. A popular television commercial for an Internet employment agency features a man writing an insulting letter to his boss only to have a toy fall off his monitor and hit the "enter" key, sending his message. Have you ever had a mishap with online communi-cation, or found yourself sending a message that you shouldn't have simply because you hit the "enter" key in the heat of the moment? Describe your experience. Did it change your use of online communication?

# 2 | Does Personal Privacy Have Limits?

**"D**o what you want, it's a free country!" is an expression that we often hear and would like to believe. Most Americans take personal freedom for granted, and are startled when our rights seem to be threatened. Over the last decade, personal privacy rights have become a subject of concern and controversy. The threat of terrorism, the advent of the Internet, and improved technology have raised new questions connected to personal privacy. Should we have national identification cards as a measure to thwart terrorism? Do Internet companies have the right to track our movements online? Do surveillance cameras in stores, parking lots, and public spaces deter criminal activity? Are we giving too much away voluntarily when we post information on blogs and social networking pages such as My-Space and Facebook? Or is less privacy simply the price we pay for more convenience and greater safety?

Most Americans assume that their right to privacy is protected by the Fourth Amendment of the Constitution, which ensures "the right of the people to be secure in their persons, houses, papers, and effects, against unreasonable searches and seizures." But does the Fourth Amendment actually protect our right to privacy in the way that we think? How do we define an "unreasonable" search? And does the Fourth Amendment protect us from things such as Internet cookies, or public surveillance cameras? Police, if they believe there is probable cause, may enter our homes or even tap our phones. Airport security guards may search our bags and our persons. Is privacy something we must sacrifice in order to participate in today's world? This unit takes a closer look at some of the privacy issues Americans face today.

## CRITICAL THINKING

1. What is happening in this cartoon? What are the people doing? What is the meaning of the signs behind the seated man, and the screens to the left of the cartoon?
2. Who do the people around the desk represent? How does the cartoonist depict them?
3. What is the author trying to say about the subject matter? What do you need to know in order to understand the point of this cartoon? Explain.

"YES, THERE'S A DEFINITE PATTERN HERE...SPEAKING FREELY, WEAPONS POSSESSION, SENSITIVITY TO SEARCHES, REFUSING TO ANSWER QUESTIONS ABOUT HIMSELF... ...HE'S OBVIOUSLY A THREAT... HAVE SOMEONE PICK UP THIS MR. BILL O. RIGHTS."

# Privacy Is Overrated

## David Plotz

David Plotz is a writer and deputy editor for Slate.com. His articles have appeared in many publications, including *Harper's Magazine*, the *New York Times Magazine*, *Rolling Stone,* and the *New Republic*. He is a recipient of the National Press Club's Sandy Hume Award for Political Journalism. This essay first appeared in *GQ* magazine in 2003.

## CONNECTING TO THE TOPIC

What privacy rights do we surrender in the name of safety, convenience, and even health? Is this sacrifice a fair exchange? For example, did you know that every time you log on to the Internet, information engines can put "cookies" on your computer to track your movements? When you visit their site again, these cookies are able to remember who you are as well as your preferences. Cookies may also gather information about you as a consumer. Is our privacy the price we pay for the convenience of the Internet? And are the rights that we give up a small price to pay when we consider the benefits we get in exchange?

## WORDS IN CONTEXT

**cookies** (7)  a collection of information stored on an Internet user's computer that identifies visitors of particular websites (n.)

**paranoia** (11)  extreme, irrational distrust of others (n.)

**pundits** (11)  critics (n.)

**Orwellian** (11)  relating to the works of author George Orwell, especially the satirical novel *1984*, which depicts a futuristic totalitarian state (adj.)

**Big Brother** (13)  a character in George Orwell's novel *1984*, who is an omnipresent figure representing an authoritarian government's total control over individual lives. The figure symbolizes a political or social situation in which one's actions are closely monitored by an authoritarian figure or group (n.).

**crusade** (14)  a campaign or concerted movement for a cause (n.)

**hypocrisy** (14)  falseness (n.)

**nostalgia** (14)  a longing for things, persons, or situations of the past (n.)

**entrepreneurship** (21)  the act of organizing, operating, and assuming the risk for a business venture (n.)

**titanic** (21)   enormous (adj.)

**stigmatized** (25)   marked as disgraceful (adj.)

**egocentric** (27)   holding the view that oneself is the center, object, and norm of all experience (adj.)

**fallacy** (27)   incorrect reasoning or beliefs (n.)

**monolithic** (28)   massive (adj.)

**encryption** (31)   the process of making information indecipherable by using a secret code to prevent access by unauthorized parties (n.)

1   Let's start by invading my privacy. I own a three-bedroom house on Cortland Place in Washington D.C. I am married to Hanna Rosin. We have a two-year-old child. I drive a 2001 Volkswagen Passat.

2   I have no criminal record. I have never been party to a lawsuit. I have no tax liens against me. I have never declared bankruptcy (unlike 2 of the 11 other David Plotzes in the United States). I have no ties to organized crime, though I do hold stock options in Microsoft.

3   The James Mintz group, a leading corporate investigation firm headquartered in New York City, learned all this about me in a few hours with a computer, an Internet connection and a single phone call—without even bending the law.

4   If you spent a bit more time, you would discover my Social Security number and how much I paid for the house. You would find out that I bank at Bank of America. You could have my listed home telephone number in two mouse clicks and my unlisted cell phone number if you paid the right data broker.

5   Corporations, meanwhile, are recording my every move. I don't watch what I eat, but Safeway does, thanks to my club card. Telecoms can pinpoint where I am when I make my cell phone calls. Clothing stores analyze my purchases in detail, recording everything from the expansion of my waist (up to 35 from 32) to my recent infatuation with three-button suits.

6   The credit reporting agencies know every time I have made a late payment to my Citibank MasterCard (number 6577 . . . I'm not that stupid) and every time I have applied for credit. This is all going on my permanent record.

7   Surveillance cameras are watching me in malls and sometimes on public streets. Even my own computer is spying on me. A scan of my hard drive turns up 141 **cookies**, deposited by companies that track me around

the Web. I recently surfed a porn site (just because a high school friend runs it, I swear). The cookies may know about it. My employer probably does too. After all, my employment contract permits my boss to track all my on-the-job Web surfing, and read all my work e-mail too.

8    If my company isn't watching, perhaps the FBI is: Its Carnivore program rafts through vast rivers of e-mail flow in search of criminal activity.

9    They—a *they* that includes the feds, a thousand corporations, a million telemarketers, my employer, my enemies and maybe even my friends—know all this about me, and more. And unless you are a technophobe hermit who pays for everything in cash, they know all this about you too.

10    To which I say, "Hallelujah!"

11    I'm in the minority. Privacy **paranoia** has become a national obsession. **Pundits**, politicians and privacy activists have been shouting about the latest government intrusion on privacy. The Defense Department's office of Total Information Awareness plans to collect massive quantities of information about all Americans—everything from what you buy to where you travel—in gigantic databases, and then sift through the information for clues about terrorism. Total Information Awareness has been denounced as **Orwellian**, and there are efforts to stop the program.

12    You could fill a library with privacy-alarmism books (*The End of Privacy*; *Privacy: How to Protect What's Left of It*). Congress and the state legislatures are awash in proposals to protect privacy. Horror stories fuel the fire of anxiety. The sailor the Navy tried to book out after he used the word *gay* in a supposedly confidential AOL profile. The stalker who bought his target's address from a Web information broker, tracked her down, and murdered her. The sale of Social Security numbers by LexisNexis.

13    You can more or less distill the essence of the privacy-rights movement to this idea: **Big Brother** and Big Business observe us too often, without our consent. The most intimate details of our lives are being sold and used secretly to make judgments about us, and we have no control over it.

14    It sounds appalling. But in fact, the privacy **crusade** is built on a foundation of **hypocrisy**, paranoia, economic know-nothingism and bogus **nostalgia**.

15    The first flaw of privacy: People care a great deal about their own, but not at all about anyone else's. We figure, why should anyone get to review my real-estate records or get to read my divorce proceedings? My life is my own business.

16      But I bet you want to know if your baby-sitter has ever been convicted of child abuse, if your business partner has a history of bankruptcy, if your boyfriend is still married. When your husband flees the state to duck child support payments, wouldn't you use his Social Security number, driving records, real estate filings and whatever else you could get your hands on to track him down?

17      You don't want the Total Information Awareness office to know what you bought at the hardware store or where you take vacations. But if your neighbor is stockpiling fertilizer and likes to holiday in Iraq, don't you want the government to notice? If government had been using even basic data-mining techniques before September 11, at least 11 of the hijackers might have been stopped, according to a report by the Markel Foundation. Wouldn't that be worth letting the feds know you bought an Xbox last month?

18      Hysteria is growing that companies are shadowing us constantly. They are. But here, too, privacy is a silly value, both because "protecting" it is enormously costly and because it's not really being violated.

19      Ignorant companies are bankrupt companies. A recent study found that restricting marketing data would raise catalog clothing prices up to 11 percent, costing shoppers $1 billion per year. By buying address lists and consumer profiles, Victoria's Secret knows to send a catalog to my house, and International Male knows not to bother. Their marketing costs plummet. We get less junk mail, lower prices, and catalogs for clothing we might buy.

20      Your father probably shopped with a clothier who knew he wore a 44 long suit and preferred a faint pinstripe. Such friendships are extinct, murdered by megastores and armchair shopping. But today, when I log on to Amazon.com, I am pitched another book about privacy, because Amazon has learned that I am the kind of guy who buys books on privacy. They are saving me time (which is money) by delivering what I like.

21      Information sharing is also an engine of **entrepreneurship**. Thanks to cheap mailing lists, upstarts can challenge **titanic** businesses, lowering prices and bringing clever products to market.

22      Losing privacy has made it much cheaper to use a credit card or buy a house. Credit card and mortgage companies collect and share information about who pays, who doesn't, etc. Because they have an idea who will default, they offer significantly lower rates to people with good records and make credit much more available to poorer customers.

23    It's true that identity theft has become easier. On the other hand, credit card fraud—a much more common crime—is harder. Companies often catch a thief before a customer even notices her card is missing. (Their observant computers notice that her buying habits have suddenly changed.)

24    Similarly, surveillance cameras reduce shoplifting and stop ATM robberies, while cameras in police cars reduce incidents of police brutality. Lack of privacy actually tends to fight crime, not cause it.

25    There is one notable exception to the argument for transparency, however. If medical records are unsealed, especially to employers, people may avoid treatment, fearing they will be **stigmatized** or fired for their health problems.

26    Philosophically, many people don't like the idea that a soulless corporation records that they buy sexy underwear, subscribe to *Penthouse* and collect heavy metal CDs. Friends were freaked out to receive ads for infant formula soon after they gave birth. How did the company know? Is the hospital selling your baby already?

27    But this worry is an example of the **egocentric fallacy**: the belief that because people know something about you, they care. One wonderful, terrible thing about modern capitalism is that companies don't care. You are not a person. You are a wallet.

28    Privacy advocates like to say, "It didn't used to be this way." They hark back to a time—it generally sounds like 19th-century rural America—when stores didn't record your every purchase and doctors didn't report your ailments to a **monolithic** insurance company. You could abandon a bad life in one state, reinvent yourself 50 miles away, and no one needed to know. Nothing went down on your permanent record, because there was no permanent record.

29    This nostalgia imagines a past that never existed. Small town America never guarded anyone's privacy. In small towns, as anyone who lives in one can attest, people can be nosy and punish nonconformity viciously.

30    The right to privacy is not mentioned in the Constitution, and was not even conceived until 1890. Censuses in the 18th and 19th centuries demanded answers to intrusive questions, such as compelling Americans to reveal any history of insanity in the family.

31    Nostalgists fail to recognize that technology is creating a golden age from what they actually care about: real privacy. This is nothing that Amazon.com cares about. Nothing that Total Information Awareness can track down. Nothing that needs to be protected by **encryption**.

32    The opposite of privacy is not invasion of privacy: it is openness. Real privacy is what allows us to share hopes, dreams, fantasies, fears, and makes us feel we can safely expose all our faults and quirks and still be loved. Privacy is the space between us and our dearest—where everything is known and does not matter.

33    There has never been a better time for real privacy. The Internet allows people who have peculiar interests, social awkwardness or debilitating health problems to create communities that never could have existed before. Online, they can find other folks who want to re-enact the Battle of Bull Run or sunbathe nude or whatever your bag is, baby.

34    By surrendering some privacy—that is, by revealing our humanity with all its peculiarity in chat rooms or on e-mail or in newsgroups—we gain a much greater privacy: an intimacy with others, a sense of belonging. To be less private sometimes is to have more privacy. To be less private is to be more ourselves. ◆

## CONSIDERING THE ISSUES

1. How much do you value your privacy? Do you ever think about this right? Plotz notes that while we tend to value our own privacy, we do not value the privacy of others. What do you feel others have a right to know about you? What do you think you have a right to know about other people? Explain.

2. Do you think we have more or less privacy than we did 50 years ago? Discuss with an older adult their perception of privacy in America now and 50 years ago. What factors, such as where we live and the lifestyle we lead, contribute to the level of privacy we have? Explain.

## CRAFT AND CONTENT

1. Why does Plotz begin his essay by revealing his personal information? How does it help support the points he outlines in his essay? As a reader, how did you react to his divulging of so much personal information? Explain.

2. Identify specific areas where Plotz uses humor in his essay. Does his use of humor help him connect with his audience, or does it trivialize a serious subject? Explain.

## CRITICAL THINKING

1. According to Plotz, why is our concern over privacy rights an "egocentric fallacy"? Do you agree with his argument? Why or why not?
2. What level of privacy do the "nostalgists" believe we enjoyed in the past? Why does Plotz say this memory is incorrect? Explain.

## WRITING ABOUT THE ISSUES

1. At the end of his essay, Plotz states, "the opposite of privacy is not invasion of privacy: It is openness." Develop your own definition of privacy. How does it compare to Plotz's viewpoint?
2. Plotz begins his article by revealing information that is easily accessible about him through the Internet. Conduct an Internet search of yourself or a parent and see how much information you can locate. You may try online phone books, a Google search, and other information systems such as www.whowhere. com. After conducting your search, write your own narrative about what someone could find about you and how you feel about the availability of personal information online.

# Invading Our Own Privacy
*David Schimke*

David Schimke is editor-in-chief of *Utne Reader*. His articles and essays have appeared in many newspapers and journals. His essay, "Rack 'Em Up," a profile of a young pool hustler, was recognized in *The Best American Sports Writing* (1999). This essay appeared in the May–June 2007 issue of *Utne Reader*.

## CONNECTING TO THE TOPIC

Tell-all blogs, party photos on Myspace and Facebook, cookies and trackers online—are we giving away too much information? As members of the digital generation come of age, they bring with them new questions regarding online privacy. Employers are using information gathered online to make hiring decisions. Online tracking devices tell marketing companies what we like to buy, where we like to eat, and with whom we like to socialize—all with the goal of steering the right advertising our way. And most online users give away information without thinking very much about it, which raises this question: are we giving our privacy away?

## WORDS IN CONTEXT

**grizzled** (1)  gray-haired, old (adj.)
**caricature** (1)  an exaggerated picture or image of a person (n.)
**blithely** (3)  exceedingly casual and carefree (adv.)
**paradigm** (4)  a new model (n.)
**proclivities** (5)  practices or inclinations (n.)
**paradoxically** (6)  seemingly contradictory (adv.)

1   It's a good guess that the last thing the newly hired editor of an alternative newspaper would want a **grizzled** group of journalists to know is that the person he'd most like to meet is Howard Stern. Yet hours after Kevin Hoffman was tapped to take the helm at *City Pages*, staffers at the Minneapolis weekly, who had yet to meet the 30-year-old in person, were reading all about their new leader's love of Stern, ultimate fighting, and *The Real World* on his MySpace page and sketching a less than favorable **caricature**.

2   That same week in late January, Jessica Blinkerd, a 22-year-old California woman charged with drunken driving and vehicular manslaughter, received a tougher-than-expected sentence, 64 months in prison. Despite having professed deep remorse in court, Blinkerd had posted pictures at MySpace of herself out on the town after the accident, drinking with friends and sporting a shirt advertising a brand of tequila. "Why would probation get your attention?" the judge asked.

3   Both cases, one comical, the other life-altering, illustrate a commercially driven cultural trend whose consequences may not be known until well after debates over the merits of wiretapping, the Patriot Act, and digital spying are resolved in Congress. People of all ages, but especially those between 18 and 34, have become so comfortable with online commerce, instant correspondence, and daily confession that personal privacy is being redefined and, some argue, **blithely** forfeited.

4    "Young people have already embraced the frenzied commercial environment of the digital marketplace," says Jeff Chester, founder and executive director of the Center for Digital Democracy. "The prevailing **paradigm** is a seamless integration of content, communication, data collection, and targeted marketing."

5    The technological assault on our anonymity is gaining speed: Surveillance cameras and now cell phones track physical movement; computer "cookies" transmit buying habits, political affiliations, and sexual **proclivities**. And now, according to *Science News* (Jan. 13, 2007), because computer users have "characteristic patterns of how they time their keystrokes [and] browse websites," researchers are learning how to use "typeprints, clickprints, and writeprints, respectively, as digital forms of fingerprints."

6    *New York* magazine (Feb. 12, 2007) points out that people of all ages are susceptible to these intrusive technologies, but it's twentysomethings who are, **paradoxically**, the most savvy about how they can be watched and the least likely to self-censor. "In essence, every young person in America has become, in the literal sense, a public figure," writes Emily Nussbaum, who posits that online differences represent the first true generation gap in nearly 50 years. "And so they have adopted the skills that celebrities learn in order not to go crazy: enjoying the attention instead of fighting it."

7    It's tempting to write off those darn kids as narcissistic or obsessed with fame, as Lakshmi Chaudhry does in the *Nation* (Jan. 29, 2007). After all, as she points out, "Celebrity has become a commodity in itself, detached from and more valuable than wealth or achievement." What's received little attention, though, is the ways corporations are stacking the digital deck.

8    "Young people are now heavily engaged in identity exploration and development well into their 20s, and the Internet has become their primary tool," says Kathryn Montgomery, professor of communications at American University and author of *Generation Digital* (MIT Press, 2007). "Companies build brands by purposely cultivating this process, creating spaces where they're encouraging people to pour their hearts out. It's like a diary—but there's no key."

9    In February of 2007, ClickZ.com reported that Fox Interactive Media, a division of Rupert Murdoch's News Corp., which owns MySpace, had hired a high-tech ad firm to mine user profiles, blog posts, and bulletins to "allow for highly refined audience segmentation and contextual

microtargeting . . . which might put it in more direct competition with the likes of Yahoo, AOL, and MSN."

10 "I don't think kids understand the long-term consequences of our surveillance culture. I'm not sure any of us do," Montgomery says. "But it's the responsibility of educators and policy makers to make sure we're educating people about the value of privacy and what it really means to give it up."

11 In that spirit, according to the *Chronicle of Higher Education* (Jan. 12, 2007), two professors at Drake University's law school, worried that their students' casual approach to digital correspondence could hinder their careers, started a class stressing online discretion. The lesson, according to one student, is simple: "If you are not comfortable with shouting your comments from a street corner, you probably shouldn't convey them via electronic print." ◆

## CONSIDERING THE ISSUES

1. Do you have a page on Facebook, MySpace, or another social networking site? If so, which one did you chose to become a member of, and why? What information do you post, and who can see it? Alternatively, if you do not have a personal page, describe why you prefer not to participate in social networking sites.

2. What unique issues and challenges do young adults growing up with the Internet face that their parents and grandparents did not? How has "growing up digital" affected how you live? Explain.

## CRAFT AND CONTENT

1. Evaluate the author's use of examples to support the point of his essay. Can you think of any areas that could be supported with more information or another point of view? Explain.

2. Summarize Schimke's article in a single paragraph. Remember to include the most important points of his article, and the point he is trying to make on the subject of online privacy.

## CRITICAL THINKING

1. In paragraph 6, Schimke notes that today's young adults are the most savvy about how they can be monitored online, yet they are the least likely group of Internet users to censor themselves.

What are the potential pitfalls of this attitude? In your opinion, what accounts for this paradox?

2. This article mentions that in February 2007, ClickZ.com was mining user profiles and posts for marketing purposes. What are your expectations regarding the personal information you choose to put online? Is it free for "data mining"? Do you think it should remain private? Is ClickZ.com violating privacy rights of users of online networking sites? Why or why not?

### WRITING ABOUT THE ISSUES

1. Lakshmi Chaudhry observes in paragraph 7 that "celebrity has become a commodity in itself." What does she mean? Read her article in *The Nation*, "Mirror, Mirror on the Web" and write a short essay responding to her assertion that today's young adults are obsessed with fame and self-promotion—to their peril.

2. Review a few pages on Facebook or MySpace and evaluate the information posted online. If you have your own page, you can discuss the information you post as well. Are the pages you review guilty of making some of the mistakes Schimke notes in his article? For example, how would a potential employer view the pages? A judge? A possible love interest? Your parents? Explain.

---

# The Case for a National ID Card

*Margaret Carlson*

Margaret Carlson has been writing the column "Public Eye" for *TIME* magazine since 1994. In addition to writing for *TIME*, she serves as a panelist on CNN's political programs *Inside Politics* and *The Capital Gang*. Her articles have appeared in many publications, including the *New Republic*, *Esquire*, and *Washington Weekly*. This column was first published in the January 14, 2002, issue of *TIME*.

### CONNECTING TO THE TOPIC

Most Americans are used to carrying identification cards: a Social Security card, a library card, a driver's license, a student college ID. Other cards we carry include credit cards, bank cards, even cards to allow us to take out DVDs and video games. After the terrorist attacks of September 11, discussion over whether we should carry "national identification cards" dramatically increased, with even Larry Ellison, chief of the information mega-giant Oracle, offering to provide the software for such cards. What would a national ID card be used for? Would it make us safer? More open to governmental scrutiny? Is this the next card we can expect to be carrying in our wallets?

## WORDS IN CONTEXT

**Nazis** (2)   the National Socialist German Workers' Party, founded in Germany in 1919 and gaining notoriety in 1933 under the direction of Adolf Hitler. (n.)
**trove** (2)   a collection of valuable items discovered or found; a treasure trove (n.)
**pertinent** (3)   relevant to the matter (adj.)
**noncommittal** (3)   refusing to commit to a particular opinion or idea (adj.)
**civil libertarian** (3)   someone who advocates for the protection of individual rights guaranteed by law (n.)
**anonymity** (8)   the state of being unknown or having one's identity unacknowledged (adj.)

1   **A**fter Michigan representative John Dingell was asked to drop his pants at Washington's National Airport, some people felt safer. Others, like me, decided that we'd lost our collective minds. A near strip search of a 75-year-old Congressman whose artificial hip has set off a metal detector—while a suspected al-Qaeda operative like Richard Reid slips onto a Paris-to-Miami flight with a bomb in his shoe—doesn't make us safer. It's making us ridiculous for entrusting our security to an unskilled police force that must make split-second decisions on the basis of incomplete data.

2   Incidents like this—and airport waits longer than the flight itself—have pushed me into the camp of the national ID card. Yes, a tamperproof ID smacks of Big Brother and **Nazis** intoning "Your papers, please," but the federal government already holds a **trove** of data on each of us. And it's less likely to mess up or misuse it than the credit-card companies or the Internet fraudsters, who have just as much data if not more.

3   The idea of a national ID card leaped into the headlines just after Sept. 11. Oracle chairman Larry Ellison offered to donate the **pertinent** software. Ellison went to see Attorney General John Ashcroft, who was **noncommittal** despite his obvious enthusiasm for expanding government powers into other areas that trouble **civil libertarians**.

4      Enter Richard Durbin. In concert with the American Association of Motor Vehicle Administrators (yes, the dreaded DMVs have their own trade group), the Illinois Senator proposed legislation that would create a uniform standard for the country's 200 million state-administered driver's licenses. Durbin noticed that the driver's license has become "the most widely used personal ID in the country. If you can produce one, we assume you're legitimate," he says. At present, nearly anyone can get a license; 13 of the 19 hijackers did. Having those licenses "gave the terrorists cover to mingle in American society without being detected."

5      Since we're using the driver's license as a de facto national ID, Durbin argues, let's make it more reliable. As it stands, the chief requirement is that one knows how to drive. This is fine if the only intent is to ensure that someone behind the wheel has mastered turn signals, but it shouldn't be sufficient to get someone into a federal building, the Olympics or an airplane. All a terrorist needs to do is shop around for a lax state (Florida still doesn't require proof of permanent residency) or resort to a forger with a glue gun and laminator.

6      A high-tech, hard-to-forge driver's license could become a national E-ZPass, a way for a law-abiding citizen to move faster through the roadblocks of post-9/11 life. It's no digitalized Supercard, but the states would have uniform standards, using bar codes and biometrics (a unique characteristic, like a palm print) and could cross-check and get information from other law-enforcement agencies. Polls show 70% of Americans support an even more stringent ID. But Japanese-American members of Congress and Transportation Secretary Norman Mineta are keenly sensitive to anything that might single out one nationality. Yet an ID card offers prospects of less profiling. By accurately identifying those who are in the U.S. legally and not on a terrorist watch list, the card would reduce the temptation to go after random members of specific groups.

7      It is not ideal to leave a national problem to the states, but because of the general squeamishness about federal "papers" in the Congress, Durbin's proposal—congressional oversight of state DMVs—may be the best way to go. And if the government doesn't act, corporations will. Delta and American Airlines already provide separate lines for premium passengers; Heathrow Airport in London has an iris scan for people who have registered their eyeballs. An airline-industry association is at work on a Trusted Traveler card. Do we really want frequent-flyer status to be the

basis for security decisions, or more plastic cards joining the too many we already have?

8     This ID would require one virtual strip search instead of many real ones. Durbin says the card would remove the **anonymity** of a Mohamed Atta but not the privacy of others. With a card, Dingell could have confirmed his identity (though he made a point of not pulling rank). With the presumption that he wasn't a terrorist, a once-over with a wand—with his pants on—would have lent credence to his claim that he possessed an artificial hip, not a gun. The Durbin card would at least let us travel with our clothes on. ◆

### CONSIDERING THE ISSUES

1. When were you last asked to produce identification? What were the circumstances? Were you asked by a person, or did you need identification of some form to access a building or pick up an item? What form of identification did you produce?
2. What personal information are you willing to give out? For example, if a cashier asks you to provide a zip code or telephone number when making a purchase, do you give out this information? What about online? Do you consider your privacy when responding to requests for personal information? Explain.

### CRAFT AND CONTENT

1. What is the position of the author on the issue of national ID cards? Identify specific areas of her essay in which she reveals her position.
2. Carlson notes that national ID cards "smack of Big Brother and the Nazis." Why does she use this reference? Who is "Big Brother"? How does the concept of Big Brother connect to the idea of a national ID card and set the tone of her essay? Explain.

### CRITICAL THINKING

1. Carlson presents congressman John Dingell's experience at Washington's National Airport as an example of a security blunder. Evaluate this example. Does it demonstrate her point? Did

the security guards act appropriately? Would a national ID card have prevented this situation in the first place? Explain.

2. In paragraph 6, Carlson states that "Japanese-American members of Congress and Transportation Secretary Norman Mineta are keenly sensitive to anything that might single out one nationality." Why are Japanese-American members of Congress particularly cautious of a national ID system? Why would they be more concerned than other groups?

### WRITING ABOUT THE ISSUES

1. Do you think that a national identification card is a good idea? Why or why not? Do you think it would deter terrorism? Make U.S. citizens safer? Explain your point of view.

2. In paragraph 6, Carlson notes that polls indicate that 70% of Americans support more stringent ID. Considering that this article was published only four months after September 11, conduct your own poll to see if Americans still feel this way. Ask at least 40 to 50 people if they support a national identification card. Based on your results, write a short essay analyzing the data. Incorporate any opinions expressed by the people you poll if appropriate.

# National ID Cards: Five Reasons Why They Should Be Rejected
*ACLU*

The American Civil Liberties Union (ACLU) was founded in 1920. Since its beginning, the nonprofit, nonpartisan ACLU has grown from a small group of civil liberties activists to an organization of nearly 400,000 members with offices in almost every state. The ACLU's mission is to fight civil liberties violations wherever and whenever they occur. It is also active in national and state government arenas and is dedicated to upholding the Bill of Rights.

## CONNECTING TO THE TOPIC

The preceding essay presented the idea that national ID cards might not be a bad idea in the post-9/11 world. The next piece explains why the ACLU believes national ID cards would be a colossal failure. Not only would such cards *not* solve the very problems that inspire them, but they would ultimately cause more harm than good.

## WORDS IN CONTEXT

**superficial** (2)   only on the surface; insubstantial (adj.)

**thwarted** (3)   prevented (v.)

**naïve** (5)   simple; lacking in experience or understanding (adj.)

**prohibition** (6)   a policy or law that forbids something (n.)

**visceral** (8)   instinctive (adj.)

**aversion** (8)   intense dislike or disgust (n.)

**totalitarian** (8)   referring to a government or political body that exercises total control over the individual lives of citizens within a state, usually with the suppression of all dissenting viewpoints (adj.)

**sentries** (8)   guards or officials with authority (n.)

**stigma** (9)   a mark of disgrace (n.)

1 The terrorist attacks of September 11 have revived proposals for a national identity card system as a way to verify the identity of airline passengers and prevent terrorists from entering the country. For example, the Chairman and CEO of Oracle Corp., Larry Ellison, recently called for the creation of a national ID system and offered to provide the software for it without charge.

2 The newest calls for a national ID are only the latest in a long series of proposals that have cropped up repeatedly over the past decade, usually in the context of immigration policy, but also in connection with gun control or health care reform. But the creation of a national ID card remains a misplaced, **superficial** "quick fix." It offers only a false sense of security and will not enhance our security—but will pose serious threats to our civil liberties and civil rights. A national ID will not keep us safe or free.

## Reason #1: A National ID Card System Would Not Solve the Problem That Is Inspiring It

3 A national ID card system will not prevent terrorism. It would not have **thwarted** the September 11 hijackers, for example, many of whom reportedly had identification documents on them, and were in the country legally.

4     Terrorists and criminals will continue to be able to obtain—by legal and illegal means—the documents needed to get a government ID, such as birth certificates. Yes, these new documents will have data like digital fingerprints on them, but that won't prove real identity—just that the carrier has obtained what could easily be a fraudulent document.

5     And their creation would not justify the cost to American taxpayers, which according to the Social Security Administration would be at least $4 billion. It is an impractical and ineffective proposal—a simplistic and **naïve** attempt to use gee-whiz technology to solve complex social and economic problems.

## Reason #2: An ID Card System Will Lead to a Slippery Slope of Surveillance and Monitoring of Citizens

6 A national ID card system would not protect us from terrorism, but it would create a system of internal passports that would significantly diminish the freedom and privacy of law-abiding citizens. Once put in place, it is exceedingly unlikely that such a system would be restricted to its original purpose. The original Social Security Act contained strict **prohibitions** against use of Social Security cards for unrelated purposes, but those strictures have been routinely ignored and steadily abandoned over the past 50 years. A national ID system would threaten the privacy that Americans have always enjoyed and gradually increase the control that government and business wields over everyday citizens.

## Reason #3: A National ID Card System Would Require Creation of a Database of All Americans

7 What happens when an ID card is stolen? What proof is used to decide who gets a card? A national ID would require a governmental database of every person in the U.S. containing continually updated identifying

information. It would likely contain many errors, any one of which could render someone unemployable and possibly much worse until they get their "file" straightened out. And once that database was created, its use would almost certainly expand. Law enforcement and other government agencies would soon ask to link into it, while employers, landlords, credit agencies, mortgage brokers, direct mailers, private investigators, civil litigants, and a long list of other parties would begin seeking access, further eroding the privacy that Americans have always expected in their personal lives.

## Reason #4: ID Cards Would Function as "Internal Passports" That Monitor Citizens' Movements

8 Americans have long had a **visceral aversion** to building a society in which the authorities could act like **totalitarian sentries** and demand "your papers please!" And that everyday intrusiveness would be conjoined with the full power of modern computer and database technology. When a police officer or security guard scans your ID card with his pocket barcode reader, for example, will a permanent record be created of that check, including the time and your location? How long before office buildings, doctors' offices, gas stations, highway tolls, subways and buses incorporate the ID card into their security or payment systems for greater efficiency? The end result could be a nation where citizens' movements inside their own country are monitored and recorded through these "internal passports."

## Reason #5: ID Cards Would Foster New Forms of Discrimination and Harassment

9 Rather than eliminating discrimination, as some have claimed, a national identity card would foster new forms of discrimination and harassment of anyone perceived as looking or sounding "foreign." That is what happened after Congress passed the Employer Sanctions provision of the Immigration Reform and Control Act of 1985: widespread discrimination against foreign-looking American workers, especially Asians and Hispanics. A 1990 General Accounting Office study found almost 20 percent of employers engaged in such practices. A national ID card would have the same effect on a massive scale, as Latinos, Asians, Caribbeans and other minorities became subject to ceaseless status and identity checks

from police, banks, merchants and others. Failure to carry a national ID card would likely come to be viewed as a reason for search, detention or arrest of minorities. The **stigma** and humiliation of constantly having to prove that they are Americans or legal immigrants would weigh heavily on such groups. ◆

### CONSIDERING THE ISSUES

1. When asked to provide proof of identity, do you consider this request an invasion of your privacy or simply a reality of modern life? Explain.
2. Many of us take the idea of privacy for granted. Think about the number of times in a given day when your actions may be tracked by others (for example, if you use a student ID card to gain access to the cafeteria or if you purchase something with a credit card). How often is your privacy at risk? Does it matter? Why or why not?

### CRAFT AND CONTENT

1. The ACLU lists five reasons why national ID cards are a bad idea. Evaluate the relevancy and logic of the reasons they cite. Are they valid points? Off track? Can you think of any additional reasons that they might have left out? Alternatively, if you do not think their reasons hold merit, explain why.
2. What is a "slippery slope"? Why would national ID cards create a "slippery slope of surveillance"? Explain.

### CRITICAL THINKING

1. Why does the ACLU believe that national ID cards would be a "superficial quick fix" that poses a serious threat to our civil liberties? What liberties do they fear will be sacrificed? Do you agree with their position? Why or why not?
2. Both this article by the ACLU and Carlson's essay before it mention the idea of totalitarian governments. In your opinion, would a national ID policy contribute to such a government or legal system? How would a national ID card be different from a driver's license or a Social Security card? A passport? Explain.

## WRITING ABOUT THE ISSUES

1. This article by the ACLU lists five arguments that a national ID system would threaten our civil liberties. Assuming the position of Oracle chairman Larry Ellison, who encouraged a national ID system, draft a list of five arguments that a national ID system is a good policy for Americans to adopt.
2. Write an essay exploring the ways a national ID system could be abused. How could it contribute to a society similar to the totalitarian state depicted in George Orwell's novel *1984*? To review this short novel, look it up at www.online-literature.com.

# VISUAL CONNECTIONS

## Identity Theft

One privacy concern of many Americans is identity theft. As more websites and retail establishments store information online, it is possible for hackers to access personal information. In 2005, many banks and credit companies reissued thousands of cards after security systems had been breached, exposing an unprecedented number of people to the possibility of identity theft. How do we protect ourselves from identity theft without unnecessarily complicating our lives? Or is this just another reason for being more vigilant than ever in safeguarding our privacy?

### CRITICAL THINKING

1. Consider the faces of the people in this ad. What sort of conclusions might a viewer draw from their expressions? Would the ad be as effective if the images were reversed? Why or why not?
2. Can you tell what this ad is trying to accomplish without reading the fine print at the bottom of the ad? Explain.
3. What does this ad imply about your privacy?
4. What is your gut reaction to this ad? How does it play into our fears and insecurities? Are these fears well founded? Why or why not?

# Smile, You're on Security Camera

*John McElhenny*

John McElhenny is a correspondent for the *Boston Globe*. His writing has appeared in dozens of newspapers, including the *New York Times* and *USA Today*. He has conducted research on business-led civic efforts across the country and is researching economic conditions in rural northern New England. This article ran in the March 2004 edition of the *Boston Globe*.

## CONNECTING TO THE TOPIC

Surveillance cameras monitor us in department stores and at ATMs. They are present in elevators and offices, parking lots, sporting arenas, and police cars. In Great Britain, over three million cameras have become fixtures in public spaces. And across the Atlantic, in Boston, cameras are everywhere. All this monitoring can seem creepy and invasive, but when a camera captures child abuse or abduction on film, such surveillance can prove to be a useful law enforcement tool. Is surveillance a price we should pay for a safer society? Is it a fair trade-off for an invasion of our personal privacy? Or is this a case where the ends do not justify the means?

## WORDS IN CONTEXT

**obtrusive** (2)   noticeable (adj.)

**elusive** (3)   difficult to capture (adj.)

**MBTA** (9)   Massachusetts Bay Transit Authority, the acronym given to Boston's public transportation system, commonly called the "T." (n.)

**ACLU** (12)   The American Civil Liberties Union, a nonpartisan organization that addresses issues connected to civil liberties (n.)

**scofflaw** (12)   someone who ignores the law or legal system ("scoffs at [the] law") (n.)

1   **P**rivate detective Rob Selevitch has been wearing out shoe leather in Boston for 25 years, interviewing witnesses and scouring crime scenes. Lately that task has been easier for one simple reason: Video cameras capture many of the city's comings and goings 24/7. "Tell me any place, and I

guarantee you there's a camera there somewhere," says Selevitch, president of the security company CEI Management Corp. and founder of the website www.bostondetective.com, which represents a consortium of licensed professional investigators in the Boston area. "If you want to get technical about it, you're pretty much under surveillance all the time."

2      Video surveillance has taken off in recent years, thanks to smaller, less **obtrusive** cameras and rising security concerns since the Sept. 11 terrorist attacks. Customers at banks, retail stores, and other businesses have long been filmed in an attempt to thwart crimes and solve them once they occur, but in recent years, camera surveillance has also made inroads at places such as churches, parking garages, and supermarkets, Selevitch says.

3      Statistics are **elusive**. The trade organization ASIS International, which lists 33,000 members and calls itself the "preeminent organization for security professionals," says nobody tracks numbers of surveillance cameras in the U.S., though it has commissioned a study to be completed by September to measure the worldwide scope of the security industry. Latanya Sweeney, director for the Carnegie Mellon Data Privacy Lab in Pittsburgh, a think tank on the relationship between technology and privacy, says she's not aware of any such figures.

4      In an unofficial count last April, two members of the Surveillance Camera Players, a New York-based group that opposes the use of surveillance cameras in public places, toured Boston on foot to spot and map cameras they saw installed in public places. Armed with binoculars, the pair led six people on a survey centered in the Financial District that located 128 such surveillance cameras. Ten were in or on government buildings, the group found, while 110 were on private property. Six other cameras were on tall buildings or otherwise elevated high off the ground, while two more were on street poles—and who knows how many more were not noticed.

5      Selevitch says there are parts of Boston where nearly all of the streets and sidewalks are covered by video cameras. Based on his work over 25 years in Boston, he estimates that 80 percent of the streets around the Federal Reserve and South Station are covered by cameras, along with perhaps 70 percent of the area around the Downtown Crossing shopping district.

6      Those percentages will almost certainly rise, he says, particularly since most new buildings built in Boston are covered by exterior cameras. "Cradle to grave, you're going to be on camera all the time," he predicts.

7    Sometimes actions recorded by cameras in public spaces end up on the Internet. The Data Privacy Lab estimates there are 10,000 webcams now broadcasting images to publicly available websites on the Internet, settings that range from beaches to university campuses to cityscapes. One such website, EarthCam.com, allows Internet surfers to view a host of live shots of Boston at any time, day or night. Taken by a camera on top of the Prudential Center, they include Fenway Park, the State House, and the Common. Another camera shows live scenes at the corner of Washington Street and Temple Place in Downtown Crossing. Boston University has several live cameras around campus. There's also one in the office of a man named John Lester who works at Massachusetts General Hospital.

8    It's difficult in some parts of Boston to walk or drive even a few blocks without being filmed. The Big Dig* already has 200 operating cameras, and 200 more will be running by the time the project is finished in a year and a half. The Massachusetts Port Authority uses about 400 cameras, most of them at Logan Airport. On the roads, 27 cameras monitor intersections around Boston, and another 15 are being installed. Jim Mansfield, spokesman for the city's Transportation Department, says the cameras monitor traffic so signals can be timed to improve the flow. The cameras aren't used to catch speeding cars.

9    Public transportation passengers on the **MBTA** better get used to smiling for the camera, too. The T currently has 79 cameras, which are located at a quarter of its 60 or so underground subway stations, with another hundred planned as the subway system largely switches to automated fare collection early next year. John Hogan, Jr., chief of the MBTA's operations control center, says every one of the stations will have a camera and most will have several. He says the cameras will save taxpayers' money by making T riders more likely to pay the fares if they know a camera is watching.

10    Jeffrey Parker, the MBTA's director of subway operations, says the cameras make the T safer by taping scenes that police can review after a crime has been committed to find suspects and witnesses. The cameras also make the T more efficient, Parker says, by allowing dispatchers to spot groups of waiting passengers and redirect trains accordingly. "From the control center, it's not important to us what someone's face looks like or what color shoes they're wearing, but we do want to see how large a crowd is," Parker says.

*The **Big Dig** is the unofficial name of a massive construction project that involved rerouting a major highway in Boston through a network of tunnels under the city and the Boston Harbor and building a bridge over the Charles River. Designed to relieve traffic nightmares, the controversial project took nearly fifteen years to complete (officially on December 31, 2007) and cost nearly 15 billion dollars—three times the original projected cost.

11     Businesses that use video cameras say they're an indispensable tool to prevent crime, ensure the safety of customers, and keep crime-related losses, which customers would ultimately have to pay for, at a minimum. Bank of America uses surveillance cameras at all of its 427 ATMs and 71 branches in the Boston area, says spokesman Jim Schepker. He says the cameras stop crimes before they happen and help investigators nab suspects when one has been committed. "We believe surveillance is a way to discourage the criminal element," says Schepker. "It's invaluable to investigators."

12     In some quarters, though, the camera eye's quiet spread is raising alarms about privacy. Carol Rose, executive director of the **ACLU** of Massachusetts, says she's concerned about "mission creep"—cameras that are set up for one purpose, such as catching traffic **scofflaws** at an intersection, and are used for another, such as identifying participants in a political rally. "The question is, who's looking at the pictures being taken and how are they using those pictures?" says Rose. "The cameras don't distinguish between the good guys and the bad guys."

13     The group has been vocal in its concern that the USA Patriot Act threatens civil liberties by giving new surveillance and other powers to law enforcement agencies. On its website, it warns, "The United States is at risk of turning into a full-fledged surveillance society. George Orwell's vision of 'Big Brother' has now become technologically possible."

14     "We have a situation where the government is increasing its power to watch the citizenry while diminishing the citizens' power to watch their government," Rose says. "The concern is that surveillance cameras that go up be used for the stated purposes they go up for, and not to invade people who have the expectation of privacy."

15     Boston-area YMCAs have taken their own step to protect against invasive surveillance. The use of cellular phones with cameras was banned last year from the 12 branches of the YMCA of Greater Boston, which host 100,000 visitors per year. YMCA Vice President of External Affairs Kelley Rice says it was common sense, not any instance of locker-room mischief, that sparked the ban. "You always see stars in embarrassing situations whose pictures end up somewhere," she says. "You could see the potential for a problem here."

16     Still, in a darkened room filled with 42 giant television screens, John Hogan Jr. is watching. Eight floors above the Financial District, in a nondescript gray building on High Street, the chief of the MBTA's operations control center looks down from what he calls the "war room." Below him are the screens, each one 5 feet tall and just as wide, a curving, constantly shifting array of lights and images that dwarfs any department store's TV

showroom. Most of the screens—38 of the 42—resemble enormous video games, with orange arrows depicting trains moving slowly along the tracks. Lighted icons show track crossings and emergency exits, while another screen shows the Weather Channel.

17    But it's the three camera-fed screens that catch the eye, rotating every few seconds from one station to the next in live, constantly changing glimpses of subway life. One follows the Blue Line. Beach Mont. Revere Beach. Another works its way up the Red Line. Harvard. Porter. Hogan says later this year, all 42 screens will be equipped to show live feeds from the cameras. As he speaks, a blonde woman in a black waist-length coat appears on one of the screens, talking on a cell phone and apparently unaware that her image is being viewed 10 miles away. A caption says the woman is standing on the inbound platform at Suffolk Downs station. In the war room, three workers talking on phones and monitoring the trains' progress pay her little attention.

18    Just off the MBTA's war room, seven videocassette recorders run 24 hours a day, seven days a week to record images from the cameras. Tapes are kept for 30 days in case police need to review them to investigate a crime. The cameras do not have microphones.

19    The MBTA is by no means alone in its increasing use of cameras. Other public agencies such as the Boston Transportation Department, Massport (which operates Logan Airport), and the Turnpike Authority (which oversees the Big Dig), have installed cameras or are adding more to improve traffic and boost security.

20    Hogan says the MBTA isn't interested in using the cameras for passenger surveillance. He says he's more interested in preventing toll-cheaters through the cameras' presence, or in using the cameras to redirect trains to cut wait times for passengers who have better things to do than wait for a train. Last year, a man fell onto the track at Broadway station and a sharp-eyed dispatcher saw it on camera just before a train rolled in. He quickly halted the train, and the fallen man was helped back onto the platform, uninjured. "The guy was lucky because he was right in the middle of the track and the train would have made contact with him," says Hogan.

21    Behind him, a screen switches to Wood Island station, where a young man in a blue-and-white plaid shirt and black winter cap gazes blankly across the tracks, unaware of the camera perched above him a few feet away.  ◆

## CONSIDERING THE ISSUES

1. Most people are aware that surveillance cameras help loss prevention officers catch shoplifters at department stores. In England,

over three million cameras are used to aid law enforcement offices to keep the peace. Would knowing you could be caught on film influence your behavior? How would you feel if you lived in a society that could track you on film up to 300 times a day in different places? Would you care? Why or why not?

2. Do you think cameras in public places are a good law enforcement tool? If you ran a municipal law enforcement operation, where would you put surveillance cameras, and why? Or would you choose to not use cameras at all? Explain.

### CRAFT AND CONTENT

1. This article ran in a newspaper. What style of writing do we expect from newspaper articles? How is it different from pieces in magazines or journals? Explain.

2. What is the author's opinion of cameras in public spaces? Can you tell? Explain.

### CRITICAL THINKING

1. Carol Rose, executive director of the American Civil Liberties Union of Massachusetts, expresses her concern that cameras that are put up for seemingly good reasons could be abused. How could camera surveillance be abused? Explain.

2. McElhenny provides many examples of sites where cameras are placed around the city of Boston and how they are used. Do you think the use of cameras makes sense? Are there areas that you think should be off limits? Refer to examples McElhenny gives in his article in your response.

### WRITING ABOUT THE ISSUES

1. Write a short article in which you express your own opinion on whether surveillance cameras should be used in public spaces. Following McElhenny's format, find out more about public surveillance where you live, and write about it.

2. Write an essay describing your views on personal freedom. How does personal freedom connect to privacy rights? Do you feel your personal freedom has been violated by public and private surveillance practices? Explain.

# VISUAL CONNECTIONS

## Flash Someone...

### FOCUS ON CONTEXT

As the previous essay by John McElhenny describes, surveillance cameras have become familiar fixtures in our lives. From department stores to airports to toll booths, cameras are everywhere. Are these cameras invading our privacy? Is it permissible for private property owners to use them, but not public law enforcement? Should we be alerted that we could be watched on camera before entering a building? Or are cameras just another way to keep us safer in a society troubled by crime and terrorism? The billboard below was part of a campaign to stop sexual harassment on public transportation in Boston. The campaign began in April 2008 and is ongoing.

(Aram Boghosian for *The Boston Globe*, April 14, 2008)

## CRITICAL THINKING

1. When you are watched on camera, do you feel your privacy is invaded, or do you accept cameras as a fact of modern life? Do law-abiding citizens need to worry about surveillance cameras at all?
2. Does knowing that surveillance cameras are located at a particular site make you feel safer? Would it make you feel better riding public transportation? Why or why not?
3. What assumptions do we make about cameras in public spaces? For example, whom do you think the camera is watching? Is it likely to deter criminal behavior? Explain.
4. What is happening in this billboard? How could a caption explaining what is happening change our opinion of the photograph? Explain.

# Blog Matters

A blog ("web log") is an online diary or commentary site that features regular entries that describe events, impressions, and viewpoints. Blogs may contain text, images, video, and often link to other websites, blogs, and online media. Most blogs allow readers to comment on the content of the post and respond to each other. As of 2007, the blog search engine estimated there were over 112 million blogs. While many blogs are maintained by individuals, some are run by journals, newspapers, and other media outlets. Remember that most blogs are not monitored for factual accuracy, and often express the opinion and views of the "blogger" writing the content.

The blog below is hosted by CollegeRecruiter.com and presents the advice of attorney George Lenard who specializes in all aspects of labor and employment law, including preventive law as well as litigation. Lenard is currently a managing partner with Harris, Dowell, Fisher & Harris, L.C., in St. Louis, Missouri, and runs employmentblawg.com.

# Is It Legal for Employers to Use Facebook for Background Checking?

*George Lenard*
*September 1, 2006*

1    There has recently been considerable attention in the media to instances of employers rejecting candidates or firing employees based on information obtained from social networking sites such as MySpace and Facebook. I may later do a review on my own blog of some of this commentary, but today I will discuss a question posed by Steven Rothberg of CollegeRecruiter.com—prefacing my remarks with a lawyerly disclaimer that I am not providing legal advice and have not thoroughly researched these issues, but am merely making some general comments.

2    Steven asked that I comment on the lawfulness of making adverse employment decisions on this basis. He raised several concerns: that with Facebook, students often have an incorrect understanding that only other students can access their profiles; that there may be false information on those sites, perhaps not even posted by the individuals themselves; and that Facebook's terms of service explicitly prohibit users from using Facebook for commercial purposes.

3    Let me start out with the comment that, like it or not, as a general proposition employers are free to make unfair, stupid, arbitrary, and wrongheaded hiring and termination decisions, even based on false information, as long as in doing so they do not violate some specific law.

## Discrimination Law

4  One category of specific laws that could be violated by an adverse employment decision based on information on a social networking site is federal and state discrimination laws. It could be evidence of unlawful discrimination if an employer checks for such Internet information on only certain types of applicants or employees—for example, African-Americans and Hispanics. It may also be evidence of unlawful discrimination if although the employer searches for such information on all applicants or employees, discriminatory bias affects the employer's evaluation of the information obtained. For example, an employer may view more negatively

photos of an African-American male, beer in hand, hanging out at a bar with a hip-hop DJ than photos of a white boy, also with beer in hand, hanging out at a rock 'n roll bar with a bunch of other white boys wearing frat T-shirts. Tell me, was it really the public evidence of drinking that disqualified the individual? How many current employees would be disqualified from employment if never getting publicly intoxicated—or even drinking in public—was a job requirement? These are the kinds of questions the EEOC would ask if discrimination was raised.

5     Sexual orientation might be another touchy area. These days, it may be frankly disclosed on social networking sites without much thought. Yet, bias remains and might cause some employers to make adverse decisions. In many states and municipalities, sexual orientation discrimination is unlawful, so such decisions will be prohibited.

## Invasion of Privacy

6  A claim that I doubt would fly is invasion of privacy. This requires a "reasonable expectation of privacy." A student may believe that Facebook access is limited to a few thousand of their schoolmates and their closest friends. Nonetheless, it would be tough to claim that this expectation of limited access, even if reasonable, is an expectation of "privacy." The Facebook FAQs do support such a belief in limited access, stating:

> Facebook was intentionally designed to limit the availability of your profile to only your friends and other people on your networks. This simple but important security measure promotes local networking and makes sure that your information is seen by people you want to share it with, and not by people you don't.

7     On the other hand, if you are using privacy features that you believe restrict access to very few specific people completely within your control, and an employer somehow hacks past such a privacy barrier, you may have a strong privacy claim.

## Terms of Service Violation

8  Now, onward to the terms of service issue raised by Steve. For sake of brevity, I will only address Facebook. MySpace may present somewhat different issues, which I may analyze in a follow-up post. The Facebook terms include the following:

> *You understand that the Service and the Web site are available for your personal, **non-commercial** use only. You represent, warrant and agree that no materials of any kind submitted through your account will violate or infringe upon the rights of any third party, including copyright, trademark, privacy, publicity or other personal or proprietary rights; or contain libelous, defamatory or otherwise unlawful material. You further agree not to harvest or collect email addresses or other contact information of Members from the Service or the Web site by electronic or other means **for the purposes of sending unsolicited emails or other unsolicited communications**. Additionally, you agree not to use **automated scripts** to collect information from the Service or the Web site or for any other purpose. You further agree that you may not use the Service or the Web site in any unlawful manner or in any other manner that could damage, disable, overburden or impair Web site. In addition, you agree not to use the Service or the Web site to:*
>
> * *impersonate any person or entity, or falsely state or otherwise misrepresent yourself or your affiliation with any person or entity; . . .*
> * *intimidate or harass another;*
> * *use or attempt to use another's account, service or system without authorization from the Company, or create a false identity on the Service or the Web site.*

9    Steven thinks it's a no-brainer that checking individuals out on Facebook for purposes of employment decisions is a commercial use. This certainly is a possible interpretation, but I believe not the only one. The next sentence focuses on materials submitted through your account, not what you do with information you learn about others. Therefore, "non-commercial use only" could be interpreted as addressing only a prohibition on *posting* information for commercial gain, such as advertisements. The paragraph goes on to specifically prohibit certain methods of obtaining and using information about others. Though it prohibits automated scraping and spamming, it does not address the issue of searching for specific individuals and using the information to make employment decisions.

10    It seems a stretch to say an employer is "intimidating or harassing" the user of Facebook by using Facebook information to make an adverse employment decision, but this certainly could be argued.

11    A more serious issue would arise if the employer misrepresented their affiliation with a college to create an account allowing them to look up certain individuals, or used another's account to do so. This would appear to be a plain violation of the terms of service.

## Consequences of Violation of Terms of Service

12  Now, let's assume the employer violated the terms of service. So what? My answer is that this fact may support a tortious interference with business expectancy claim, but probably only if it was a third-party recruiter or investigator who committed a violation. This is because interference by a third party is required. Perhaps, such a claim against the individual who obtained the information improperly, not the company, would satisfy this requirement, but that is still somewhat iffy.

13    Other elements of this type of client might also be difficult to prove, such as whether the candidate has a reasonable expectancy of employment.

14    There might also be a federal cause of action under the Federal Computer Fraud And Abuse Act to the extent the recruiter/employer exceeds authorized access (as authorized in the terms of service) in obtaining data from a computer system (the Facebook server).

## Thinking Practically

15  Those are a few of my well-educated, but still speculative, legal thoughts. Long ago, one of my mentors taught me to always ask not only what the law requires my client to do, but also what the client *should* do, taking into account extra-legal factors such as business realities, employee morale, employee and public perceptions, etc. Here, I have some thoughts on what both employers and applicants/employees *should* do, in the face of this growing trend of employers checking social networking sites.

16    I would advise applicants/employees to assume future employers will read everything you post. So when you put something about yourself out there, you can be yourself, but avoid obvious negatives like saying you hate to work or posting sleazy or drunken photos. It may help to ask yourself whether you would want your mother to see your site. Sorry to say, but you may not even want to admit homosexuality or *extreme* political or religious views. On a positive note, use your Internet postings, including blogs as well as social networking sites, affirmatively, to build visibility

and credibility as an expert in your field (or hobby). Join more "serious" networking sites like LinkedIn even if you are still a student—and work at building a network there that can help you in future job searches.

17    I would advise employers to cut applicants and employees some slack. You were once young too and maybe did similar things—if not publicly on the Internet. Ask yourself how relevant the information creating the negative impression is to job performance. If you are going to do Internet searches and use them as a basis for employment decisions, you better document them and do it consistently, without regard to any legally protected classifications, e.g., race, sex, age. I also agree 100% with Steven's suggestion to use social networking sites and blogs in a positive fashion in your search to find good candidates. Consider the whole person, of whom the Internet persona is not always a fully accurate reflection. ◆

### RESPOND TO THE BLOG:

What do you think? Are we giving away too much information online? Should employers be able to consider the behavior expressed on a social networking site in its hiring decisions? If you have a MySpace or Facebook page, what would an employer learn about *you*?

## TOPICAL CONNECTIONS

### GROUP PROJECT

1. In the first essay in this section, David Plotz states that the infringements on our privacy are a small price to pay for the protections we enjoy in return for this sacrifice. As a group, compile a list of ways that you must sacrifice your privacy. You may include airport security checks, locker searches, and even having to produce identification to pay with a check. Is this forfeiture of privacy rights worth it? Are some more invasive than others? Discuss your list and assess the costs and benefits of privacy loss. After group discussion, share your opinions with the rest of the class.

### WEB PROJECT

1. This chapter addresses many issues connected to our concept of privacy. Many of us are unclear about what our privacy rights

actually are. Visit the Privacy Rights Clearinghouse website at www.privacyrights.org for fact sheets on privacy and your privacy rights. What assumptions do you make about your privacy? Write an essay in which you explore privacy rights in American society.

## FOR FURTHER INQUIRY

1. While some authors in this section imply that we are subjected to more invasions of privacy than ever before, others infer that we are more anonymous now than we were a century ago. What are your impressions of this issue? Interview fellow students, parents, grandparents, and older relatives and ask them for their viewpoints on privacy. Assess whether we have more or less privacy today than in the past. Then address how Americans feel about privacy.

2. Watch the movie *The Net,* starring Sandra Bullock, or *The Truman Show,* with Jim Carrey. Write a short review of either film, addressing specifically how the movie illuminates privacy issues in modern life.

# 3 | How Does Advertising Influence Us?

**A**dvertising surrounds us, permeating our daily lives—on television, billboards, newspapers, magazines, the Internet, the sides of buses and trains, T-shirts, sports arenas, even license plates. Advertising is the driving force behind our consumptive economy, accounting for more than 150 billion dollars worth of commercials and print ads each year in the United States. Commercials fill 15 to 20 minutes of television airtime per hour (more for sporting events such as football games). They form the bulk of most newspapers and magazines. Advertising is everywhere we are, appealing to the root of our desires—our fantasies, hopes, wishes, and dreams—while promising us youth, beauty, social acceptance, power, sex appeal, and happiness. Through carefully selected images and words, advertising may be the most powerful manufacturer of meaning in our society. And many of us are not even aware of how it influences our lives.

Most of us are so accustomed to advertising that we barely notice its presence around us. However, if we stopped to think about how it works on our subconscious, we might be amazed at how powerful and complex a force it is. This chapter examines how advertising tempts us to buy, feeds our fantasies, and convinces us to part with our money.

The chapter closes with some sample ads for popular products and services. Use a critical eye when reviewing these advertisements, and consider some of the points about persuasion and advertising described in this chapter.

## CRITICAL THINKING

1. This editorial cartoon features a great deal of visual material. What is happening in this cartoon? What does it seek to demonstrate? How effective is it in relaying its message? Explain.
2. How many scenarios exhibited in this cartoon can you relate to? Cite a few examples of how this cartoon reflects your own life experience.
3. Can you tell how the person in the cartoon feels about the issue depicted? Explain.

# A Brand by Any Other Name
*Douglas Rushkoff*

Douglas Rushkoff is a writer and columnist who analyzes, writes, and speaks about the way people, cultures, and institutions share and influence each other's values. He is the author of many books on new media and popular culture, including *Media Virus* and *Coercion: Why We Listen to What "They" Say*. His column on cyberculture appears monthly in the *New York Times*. This essay appeared in the April 30, 2000, edition of the *London Times*.

## CONNECTING TO THE TOPIC

Brand-name products target groups of consumers—Pepsi and Levi appeal to large, diverse populations, while Fendi, Coach, or Gucci appeal to very elite ones. Brands depend on image—the image they promote, and the image consumers believe they will project by using the product. For many teens, brands can announce membership in a particular group, value systems, personality type, and personal style. Today's youth are more consumer and media savvy than previous generations, forcing retailers to rethink how they brand and market goods to this group. While teens like to think that they are hip to advertising gimmicks, marketers are one step ahead of the game—a game that teens are likely to lose as they strive to "brand" themselves.

## WORDS IN CONTEXT

**affiliation** (1)   connection; association (n.)
**psycho-physical** (2)   mind-body (adj.)
**phenomenon** (2)   a circumstance or fact that can be felt by the senses (n.)
**utilitarian** (3)   practical (adj.)
**esoteric** (3)   confined to and understood by a small group only (adj.)
**affinity** (3)   natural attraction and liking (n.)
**existential** (4)   relating to or dealing with existence (adj.)
**anthropology** (5)   the study of the behavior and physical, social, and cultural development of humans and human groups (n.)
**predilections** (6)   preferences (n.)
**angst** (8)   anxiety (n.)
**compunction** (8)   sense of guilt (n.)

**deconstruct** (8)  to break down and analyze (v.)
**arsenal** (9)  a store of weapons of defense (n.)
**opaque** (10)  impenetrable; difficult to see through and understand (adj.)
**sensibility** (11)  awareness and sense of feeling (n.)
**coerce** (12)  to force to act or think in a certain way by use of pressure or intimidation; to compel (v.)
**conflation** (13)  a mix of several things together (n.)

1   was in one of those sports "superstores" the other day, hoping to find a pair of trainers for myself. As I faced the giant wall of shoes, each model categorized by either sports **affiliation**, basketball star, economic class, racial heritage or consumer niche, I noticed a young boy standing next to me, maybe 13 years old, in even greater awe of the towering selection of footwear.

2   His jaw was dropped and his eyes were glazed over—a **psychophysical** response to the overwhelming sensory data in a self-contained consumer environment. It's a **phenomenon** known to retail architects as "Gruen Transfer," named for the gentleman who invented the shopping mall, where this mental paralysis is most commonly observed. Having finished several years of research on this exact mind state, I knew to proceed with caution. I slowly made my way to the boy's side and gently asked him, "What is going through your mind right now?"

3   He responded without hesitation, "I don't know which of these trainers is 'me.'" The boy proceeded to explain his dilemma. He thought of Nike as the most **utilitarian** and scientifically advanced shoe, but had heard something about third world laborers and was afraid that wearing this brand might label him as too anti-Green. He then considered a skateboard shoe, Airwalk, by an "indie" manufacturer (the trainer equivalent of a micro-brewery) but had recently learned that this company was almost as big as Nike. The truly hip brands of skate shoe were too **esoteric** for his current profile at school—he'd look like he was "trying." This left the "retro" brands, like Puma, Converse and Adidas, none of which he felt any real **affinity** for, since he wasn't even alive in the 70's when they were truly and non-ironically popular.

4   With no clear choice and, more importantly, no other way to conceive of his own identity, the boy stood there, paralyzed in the modern youth equivalent of an **existential** crisis. Which brand am I, anyway?

5    Believe it or not, there are dozens, perhaps hundreds of youth culture marketers who have already begun clipping out this article. They work for hip, new advertising agencies and cultural research firms who trade in the psychology of our children and the **anthropology** of their culture. The object of their labors is to create precisely the state of confusion and vulnerability experienced by the young shopper at the shoe wall—and then turn this state to their advantage. It is a science, though not a pretty one.

6    Marketers spend millions developing strategies to identify children's **predilections** and then capitalize on their vulnerabilities. Young people are fooled for a while, but then develop defense mechanisms, such as media-savvy attitudes or ironic dispositions. Then marketers research these defenses, develop new countermeasures, and on it goes.

7    The battle in which our children are engaged seems to pass beneath our radar screens, in a language we don't understand. But we see the confusion and despair that results. How did we get in this predicament, and is there a way out? Is it your imagination, you wonder, or have things really gotten worse? Alas, things seem to have gotten worse. Ironically, this is because things had gotten so much better.

8    In olden times—back when those of us who read the newspaper grew up—media was a one-way affair. Advertisers enjoyed a captive audience, and could quite authoritatively provoke our **angst** and stoke our aspirations. Interactivity changed all this. The remote control gave viewers the ability to break the captive spell of television programming whenever they wished, without having to get up and go all the way up to the set. Young people proved particularly adept at "channel surfing," both because they grew up using the new tool, and because they felt little **compunction** to endure the tension-provoking narratives of storytellers who did not have their best interests at heart. It was as if young people knew that the stuff on television was called "programming" for a reason, and developed shortened attention spans for the purpose of keeping themselves from falling into the spell of advertisers. The remote control allowed young people to **deconstruct** TV.

9    The next weapon in the child's **arsenal** was the video game joystick. For the first time, viewers had control over the very pixels on their monitors. The television image was demystified. Then, the computer mouse and keyboard transformed the TV receiver into a portal. Today's young people grew up in a world where a screen could as easily be used for expressing oneself as consuming the media of others. Now the media was

up-for-grabs, and the ethic, from hackers to camcorder owners, was "do it yourself."

10      Likewise, as computer interfaces were made more complex and **opaque**—think Windows—the do-it-yourself ethic of the Internet was undone. The original Internet was a place to share ideas and converse with others. Children actually had to use the keyboard! Now, the World Wide Web encourages them to click numbly through packaged content. Web sites are designed to keep young people from using the keyboard, except to enter in their parents' credit card information.

11      But young people had been changed by their exposure to new media. They constituted a new "psychographic," as advertisers like to call it, so new kinds of messaging had to be developed that appealed to their new **sensibility**.

12      Anthropologists—the same breed of scientists that used to scope out enemy populations before military conquests—engaged in focus groups, conducted "trend-watching" on the streets, in order to study the emotional needs and subtle behaviors of young people. They came to understand, for example, how children had abandoned narrative structures for fear of the way stories were used to **coerce** them. Children tended to construct narratives for themselves by collecting things instead, like cards, bottlecaps called "pogs," or keychains and plush toys. They also came to understand how young people despised advertising—especially when it did not acknowledge their media-savvy intelligence.

13      Thus, Pokemon was born—a TV show, video game, and product line where the object is to collect as many trading cards as possible. The innovation here, among many, is the marketer's **conflation** of TV show and advertisement into one piece of media. The show is an advertisement. The story, such as it is, concerns a boy who must collect little monsters in order to develop his own character. Likewise, the Pokemon video game engages the player in a quest for those monsters. Finally, the card game itself (for the few children who actually play it) involves collecting better monsters—not by playing, but by buying more cards. The more cards you buy, the better you can play.

14      Kids feel the tug, but in a way they can't quite identify as advertising. Their compulsion to create a story for themselves—in a world where stories are dangerous—makes them vulnerable to this sort of attack. In marketer's terms, Pokemon is "leveraged" media, with "cross-promotion" on "complementary platforms." This is ad-speak for an assault on multiple fronts.

15    Moreover, the time a child spends in the Pokemon craze amounts to a remedial lesson in how to consume. Pokemon teaches them how to want things that they can't or won't actually play with. In fact, it teaches them how to buy things they don't even want. While a child might want one particular card, he needs to purchase them in packages whose contents are not revealed. He must buy blind and repeatedly until he gets the object of his desire.

16    Meanwhile, older kids have attempted to opt out of aspiration altogether. The "15–24" demographic, considered by marketers the most difficult to wrangle into submission, have adopted a series of postures they hoped would make them impervious to marketing techniques. They take pride in their ability to recognize when they are being pandered to, and watch TV for the sole purpose of calling out when they are being manipulated.

17    But now advertisers are making commercials just for them. Soft drink advertisements satirize one another before rewarding the cynical viewer: "image is nothing," they say. The technique might best be called "wink" advertising for its ability to engender a young person's loyalty by pretending to disarm itself. "Get it?" the ad means to ask. If you're cool, you do.

18    New magazine advertisements for jeans, such as those created by Diesel, take this even one step further. The ads juxtapose imagery that actually makes no sense—ice cream billboards in North Korea, for example. The strategy is brilliant. For a media-savvy young person to feel good about himself, he needs to feel he "gets" the joke. But what does he do with an ad where there's obviously something to get that he can't figure out? He has no choice but to admit that the brand is even cooler than he is. An ad's ability to confound its audience is the new credential for a brand's authenticity.

19    Like the boy at the wall of shoes, kids today analyze each purchase they make, painstakingly aware of how much effort has gone into seducing them. As a result, they see their choices of what to watch and what to buy as exerting some influence over the world around them. After all, their buying patterns have become the center of so much attention!

20    But however media-savvy kids get, they will always lose this particular game. For they have accepted the language of brands as their cultural currency, and the stakes in their purchasing decisions as something real. For no matter how much control kids get over the media they watch, they are still utterly powerless when it comes to the manufacturing of brands. Even a consumer revolt merely reinforces one's role as a consumer, not an autonomous or creative being.

21    The more they interact with brands, the more they brand themselves. ◆

## CONSIDERING THE ISSUES

1. When you were in junior and senior high school, did you have particular brands to which you were most loyal? Did this brand loyalty change as you got older? Why did you prefer certain brands over others? What cultural and social influences, if any, contributed to your desire for that brand?
2. How would you define your personal style and the image you wish to project? What products and/or brands contribute to that image? Explain.
3. What can a brand tell you about the person who uses it? Explain.

## CRAFT AND CONTENT

1. How does Rushkoff support his argument? Evaluate his use of supporting sources. Identify some of the essay's particular strengths.
2. In paragraph 7, Rushkoff notes that things have gotten worse because they have gotten better. What does he mean by this statement? Explain.

## CRITICAL THINKING

1. Look up the phrase "Gruen transfer" on the Internet. Were you aware of this angle of marketing practice? Does it change the way you think about how products are sold to you? Explain.
2. In order to stay in business, marketers have had to rethink how they sell products to the youth market. How have they changed to keep pace with the youth market? Explain.
3. In his conclusion, Rushkoff predicts that even media-savvy kids will still "lose" the game. Why will they fail? Explain.

## WRITING ABOUT THE ISSUES

1. Rushkoff notes in paragraph 11 that the youth generation "constitutes a new psychographic." First, define what you think "psychographic" means in the advertising industry. What makes this generation different from previous generations of consumers? If you are part of this generation (ages 14–24), explain

why you do or don't think you indeed represent a new "psycho-graphic." If you are older than this group, answer the same question based on your own experience and observation of younger consumers.

2. Teens and young adults covet certain brand-name clothing because they believe it promotes a particular image. What defines brand image? Is it something created by the company, or by the people who use the product? How does advertising influence the social view we hold of ourselves and the brands we use? Write an essay on the connection between advertising, image, and cultural values of what is "in" or popular and what is not.

3. Did marketing techniques such as the one described by Rushkoff for the Pokemon trading cards and games influence your consumer habits as a child or teen? Were you aware of such techniques? Write an essay exploring the way advertising targets specific age groups. Support your essay with information from the article and your own experience. You may wish to identify particular products that use specific marketing techniques to target young consumers.

# Black Friday . . . Gray Thursday
*Benjamin R. Barber*

Benjamin R. Barber is a democratic theorist, and the author of *Strong Democracy, Jihad vs. McWorld, Consumed: How Markets Corrupt Children, Infantilize Adults, and Swallow Citizens Whole* (2007). He is a Distinguished Senior Fellow at Demos: A Network for Ideas and Action, and President of CivWorld at Demos. This editorial was posted on the *Huffington Post* on November 26, 2007.

## CONNECTING TO THE TOPIC

Black Friday is the name given to the day after Thanksgiving where it is recognized as kicking off the holiday shopping season. While it is not an official holiday, many people take this day off and devote it to shopping, making it one of the most profitable retail days of the year. Many stores open their doors very early (some as early as 5 AM) and hold "early-bird specials" featuring discounts on merchandise that can range from video game consoles to cashmere sweaters. Such great buys can lead to store stampedes when shop doors open. The name originally reflected the huge traffic jams that often developed on that day, but its contemporary meaning is now connected to the concept of "being in the black" (making a profit). The dark phrasing may hold another meaning for some consumers, who are disgusted by the long lines, the mad grabs for merchandise, and the hoarding of popular items for resale online.

## WORDS IN CONTEXT

**solidarity** (2)   a union of among members of a group who share similar views or interests (n.)

**mantra** (5)   a repeated word or phrase that holds mystical properties (n.)

**anomaly** (9)   a deviation from what is normal or expected (n.)

**incarnate** (9)   given a human form, personified (adj.)

**compliant** (9)   submissive, willing to go along with (adj.)

**instigate** (9)   to stir up, urge on (v.)

1    **O**n this blue Monday following Black Friday, can anyone remember Thursday?

2    Thanksgiving, once America's holiday of gratitude and family **solidarity**, has become the staging area for Christmas shopping. It is no longer just the day after Thanksgiving—Black Friday (as in "in the black, or profitable")—that is devoted to consumerism, but Thanksgiving Day itself, on which more and more stores are now staying open for pre-Black Friday sales. Call it gray Thursday.

3    America's retail industry, now indistinguishable from its marketing industry, sees in every blank space a billboard, in every suburban meadow, a mall, in every screen—big or small—a banner ad. And in every "non-working" holiday, a time for more shopping. The Thanksgiving weekend comprises four non-working days: that's ninety-six hours available for non-stop shopping. Ditto for Halloween, Ramadan, Christmas, you name it—the "holy days" are now all shopoholy days. And whose fault is that?

4    I had a half-dozen calls from radio and TV stations over this long shopping weekend asking me to talk about why consumers are so hungry to shop, why housewives were camping out at 3 AM Friday morning to make the 4 AM opening of mega-stores like Target. The assumption of the reporters

who called was that Black Friday was a demand-side phenomenon—moms deciding there wasn't enough time in the day for all the shopping they wanted to do, dads insisting that stores stay open on Thanksgiving and open again at midnight on Black Friday' 'cause they just couldn't get enough of those bargains, kids leaping from bed at midnight as if they'd spotted Peter Pan in the window and shouting, "Let's go shopping!"

5    See, the point seems to be, the retail industry is just saying—after all, this is its **mantra**—we're just giving people what they want.

6    Well, not quite: Americans like to shop, but they also like to pray, read, play, talk, make art, make love, take walks, and spend time munching turkey with loved ones. They like to shop but not 24/7. The shopping fanaticism we see on Black Friday, and throughout the year, is a supply-side phenomenon: the result of corporations "pushing," not consumers "pulling."

7    That's why marketing and advertising are capitalism's main industries today, why they expend a quarter of a trillion every year to get people to "want" all the stuff they sell. It's why they target children and encourage shopaholism (a serious problem for more than 20 million Americans who regularly go shopping without a particular purchase in mind).

8    Where capitalism once produced goods and services to meet real needs and wants, today it produces needs and wants to sell all the goods, wanted or not, it must sell to stay in business. Real needs (clean water in the third world) go wanting, while manufactured needs (bottled water) are pushed on first-world consumers who can get free clean water from their taps.

9    So Black Friday is no **anomaly;** it is consumer capitalism **incarnate.** It is not a **compliant** response by polite retailers to consumer demand, it is part of a massive world-wide campaign to **instigate** and sustain consumer demand beyond any reasonable definition of need or want. To satisfy shareholders, not citizens.

10    Our hyper-consumerism is actually consuming us (sub-prime mortgage anyone?). It's time we understand that Black Friday is not something we do; it something being done to us. And comprehend that, left to the marketplace, Black Friday will eat Thursday as well and annihilate what is left of Thanksgiving and the American spirit it represents. ◆

## CONSIDERING THE ISSUES

1. How do you approach the holiday season? Do you plan to shop on the day after Thanksgiving? Why or why not?

2. What is our social attitude about people who spend a lot of money on items they don't really need? Do we send mixed messages that consumerism is a bad thing, but then urge consumers to keep spending?

## CRAFT AND CONTENT

1. Evaluate the author's tone in this piece. Identify specific words and phrases that convey his personal opinion on the subject of consumerism and "Black Friday."
2. At various points throughout his editorial, Barber asks his readers a question. What questions does he pose to his reader, and how does he answer these questions? Is this a good writing technique? Explain.

## CRITICAL THINKING

1. In his conclusion, Barber asserts, "Black Friday is not something we do; it is something being done to us." What does he mean?
2. Barber argues that corporations are not really giving consumers what they want—rather, they are pushing consumers to buy more than they need. What is your own reaction to this point? Do you feel pushed by advertisers to buy things you don't really want?

## WRITING ABOUT THE ISSUES

1. Research the topic of consumer spending during the holiday season. How important is "Black Friday" to the economy? What are the origins of the term, and how has this day changed over the last 20 to 30 years (for example, what is "Cyber Monday"?). Based on what you know already and what you learn from research, how might this day change over the next decade?
2. Write a personal narrative describing your Thanksgiving break and any consumer practices you associate with this four-day period (Thursday to Sunday). Connect your narrative to points Barber raises in his editorial.

# On Sale at Old Navy: Cool Clothes for Identical Zombies!

*Damien Cave*

> Damien Cave is a writer and Phillips Foundation Fellow. This article first appeared in the November 22, 2000, issue of the e-zine *Salon*.

## CONNECTING TO THE TOPIC

Mass-market retail stores like Old Navy, Gap, Pottery Barn, and Ikea have enjoyed enormous popularity in recent years. Part of their appeal is that they market the concept of "cool." We believe that they represent a "with-it" lifestyle that we literally buy into. But are these stores just marketing conformity under the guise of "cool"? Are they crushing our individuality? Are we moving rapidly to the day where we will all dress the same, have the same furniture, and want the same things? If the things we own and the clothes we wear help create our identity, are chain stores just helping us join the cult of conformity?

## WORDS IN CONTEXT

**pugnacious** (2)  scornful or hostile; disapproving and critical (adj.)

**homogenous** (4)  of the same or similar nature or kind (adj.)

**urbanite** (5)  a city dweller (n.)

**equate** (8)  to consider, treat, or depict as equal or equivalent (v.)

**Pavlovianly** (10)  referring to Russian scientist Ivan Petrovich Pavlov, known for discovering the conditioned response. In one experiment, by ringing a bell when feeding dogs, he eventually was able to get the dogs to salivate just by hearing the bell, even when no food was present. His experiment proved that animals could be conditioned to expect a consequence on the results of previous experience. (adj.)

**commodify** (14)  to turn into or treat as a product that can be sold; make commercial (v.)

**pessimistic** (16)  tending to stress the negative or unfavorable viewpoint (adj.)

**duality** (19)  state of having two sides (n.)

**insidious** (20)  sinister; intended to entrap by stealth; having a harmful allure (adj.)

1    **T**homas Frank walks by the candy-cane-adorned displays of Old Navy, passing the sign exclaiming "priced so low, you can't say no," and into the chain's San Francisco flagship store. The all-devouring Christmas rush hasn't started yet, but it's clear from the frown on Frank's face that he's not being seduced by the cheap but stylish clothes, the swirling neon and the bass-heavy hip-hop pounding in his ears.

2    "Oh God, this is disgusting," Frank says. This reaction isn't surprising. The bespectacled Midwesterner is a pioneering social critic—one of the first writers to document how, starting in the '60s, American businesses have co-opted cool anti-corporate culture and used it to seduce the masses. His arguments in the *Baffler*, a **pugnacious** review Frank founded in 1988, and in 1997's "The Conquest of Cool" read like sermons, angry wake-up calls for consumers who hungrily ingest hipper-than-thou ("Think Different") marketing campaigns without ever questioning their intent.

3    Old Navy and other cheap but tasteful retailers provide perfect fodder for Frank's critique. Their low prices and hip-but-wholesome branding strategy are supposed to present a healthy alternative to the conspicuous consumption of a Calvin Klein. But critics like Frank and Naomi Klein, author of "No Logo," argue that the formula is really nothing more than the wolf of materialism wrapped in cheaper sheep's clothing.

4    Consumers are being scammed, says Klein, arguing that stores like Old Navy and Ikea are duping millions, inspiring mass conformity while pretending to deliver high culture to the masses. "It's this whole idea of creating a carnival for the most **homogenous** fashions and furniture," says Klein. "It's mass cloning that's being masked in a carnival of diversity. You don't notice that you're conforming because everything is so colorful."

5    Klein and Frank say that few consumers recognize just how conformist their consumption habits have become. And certainly, it's hard to argue that Ikea's and Old Navy's items haven't become icons of **urbanite** and suburbanite imagination. Watch MTV, or rent "Fight Club," to see Ikea's candy-colored décor, then truck down to your local Old Navy flagship store. When you arrive, what you'll find is that hordes of people have beaten you there. At virtually every opening of Old Navy's and Ikea's stores—in the New York, Chicago and San Francisco areas, for example—tens of thousands of people appeared in the first few days. Even now, long after the stores first opened, lines remain long.

6    What's wrong with these people? Nothing, say defenders of the companies. The popularity of brands like Ikea and Old Navy, they argue,

derives from the retailers' ability to offer good stuff cheap. "They provide remarkable value," says Joel Reichart, a professor at the Fordham School of Business who has written case studies on Ikea. "They're truly satisfying people's needs."

7    Despite his irritation with the way companies like Old Navy market themselves, Frank acknowledges that businesses have always sought to offer cheap, relatively high-quality merchandise and concedes that there is some value in their attempts. He even admits that consumerism is good for the economy.

8    But he and other critics argue that in the end we're only being conned into thinking that our needs are being satisfied. What's really happening, they argue, is that clever marketers are turning us into automatons who **equate** being cool with buying cheap stuff that everyone else has. Under the stores' guise of delivering good taste to the general public, any chance we have at experiencing or creating authenticity is being undermined. Ultimately, our brave new shopping world is one in which we are spending more time in the checkout line than reading books, watching movies or otherwise challenging ourselves with real culture.

9    "Shopping is a way of putting together your identity," laments "Nobrow" author John Seabrook. And the "homogenized taste" of today's Old Navy and Ikea shoppers proves, he says, that Americans either are consciously choosing to look and live alike or are determined not to notice that that is what they're doing.

10   According to Christine Rosen, a professor in the Haas School of Business at UC-Berkeley, people who fill their closets, homes and lives with Old Navy and Ikea—or Pottery Barn or a host of other slick stores—are simply new examples of the trend toward conformity that started when the first "brands" appeared in the 1910s and '20s. "We're **Pavlovianly** trained to respond to this," she says.

11   And we're also just too damn lazy. That's the theory floated by Packard Jennings, an anti-consumerism activist who says that stores like Old Navy are designed to numb the brain and remove all semblance of creativity from the purchasing process. "Ikea pre-arranges sets of furniture in its stores, thereby lessening individual thought," he says. Once people are in the store, they can't resist. "Entire households are purchased at Ikea," he says.

12   Indeed, Janice Simonsen, an Ikea spokeswoman, confirmed that a large part of the chain's demographic consists of "people who come in and say, 'I need everything.'" Meanwhile, those who don't want everything

usually end up with more than they need, says Fordham's Reichart. "The way they design their stores"—with an up escalator to the showroom and no exit until the checkout—"you end up going through the entire store," he says.

13    Old Navy plays by the same sneaky rules. When Frank and I entered the San Francisco store, clerks offered us giant mesh bags. Ostensibly, this is just good service, but since the bags are capable of holding at least half a dozen pairs of jeans and a few shirts, it's obvious that they're also meant to encourage overconsumption.

14    Frank called the bags "gross" but not out of line with other state-of-the-art retailing practices. But according to Klein, the sacks, in conjunction with Old Navy's penchant for displaying T-shirts in mock-1950s supermarket coolers, prove that the company is aiming to do something more. The idea behind this "theater for the brand" architecture is to **commodify** the products, to make them "as easy to buy as a gallon of milk," Klein says. "The idea is to create a Mecca where people make pilgrimages to their brand," Klein says. "You experience the identity of the brand and not the product."

15    Disney, which opened its first store in 1987, was the first to employ this strategy. And since then others have appeared. Niketown, the Body Shop, the Discovery Store—they all aim to sell products by selling a destination.

16    Old Navy and Ikea, however, are far more popular than those predecessors—and, if you believe the more **pessimistic** of their critics, more dangerous. Not only are the two chains remaking many closets and homes into one designer showcase, says Klein, but they are also lulling consumers to sleep and encouraging them to overlook some important issues.

17    Such as quality. People think they're getting "authenticity on the cheap," says David Lewis, author of "The Soul of the New Consumer." But the truth may be that they're simply purchasing the perception of quality and authenticity. "Because [Ikea and Old Navy] create these self-enclosed lifestyles," Klein explains, "you overlook the fact that the products are pretty crappy and fall apart." Adds Jennings, "Things may be cheaper, but you keep going back to replace the faulty merchandise."

18    Then there is the trap of materialism. Survey after survey suggests that people who place a high value on material goods are less happy than those who do not, says Eric Rindfleisch, a marketing professor at the University of Arizona. The focus on bargains, incremental purchases and commodification plays to a uniquely American blind spot.

19    "We operate with a **duality**," explains Rindfleisch, who has conducted studies linking materialism with depression. "Americans know that money doesn't buy happiness, but most people somehow believe that increments in pay or goods will improve our lives. It's a human weakness—particularly in America."

20    The most **insidious** danger may be more abstract. The anti-consumerism critics argue that by elevating shopping to cultural status, we are losing our grip on real culture. We live in a time where college kids think nothing of decorating their rooms with Absolut vodka ads and fail to realize that they're essentially turning their rooms into billboards. Meanwhile, museum stores keep getting larger, Starbucks sells branded CDs to go with your coffee and because Ikea and other stores now look like movie theaters or theme parks, we don't just shop, "we make a day of it," as Klein puts it.

21    This only helps steer us away from other endeavors. When people spend so much time buying, thinking and talking about products, they don't have time for anything else, for real conversations about politics or culture or for real interaction with people.

22    Ultimately, the popularity of Old Navy, Ikea and their ilk proves that we're stuck in what Harvard professor Juliet Schor calls "the cycle of work and spend." Breaking that cycle may not be easy, but if one believes critics like Frank, it's essential if we are to control our own culture, instead of allowing it to be defined by corporations.

23    The cycle may not be possible to break. Frank, for one, is extremely pessimistic about our chances for turning back the tide of conformity and co-opted cool. Maybe that's one reason why he wanted to get out of Old Navy as fast as he could.

24    But I'm not so sure. When "Ikea boy," Edward Norton's character in "Fight Club," watched his apartment and his Swedish furniture explode in a blaze of glory, I wasn't the only one in the theater who cheered.  ◆

### CONSIDERING THE ISSUES

1. Cave notes several businesses in his essay that he calls "mass-market" sellers of "cool." What stores does he specifically identify? Do you shop at any of these stores? If so, why do you shop there? Because they are "cool"? Affordable? Hip? Popular? Explain.

2. In paragraph 20, Cave observes that "college kids think nothing of decorating their rooms with Absolut vodka ads and fail to realize that they're essentially turning their rooms into billboards."

What decorating choices have you made for your personal space? In what ways has your decorating style been influenced by outside forms of advertising? Explain.

## CRAFT AND CONTENT

1. Cave quotes many different people in his essay. Identify all of his sources and group them as either "inside advertising/marketing," or "outside critics/academics." Whom does he rely upon more? How do the quotes he uses from both groups support his argument?
2. Can you tell what position Cave supports on the issue of mass consumption and on the stores he describes in his essay? Identify a few specific statements he makes in his essay that reveal his point of view.
3. How does Cave's title connect to his subject matter? What images does it create? How does it influence the reader's interpretation of his argument? Explain.

## CRITICAL THINKING

1. In paragraph 2, Cave notes that American businesses have "co-opted cool anti-corporate culture." What does he mean? What is "anti-corporate" culture and why is it "cool"? What started it and how are businesses using it to their advantage? In what ways is this ironic? Explain.
2. What techniques do mass-market stores employ to squeeze the maximum profit from consumers who enter them? Were you aware of these techniques? Have you fallen victim to them yourself? Explain.

## WRITING ABOUT THE ISSUES

1. In paragraph 9, author John Seabrook comments, "Shopping is a way of putting together your identity." Consider the ways your shopping habits put together your identity. Are you influenced by some of the techniques described in this essay? Consider in your response not just what you buy, but where you shop, why you shop, and with whom. How do your shopping companions influence your choices? How does advertising appeal to your

desire to buy particular things as part of your own personal identity? Explain.

2. Several critics in this essay fear that mass-marketing chains aim
to make shopping the primary characteristic of American culture. "By elevating shopping to cultural status, we are losing our
grip on real culture. When people spend so much time buying,
thinking, and talking about products, they don't have time for
anything else, for real conversations about politics or culture or
for real interaction with people." Write a response to this assertion, expressing your own point of view.

# With These Words I Can Sell You Anything

*William Lutz*

William Lutz teaches English at Rutgers University and is the author of sev-
eral books, including *Beyond Nineteen Eighty-Four* (1984) and *Doublespeak
Defined* (1999). The following essay is an excerpt from Lutz's book
*Doublespeak*.

## CONNECTING TO THE TOPIC

Words such as "help" and "virtually" and phrases such as "new and improved" and "acts fast" seem like innocuous weaponry in the arsenal of advertising. But not to William Lutz, who analyzes how such words are used in
ads—how they misrepresent, mislead, and deceive consumers. In this essay,
he alerts us to the special power of "weasel words"—those familiar and
sneaky little critters that "appear to say one thing when in fact they say the opposite, or nothing at all." The real danger, Lutz argues, is how such language
debases reality and the values of the consumer.

1    One problem advertisers have when they try to convince you that the
product they are pushing is really different from other, similar products is
that their claims are subject to some laws. Not a lot of laws, but there are

some designed to prevent fraudulent or untruthful claims in advertising. Generally speaking, advertisers have to be careful in what they say in their ads, in the claims they make for the products they advertise. Parity claims are safe because they are legal and supported by a number of court decisions. But beyond parity claims there are weasel words.

2    Advertisers use weasel words to appear to be making a claim for a product when in fact they are making no claim at all. Weasel words get their name from the way weasels eat the eggs they find in the nests of other animals. A weasel will make a small hole in the egg, suck out the insides, then place the egg back in the nest. Only when the egg is examined closely is it found to be hollow. That's the way it is with weasel words in advertising.

## "Help"—The Number One Weasel Word

3   The biggest weasel word used in advertising doublespeak is "help." Now "help" only means to aid or assist, nothing more. It does not mean to conquer, stop, eliminate, end, solve, heal, cure, or anything else. But once the ad says "help," it can say just about anything after that because "help" qualifies everything coming after it. The trick is that the claim that comes after the weasel word is usually so strong and so dramatic that you forget the word "help" and concentrate only on the dramatic claim. You read into the ad a message that the ad does not contain. More importantly, the advertiser is not responsible for the claim that you read into the ad, even though the advertiser wrote the ad so you would read that claim into it.

4    The next time you see an ad for a cold medicine that promises that it "helps relieve cold symptoms fast," don't rush out to buy it. Ask yourself what this claim is really saying. Remember, "helps" means only that the medicine will aid or assist. What will it aid or assist in doing? Why, "relieve" your cold "symptoms." "Relieve" only means to ease, alleviate, or mitigate, not to stop, end, or cure. Nor does the claim say how much relieving this medicine will do. Nowhere does this ad claim it will cure anything. In fact, the ad doesn't even claim it will do anything at all. The ad only claims that it will aid in relieving (not curing) your cold symptoms, which are probably a runny nose, watery eyes, and a headache. In other words, this medicine probably contains a standard decongestant and some aspirin. By the way, what does "fast" mean? Ten minutes, one hour, one day? What is fast to one person can be very slow to another. Fast is another weasel word.

5 Look at ads in magazines and newspapers, listen to ads on radio and television, and you'll find the word "help" in ads for all kinds of products. How often do you read or hear such phrases as "helps stop . . .," "helps overcome . . .," "helps eliminate . . .," "helps you feel . . .," or "helps you look . . ."? If you start looking for this weasel word in advertising, you'll be amazed at how often it occurs. Analyze the claims in the ads using "help," and you will discover that these ads are really saying nothing.

## Virtually Spotless

6 One of the most powerful weasel words is "virtually," a word so innocent that most people don't pay any attention to it when it is used in an advertising claim. But watch out. "Virtually" is used in advertising claims that appear to make specific, definite promises when there is no promise. After all, what does "virtually" mean? It means "in essence of effect, although not in fact." Look at that definition again. "Virtually" means not in fact. It does not mean "almost" or "just about the same as," or anything else.

7 The next time you see the ad that says that this dishwasher detergent "leaves dishes virtually spotless," just remember how advertisers twist the meaning of the weasel word "virtually." You can have lots of spots on your dishes after using this detergent and the ad claim will still be true, because what this claim really means is that this detergent does not in fact leave your dishes spotless. Whenever you see or hear an ad claim that uses the word "virtually," just translate that claim into its real meaning. So the television set that is "virtually trouble free" becomes the television set that is not in fact trouble free, the "virtually foolproof operation" of any appliance becomes an operation that is in fact not foolproof, and the product that "virtually never needs service" becomes the product that is not in fact service free.

## New and Improved

8 If "new" is the most frequently used word on a product package, "improved" is the second most frequent. In fact, the two words are almost always used together. It seems just about everything sold these days is "new and improved." The next time you're in the supermarket, try counting the number of times you see these words on products.

9 Just what do these words mean? The use of the word "new" is restricted by regulations, so an advertiser can't just use the word on a product or in

an ad without meeting certain requirements. For example, a product is considered new for about six months during a national advertising campaign. If the product is being advertised only in a limited test market area, the word can be used longer, and in some instances has been used for as long as two years.

10    What makes a product "new"? Some products have been around for a long time, yet every once in a while you discover that they are being advertised as "new." Well, an advertiser can call a product new if there has been "a material functional change" in the product. What is "a material functional change," you ask? Good question. In fact it's such a good question it's being asked all the time. It's up to the manufacturer to prove that the product has undergone such a change. And if the manufacturer isn't challenged on the claim, then there's no one to stop it. Moreover, the change does not have to be an improvement in the product. One manufacturer added an artificial lemon scent to a cleaning product and called it "new and improved," even though the product did not clean any better than without the lemon scent. The manufacturer defended the use of the word "new" on the grounds that the artificial scent changed the chemical formula of the product and therefore constituted "a material functional change."

11    Which brings up the word "improved." When used in advertising, "improved" does not mean "made better." It only means "changed" or "different from before." So, if the detergent maker puts a plastic pour spout on the box of detergent, the product has been "improved," and away we go with a whole new advertising campaign. Or, if the cereal maker adds more fruit or a different kind of fruit to the cereal, there's an improved product. Now you know why manufacturers are constantly making little changes in their products. Whole new advertising campaigns, designed to convince you that the product has been changed for the better, are based on small changes in superficial aspects of a product. The next time you see an ad for an "improved" product, ask yourself what was wrong with the old one. Ask yourself just how "improved" the product is. Finally, you might check to see whether the "improved" version costs more than the unimproved one.

12    "New" is just too useful and powerful a word in advertising for advertisers to pass it up easily. So they use weasel words that say "new" without really saying it. One of their favorites is "introducing," as in, "Introducing improved Tide," or "Introducing the stain remover." The first is simply saying, here's our improved soap; the second, here's our new advertising campaign for our detergent. Another favorite is "now," as in, "Now there's

**Advertising Doublespeak**
**Quick Quiz**

Test your awareness of advertising doublespeak. The following is a list of statements from some recent ads. Your job is to figure out what each of these ads really says.

DOMINO'S PIZZA: "Because nobody delivers better."
SINUTAB: "It can stop the pain."
TUMS: "The stronger acid neutralizer."
LISTERMINT: "Making your mouth a cleaner place."
CASCADE: "For virtually spotless dishes"
NUPRIN: "Little. Yellow. Different. Better."
ANACIN: "Better relief."
ADVIL: "Advanced medicine for pain."
ALEVE COLD AND SINUS: "12 hours of relief."
PONDS COLD CREAM: "Ponds cleans like no soap can."
MILLER LITE BEER: "Tastes great. Less filling."
PHILIPS MILK OF MAGNESIA: "Nobody treats you better than MOM."
BAYER: "The wonder drug that works wonders."
KNORR: "Where taste is everything."
ANUSOL: "Anusol is the word to remember for relief."
DIMETAPP: "It relieves kids as well as colds."
LIQUID DRANO: "The liquid strong enough to be called Drano."
JOHNSON & JOHNSON BABY POWDER: "Like magic for your skin."
PURITAN: "Make it your oil for life."
PAM: "Pam, because how you cook is as important as what you cook."
TYLENOL GEL-CAPS: "It's not a capsule. It's better."
ALKA-SELTZER PLUS: "Breaks up your worst cold symptoms."

Sinex," which simply means that Sinex is available. Then there are phrases like "Today's Chevrolet," "Presenting Dristan," and "A fresh way to start the day." The list is really endless because advertisers are always finding new ways to say "new" without really saying it.

## Acts Fast

13  "Acts" and "works" are two popular weasel words in advertising because they bring action to the product and to the advertising claim. When you see the ad for the cough syrup that "Acts on the cough control center," ask

yourself what this cough syrup is claiming to do. Well, it's just claiming to "act," to do something, to perform an action. What is it that the cough syrup does? The ad doesn't say. It only claims to perform an action or do something on your "cough control center." By the way, what and where is your "cough control center"? I don't remember learning about that part of the body in human biology class.

14    Ads that use such phrases as "acts fast," "acts against," "acts to prevent," and the like are saying essentially nothing, because "act" is a word empty of any specific meaning. The ads are always careful not to specify exactly what "act" the product performs. Just because a brand of aspirin claims to "act fast" for headache relief doesn't mean this aspirin is any better than any other aspirin. What is the "act" that this aspirin performs? You're never told. Maybe it just dissolves quickly. Since aspirin is a parity product, all aspirin is the same and therefore functions the same.

## Works Like Anything Else

15    If you don't find the word "acts" in an ad, you will probably find the weasel word "works." In fact, the two words are almost interchangeable in advertising. Watch out for ads that say a product "works against," "works like," "works for," or "works longer." As with "acts," "works" is the same meaningless verb used to make you think that this product really does something, and maybe even something special or unique. But "works," like "acts," is basically a word empty of any specific meaning.

## Like Magic

16    Whenever advertisers want you to stop thinking about the product and to start thinking about something bigger, better, or more attractive than the product, they use that very popular weasel word, "like." The word "like" is the advertiser's equivalent of a magician's use of misdirection. "Like" gets you to ignore the product and concentrate on the claim the advertiser is making about it. "For skin like peaches and cream" claims the ad for a skin cream. What is this ad really claiming? It doesn't say this cream will give you peaches-and-cream skin. There is no verb in this claim, so it doesn't even mention using the product. How is skin ever like "peaches and cream"? The ad is making absolutely no promise or claim whatsoever for this skin cream. If you think this cream will give you soft,

smooth, youthful-looking skin, you are the one who has read that meaning into the ad.

17    The wine that claims "It's like taking a trip to France" wants you to think about a romantic evening in Paris as you walk along the boulevard after a wonderful meal in an intimate little bistro. Of course, you don't really believe that a wine can take you to France, but the goal of the ad is to get you to think pleasant, romantic thoughts about France and not about how the wine tastes or how expensive it may be. That little word "like" has taken you away from crushed grapes into a world of your own imaginative making. Who knows, maybe the next time you buy wine, you'll think those pleasant thoughts when you see this brand of wine, and you'll buy it. Or, maybe you weren't even thinking about buying wine at all, but now you just might pick up a bottle the next time you're shopping. Ah, the power of "like" in advertising.

## The World of Advertising

18    A study some years ago found the following words to be among the most popular used in U.S. television advertisements: "new," "improved," "better," "extra," "fresh," "clean," "beautiful," "free," "good," "great," and "light." At the same time, the following words were found to be among the most frequent on British television: "new," "good-better-best," "free," "fresh," "delicious," "full," "sure," "clean," "wonderful," and "special." While these words may occur most frequently in ads, and while ads may be filled with weasel words, you have to watch out for all the words used in advertising, not just the words mentioned here.

19    Every word in an ad is there for a reason; no word is wasted. Your job is to figure out exactly what each word is doing in an ad—what each word really means, not what the advertiser wants you to think it means. Remember, the ad is trying to get you to buy a product, so it will put the product in the best possible light, using any device, trick, or means legally allowed. Your only defense against advertising (besides taking up permanent residence on the moon) is to develop and use a strong critical reading, listening, and looking ability. Always ask yourself what the ad is really saying. When you see ads on television, don't be misled by the pictures, the visual images. What does the ad say about the product? What does the ad not say? What information is missing from the ad? Only by becoming an active, critical consumer of the doublespeak of advertising will you ever be able to cut through the doublespeak and discover what the ad is really saying. ◆

## CONSIDERING THE ISSUES

1. Consider the phrases used in advertising such as "new and improved" and "cleans like a dream." Do you think about such advertising phrases? How much do such phrases influence you as a consumer? Explain.

2. Do you think that most people fail to comprehend how advertising works on them? When you read or watch ads, do you see through the gimmicks and weasel words?

## CRAFT AND CONTENT

1. What do you think of Lutz's writing style? Is it humorous? Informal? Academic? What strategies does he use to involve the reader in the piece?

2. The author uses "you" throughout the article. Do you find the use of the second person stylistically satisfying? Do you think it is appropriate for the article?

3. Review Lutz's "Doublespeak Quick Quiz." Choose five items and analyze them using dictionary meanings to explain what the ads are really saying.

## CRITICAL THINKING

1. How did "weasel words" get their name? Does it sound like an appropriate label? Why, according to Lutz, do advertisers use them?

2. According to the author, how can consumers protect themselves against weasel words?

## WRITING ABOUT THE ISSUES

1. As Lutz suggests, look at some ads in a magazine or newspaper (or television and radio commercials). Then make a list of all uses of "help" you find over a 24-hour period. Examine the ads to determine exactly what is said and what the unwary consumer thinks is being said. Write up your report.

2. Invent a product and have some fun writing an ad for it. Use as many weasel words as you can to make your product shine.

3. Lutz characterizes the language used in ads as "weasel words," that is, language that pretends to do one thing while really doing another. Explore your campus for examples of "weasel words." Look not only at ads, but at material such as university brochures and pamphlets that are sent to prospective students, and/or any political contests taking place (e.g., students running for the student government or candidates for office speaking at your campus). Write down all examples of weasel words and explain why they are empty words.

# SAMPLE ADS AND STUDY QUESTIONS

The following section features five magazine advertisements. Diverse in content and style, some ads use words to promote the product, while others depend on emotion, name recognition, visual appeal, or association. They present a variety of sales pitches and marketing techniques.

Following each ad is a list of questions to help you analyze how the ads work their appeal to promote their products. When studying them, consider how they target our social perception and basic desires for happiness, beauty, and success. Approach each as a consumer, an artist, a social scientist, and a critic with an eye for detail.

**JIMMY CHOO**

1. Examine this advertisement carefully. What is happening in this ad? How does it sell the product? Can you tell what product the ad promotes?
2. How does the desert setting and mountains and cracked earth contribute to the image? Do these elements tap into audience expectations about the product? Are they confusing? Entertaining? Explain.
3. Would you know what this ad was selling if there were no brand name mentioned in the ad? Explain.
4. If you were leafing through a magazine and saw this ad, would you stop to read it? Why or why not?
5. In January 2007, Dolce & Gabbana pulled an ad that depicted an image that could have been interpreted as promoting violence against women. Could this ad be viewed similarly? Why or why not?

ACLU

1. Who is featured in the picture? How does this image play upon our cultural and historical expectations and twist them?
2. Who is the ACLU? What mission do they support? Does this ad motivate you to take action? Why or why not?
3. Who do you think is the target audience for this advertisement? How do you think a young adult would respond to it? a married man? a politician or government worker? a teenage girl? a lawyer? Explain.

## SHELL OIL

1. Would you know what this ad was promoting if the company's logo was not located at the lower-right section of the ad? Would there be any ambiguity about what was being "sold" in the advertisement? How much does this ad depend on name recognition? Explain.
2. Where would you expect to see an ad like this and why? If you were an advertising executive, where would you place this ad? How would you target your public? Explain.
3. What connection does the tag line, "Say No to No" have to the product? What association or product image is the company trying to promote?
4. Review the list of items that the girl has imagined will be a "yes" by responding to the directive "say no to no." What does the list mean? How does it relate to the company sponsoring the advertisement? Explain.

STOLICHNAYA

1. How do the young women in the photograph connect to the product being promoted in this ad?
2. Who is the likely target audience for this ad? In what magazines would you expect to see it? Is it an effective ad? Explain.
3. What are the young women doing in the ad? What lifestyle does the ad promote? What is the product's implied promise? Explain.
4. What does the text below the photograph say about the product? Is the text about the women, or directed to the reader? Who do we presume the reader to be?

**VANS**

1. Analyze the different images featured in the ad. What do they depict? How do the different photos contribute to the overall tone of the ad?
2. Do you know who the man is in the ad? How does he connect to the product—sneakers? Is it important that he connect at all?
3. What is the meaning of the skull photo behind the man? Would the tone of the ad be different without it? Why or why not?
4. Who would you say is the target audience for this ad, and why? Consider age, gender, lifestyle, etc., in your response.

# VISUAL CONNECTIONS

## Follow the Flock

### CONNECTING TO THE TOPIC

*Adbusters* magazine is a nonprofit, reader-supported, 120,000-circulation journal that provides critical commentary on consumer culture and corporate marketing agendas. Articles and issues from the magazine have been featured on MTV and PBS, the *Wall Street Journal, Wired,* and in hundreds of other newspapers, magazines, and television and radio shows around the world. They are "dedicated to examining the relationship between human beings and their physical and mental environment" and striving to create a "world in which the economy and ecology resonate in balance." This ad, a spoof on the Tommy Hilfiger brand, appeared both in its magazine and on its website at www.adbusters.org.

## CONSIDERING THE ISSUES

1. What expectations do we have of brand names and brand name products? Do we expect them to be better quality? To promote an image? To convey status? To be admired by others? Explain.
2. What brands do you use and why?

## CRITICAL THINKING

1. What message is *Adbusters* trying to convey with this ad? Explain.
2. Locate a few real Tommy Hilfiger ads from popular magazines and compare them to this one. What similarities exist? How does the spoof ad play on conventional images and messages used in the real ones? Explain.

# Blog Matters

A blog ("web log") is an online diary or commentary site that features regular entries that describe events, impressions, and viewpoints. Blogs may contain text, images, video, and often link to other websites, blogs, and online media. Most blogs allow readers to comment on the content of the post and respond to each other. As of 2007, the blog search engine estimated there were over 112 million blogs. While many blogs are maintained by individuals, some are run by journals, newspapers, and other media outlets. Remember that most blogs are not monitored for factual accuracy, and often express the opinion and views of the "blogger" writing the content.

    The blog below is hosted by "The Daily Galaxy—News from Planet Earth & Beyond," a blog site syndicated by Reuters News and created and produced by Galaxy Media, LLC.

# Scientists Find that Low Self-Esteem and Materialism Go Hand in Hand

*Rebecca Sato*
*November 13, 2007*

> *"Advertising has us chasing cars and clothes, working jobs we hate so we can buy shit we don't need."*
>
> —*Fight Club* by Chuck Palahniuk

1    Researchers have found that low self-esteem and materialism are not just a correlation, but also a causal relationship where low self-esteem increases materialism, and materialism can also create low self-esteem. They also found that as self-esteem increases, materialism decreases. The study primarily focused on how this relationship affects children and adolescents. Lan Nguyen Chaplin (University of Illinois Urbana-Champaign) and Deborah Roedder John (University of Minnesota) found that even a simple gesture to raise self-esteem dramatically decreased materialism, which provides a way to cope with insecurity.

2    "By the time children reach early adolescence and experience a decline in self-esteem, the stage is set for the use of material possessions as a coping strategy for feelings of low self-worth," they write in the study, which will appear in the *Journal of Consumer Research*.

3    The paradox that findings such as these bring up is that consumerism is good for the economy but bad for the individual. In the short run, it's good for the economy when young people believe they need to buy an entirely new wardrobe every year, for example. But the hidden cost is much higher than the dollar amount. There are costs in happiness when people believe that their value is extrinsic. There are also environmental costs associated with widespread materialism.

4    In the book "Happiness: Lessons from a New Science," Richard Layard exposes a paradox at the heart of our lives. Most of us want more income so we can consume more. Yet as societies become richer, they do not become happier. In fact, the First World has more depression, more alcoholism and more crime than 50 years ago. This paradox is true of Britain, the United States, continental Europe and Japan.

5    Statistically people have more things than they did 50 years ago, but they are actually less happy in several key areas. There is also the considerable cost of what materialism does to the environment. We don't yet know what final toll that could take in terms of quality of life and overall happiness. What many people don't understand is that if we want to save the environment then at some level we have to buy and consume less. We don't need to buy so much bottled water, for example. Studies have shown it's usually not any purer than city tap water, which doesn't leave mountains of plastic bottles strewn across the nation's landfills. It also wastes energy and resources to make those plastic bottles and the many other unnecessary things that both youth and adults alike believe they need to have in order to enjoy life and feel good about themselves.

6    *Mad Magazine* summed it up with the statement, "The only reason a great many American families don't own an elephant is that they have never been offered an elephant for a dollar down and easy weekly payments."

7    That funny statement is only funny because it's somewhat true. The reason people want whatever is currently "hot" is because they believe it will contribute toward their satisfaction and happiness in life. The word "believe" is the key here. People believe that buying more and more things will make them happy, when in fact research has shown time and time again that this simply isn't the case. What we do know for sure is that buying more and more unnecessary things is damaging our planet and contributing to global warming.

8    Sure, one person being less materialistic isn't going to make a noticeable impact on the environment, but it will make a positive impact in that one life. Once entire nations start to understand the myths about what really makes individuals happy, the world will stand a fighting chance. ◆

*Posted by: Brweb*
*November 13, 2007 at 12:53 PM*

Good article, I think we all know deep down it's true, but at the same time it can be hard to fight the propaganda and not get suckered into wanting a flashy car or 82-inch flat screen TV.

There's another Gandhi quote that seems appropriate here. "Earth provides enough to satisfy every man's need, but not every man's greed."

*Posted by: closet.hippy*
*November 14, 2007 at 02:17 AM*

I noticed this myself when I asked myself after another of those useless "what would you buy if you won the power ball jackpot" questions.

The chance of that happening is negligible [I'd have to buy a ticket first], but it got me thinking. What would I buy if I won the jackpot? And the answer to that was quite surprising. I would buy very little. Aside from a house [which I don't think is a luxury] that was reasonably equipped, but not luxurious, I need very little. There would be the occasional upgrade of aging gear but nothing "to feel better." It's just not essential to my well-being.

Ok, here's one: I'd pay top dollar for an awesome bathroom with a quality shower and a Jacuzzi. That would be my luxury.

And time. Not having to work a dumb job to pay the bills would be a blessing. The time that is allotted to me, however much or little there is left. That would be all I really needed. I can only eat one meal at a time, I have no need to impress anyone, and inventory does not equal happiness for me.

*Posted by: Karl Frank*
*November 14, 2007 at 06:43 AM*

"If you have ever lived in some war-torn third world (like Iraq), then you will learn that money and possessions DOES equal more happiness in life."

You're way off track. Having money and possessions AS COMPARED to having NOTHING or being in extreme poverty will obviously make a person happier. However, research shows that amassing MORE possessions and money when a person has already achieved some basic amount of middle-class status and self-sufficiency actually doesn't make them happier.

The issue isn't should we have ANY possessions compared to nothing, it's wanting "more, more, more."

**RESPOND TO THE BLOG:**

What do you think? Is consumer culture making children less happy and more likely to be dissatisfied with life? Have you experienced this paradox yourself?

# TOPICAL CONNECTIONS

## GROUP PROJECTS

1. Working in a group, develop a slogan and advertising campaign for one of the following products: sneakers, soda, a candy bar, or jeans. How would you apply the principles of advertising language to market your product? After completing your marketing plan, "sell" your product to the class. If time permits, explain the reasoning behind your selling technique.

2. With your group, think of some advertising campaigns that created controversy (Camel cigarettes, Calvin Klein, Carl's Jr., etc.) What made them controversial? What was the impact on sales?

## WEB PROJECTS

1. Access the websites for several popular soft drinks, such as www.pepsi.com, www.coke.com, www.drpepper.com, etc. How do the websites promote the product? Who is the target audience, and how do the sites reflect this audience? What techniques do they use to sell? Write an essay on the differences between online and paper advertising for soft drinks. Will the Web be the next great advertising venue? Will paper ads become obsolete? What considerations are unique to each? Is advertising on the Web a passing fad or the wave of the future? Consider the information on advertising provided in this chapter when developing your response.

2. *Adbusters* addresses the unethical ways advertisers manipulate consumers to "need" products. However, if we consider ads long enough, we can determine for ourselves the ways we may be manipulated. Write a paper in which you consider the techniques of advertising. Support your evaluation with examples of advertising campaigns with which you are familiar. Make an argument for the effectiveness or exploitative nature of such campaigns. You may draw support from the articles by authors such as Rushkoff, Barber, Cave, and Lutz, as well as from your personal experience as a consumer.

## FOR FURTHER INQUIRY

1. You are an advertising executive. Select one of the products featured in the sample ads section and write a new advertising campaign for it. Do you use "weasel words" or tap into popular consciousness? Do you use sex appeal or power to promote your product? How do you create a need or desire for the product? Defend your campaign to your supervisors by explaining what motivates your creative decisions.

2. Write an essay evaluating advertising techniques in the twentieth and twenty-first centuries. Have ads changed over the last 50 years or so? What accounts for similarities or differences? Has advertising become more or less ethical? Creative? Focused? Be sure to explain your position and support it with examples from real advertisements.

# 4 | Do the Media Promote a Culture of Fear?

**W**e live in a media-driven world. We are constantly under the influence of newspapers, magazines, television and radio programs, music, the Internet, and advertising. The mass media competes for our eyes and ears to ensure that we are exposed to the advertising that forms its backbone. Newspapers, television programs, magazines, and most radio programs are all supported by the marketing industry. The goal is getting us to pay attention. And in today's world, we seem to pay attention to scary stories.

It is human nature to pay attention to that which is distressing—whether a car wreck on the freeway, a mass murder in a restaurant in the Midwest, or a child abduction a few states away. And while such incidents are indeed distressing, we also pay attention to other "horror" stories—from moldy basements making people sick, to high mercury levels in tuna, to exploding cigarette lighters, to dangerous trans fats in our doughnuts. We are drawn to violent programs and music, even though many of us feel that such media can cause harm—especially to impressionable children.

To sift through the hype, it is important that we understand how to critically analyze different media, to use and maximize its many benefits, and to defend ourselves against its sneaky manipulations. The articles in this unit examine the ways the media grabs our attention and preys on our deepest fears and natural tendency to worry about what a dreadful world we live in. These pieces also raise questions about violence on television and music, and the impressions such violence can make on us. Do the media have a responsibility to the public to balance hype with fact? Are the media creating a culture of fear and violence in order to sell airtime, music, magazines? And how do we distinguish fact from fiction?

142

## CRITICAL THINKING

1. What is the effect of the boy's single word in such a large bubble? If the word was larger, or the bubble smaller, would the effect be the same? Explain.
2. Is there more than one possible interpretation of this cartoon? What do you think the cartoonist is trying to say here? Can you think of other interpretations in addition to your first one? Explain.
3. How does this cartoon connect to the larger theme of "media hype"? Explain.

# Extreme Reality: How Media Coverage Exaggerates Risks and Dangers

*John Stossel*

> John Stossel is coanchor of ABC's *20/20* and the recipient of 19 Emmy awards for reporting. He is the author of *Give Me a Break: How I Exposed Hucksters, Cheats, and Scam Artists and Became the Scourge of the Liberal Media* (2004). The article that follows was part of a *20/20* segment airing on July 12, 2002.

## CONNECTING TO THE TOPIC

News programs such as *20/20*, *Dateline*, *60 Minutes*, and *48 Hours*, and news magazines such as *Time* and *Newsweek*, tend to rely on sensational stories to grab viewers' attention and keep it for the hour. Sometimes the information they provide can be quite helpful and illuminating. Yet sometimes they twist an obscure incident into a national epidemic. The trick for the audience, of course, is to figure out which is which.

## WORDS IN CONTEXT

**amid** (4)  surrounded by; in the middle of (prep.)

**circular logic** (8)  a fallacy in reasoning in which the premise is used to prove the conclusion, and the conclusion used to prove the premise—e.g., *steroids are dangerous because they ruin your health* (n.)

**conglomerate** (10)  a corporation made up of a number of different companies that operate in diversified fields (n.)

**infinitesimally** (11)  immeasurably or incalculably (adv.)

**mundane** (12)  relating to or concerned with the commonplace and the ordinary (adj.)

**ramp up** (14)  to increase, usually in violence (n.)

**rivet** (14)  to engross or hold (as in one's attention) (n.)

1   If you watch television news regularly, you can't help but think that the world is a very scary place.

2       You'll be hammered with a whole host of frightening stories about crime, terror threats, strange new diseases, or scary old ones. It's the media's

job to inform us of these dangers, but does the amount of coverage reflect the risk we really face?

3    Remember 2001's coverage of shark attacks? It seemed everywhere you looked someone in the press was talking about the "Summer of the Shark." You may have believed that shark attacks were on the rise. That's what some television stations reported. But it wasn't true.

4    In 2002, shark attacks off American beaches were hardly different from previous years. Most of the reports mentioned that, but that important truth got lost **amid** the blare and blur of frightening headlines and images. While the media were busy scaring us out of the water, scientists said there was no increase in the number of sharks off our beaches and stressed that sharks were so unlikely to kill you that you're about 25 times more likely to be killed by lightning.

5    If television isn't frightening you, then news magazines are ready to step in and fill that void. *Newsweek*, for example, claimed Americans were being "driven to destruction" by road rage. In their report, they quoted a study saying we were "increasingly being shot, stabbed, beaten and run over." Then television echoed with its own flurry of road-rage reports. On *20/20*, ABC NEWS introduced a story by telling viewers that they're surrounded by "strangers in their cars, ready to snap." We called road rage a frightening trend and a growing American danger.

6    The hype surrounding the reporting blew the real dangers out of proportion. Bob Lichter, president of the Center for Media and Public Affairs, which studies media coverage, has concluded that the media often distort or exaggerate threats. He said, "If road rage is something that's increasing . . . we should see more fatalities on the road. There should be more reports of reckless driving. But these things are going down instead of up."

7    A justification for the media hype surrounding road rage was a study sponsored by the American Automobile Association (AAA) that chronicled reports of aggressive driving. According to a *Time* magazine story, which based its information on the AAA report, road rage was up 51 percent in the first half of the 1990s.

8    Stefanie Faul, a spokeswoman for the AAA, said the consumer group based its analysis mostly on the number of road rage and aggressive driving incidents reported in the press. It was a strange sort of **circular logic** that fueled the spiraling coverage of road rage. The AAA study looked at police reports as well, but was largely based on media accounts.

9    Lichter said people have been yelling at each other in their cars for years. Journalists just found a term for it. A few years back, Lichter noted,

a person might come and complain that somebody yelled at them from his car. Today, people go home and say they're victims of "road rage."

10   AAA's Faul said that the idea of violent death by strangers is a very common topic in news reports. "You know that if you get people excited about an issue . . . that's what makes it appealing as a topic." She also added that small organizations like hers can't take on huge media **conglomerates**. Still, she admits that she didn't make an effort to correct the mischaracterization she saw in the press.

11   And before there was road rage, there were carjackings. The media told us that carjackings were making a comeback on Americans streets in the '90s. Greg McCrary, of the Threat Assessment Group, which works to point out that life's real dangers are far less dramatic than what the media may lead you to believe, said the chance of being killed in a carjacking is **infinitesimally** small.

12   McCrary said the **mundane** things pose greater risks on the road—things like drunken driving and failing to fasten our seat belts. Like Faul, McCrary said these sorts of things just aren't attention-grabbing. "It doesn't sell on TV. Sex and violence sells," he said.

13   Lichter agrees with McCrary's assessment. His organization noted that press coverage of murders increased by 700 percent in the 1990s, but the murder rate had fallen by half during the decade. Lichter said, "It's easier to point a camera at a blood-stained wall where a victim has just been taken away, than it is to dig into a book of dull, dry statistics."

14   According to Lichter, when there's not a major news story that has some dramatic element to it, newspapers and television stations will **ramp up** their coverage of things like shark attacks and carjackings to keep us buying papers and tuning in. Lichter said, "Journalists unconsciously train themselves to look for the story that really **rivets** your attention. And that story is, 'Wow, here's a disaster, oh my God.'"

15   A few years ago, for example, there were as many shark attacks, but it wasn't a summer of the shark. Perhaps because the media were busy covering the election. Back in 1995 there were 46 shark attacks, but the spotlight was on O.J. Simpson's murder trial. In 1998, the Monica Lewinsky story kept the shark attacks in the shadows.

16   Lichter said that reporters may have the best of intentions when they pursue a story, but often they stir up problems that really aren't there. This, Lichter said, poses a real danger to the public. Lichter said, "Bad journalism is worse than no journalism, because it leaves people thinking they know something that is, in fact, wrong." ◆

## CONSIDERING THE ISSUES

1. In his article, Stossel notes several media-hyped issues: shark attacks, road rage, and carjackings. Coverage of these issues contributes to our perception that it is a very dangerous world out
there. What fears do you have regarding the society in which we
live? For example, are you afraid that you could be a victim of
road rage? Murder? Make a list of the things that worry you
about today's society. Include even small things that may not
seem dangerous but concern you nonetheless.
2. Have you ever changed your behavior based on a news report?
For example, did you avoid swimming because of shark attacks,
or avoid driving in a certain area for fear of road rage or carjackings? Or stop eating a particular food because it might cause
cancer or another disease? Explain.

## CRAFT AND CONTENT

1. What was the "circular logic" of the media hype surrounding
road rage (paragraphs 5–7)? What was faulty about this logic,
and how did it mislead the public's perception of road rage?
2. Review Stossel's last paragraph in which he paraphrases Bob
Lichter: "[The media] stir up problems that really aren't there . . .
this . . . poses a real danger to the public." Can this paragraph be
viewed as making some of the same media errors Stossel challenges in his essay? Explain.

## CRITICAL THINKING

1. John Stossel is a media journalist. Does the fact that he is reporting on a problem in his own industry make his comments seem
more credible? Why or why not?
2. Greg McCrary, of the Threat Assessment Group, observes, "Sex
and violence sells." Why do we find these things more interesting than more mundane things? What is it about sex and violence that holds such appeal?

## WRITING ABOUT THE ISSUES

1. In the closing paragraph, Bob Lichter states, "Bad journalism is
worse than no journalism, because it leaves people thinking they
know something that is, in fact, wrong." Write a response to this

statement from the viewpoint of a television journalist. You may agree or disagree with his comment. (Remember that Stossel seems to agree and he is a television journalist himself.)

2. Stossel notes that the summer of 2002 was "the summer of the shark." Review the news from the past year and try to identify the sensationalized stories that marked certain seasons. For example, some people may think that the winter of 2004 was marked by stories about Lacey Peterson and the Atkins diet ("Carb Wars"). Visit Web sites such as www.cnn.com and www.msnbc.com/top10.asp for current hot news topics. After compiling your list, try to determine which topics were likely hyped up for the consumer audience.

# The Female Fear Factor
*Myrna Blyth*

Myrna Blyth served as the editor for the magazine *Ladies' Home Journal* from 1981 to 2002. Before joining *Ladies' Home Journal*, Blyth was the executive editor of the women's magazine *Family Circle*. This article is excerpted from her 2004 exposé book, *Spin Sisters: How the Women of the Media Sell Unhappiness and Liberalism to the Women of America.*

## CONNECTING TO THE TOPIC

American women today are the most prosperous, healthy, well-educated, and advantaged ever. Yet many feel unhappy—overwhelmed, unsafe, stressed, and even victimized. From morning shows to women's magazines, journalists influence how women see the world. As a member of the female journalistic elite, Myrna Blyth knew firsthand just how to twist a story to sell magazines. This twisting of information, or *spin* as it is known in the industry, promotes sensationalized stories in order to get women to watch a program, read an article, or listen to a news broadcast. Do the media feed on women's natural insecurities? If so, is such manipulation unethical, or simply part of media culture? And, to take a page out of the media hype playbook, could spin be creating a culture of fear?

## WORDS IN CONTEXT

**solemnly** (2)   earnestly, with grave seriousness (adv.)

**wont** (4)   likely (adj.)

**chaser** (4)   something closely following another thing, from the informal reference to a drink, such as beer or water, taken after hard liquor (n.)

**incensed** (5)   extremely angry; infuriated (adj.)

**Alar** (12)   the trade name for daminozide, a chemical plant growth regulator, formerly used to increase the storage life of fruit (n.)

**asbestos** (12)   a chemical-resistant, fibrous mineral form of impure magnesium silicate, used for fireproofing, electrical insulation, building materials, brake linings, and chemical filters (n.)

**Alzheimer's** (13)   a degenerative brain disease marked by memory loss and dementia (n.)

**mitigate** (16)   to moderate (a quality or condition) in force or intensity; alleviate (v.)

**tuberculosis** (18)   an infectious disease usually of the lungs (n.)

**diluted** (18)   made thinner or less concentrated by adding a liquid such as water (adj.)

1   When Diane Sawyer looks me in the eye and tells me "sleeping on a conventional mattress is like sleeping on kerosene," she gets my attention—and that's the point. It was a March 30, 2000, *Good Morning America* segment. I stopped making the bed, grabbed my coffee, and sat glued to the set watching a fairly typical and typically scary network report on the dangers of non-flame-resistant mattresses.

2   Watching, with a pro's eye—hey, maybe this is a story for my magazine, too—I noted that the report had everything a woman needs . . . to start the day wrong. It had:

1. **Fear**—"This is a mattress study called 'The Big Burn' conducted by the California Bureau of Home Furnishings back in 1991." (Meaning nine whole years had passed before the show, but who's counting?) "It was a test to see how long it would take for a fire to consume a mattress like the one you just spent the night on. Firefighters . . . say they are well aware of the risk," **solemnly** intoned reporter Greg Hunter.

2. **A threat that endangers children**—"Stacey Hernandez's son, Damon, set a polyurethane foam mattress on fire in California back

in 1993 . . ." (Seven years before the show.) "Third-degree burns over half his body."

   3. **A distraught mother**—"If I had known that that was so unsafe I would rather we had slept on the floor."

3     The story also featured a bit of a debate and a doubter or two, but any and all criticisms of the story's basic premise were passed over faster than a size 14 at a fashion shoot. "The Consumer Product Safety Commission and the mattress industry insist that the greater fire hazard is what's on the mattress, [namely] the bedclothes. Not the polyurethane on the inside." Great. Now, what are the odds of finding a comforting little fire-resistant tag still on those sheets I've slept on through at least three presidents?

4     Then, as television is **wont** to do, we were given a **chaser** of reassurance after the scare session: "The federal government has required mattresses to be cigarette resistant since 1973," which I had already guessed is the cause of most bedroom fires.

5     Still, I sat there watching a terribly disfigured child, a weeping mom, and an **incensed** Diane. "This is really stunning," she said.

6     But what should be done about it? If I wanted to get a flame-retardant mattress right away, like before tonight when I might once again be "sleeping on kerosene," where do I find one?

7     "Only in some state prisons," Greg tells me.

8     Now, that's very helpful. Let me run right out and rob a bank.

9     That short *Good Morning America* piece was pretty standard fare, and a good illustration of the way editors and television producers construct human interest stories and consumer reports that are the bread and butter of media aimed at women. Next time you watch *48 Hours* or *Dateline NBC*, look at the way the story is told. They all tend to have the same format: High volume on the emotions, low volume on everything else (facts, balance, debate, assessment of risks, advice you can really use).

10     But even knowing how the media overdoes stories, my basic reaction to the *GMA* piece was probably just what yours would have been. How very sad about that child. And even though I know that most safety officials are neither uncaring nor unwise, I was left with the uneasy feeling that we are often in danger, even in our own beds.

11     And that's what *GMA*, *20/20*, *Today*, *Dateline*, *Lifetime*, and other network series—all of them—want you to feel. Afraid. Worried that the next victim might be you or your child. When it comes to selling fear,

television and women's magazines live by one rule—there's no such thing as overkill, no pun intended.

12    For years, we have been warned and warned again about so many terrible things—benzene in our bottled water, Alar on our apples. We may not have **Alar** to be afraid of anymore but never fear, there's always **asbestos** in our school buildings, secondhand smoke in our environment, the hole in the ozone layer, the ozone in the ozone layer, high-tension power lines, cell phones that cause brain cancer, and lead paint peeling off our walls. That old lead paint fear was recycled in a recent *Redbook* article that claimed that living in any house built before 1978—which means 40 percent of all homes in America—could be a serious danger to your children. So now I know my kids spent their entire childhood in danger, not just when they came home after curfew.

13    We have also been warned by the Center for Science in the Public Interest, a.k.a. the food police, that popcorn, margarine, red meat, Chinese, Italian, French, and Mexican food along with McDonald's French fries

contribute to heart disease. Still ordering fettuccine Alfredo? Heart attack on a plate, sister! Aluminum and zinc may contribute to **Alzheimer's**. And almost everything else including alcohol, birth control pills, bottled water, silicone breast implants, exhaust fumes, chlorine, caffeine, dairy products, diet soda, hot dogs, fluoridation, grilled meat, hair dyes, hydrogen peroxide, incense, jewelry, kissing, laxatives, low-fiber diets, magnetic fields, marijuana, olive oil, orange juice, peanut butter, playground equipment, salt, "sick" buildings, sun beds, sunlight, sunscreen, talc, testosterone, tight bras, toast, tooth fillings, vinyl toys, and wallpaper may cause cancer.

14    More than twenty years ago, political scientist Aaron Wildavsky looked around America and wrote, "How extraordinary! The richest, longest-lived, best-protected, most resourceful civilization with the highest degree of insight into its own technology is on its way to becoming the most frightened." We have arrived.

15    And the media is largely to blame; even media reporters fess up to that. As David Shaw wrote in the *Los Angeles Times*, "The media, after all, pays the most attention to those substances, issues and situations that most frighten their readers and viewers. Thus, almost every day, we read and see and hear about a new purported threat to our health and safety."

16    Says TV commentator Jeff Greenfield, "It's a basic rule of journalism— to get the human angle. But with a complicated technical story . . . the concerns, the worries, the fears of people . . . will always carry more weight than the disputes and the cautions of the experts." In other words, let's not clutter up a perfectly good horror story with any **mitigating** facts.

17    Human drama, human emotions are what work. And pictures— dramatic pictures of a sobbing mother, an injured child, a disfigured teenager. Such pictures and the stories that go with them are easy for women to empathize with and understand. And that's the name of the game—attracting women. So why should we be surprised that so many of these pieces are for and about women. For example, on *20/20* there was a segment, in the early summer of 2001, introduced by Barbara Walters telling us:

> How do you like to be pampered? For millions . . . especially women, especially as summer approaches, the answer is a visit to a nail salon. Maybe you're headed there tomorrow. Well, we have to warn you, you may come home with more than beautiful fingers and toes, because there is something ugly going on at some nail salons. Customers who don't know how to protect themselves are really getting nailed.

18    "Getting Nailed" was about a California nail salon where a group of women were infected by **tuberculosis**-related bacteria that were found in the drain of the foot basin, which had not been carefully cleaned. The rest of the piece took us along as undercover inspectors raided other salons in various states. Many, owned by immigrants, were found to be violating local health codes, reusing emery boards and swabbing counters down with **diluted** disinfectant. Only one salon was shown to have seriously injured any clients, but the legs of the women who had become infected did, I grant you, look quite gruesome.

19    At the end of the piece, Barbara Walters shared that "I wanted to have a pedicure this week," but she said she didn't. Why not? Did the *20/20* piece make her as fearful as it was supposed to make us? Not really. Barbara told us, "Once and again I've been too busy." She didn't say she would be sure to do a safety check the next time she hits Frederic Fekkai's exclusive salon as she advised her loyal viewers to do.

20    Still, e-mails flew around my office and across the Internet—the world's biggest party line—as women warned their sister sandal wearers of the newly discovered dangers of the pedicure. This was real news we can use from one of television's most respected women journalists warning us that pampering can be hazardous to your health.

21    And we do depend on media to tell us what's important in the world, good news and bad. Whether it's *Dateline NBC* or Peter Jennings or *Ladies' Home Journal*, the media is our information source, and we want the truth. And there's the rub. Although we might like to think so, journalists and editors don't just transmit the facts, ma'am. They select and shape it and make facts fit into emotional stories that tug at our heartstrings or send a chill up our spines. I've done it myself. That's because news is most effective when it tells a story that confirms our deep-seated beliefs and stokes our deep-seated fears. As psychology professor Paul Slovic of the University of Oregon says, "We trust people who tell us we're in danger more than people who tell us we're not in danger." And when we hear someone is harmed, we want a simple explanation for her pain. A very simple explanation. Editors and producers know that.

22    Look, I'm not telling you that all these "fear factor" pieces you read in magazines and see on the networks are untrue. Those women on *20/20* did get a nasty infection from their pedicures. Through the years I published many articles about wrongs against women and families, and stories about health that were fair and honest. I believed I was giving good sensible information. But there is always the temptation to play gotcha! To simplify

and dramatize in order to hold the attention of the reader or viewer. And I can't deny that those of us in media, like a little girl who keeps crying long after her stubbed toe has stopped hurting, tend to exaggerate and do a lot of it for effect.

23    That's why even though women and men are safer and healthier than we have ever been, we are also more afraid of what we eat, drink, touch, and breathe. Eleanor Singer and Phyllis Endreny, two social scientists, did a study of risk coverage by the media and concluded, "A direct comparison between hazards as topics of news stories and as causes of death show essentially no relationship between the two." So we're really okay, but we are being told not to feel okay. That's because the media, in order to attract readers and viewers, "often overplays risks of dubious legitimacy. Scientific studies show that many of the alleged hazards the media trumpet are either misstated, overstated, nonexistent or there just is not enough scientific evidence yet to yield reliable guidance on the true risk for the average American." Which, I admit, is a kind of shabby way to get readers or ratings.  ◆

## CONSIDERING THE ISSUES

1. Blyth's introduction describes a television program segment that drew her to sit and watch. What types of news story "hooks" are likely to get your attention? Have you stayed up later than you intended or watched a news program because the "hook" statement before the show or news segment grabbed your interest? Explain.

2. What makes you buy a particular magazine? Is it the content? The advertisements? The stories? The layout? Do the headlines on the magazine influence you to buy it? Do you ever think about how the headlines might be manipulating you? Explain.

## CRAFT AND CONTENT

1. In paragraph 2, Blyth notes three things that Diane Sawyer's story used to hold a woman riveted to the television set. Analyze these elements and explain why they work to capture the intended audience. Would they work on you to grab and hold your attention? Why or why not?

2. Like John Stossel at the beginning of this chapter, Myrna Blyth is an "insider" to the journalism industry. Drawing from your

experience with the format of most stories in popular magazines, in what ways does Blyth's article resemble the story format typical in many women's magazines? Does this format make her argument more accessible to her readers? (If you are unfamiliar with this format, take a look at some articles from the magazines she cites in your library or at a newsstand, and then review the article again.)

## CRITICAL THINKING

1. In paragraph 15, Blyth quotes *Los Angeles Times* reporter David Shaw, "The media, after all, pays the most attention to those substances, issues, and situations that most frighten their readers and viewers. Thus, almost every day, we read and see and hear about a new purported threat to our health and safety." Respond to Shaw's statement with your own opinion. Is this practice acceptable? Does it allow the reader to determine what information is important, and what is not? Explain.

2. Blyth reveals how women's magazines target women's fears in order to sell magazines. What techniques are used to hook men's attention on magazines? How do men and women's magazines differ? Can the same principles be applied to popular men's magazines such as *Details, Maxim, GQ,* and *Esquire?* Explain.

## WRITING ABOUT THE ISSUES

1. Blyth notes that "When it comes to selling fear, television and women's magazines live by one rule—there's no such thing as overkill, no pun intended." Visit your local library and scan the headlines on some popular women's magazines. Write down any headlines that seem to fit Blyth's assertion. How does the magazine twist the story to grab the viewer's attention? Is this technique ethical? Is it simply the way magazines market their material? Explain.

2. Create your own magazine cover for a women's magazine presenting stories in a factual and unsensationalized way. Select a real magazine and create an alternative cover for it after reading the articles and analyzing them with a critical eye.

# Blog Matters

A blog ("web log") is an online diary or commentary site that features regular entries that describe events, impressions, and viewpoints. Blogs may contain text, images, video, and often link to other websites, blogs, and online media. Most blogs allow readers to comment on the content of the post and respond to each other. As of 2007, the blog search engine estimated there were over 112 million blogs. While many blogs are maintained by individuals, some are run by journals, newspapers, and other media outlets. Remember that most blogs are not monitored for factual accuracy, and often express the opinion and views of the "blogger" writing the content.

The blog below is maintained by danah boyd, a doctoral student in the School of Information at the University of California–Berkeley and a fellow at the Harvard University Berkman Center for Internet and Society.

# Growing Up in a Culture of Fear: From Columbine to Banning of MySpace

*danah boyd\**
*November 2, 2005*

1   I'm tired of mass media perpetuating a culture of fear under the scapegoat of informing the public. Nowhere is this more apparent than how they discuss youth culture and use scare tactics to warn parents of the safety risks about the Internet. The choice to perpetually report on the possibility or rare occurrence of kidnapping/stalking/violence because of Internet sociability is not a neutral position—it is a position of power that the media chooses to take because it's a story that sells. There's something innately human about rubbernecking, about looking for fears, about reveling in the possibilities of demise. Mainstream media capitalizes on this, manipulating the public and magnifying the culture of fear. It sells horror films and it sells newspapers.

2   A few days ago, I started laying out how youth create a public in digital environments because their physical publics are so restricted. Since then, I was utterly horrified to see that some school officials are requiring students to dismantle their MySpace and Xanga accounts or risk suspension. The reason is stated simply in the article: "If this protects one child from being near-abducted or harassed or preyed upon, I make no apologies for this stance." OMG, this is insane.

3   In some ways, I wish that the press had never heard of these sites. . . I wish that I had never participated in helping them know of its value to youth culture. I wish that it remained an obscure teenage site. Because I'm infuriated at how my own participation in information has been manipulated to magnify the culture of fear. The culture of fear is devastating; it is not the same as safety.

4   Let's step back a few years. Remember Columbine? I was living in Amsterdam at the time and the coverage was brilliant—the Dutch press talked about how there was a school shooting by kids who felt alienated from their community. And then the US coverage started pouring in. Goths (or anyone wearing black, especially black trench coats) were marked as the devil incarnate. Video games were evil and were promoting

---

*For personal and political reasons, the author says that she legally changed her name to be spelled without initial capital letters.

killing. Everything was blamed except the root cause: alienation. There were exceptions though. I remember crying the first time I read Jon Katz's *Voices from the Hellmouth* where numerous youth poured out their souls about how they were treated in American education systems. Through his articles, he was able to capture the devastation of the culture of fear. My professor Henry Jenkins testified in Washington about how dangerous our culture has become, not because there are tools of rage, but an unchecked systematic creation of youth alienation. He pleaded with Congress: "Listen to our children. Don't fear them." And yet, we haven't. In response, youth went underground. Following one of his talks, a woman came up to him dressed in an array of chaotic pink. She explained to Henry that she was a goth, but had to go underground. What kind of world do we live in where a color symbolizes a violent act?

5    We fear our children. We fear what they might do in collectives. We ban them from public spaces. We think that we are protecting them, but we're really feeding the media industry and guaranteeing the need for uncountable psychiatrists. Imagine the weight that this places on youth culture. Imagine what it's like to grow up under media scrutiny, parental protectionism and formalist educational systems.

6    During the summer of 1999, I was driving cross-country and ended up at an outdoor rave outside of Denver, Colorado. I was sitting in my tent, writing in my diary when a group of teens rapped at my door asking if they could come in and smoke because it was too windy outside to light the damn thing. I invited them in and we started talking. They were all from Littleton and had all dropped out of school shortly following Columbine and were now at a loss for what to do. I asked them why they dropped out, expecting that they would tell me about how eerie the school was or how they were afraid of being next. No. They dropped out because the media was hounding them everywhere they went. They couldn't get into the school without being pestered; they couldn't go to the mall or hang out and play basketball. They found underground venues for socialization. Here we were, in the middle of a field outside town at a rave, the only place that they felt safe to be themselves. The underground rave scene flourished in the summer of 1999 outside Denver because it was a safe haven for teens needing to get away from adult surveillance and pressure. Shortly later, the cops busted the party. I went and pleaded with them, asking them to let the kids camp there without the music; they had the permits for camping. No; they had heard that there were kids doing ecstasy. Let's say they are—you want them to drive on drugs? Why not let them just camp? The cops ignored me and turned on bright lights and told the kids

that they needed to leave in 10 minutes or they would be arrested. Argh! I'm not going to condone teenage drug use, but I also know that it comes from a need to find one's identity, to make sense of the world removed from adult rules. These kids need a safe space to be themselves; overzealous police don't help a damn thing.

7    How do youth come of age in this society? What good is it to restrict every social space that they have? Does anyone actually think that this is a good idea? Protectionist actions tend to create hatred, resentment. It destroys families by failing to value trust and responsibility. Ageist rhetoric alienates the younger generation. And for what purpose?

8    The effects are devastating. Ever wonder why young people don't vote? Why should they? They've been told for so damn long that their voices don't matter, have been the victims of an oppressive regime. What is motivating about that? How do you learn to use your voice to change power when you've been surveilled and controlled for so long, when you've made an art out of subversive engagement with peers? When you've been put on drugs like Strattera that control your behavior to the point of utter obedience?

9    We drug our children the whole way through school as a mechanism of control and wonder why drug abuse and alcoholism is rampant when they come of age. I've never seen as many drugs as I did at pristine prestigious boarding schools. The wealthy kids in our society are so protected, pampered. When given an ounce of freedom, they go from one extreme to the other instead of having healthy exploratory developments. Many of the most unstable, neurotic and addicted humans i have met in this lifetime come from a position of privilege and protectionism. That cannot be good.

10    We need to break this culture of fear in order to have a healthy society. Please, please . . . whenever you interact with youth culture (whether you're a parent, a schoolteacher or a cafe owner), learn from them. Hear them from their perspectives and stop trying to project your own fears onto them. Allow them to flourish by giving them the freedom to make sense of their identity and culture. It doesn't mean that there aren't risks—there are. But they are not as grandiose as the press makes them out to be. And besides, youth need to do stupid things in order to learn from their own mistakes. Never get caught up in the "I told you so" commentary that comes after that "when I was your age" bullshit. People don't learn this way—they learn by putting their hand in the fire and realizing it really is hot and then stepping back.

11    Post-Columbine, we decided to regulate the symptoms of alienation rather than solve the problem. Today, we are trying to regulate youth efforts to have agency and public space. Both are products of a culture of fear and completely miss the point. We need to figure out how to support

youth culture, exploration and efforts to make sense of the social world. The more we try to bottle it into a cookie-cutter model, the more we will destroy that generation.

12    In line with Henry's claim to Congress, I want to plead to you (and ask you to plead to those you know): Listen to the youth generation— don't fear them and don't project your fear onto them.

13    *(Note: My use of the term "kids" references the broader youth population using a slang very familiar to subcultures where an infantilized generation reclaimed the term for personal use. I am 27 and I still talk about my friends as kids. What I'm referencing is youth culture broadly, not children and not just teens.)* ◆

### RESPOND TO THE BLOG:

What do you think? Are the media programming us to fear American life? Are they promoting a world that is cold, heartless, violent, corrupt, and dangerous? Why? How do we slog through the hype to get to the truth? Present your own view here.

# Violence on Television—What Do Children Learn? What Can Parents Do?
*American Psychological Association*

Based in Washington, DC, the American Psychological Association (APA) is a scientific and professional organization that promotes the advancement and distribution of psychological knowledge to promote health, education, and public welfare. This fact sheet is available on its website: www.apa.org.

### CONNECTING TO THE TOPIC

Almost 20 years ago, the National Institute of Mental Health reported that television violence could be dangerous for children. Since then, and despite such warnings, violence on television has significantly increased both in quantity and intensity. Studies indicate that children who watch a lot of violent television programming tend to be less bothered by violence. Other studies reveal that children who watch violent programming are less likely to call for help or intervene when they witness violent acts among their peers. Should the television industry be more responsible for its programming? Is this an issue for parents or the medium of television itself? And is society as a whole at risk?

## WORDS IN CONTEXT

**National Institute of Mental Health** (2)   a division of the National Institutes of Health (NIH), the federal government's principal biomedical and behavioral research agency. Its mission is to reduce the burden of mental illness and behavioral disorders through research on mind, brain, and behavior. (n.)

**psychological** (3)   involving the study of the mind and behavior (adj.)

1   **"V**iolent programs on television lead to aggressive behavior by children and teenagers who watch those programs."

2   That was the word from a 1982 report by the **National Institute of Mental Health**, a report that confirmed and extended an earlier study done by the surgeon general. As a result of these and other research findings, the American Psychological Association passed a resolution in February of 1985 informing broadcasters and the public of the potential dangers that viewing violence on television can have for children.

## What Does the Research Show?

3   **Psychological** research has shown three major effects of seeing violence on television:

- Children may become less sensitive to the pain and suffering of others.
- Children may be more fearful of the world around them.
- Children may be more likely to behave in aggressive or harmful ways toward others.

4   Children who watch a lot of TV are less aroused by violent scenes than are those who only watch a little; in other words, they're less bothered by violence in general, and less likely to see anything wrong with it. One example: in several studies, those who watched a violent program instead

of a nonviolent one were slower to intervene or to call for help when, a little later, they saw younger children fighting or playing destructively.

5        Studies by George Gerbner, Ph.D., at the University of Pennsylvania, have shown that children's TV shows contain about 20 violent acts each hour and also that children who watch a lot of television are more likely to think that the world is a mean and dangerous place.

6        Children often behave differently after they've been watching violent programs on TV. In one study, done at Pennsylvania State University, about 100 preschool children were observed both before and after watching television; some watched cartoons that had a lot of aggressive and violent acts in them, and others watched shows that didn't have any kind of violence. The researchers noticed real differences between the kids who watched the violent shows and those who watched nonviolent ones.

7        "Children who watch the violent shows, even 'just funny' cartoons, were more likely to hit out at their playmates, argue, disobey class rules, leave tasks unfinished, and were less willing to wait for things than those who watched the nonviolent programs," says Aletha Huston, Ph.D., now at the University of Kansas.

## Real-Life Studies

8  Findings from the laboratory are further supported by field studies which have shown the long-range effects of televised violence. Leonard Eron, Ph.D., and his associates at the University of Illinois found that children who watched many hours of TV violence when they were in elementary school tended to also show a higher level of aggressive behavior when they became teenagers. By observing these youngsters until they were 30 years old, Dr. Eron found that the ones who'd watched a lot of TV when they were eight years old were more likely to be arrested and prosecuted for criminal acts as adults.

## A Continuing Debate

9  In spite of this accumulated evidence, broadcasters and scientists continue to debate the link between viewing TV violence and children's aggressive behavior. Some broadcasters believe that there is not enough evidence to prove that TV violence is harmful. But scientists who have studied this issue say that there is a link between TV violence and aggression, and in 1992,

the American Psychological Association's Task Force on Television and Society published a report that confirms this view. The report, entitled *Big World, Small Screen: The Role of Television in American Society*, shows that the harmful effects of TV violence do exist.

## What Parents Can Do

10 While most scientists are convinced that children can learn aggressive behavior from television, they also point out that parents have tremendous power to moderate that influence.

11     Because there is a great deal of violence in both adult and children's programming, just limiting the number of hours children watch television will probably reduce the amount of aggression they see.

12     Parents should watch at least one episode of the programs their children watch. That way they'll know what their children are watching and be able to talk about it with them.

13     When they see a violent incident, parents can discuss with their child what caused the character to act in a violent way. They should also point out that this kind of behavior is not characteristic, not the way adults usually solve their problems. They can ask their children to talk about other ways the character could have reacted, or other nonviolent solutions to the character's problem.

14     Parents can outright ban any programs that they find too offensive. They can also restrict their children's viewing to shows that they feel are more beneficial, such as documentaries, educational shows and so on.

15     Parents can limit the amount of time children spend watching television, and encourage children to spend their time on sports, hobbies, or with friends; parents and kids can even draw up a list of other enjoyable activities to do instead of watching TV.

16     Parents can encourage their children to watch programs that demonstrate helping, caring and cooperation. Studies show that these types of programs can influence children to become more kind and considerate. ◆

### CONSIDERING THE ISSUES

1. Think about the level and frequency of violence in the programs you watch on television. Is violence a common theme? What types of television programs do you like to watch, and why?

2. In this article, the APA provides recommendations to parents, but not to television broadcasters. In your opinion, does control over television's violent content belong at home or at the network? Explain.

## CRAFT AND CONTENT

1. This article was produced by the APA to provide guidance and information for parents on the issue of children and television violence. Does the fact that the APA is a scientific body make its statements seem more credible? What sources of information do we tend to trust, and why?

2. What information does this document convey most strongly? What visual and organizational devices does it use to make certain points stand out? Explain.

3. What authorities and sources does the APA cite to support its point? How do these authorities influence the reader?

## CRITICAL THINKING

1. The APA notes that George Gerbner's research indicates that children who watch violent television programs are more likely to think that the world is "a mean and dangerous place." What effect might such a belief have on a child? What about when that child grows up? Explain.

2. According to the APA, what are the real-life ramifications for children who view violent television programming?

## WRITING ABOUT THE ISSUES

1. The APA article notes that despite significant evidence indicating that television violence influences children, the issue continues to be debated. Why do you think that is? Why is this issue so controversial?

2. The APA provides some recommendations to parents at the end of its article. Evaluate the practicality and logic of the advice they offer. Respond to each recommendation with your own viewpoint.

# Hate Violence? Turn It Off!

*Tim Goodman*

Columnist Tim Goodman is a television and media critic for the *San Francisco Chronicle,* in which this article first appeared on April 29, 2001.

## CONNECTING TO THE TOPIC

Not everyone agrees that television violence is a problem. Some people argue that if you don't like what you see on television, you should change the channel or turn it off. The author of the next piece is tired of critics complaining that television violence is damaging to children. He says, "Vote with your remote" and stop trying to ruin television for everyone else.

## WORDS IN CONTEXT

**plethora** (2)  a superabundance; an excess (n.)
**censorship** (4)  the practice of restricting, suppressing, or removing material that is considered morally, politically, or socially objectionable (n.)
**scapegoat** (4)  one that is made to bear the blame of others (n.)
**lax** (4)  lacking in strictness; overly permissive; negligent (adj.)
**vaunted** (5)  boasted or bragged about (adj.)
**pap** (6)  material lacking real value or substance (n.)
**prominent** (10)  immediately noticeable; conspicuous (adj.)
**ratcheted** (11)  increased or decreased by increments (v.)
**erode** (13)  wear away (v.)
**chaos** (13)  condition or place of great disorder or confusion (n.)

1    Perhaps it's a sign of progress that Americans are becoming just as concerned about violence on television as they are about sex. For years, a barely concealed nipple or a tame bed scene was deemed worse than hundreds of people being brutally shot down on cop shows and the like.

2    Now you can't pick up the paper without some watchdog group denouncing Hollywood for ruining their children's lives with a **plethora** of violent images nightly. Some kid goes postal at his high school and "Starsky and Hutch" is the root cause.

3    We're getting our priorities right and wrong simultaneously. If sexuality is now not the enemy, great. But to continue to demonize Hollywood for its portrayals of violence is to put our heads in the sand about the world we live in.

4    Worse, it's just plain wrong, reeks of **censorship** and, in the context of parents worried about their children, it's looking for a **scapegoat** when **lax** parenting skills are more to blame.

5    For example, parents have put pressure on their elected officials to "do something" about violence, and the result has been a ratings system that surveys suggest most parents never use. And then there's the **vaunted** "V-chip," which effectively shifted parental responsibility to the government and doesn't consider the simplest way for everyone to solve this problem: Vote with your remote.

6    Some of us like violence. Some of us like shows that have a gritty realism to them, rather than the glossy **pap** offered up by most networks. And think of all the people without children who, as grown-ups, choose to watch programming clearly geared to adults. Just because you've given little Jimmy his own TV set upstairs and now you can't stop him from watching "Jackass" on MTV or "Oz" on HBO, don't cry foul and ruin it for the rest of us.

7    This is an old and now increasingly tired defense of art, anti-censorship and the need for parents to take more responsibility for what their children are watching. Don't like it? Don't watch it. There are enough elements in place now—blocking devices, ratings, V-chips, etc.—that to whine about how Hollywood should tone it down (as you allow the blood-and-guts nightly news to waft over dinner) completely misses the point about whose kid it is.

8    Then again, many adults also dislike violence. Fine. Vote with the remote. Go to PBS, the History Channel, Disney—whatever—just stop writing letters to politicians who have already had a chilling effect (thus a watering- and dumbing-down of content) on what we already see.

9    Most recently, there has been a backlash against "The Sopranos," with many people thinking there's been an amping up of the violence and at least two very disturbing episodes filled with violence toward women.

10    First off, yes, those were difficult to watch. But HBO runs a very **prominent** content advisory at the front of every episode. And, more important, "The Sopranos" is not "Leave It to Beaver," despite near universal acclaim from critics and an almost scary loyalty among viewers.

11    It's just a hunch, but perhaps creator David Chase, sensing this weird, uncomfortable embracing of—let's be honest here—bad people, **ratcheted** up the violence as a reminder of what exactly it is we're watching.

12    If this moved people out of their comfort zones, they should stop watching. Many have. Others have complained to HBO and some are asking that such behavior be toned down. The short answer to that is this: No. "The Sopranos" is art. As a viewer, your reaction to that art can be anything you want it to be, but restricting it instead of looking away is not the right course.

13    This goes beyond freedom of expression, of course, and those who do not embrace their own freedom to choose other programming. People assume that television has somehow helped **erode** the social contract that keeps **chaos** and horror at bay. They blame television for the downfall of the nation's morals.

14    But we have always been a violent country. People were killed at a pretty good clip before television appeared. It's the dark side of our nature, but it didn't come out of the bogeyman's closet 50 years ago.

15    Violence as entertainment, or as a realistic expression of what is really going on in our world, will never appeal to some people. But no one is forcing them to watch. There are dozens of other channels, hundreds of other programs.

16    There's also an off button. Sometimes that gets forgotten.

17    Television is not the problem in our society. It may always be the scapegoat, but it's nothing more than a bastard machine, not half as disturbing as the real thing. ◆

## CONSIDERING THE ISSUES

1. Goodman states that pressuring Hollywood to change violent programming "reeks of censorship." Do you agree with Goodman? What do you think censorship means? Are you opposed to censorship of this kind? Why or why not?

2. Do you enjoy watching violent television programs? Would you be upset if a "watchdog" group forced one of your favorite programs off the air? Explain.

## CRAFT AND CONTENT

1. Evaluate the author's use of language in paragraphs 6, 7, 16, and 17. What does it reveal about people who wish to change television programming? Is this language likely to appeal to or anger his readers? Or does the answer depend on who is reading his column? Explain.

2. What phrases does Goodman repeat in his essay? Why do you think he repeats certain words?

## CRITICAL THINKING

1. What is Goodman's opinion of parents who want to influence television programming? Do parents have a right to pressure Hollywood to change violent shows?
2. How might the other side respond to Goodman's claim that he has a right to watch violent programs if he wants to?
3. Goodman urges people to "vote with your remote." Is changing the channel the equivalent of "voting" on what programs should air on television? Is it a solution that could work, or is it just a catchy phrase? Explain.
4. Goodman notes that "we have always been a violent country" (paragraph 14). Does this statement justify television violence? Why or why not?

## WRITING ABOUT THE ISSUES

1. Goodman argues that if parents or other adults object to a television program, they should change the channel or just turn off the television. Is this a reasonable solution? Why or why not? Write about your thoughts on this issue in a short essay.
2. What is "art"? Are violent television programs, such as the ones Goodman cites, art? Does the claim that these programs are a form of artistic expression support Goodman's argument? Explain.
3. Write a short essay exploring the connection between censorship and television programming. Who is likely to control the airwaves? What programs would survive, and what would be cut? Explain.

# VISUAL CONNECTIONS

## It's a Scary World

Pulitzer Prize–winner Jim Borgman's comic strip "Zits" has described the teen-angst-ridden life of 15-year-old Jeremy and his family and friends since its debut in July 1997. The syndicated strip appears in 875 newspapers around the world and is translated into at least seven languages, including German, Chinese, Spanish, and Finnish.

## CONSIDERING THE ISSUES

1. Can you recall a time when you knew your parents were frightened? How did you react? Explain.
2. Usually, children end up in their parents' room after having a nightmare. Is it significant that the parents turn to their teenage son for "protection" from their "nightmare"? Explain.

## CRITICAL THINKING

1. What is this cartoon about? What cultural theme does it employ? What does the audience need to understand in order to "get" the comic's twist?
2. Who is the audience for this cartoon? How does it tap into popular fears? Explain.

# In Search of Notorious Ph.D.s

*Lindsay Johns*

Lindsay Johns is a social commentator and cultural critic on Colourful Radio, London. This essay appeared in the *New Black Magazine* in the Spring 2007 issue.

## CONNECTING TO THE TOPIC

Deadly shootings both on the street and in the schools are putting kids—especially young males—in front of and behind the trigger. Music glorifying violence and promoting "gangsta life" is giving a soundtrack to the violent street dramas that unfold daily in the nation's neighborhoods and suburbs. Could hip-hop music and its preoccupation with violence be fueling the fire? In this next essay, Lindsay Johns takes a look at the connection between hip-hop, violence, and black masculinity.

## WORDS IN CONTEXT*

**priapic** (2)  phallic; having to do with male sexuality (adj.)
**über** (3)  German, "ultra" or "over" (adj.)
**hackneyed** (3) cliched, boring (adj.)
**malaise** (3)  weariness, boredom, lack of energy or initiative (n.)
**histrionic** (10)  overly dramatic (adj.)
**trope** (10)  a rhetorical use of words in anything other than their literal sense (n.)
**redolent** (10)  fragrant, suggestive of something (adj.)
**striations** (10)  parallel lines or grooves (n.)
**hyperbolized** (13)  to exaggerate (v.)
**tranche** (14)  French, "slice" (n.)

---

*The vocabulary in this essay is challenging but part of the author's unique style. Some words are defined above. Students may look up additional words (also bolded in the text) as necessary.

**elegiac** (14)  like an elegy; expressing sadness (adj.)

**carapace** (14)  a hard, protective covering or shell (n.)

**misogynistic** (15)  anti-woman or anti-female; disrespecting of women (adj.)

**ensconced** (16)  firmly settled in or nested in a place (adj.)

**concomitants** (16)  accompanying (n.)

**churlish** (24)  rude, unpleasant, vulgar (adj.)

**ostracism** (24)  boastful display or attitude (n.)

**alacrity** (28)  speed, alertness (n.)

**antediluvian** (31)  literally, "before the Flood," before the time of Noah in the Bible

**cornell West** and **DuBois** (34)  Cornell West (b. 1953) is a prominent African-American philosopher and civil rights activist who teaches at Princeton University; W. E. B. Du Bois (1868–1963) was an African-American civil rights activist and author of the hugely influential *The Souls of Black Folk* (1903).

1　Look around. It only takes a nano-second of exposure to modern mass media to discern a dazzlingly disturbing trend.

2　From the glistening pecs and ridiculously chiseled abs of LL Cool J on a billboard to the cringingly pimpilicious demeanor of Snoop Dogg on MTV Base, or the tediously **priapic** and rabidly homophobic lyrics of Beenie Man, we are constantly bombarded by stylized images of hyper-masculine black men.

3　Name your cliché. **Über**-physical, über-feral or über-sexually potent: they all apply. It doesn't take a genius to see what trite, **hackneyed** and ultimately depressing images of blackness these all are. What is more, they are unfortunately symptomatic of a much greater social and racial **malaise**, one which, like a rotten timber supporting the **precariously** balanced **edifice** of our society, threatens to bring it crashing down upon our heads very soon.

4　Heterosexual black masculinity, as a social construction in the twenty-first century, is at best deeply problematic, and at worst hideously flawed.

5    From Mike Tyson to Tupac, via 50 Cent, Shaquille O'Neill and Shabba Ranks, black male icons (invariably from the arenas of sport or music) are right now **indubitably** doing more harm than good.

6    But what's wrong with the likes of Fifty, Beenie Man, I hear you cry? What's so wrong with being big'n' buff or being able to handle your business in the bedroom and, in the memorable words of Sean Paul, able *to do the wuk*?

7    The answer is devastatingly simple, yet is constantly ignored.

8    Black musicians who indulge in representations of hypermasculinity are simply conceding much-sought-after gains in racial equality. Icons such as 50 Cent, Snoop Dogg, and Elephant Man persist in trading racial dignity for a quick buck, and are willingly conforming to the oldest, most **pernicious** (but perhaps the most **lucrative**) racial stereotype of all: the most execrable of old chestnuts: that black is wholly physical, and that by implication in the system of **binary** opposition, white is cerebral.

9    Why does so much contemporary black music persist in presenting to the world at large such a limiting and psychologically harmful (not to mention erroneous) caricature of black hypermasculinity?

10    The **histrionic** (and oh-so-easy to be ridiculed by white people) hip-hop hand gestures, the tedious and repetitious physical and verbal posturing, based on empty self-aggrandizement, the **trope** of mythical sexual prowess, all are images **redolent** of ignorance, and all are indicative of a deeply troubled psyche, a psyche visibly manifesting the scars and **striations** of centuries of slavery and oppression.

11    Where power, control and authority (traditional definitions of masculinity) have been historically denied to black men since slavery, it is perhaps historically understandable that the knee-jerk reaction is to present oneself as all that one has lacked.

12    Thus, the rapper or the reggae singer's conscious embrace of a hypermasculine image as a means of resisting the emasculation of racism is understandable, but ultimately misguided. Unwittingly he plays into the arms of the oppressor yet again. At the risk of gaining the physical, he spectacularly concedes the cerebral.

13    The **ubiquitous** and seemingly **omnipotent** MTV-based culture which peddles *ad nauseam* this **hyperbolized** and grossly distorted image of black masculinity simply reinforces these negative stereotypes in the most harmful, demeaning and detrimental of ways. Thus a whole generation of both white and black kids has now been successfully indoctrinated

to think that the only way for black masculinity to manifest itself is through physical posturing, sexual **braggadocio**, **feral** violence, and general anti-social behavior.

14   Very soon (if not already) a massive **tranche** of white people will only be able to relate to black men through the prism of hypermasculinity, not to mention the generation of young black men, some barely into their teens, for whom the *pimp roll*, the *Yo, bitch!* and the *bedroom bully* persona are sadly now the only ways of relating to themselves: the **elegiac carapaces** behind which they hide from an unforgiving, hostile universe.

15   New York rapper Nas' hit song *Oochie Wally* (despite its infectious hook and chorus) exemplifies the long list of anthemic songs built upon deeply troubling **misogynistic** and hypermasculine foundations. Let's be honest: "*I long dicked the bitch all night*" might be a great line to share with your boys at the gym in a moment of locker room bravado or *esprit de corps masculin* when regaling them with tales of your bedroom exploits, but seriously people . . . . . . are we making any progress here?

16   Similarly, Mad Cobra, another legendary luminary firmly **ensconced** in the **pantheon** of dancehall deities (famous for hits such as *Flesh Dagger* and *Plant It*) is one of the most sexually brutal lyricists in the reggae business. Yet he is hailed as an **avatar** of all that is good about dancehall music. Hypermasculinity (and its **concomitants** misogyny and homophobia) are all decidedly *de rigueur* in reggae culture, and, what is worse, continue to go unchallenged.

17   And where does this depiction of black hypermasculinity ultimately lead?

18   Well, in the first instance, it leads to [the youth who want to play the "bad boy"] **ostentatiously** pimp rollin' down the streets, bouncing along as if he has dislocated his pelvis, belligerently kissing his teeth in some old granny's face because he thinks his *respect* has been compromised by her accidental nudge or stray glance. Result: intimidating or laughable, depending on your point of view.

19   On another level, the **endemic** gun violence in the black community can be directly traced back to the wholly irresponsible image of black masculinity which is fed to us through music.

20   I will happily wager that Miles Davis *Birth of Cool* or George Benson's *The Guitar Man* are not the musical accompaniments of choice in the majority of drive-by shootings (auto-tuning into Classic FM by accident notwithstanding).

21    Ceaseless macho posturing and the absorption of violent imagery results in the playing out of violence in real life. Art mirrors life, but also life
mirrors art.

22    As a direct result of the hypermasculine lyrics in garage, grime, hip-
hop or reggae music, we are witnessing a culture of deeply-ingrained self-
loathing which is **imbuing** in black youngsters the notion that to be black
means to be physical, violent, homophobic, and über macho (with at least
three women). From Ludacris' *I've got hos in different area codes* to Beenie Man's *Nuff Gal*, the hypermasculine predominates. Anything else is
seen as quite frankly effeminate.

23    These **nefarious** lies of black masculinity, no doubt **expediently prop-
agated** over the centuries by white opportunists (first anti-abolitionists, and
now, in their most contemporary guise, the music executives who control
the distribution and marketing of black music, knowing that these raw ingredients will ensure more record sales to the white teenagers who are their
target audience) need to be swiftly exposed, dispelled and eradicated.

24    Is the hypermasculinity expounded in black music a mask for historical pain? It would be both **churlish** and naïve to say that it isn't. It clearly
functions as a mask for the pain engendered by centuries of social
**ostracism**, oppression and cultural alienation dating back to slavery and
also as a mask for chronically low self-esteem.

25    [But] The days of slavery are over. And what may have been once a
*bona fide* psychological crutch is now being lucratively peddled as an ex-
pedient sales gimmick. Is it any wonder that so much of the educated
Black American middle class has a healthy disdain for hip-hop?

26    It is time to smell the coffee and to realize that, although the physical
shackles of slavery are off, we still need liberating from the debilitating
mental shackles, and that by falling into the trap of complying with and
buying into these heinous stereotypes, black people are themselves setting
back the notion of racial equality decades, if not centuries.

27    So what next?

28    We need to redefine notions of black masculinity with **alacrity** and to
directly incorporate more progressive ideas of what it means to be black
and male into our music. There is, of course, no one **monolithic** notion of
black masculinity. There are as many manifestations of black masculinity
as there are shades of black.

29    But of paramount importance is the need to present more viable and more
visibly cerebral alternatives. We urgently need to create new **paradigms**
of black masculinity which do not give voice to the old lie of black as
physical and by implication, white as cerebral.

30    The sooner we acknowledge that the black male hip-hop or reggae **aesthetic** is fundamentally limiting and ironically intellectually emasculating, as opposed to actually empowering, then, and only then, we will begin to progress as a people.

31    Because, hard though it is to hear, while these **antediluvian** beliefs persist, we are still simply playing ourselves. As the conscious rapper Jeru The Damaja so eloquently said back in 1996:

32    *"With all that big willy talk, ya playin' yaself.*

33    *With all that big gun talk, ya playin' yaself."*

34    At the dawn of the twenty-first century, if we are to stand even a chance of leveling the playing field and making tangible progress, we need (as was said of the teaching methods of **Cornell West** at Harvard) less of *da boyz* and more of **DuBois.**

35    In short, we need much less Notorious B.I.G. and much more Notorious Ph.D. ◆

## CONSIDERING THE ISSUES

1. In this essay, Johns notes that MTV "peddles *ad nauseam*" distorted images that reinforce negative stereotypes. In your opinion, is Johns taking MTV culture too seriously, or can this medium be harmful to society? Explain.

2. Do you think that music can influence behavior? Write about a time when music—or another medium such as drama in a film or image in a piece of art—influenced the way you behaved. Describe the incident and your behavior, and discuss why the medium influenced you the way it did.

## CRAFT AND CONTENT

1. What does the author's title mean? What do you need to know about hip-hop to understand the title?

2. What can you guess about the author based on his language, word choice, and style of writing? Explain.

3. What is Johns's argument? Who is he trying to convince? Do you think his sophisticated use of vocabulary reaches his target audience, or could it miss the mark? Explain.

## CRITICAL THINKING

1. Johns comments "Heterosexual black masculinity, as a social construction in the twenty-first century, is at best deeply problematic, and at worst hideously flawed." In your own words, describe what image of black masculinity is promoted in the media in America today. Do you agree or disagree with Johns's assessment? Why or why not?

2. Why does Johns feel hip-hop artists who cash in on hypermasculinity are setting back racial equality? Explain.

## WRITING ABOUT THE ISSUES

1. In this essay, Lindsay Johns expresses his concern about the way some hip-hop artists glorify music that conveys the message that "to be black means to be physical, violent, homophobic, and über macho." Write an essay expressing your own viewpoint on this issue. Can lyrics and images be harmful? Are they just in fun, or maybe intended to shock but not to be taken seriously? Explain.

2. Compare the images of females on hip-hop music covers and videos with real women. What images of women are they promoting? Imagine you are a foreign visitor to the United States who has never seen a music video or listened to hip-hop music. What might you assume about the cultural attitude toward American women based on what you see and hear? Explain.

# VISUAL CONNECTIONS

## Young Jeezy

### CONNECTING TO THE TOPIC

In the preceding article, Lindsay Johns discussed the violence, sexism, and hypermasculinity promoted by some very popular hip-hop artists. The lyrics in this type of music, and the glorification of violence, he fears, send a message to youth that such traits are not only permissible, they are cool. Do we take such images seriously, or are they just a marketing ploy? Do they hurt anyone? Consider this photo of rapper Young Jeezy in the audience at the 2008 BET Awards held at the Shrine Auditorium on June 24, 2008, in Los Angeles, California. As you analyze the image, consider the points Johns makes in his essay as well as your own personal perspective.

## CONSIDERING THE ISSUES

1. Who are your favorite music artists? How are men and women portrayed in videos and music jackets by these artists? How do the artists portray themselves?
2. Despite warnings to the contrary, we often judge people by how they look and the images they project. How does the body language of the recording artist in this photo reinforce points that Johns makes in his essay? For example, what sort of personality do you expect the young men in the photo to have and why?

## CRITICAL THINKING

1. Do you think men would react differently than women to this photo? Why or why not?
2. What is happening in this photo? If you were leafing through a magazine and were unfamiliar with Young Jeezy, would you stop and take a closer look at the picture? Why or why not?

# TOPICAL CONNECTIONS

### GROUP PROJECTS

1. Visit the Media Awareness website and read more about the television violence debate (www.media-awareness.com). Each member of your group should evaluate a different current argument posted on this site. Are there any perspectives with which members particularly agree or disagree? Evaluate the arguments and discuss them as a group.
2. With your group, view the clips and read about the independent movie *HIP-HOP: Beyond Beats and Rhymes* by lifelong hip-hop fan and former college football quarterback turned activist Byron Hurt. Hurt decided to make a film about the gender politics of hip-hop, the music and the culture that he grew up with. "The more I grew and the more I learned about sexism and violence and homophobia, the more those lyrics became unacceptable to me," he says. After visiting all parts of the website [www.pbs.org/independentlens/hiphop/], give a presentation to the class on this issue.
3. Using a major metropolitan newspaper, make a list of the headlines in each section. Using this list, conduct a poll on which sto-

ries grab attention or seem the most interesting. Ask the participants of your survey to rank the headlines from most to least interesting. Then, ask them to explain why they picked the top three headlines they ranked as most compelling. Based on the information you gather, what conclusions can you make about the media and the public's appetite for information?

4. Question 3 asked you to make a list of all the headlines included in a major metropolitan newspaper. Working with such a list, analyze the language used in each headline. Are the headlines straightforward and factual, or do they put some "spin" on language in order to hook the reader? How does the headline connect to the actual content of the story? As a group, rewrite each headline in your own words to better reflect the content of the corresponding story.

### WEB PROJECT

1. The evening news broadcast that is a staple in many American homes is more than simply a recounting of the day's events. Most programs carefully consider what they will present in order to catch—and hold—viewers' attention. Visit the PBS website "Inside the Local News," which examines how media pick and present stories to the public. Examine the entire site, but carefully read the sections entitled "Behind the Story" and "The Ratings Game." Based on research gathered on this site, design your own news broadcast based on current events and explain in detail the reasons behind your design and story selection.

### FOR FURTHER INQUIRY

2. While a critical eye may be able to cut through media hype that helps "sell" a story, media bias may be harder to decipher. Read the article on bias featured on the Rhetorica Network's website at http://rhetorica.net/bias.htm. Apply the questions Rhetorica lists in its six "Critical Questions for Detecting Media Bias" to a television, newspaper, or magazine journal article. Choose a "hot" issue that has received a great deal of press coverage in recent weeks. How does the article stand up to the test? What media bias can you detect, if any?

# 5 | What Does Freedom of Speech Really Mean?

"*Congress shall make no law . . . abridging the freedom of speech, or of the press.*" With these simple words, the writers of the Constitution created one of the pillars of our democratic system of government—the First Amendment guarantee of every American's right to the free exchange of ideas, beliefs, and political debate. Most students support their right to express themselves without fear of government reprisal. However, over the years questions have arisen about whether limits should be imposed on our right to free expression when the exercise of that right imposes hardship or pain on others. What happens when the right of one person to state his or her beliefs conflicts with the rights of others to be free from verbal abuse? What happens when free expression runs counter to community or university values? At what point does the perceived degree of offensiveness warrant censorship? And who decides what is acceptable speech? In this unit, we look at the controversial issue of censorship and free speech, both on and off campus.

Many students arrive on campus eager to learn and eager to debate issues that matter. But are college campuses truly a haven for the exchange of ideas and free expression, or are some ideas more acceptable than others? And what happens if you express an unpopular point of view? Administrators on many campuses are imposing limits on the right to free expression when the exercise of that right imposes hardship or pain on others. How should administrators respond when free expression runs counter to community and university values? Are campus speech codes appropriate, or are they a violation of free speech? This unit focuses on this issue in depth.

### CRITICAL THINKING

1. What is happening in this cartoon? To what events does it refer?
2. How does this cartoon relate to the issue of free speech on campus? Explain.
3. What name does the cartoonist give to the security officer? How does this name connect to the event the cartoon is reflecting?
4. What point is the cartoonist trying to make with this cartoon? Is it funny? Why or why not?

## What Does "Freedom of Speech" Really Mean?

Brian Fairrington—Cagle Cartoons—09/19/2007

# Free Inquiry? Not on Campus

*John Leo*

Writer John Leo is contributing editor at the Manhattan Institute's *City Journal*, in which this essay appeared in the Winter 2007 issue. He is a former syndicated columnist and author of three books, *How the Russians Invented Baseball and Other Essays of Enlightenment* (1989), *Two Steps Ahead of the Thought Police* (1994), and *Incorrect Thoughts* (2001). For many years his commentary appeared in *Time* magazine and *U.S. News and World Report*. He is currently working on a book about colleges and universities.

## CONNECTING TO THE TOPIC

In only a generation, claims John Leo in the next essay, college campuses have transformed from havens supporting the sanctity of free speech to "politically correct" asylums in which conservative points of view are silenced. Campus speech codes protect students' feelings. Liberal administrators covertly support—and even finance—the disruption of conservative speeches and demonstrations. Students are learning to keep their mouths shut out of fear of expressing the "wrong" point of view. Are the college speech police threatening the liberty of us all?

## WORDS IN CONTEXT

**Right** (1)   politically right wing, conservative (n.)
**Left** (1)   politically left wing, liberal (n.)
**secular** (1)   not relating to the spiritual but to the worldly (adj.)
**tacit** (2)   not spoken but implied (adj.)
**partisan** (6)   biased in support of a party or group (adj.)
**academe** (8)   the academic community (n.)
**dogma** (9)   a principle or belief (n.)
**effusive** (10)   excessively emotional expression (adj.)
**proliferate** (12)   to grow rapidly, spread (v.)
**reproof** (13)   criticism, correction (n.)
**satirical** (17)   of or relating to sarcasm (adj.)

1   **R**emember when the **Right** had a near-monopoly on censorship? If so, you must be in your sixties, or older. Now the champions of censorship are

mostly on the **Left**. And they are thickest on the ground in our colleges and universities. Since the late 1980s, what should be the most open, debate-driven, and tolerant sector of society has been in thrall to the diversity and political correctness that now form the aggressive **secular** religion of America's elites.

2    The censors have only grown in power, elevating antidiscrimination rules above "absolutist" free-speech principles, silencing dissent with anti-harassment policies, and looking away when students bar or disrupt conservative speakers or steal conservative newspapers. Operating under the **tacit** principle that "error has no rights," an ancient Catholic theological rule, the new censors aren't interested in debates or open forums. They want to shut up dissenters.

3    In October 2007, for instance, a student mob stormed a Columbia University stage, shutting down speeches by two members of the Minutemen, an anti-illegal-immigration group. The students shouted: "They have no right to speak!" Campus opponents of Congressman Tom Tancredo, an illegal-immigration foe, set off fire alarms at Georgetown to disrupt his planned speech, and their counterparts at Michigan State roughed up his student backers. Conservative activist David Horowitz, black conservative columnist Star Parker, and Daniel Pipes, an outspoken critic of Islamism, frequently find themselves shouted down or disrupted on campus.

4    School officials seem to have little more interest in free speech. At Columbia this fall, officials turned away most of a large crowd gathered to hear former PLO terrorist-turned-anti-jihadist Walid Shoebat, citing security worries. Only Columbia students and 20 guests got in. Colleges often cite the danger of violence as they cancel controversial speeches—a new form of heckler's veto: shrinking an audience so that an event will seem unimportant is itself a way to cave to critics. In 2003, Columbia, facing leftist fury at the scheduled speeches of several conservatives (myself included), banned scores of invited non-students who had agreed to attend. Though some schools cancel left-wing speakers, too—including Ward Churchill and Michael Moore, or abortion-supporters Anna Quindlen and Christie Whitman at Catholic universities—right-of-center speakers are the campus speech cops' normal targets.

5    Official censorship—now renamed speech codes and anti-harassment codes—pervades the campuses. The Foundation for Individual Rights in Education (FIRE) recently surveyed more than 300 schools, including the top universities and liberal arts colleges, and found that over 68 percent explicitly prohibit speech that the First Amendment would protect if uttered

off campus. At 229 schools, FIRE found clear and substantial restriction of speech, while 91 more had policies that one could interpret as restricting speech. Only eight permitted genuine free expression.

6      A 2002 *New York Times* article reported that today's college kids seem more guarded in their views than previous generations of students. The writer suggested several possible explanations—disgust with **partisan** politics and uncivil debates on cable news shows, perhaps, or simple politeness. A more likely reason is that universities have made honest disagreement dangerous, making students fearful of saying what they think.

7      Much campus censorship rests on philosophical underpinnings that go back to social theorist Herbert Marcuse, a hero to sixties radicals. Marcuse argued that traditional tolerance is repressive—it wards off reform by making the status quo . . . well, tolerable. Marcuse favored intolerance of established and conservative views, with tolerance offered only to the opinions of the oppressed, radicals, subversives, and other outsiders. Indoctrination of students and "deeply pervasive" censorship of others would be necessary, starting on the campuses and fanning out from there.

8      By the late 1980s, many of the double standards that Marcuse called for were in place in **academe**. Marcuse's candor was missing, but everyone knew that speakers, student newspapers, and professors on the right could (make that should) receive different treatment from those on the left. The officially oppressed—designated race and gender groups—knew that they weren't subject to the standards and rules set for other students.

9      Confusing speech and action has a long pedigree on the PC campus. At the time of the first wave of speech codes 20 years ago, Kenneth Lasson, a law professor at the University of Baltimore, argued that "racial defamation does not merely 'preach hate'; it is the practice of hatred by the speaker"—and is thus punishable as a form of assault. Indeed, the Left has evolved a whole new vocabulary to blur the line between acts and speech: "verbal conduct" and "expressive behavior" (speech), "non-traditional violence," and "anti-feminist intellectual harassment" (rolling one's eyeballs over feminist **dogma**).

10     Campus censors frequently emulate the Marcusian double standard by combining **effusive** praise for free speech with an eagerness to suppress unwelcome views. "I often have to struggle with right and wrong because I am a strong believer in free speech," said Ronni Santo, a gay student activist at UCLA in the late nineties. "Opinions are protected under the First Amendment, but when negative opinions come out of a person's fist,

mouth, or pen to intentionally hurt others, that's when their opinions should no longer be protected."

11    In their 1993 book, *The Shadow University*, Alan Charles Kors and Harvey Silverglate turned some of the early speech codes into national laughingstocks. Among the banned comments and action they listed: "intentionally producing psychological discomfort" (University of North Dakota), "insensitivity to the experience of women" (University of Minnesota), and "inconsiderate jokes" (University of Connecticut). Serious nonverbal offenses included "inappropriate laughter" (Sarah Lawrence College), "eye contact or the lack of it" (Michigan State University), and "subtle discrimination," such as "licking lips or teeth; holding food provocatively" (University of Maryland). Later gems, added well after the courts struck down campus codes as overly broad, included bans on "inappropriate non-verbals" (Macalester College), "communication with sexual overtones" (Lincoln University), and "discussing sexual activities" (State University of New York–Brockport). Other codes bar any comment or gesture that "annoys," "offends," or otherwise makes someone feel bad. Tufts ruled that attributing harassment complaints to the "hypersensitivity of others who feel hurt" is itself harassment. Brockport, which banned "cartoons that depict religious figures in compromising situations," "jokes making fun of any protected group," and "calling someone an old hag," helpfully described for students what does not constitute sexual harassment: "non-coercive interaction(s) . . . that are acceptable to both parties." Commented Greg Lukianoff of FIRE: "The wonder is that anyone would risk speaking at all at SUNY Brockport."

12    Despite numerous court decisions overturning these codes, they have **proliferated**. College officials point to the hurt feelings of women or minorities as evidence that a violation must have occurred, in part because they want to avoid charges of racism, sexism, and homophobia— an overriding fear in today's academe, where diversity offices can swarm with 40 or 50 administrators. Georgia Tech went so far as to ban "denigrating" comments on "beliefs," which would make almost any passionate argument over ideas a violation. Needless to say, the targets here are usually conservative. Ohio State University at Mansfield launched a sexual harassment investigation of a research librarian, Scott Savage, for recommending the inclusion of four conservative books, including popular works by David Horowitz and ex-senator Rick Santorum, on a freshman reading list. Two professors had complained that one of the books, *The Marketing of Evil*, by journalist David Kupelian, was "homophobic tripe" and "hate literature." This may have been the first time that a campus charged that a book

recommendation qualified as sexual harassment. After a burst of publicity and a threat to sue, the university dropped the investigation.

13    Student censors regularly spirit away whole print runs of conservative student newspapers, almost always without **reproof** from administrators. Over the years, campus officials, including a few university presidents, have even encouraged such stealing. After repeated thefts of the *Dartmouth Review*, an official egged on the thieves by calling the paper "litter" and "abandoned property." In a commencement speech, former Cornell president Hunter Rawlings III praised students who seized and burned copies of the conservative *Cornell Review* in retaliation for printing a gross parody of Ebonics.

14    Once in a blue moon, a college president vigorously defends free speech. At Northern Kentucky University, president James Votruba rebuked and suspended a tenured feminist professor, Sally Jacobsen, who led a group that demolished a campus-approved right-to-life display. Jacobsen cited two justifications: her deep feelings and her alleged free-speech right to tear down displays that offend her. "I did invite students to express their freedom of speech rights to destroy the display if they wished," she said. "Any violence perpetrated against that silly display was minor compared to how I felt when I saw it."

15    Nothing makes the campus censors angrier than someone who dares to question race and gender preferences, especially if he uses satire to do it. That's why the anti-affirmative-action bake sales that conservative students have sponsored at many schools—white male customers can buy cookies for $1, with lower prices for women and various minorities—have provoked such ferocious responses from campus authorities.

16    Grand Valley State University in Allendale, Michigan, provides a typical example. A Republican club there staged a bake sale, and several students then said that they felt offended. This amounted to a powerful argument, since hurt feelings are trump cards in the contemporary campus culture. Next came the usual administrative scramble to suppress free speech while expressing great respect for it. The university charged the club with a violation of the student code and threatened sanctions. The students folded under administrative pressure and apologized. When the Republican club president refused to back down, club members asked him to resign, and he did. The students' retreat was understandable, if not very courageous. The university in effect was trying them for bias, with the likelihood that a notation of racism would become part of their academic record and follow them to post-college job interviews.

17    The College Republicans at Northeastern Illinois University canceled an announced affirmative-action bake sale after the administration threatened punishment. Dean of students Michael Kelly announced that the cookie sellers would be violating university rules and that "any disruption of university activities that would be caused by this event is also actionable." This principle—politically incorrect speakers are responsible for attacks on them by students who resent their speech—is dear to campus censors' hearts. The university didn't view itself as engaging in censorship—and double-standard censorship at that, since it freely allowed a satirical wage-gap bake sale run by feminists. Absurdly, Kelly said that the affirmative-action sale would be fine—if cookie prices were the same for whites, minorities, and women. Other administrators complained that differential pricing of baked goods is unfair, thus unwittingly proving the whole point of the parody.

18    Schools will use almost any tactic to shut the bake sales down. At the University of Washington, the administration said that the sponsor had failed to get a food permit. At Grand Valley, the university counsel argued that the sale of a single cupcake would convert political commentary into forbidden campus commerce. At Texas A&M, the athletics director argued that a satirical bake sale would damage the sports teams by making it harder to recruit minorities. [. . .]

19    We are very lucky to have the First Amendment. Without it, our chattering classes would be falling all over themselves to ban speech that offends sensitive groups. We know this because our campus speech codes, the models for the disastrous hate-speech laws elsewhere, were the inventions of our own elites. Without a First Amendment, the distortions and suppressions of campus life would likely have gone national. Mel Gibson, Michael Richards, and many rap artists would be in jail, or at least facing charges.

20    The cause of free speech can no longer expect much help from the American Civil Liberties Union, more concerned today with civil rights and multicultural issues than with civil liberties and free speech. True, the ACLU still takes some censorship cases—it led the fight against the first wave of campus speech codes circa 1990, for instance. But the rise of the ACLU's internal lobbies or "projects," such as the Lesbian and Gay Project and the Immigrants' Rights Project, has made the organization look more and more like a traditional left-wing pressure group, with little passion for the First Amendment. The ACLU is also following the money: funds flow in because the group responds to concerns of feminist, gays, and other

identity groups, not because of its historical defense of free speech and civil liberties.

21 These days, the ACLU visibly stands aloof from obvious First Amendment cases—such as the college speech and harassment codes—and even comes down on the anti-free-speech side. Consider the group's stance in *Aguilar v. Avis Rent-A-Car System,* a case involving ethnic epithets aimed by supervisors at Latino employees of Avis in San Francisco. A California court ruled that Avis had permitted a hostile environment. The California Supreme Court, abetted by both the northern Californian and the national ACLU, agreed, and upheld the lower court's startling speech restriction: prior restraint on workers' speech, forbidding a judge-made list of specific words. These words, not yet revealed or promulgated, will soon be taboo in every California workplace, even outside the earshot of Latino employees, and even if they are welcome. As civil libertarian Nat Hentoff wrote: "This may be the broadest and vaguest restriction of speech in American legal history."

22 Even with the ACLU, the mainstream media, school officials, and much of the professorate AWOL, the speech police haven't gone unopposed. Just ask former Clinton official Donna Shalala. As chancellor of the University of Wisconsin in the late eighties, she proved a fervent early advocate of campus speech restrictions. Though Shalala occasionally praised free speech, she and her team imposed not only a full-fledged student speech code, later struck down in federal court, but also a faculty code that provoked the first (and so far, only) pro-free-speech campus campaign strong enough to repeal such repressive restrictions. The Wisconsin faculty code was a primitive, totalitarian horror. Professors found themselves under investigation, sometimes for months, without a chance to defend themselves or even to know about the secret proceedings. One female professor said: "It was like being put in prison for no reason. I had no idea what it was that I was supposed to have done."

23 A small group of free-speech-minded faculty formed the Committee for Academic Freedom and Rights (CAFR). The group asked for help from the Wisconsin chapter of the pro-free-speech National Association of Scholars, which enlisted as speakers such celebrated allies as Alan Dershowitz and *National Journal* columnist Jonathan Rauch.

24 The First Amendment forces got a lucky break when the university signed a foolish contract with Reebok, in which it received millions of dollars in exchange for the use of the company's footwear by campus sports teams. The contract included a clause forbidding negative comments on Reebok products by any "University employee, agent or representative."

The clause greatly irritated the anticorporate campus Left, which had usually been lukewarm or indifferent to free-speech concerns, helping convert some of its members to the anti-speech-code side. Later, a strong defense of free speech by a homosexual professor, called a traitor to his identity group for his courage, brought in other campus leftist allies. CAFR was amazed at how quickly many would-be censors backed down when confronted with controversy and threatened lawsuits. Wisconsin rescinded its faculty code—the first university to do so without a court order.

25    New national groups have joined the fight for free speech on campus (and off), among them the Center for Individual Rights, the Alliance Defense Fund, and FIRE, the most relentless of the newcomers. FIRE usually starts a campaign with a polite letter to a university president, noting that some policy is either unconstitutional or a clear violation of civil liberties. If it doesn't get the change it wants, it will then write to trustees, parents, and alumni, and take its case to the media.

26    FIRE now has an extensive network of campus free-speech "spies," as its cofounder, Harvey Silverglate, jauntily calls them (Alan Charles Kors, the other cofounder, prefers "concerned members of the community"). The organization is seeking new ways to open up closed campus systems, too, such as suing administrators as individuals, which FIRE believes will get their full attention. Another new tactic is to publicize what colleges spend on fighting for unconstitutional speech codes. Most of all, FIRE is trying to show stubborn administrators that the era of hiding gross civil liberties violations behind a PC wall of silence is over: the group wins more than 95 percent of its cases.

27    Political correctness took hold when there were 40 radio talk shows, three networks, and no bloggers. Today, the cross-referencing of PC outrages among bloggers, radio talkers, and rights groups makes it hard to run an old-fashioned repressive campus. University presidents now understand that their reputations do not rest entirely with the PC platoons.

28    Perhaps the battle to release the campuses from the iron grasp of PC will take decades, but the struggle for free speech is being fought—and won—now. ◆

### CONSIDERING THE ISSUES

1.  Have you ever participated in or witnessed a demonstration on campus? What was the demonstration about? Was it restricted to a particular area? Could the participants speak freely, or were

they restricted in what they could say? Were they of a liberal or conservative viewpoint?

2. Should leaders of controversial groups be allowed to speak on campus? For example, should a person with extremist views, such as a member of the Ku Klux Klan or Hammas be allowed to speak? What about staunchly pro-life and pro-choice groups? Anti-war demonstrators? Who decides what is extremist? Students? Administrators? What do you think?

## CRAFT AND CONTENT

1. What is Leo's opinion of college administrators? Identify areas of his essay that use "us" and "them" rhetoric.
2. Review the list of speech codes (paragraph 11). Explain whether you feel any or all of the "banned comments and actions" are justifiable and should indeed be banned from public discourse.
3. What does the phrase "error has no rights" mean? How does it connect to censorship and free speech? Explain.

## CRITICAL THINKING

1. Why does Leo think that censorship is "thickest on the ground" at colleges and universities? How does he support this view? Do you agree?
2. Leo points out that the voices of conservatives are being censored from campus. In your view, is this fair? Should a university setting support all viewpoints, or is the nature of a university simply more liberal and thus, less welcoming to conservative views? Can there be a balance between the two that promotes a climate of mutual respect? Why or why not?
3. Who is Herbert Marcuse? How have his theories influenced modern campuses today?

## WRITING ABOUT THE ISSUES

1. Imagine that a controversial or conservative speaker was going to speak at your school. Explain why you would or would not protest such a speaker. Alternatively, you could explain why you would support his or her right to speak.

2. In paragraph 6, Leo comments, "Universities have made honest disagreement dangerous, making students fearful of saying what they think." Respond to his statement with your own viewpoint. Reference instances on campus or from your personal experience that support or challenge this assessment.

# Hate Cannot Be Tolerated

*Richard Delgado*

Richard Delgado is a law professor at the University of Pittsburgh. He is widely published and often appears on television and radio programs including *Good Morning America*, NPR, and the *MacNeil-Lehrer Report*. He has authored 15 books and has published articles in the *Nation*, the *New Republic*, the *New York Times*, the *Washington Post*, and the *Wall Street Journal*. His most recent book is *Race and Races, Cases and Resources for a Diverse America* (2007). This article appeared in *Insight on the News*, a national biweekly news magazine published as the sister publication of the *Washington Times*.

## CONNECTING TO THE TOPIC

Speech codes and harassment policies have been adopted by many U.S. colleges and universities in an effort to stop racist, sexist, or other types of offensive language. The rationale is that racial and other offensive slurs are violent verbal assaults that interfere with students' rights. Many civil liberties activists, students, college faculty, and administrators fear that such codes violate First Amendment rights. Who decides what is offensive language and what is not? Should "hate speech" be protected, or can it lead to violence? Are there limits to free speech in favor of greater good and greater safety for the campus body?

## WORDS IN CONTEXT

**epithet** (1)  abusive, disdainful, or condescending word or phrase (n.)
**elicit** (3)  to provoke or draw out (v.)
**revile** (4)  to assault or attack with abusive language (v.)

**evolution** (5)  in biology, the gradual change in the genetic composition of a
species over generations, resulting in the improvement of existing species
or the development of new ones (n.)
**hone** (6)  to focus on or advance toward a target or goal (v.)

1   **A**nonymous vandals scrawl hate-filled graffiti outside a Jewish student
center. Black students at a law school find unsigned fliers stuffed inside their
lockers screaming that they do not belong there. At a third campus, a group
of toughs hurls **epithets** at a young Latino student walking home late at night.

2   In response to a rising tide of such incidents, some colleges have enacted hate-speech codes or applied existing rules against individuals
whose conduct interferes with the educational opportunities of others.
Federal courts have extended "hostile environment" case law to schools
that tolerate a climate of hate for women and students of color.

3   Despite the alarm these measures sometimes **elicit**, nothing is wrong
with them. In each case, the usual and preferred response—"more
speech"—is unavailable to the victim. With anonymous hate speech such
as the flier or graffiti, the victim cannot talk back, for the hate speaker delivers the message in a cowardly fashion. And talking back to aggressors
is rarely an option. Indeed, many hate crimes began just this way: The victim talked back—and paid with his life.

4   Hate speech is rarely an invitation to a conversation. More like a slap
in the face, it **reviles** and silences. College counselors report that campuses where highly publicized incidents of hate speech have taken place
show a decline in minority enrollment as students of color instead choose
to attend schools where the environment is healthier.

5   A few federal courts have declared overly broad hate-speech codes
unconstitutional, as well they should. Nothing is gained by a rule so broad
it could be construed as forbidding the discussion of controversial subjects
such as **evolution** or affirmative action.

6   But this is not what most people mean by hate speech, nor are colleges barred from drafting narrow rules that **hone** in on the conduct they
wish to control. And when they do, courts are very likely to find in their
favor. Recent Supreme Court rulings striking down laws upholding affirmative action and approving punishment for cross-burning show that the
court is not unaware of current trends. Society is becoming more diverse.
Reasonable rules aimed at accommodating that diversity and regulating
the conduct of bullies and bigots are to be applauded—not feared. ◆

## CONSIDERING THE ISSUES

1. Does the saying "sticks and stones may break my bones, but names will never hurt me" apply to racist and hate speech? Have you ever witnessed or experienced a verbal assault based on race or gender? What was the impact, if any, on you? How did you react?
2. In your opinion, when racist or hate speech is used on campus, should it be ignored or dealt with formally? If you feel racist or hate speech should be banned from campus, do you think *all* such speech should be prohibited in *any* situation, or only in public forums? Explain your point of view.

## CRAFT AND CONTENT

1. This piece is called an opinion editorial that allows the writer to offer an opinion or viewpoint on an issue. Summarize Delgado's opinion in this editorial. What is his position on hate speech and on campus speech codes, and why?
2. Delgado identifies several "cowardly" methods people use to promote hate speech. What are they? Why does Delgado feel such speech is cowardly? Does he object to the speech itself, or the method of delivery, or both?

## CRITICAL THINKING

1. What reasons does Delgado offer for banning hate speech from campus and from general public discourse? Do you agree? Explain.
2. Do you think hate speech deserves First Amendment protection? If not, why? If so, can you think of any circumstances when hate speech should be protected? Explain.
3. Delgado observes that "hate speech is rarely an invitation to a conversation." Why do you think he makes this comment? To what free speech argument is he referring? Explain.

## WRITING ABOUT THE ISSUES

1. Many legal scholars view restrictions on hate speech as a form of censorship and contrary to the democratic spirit of pluralism and tolerance. Write a paper in which you argue that hate speech should be protected if we are to remain a legitimate democracy.

2. Taking an opposing view expressed in the last assignment, write a paper in which you argue that hate speech should be banned. In your discussion, explain what types of hate speech should be banned, and why. How would bans on hate speech be enforced?

# Free Speech Causes Problems, but Censorship Causes More

*Denise Chaykun*

Denise Chaykun wrote this editorial in 2003 when she was a senior at Bucknell University in Lewisburg, Pennsylvania, where she served as deputy editor of *The Counterweight,* a publication of the Bucknell Conservatives Club. She appeared on the cover of the May 25, 2003, issue of the *New York Times Magazine,* "The Young Hipublicans: What Campus Conservatives Learned from the 60's Generation," by John Colapinto.

## CONNECTING TO THE TOPIC

In recent years, many colleges and universities across the nation have implemented rules and speech codes restricting or banning words and expressions that may prove hurtful, offensive, or insulting to others, especially to minority groups and women. Few people would argue that racist and sexist speech is good speech. But does that mean that such speech should be banned entirely? Who decides what constitutes offensive speech? Are speech codes restricting the free flow of ideas? In the next essay, a student attending a school with a speech code explains why she feels that restricting free speech is a bad idea.

## WORDS IN CONTEXT

**reprehensible** (1)   deserving rebuke or censure (adj.)
**partisan** (1)   devoted to or biased in support of a party, group, or cause, as in *partisan politics* (adj.)
**eradication** (1)   abolishment; elimination (n.)
**abolitionist** (3)   one who advocates for the abolishment of slavery (n.)
**audacity** (3)   boldness, unhindered by a sense of propriety or convention (adj.)
**status quo** (7)   the existing condition or state of affairs (n.)

1   Free speech can really suck sometimes. If not for the First Amendment, there are so many awful things that we would never have to bother with—like the absolutely **reprehensible** and downright wrong Ku Klux Klan. In this ideal world, we could outlaw all gatherings of the KKK. This elimination of speech doesn't have to be a **partisan** sort of thing, either. We could also choose to get rid of all speech that calls for the **eradication** of the white race and any kind of comment that really makes people feel uncomfortable—no more insults, no more criticizing each other's religions, none of this offensive speech business.

2   If only it were that easy. As logical as it may seem to get rid of certain kinds of speech, it's happened before and hasn't worked too well. Remember that Galileo guy? The one who said that the universe didn't revolve around the Earth? The things he said were really offensive—he totally rocked medieval people's world views. He was threatening Christian norms, and since they didn't have to deal with speech they didn't like, they could imprison him for life.

3   Something similar also happened with **abolitionists** before the Civil War. They had the **audacity** to say that black people were, well, people—not property. Again, this offensive speech didn't have to be tolerated—the South barred abolitionist material from the mail and Congress imposed the "gag rule." Since everyone was so sure that those crazy abolitionists were wrong, it was okay to make laws that kept them from helping black people succeed.

4   There were also rules sort of like that back in kindergarten—for example, "Don't be mean." Was it always wrong to insult someone? There was a kid in my kindergarten class who got in trouble for calling the class bully a butthead, for example. While that's never the best choice of words for a kindergartener, he was right, wasn't he?

5   Wouldn't you know that we even have some great rules and scenarios like that here? Like the kid who made fun of a dean on the AIM [AOL instant messenger] last year and got taken to the Community Judicial Board for it? That certainly wasn't nice of him. I think he hurt the dean's feelings. Thank goodness that we don't have the freedom to make fun of others, lest the administration's "AIM stalking" go to waste.

6   I think you get the point. Allowing free speech always sucks for someone. If free speech had been allowed in the cases I've mentioned, medieval people would have had to deal with the concept that maybe the universe didn't revolve around them, the South might have had to give up on slavery a bit sooner, the kindergarten bully would have had to hear the

truth about himself, and the deans would have had to deal with students making fun of them on AIM. It would really suck to be them.

7    The tough part about this is that all of those restrictions were made with good intentions. Speech can hurt feelings, change the **status quo**, or even lead to changing someone's point of view. Sometimes these effects can be good, but not always.

8    With this in mind, how are we going to be able to make rules that keep these things from happening?

9    Well, for starters, the Supreme Court has put some pretty good limitations on free speech. According to the Supreme Court, there can be restrictions on "time, place, and manner"—when we speak, where we speak, and how we speak. So with these rules in mind we can all sleep peacefully in our dorms at night. Other than perhaps yelling "fire" (assuming there was one), yelling in a dorm hall at 3 a.m. is unacceptable. Three in the morning is an unacceptable time. A dorm hall is an unacceptable place. Yelling is an unacceptable manner. These rules can be applied to most sorts of extremely obnoxious behavior.

10    Harassment is another form of unprotected speech. As a legal matter, harassment is a behavior done to cause substantial emotional distress to someone. Sexual harassment, behavior that results in unreasonable interference with work performance or creates a severe and pervasively hostile environment, also fits into this category of unprotected speech.

11    So these are the legal restrictions on speech. I think they're pretty good. They make sense, but they don't restrict *what* you say. You can express any sort of idea as long as you do it in an acceptable manner.

12    We're still left with the fact that you can use speech to do all sorts of awful things to people. And because of this we're left with two options. We can accept that people are going to be mean and upset us sometimes, or we can try to keep this from happening. While it would be great to keep this from happening in lots of cases, what about those times when those upsetting things are true? Based on history, it doesn't seem like anyone can objectively be sure that there is no worth in having a certain idea expressed.

13    Hey, my life would be a lot easier if Bucknell added conservatives to the group of people you can't insult. But then again, how am I sure I'm right? While it might be upsetting or annoying to get hate mail from readers, shouldn't you have the opportunity to try to convince me that I'm wrong? Maybe I am wrong, and if I am, I hope that someone can show me why I am. That's the fair and right thing to have the freedom to do.

14    So Bucknell has also been faced with the dilemma of whether to protect feelings or ideas and has chosen feelings. I can understand why. Feelings matter. But we're a university—we should be all about ideas. If we allow free speech, there's nothing saying that there can't be more speech that opposes whatever may have been offensive or hurtful. If we do this we then all have the opportunity to learn from each other.

15    So we have a choice: we can choose to protect feelings or ideas. Hurt feelings can be mended by ideas, but lost ideas might never be recovered. With this in mind, I propose that we protect ideas. ◆

## CONSIDERING THE ISSUES

1. Chaykun recalls rules that governed how students were allowed to speak to each other in grade school. Do you recall any speech codes or rules about acceptable speech from your childhood? Were any reasons given for why some words or phrases were unacceptable? How did you learn about "incorrect" speech?

2. In her essay, Chaykun observes that many opinions that are unpopular often turn out to be true. Can you think of any unpopular opinions that follow this principle? What made the opinions unpopular? How were people treated for expressing unpopular opinions? Have you ever expressed a viewpoint that opposed popular opinion? Explain.

## CRAFT AND CONTENT

1. Chaykun cites four examples of how some individuals have had their free speech curtailed. List these examples and explain why you think they are either effective or ineffective support for her argument.

2. Who is Chaykun's audience for this essay? In what ways does her writing reflect her expectations of her audience? Consider her use of language, tone, and style in your response.

## CRITICAL THINKING

1. In her opening paragraph, Chaykun comments that the elimination of speech "doesn't have to be a partisan sort of thing, either." What does she mean? Who supports free speech and who encourages greater control?

2. In paragraph 12, Chaykun wonders if true statements should still be censured if they are upsetting. What do you think? Is it permissible in your opinion to say something harsh or upsetting if it is true? Who decides what is true or not? What about unpleasant opinions? Explain.

3. What restrictions are there on free speech that are not protected by the First Amendment? Chaykun feels that these restrictions are "pretty good" (paragraph 11). What do you think?

### WRITING ABOUT THE ISSUES

1. In paragraph 13, Chaykun notes that her life would be a lot easier if her college "added conservatives to the group of people you can't insult." Most speech codes do not cite specific groups of people that are protected by them. What does Chaykun's statement imply about who is protected by speech codes and who is not? Is a racist or sexist remark worse than saying "conservatives are stupid" or "men are jerks"? Write a short essay exploring how speech codes protect certain groups of students more than others, and whether such protection is justifiable due to the nature of the offensive speech.

2. Chaykun argues that students have a choice—they can choose to protect feelings or ideas. In your own words, write a response to her statement, explaining what you would choose to protect—feelings or ideas—and why.

# The Dark Side of Web Anonymity
*Catherine Holahan*

Catherine Holahan covers technology and the web for BusinessWeek.com. She was previously a reporter and columnist for the *Record* in New Jersey. She is a winner of the 2000 New Jersey Press Association's Robert P. Kelly Memorial Award for Reporting and Writing for first-year reporters. This article was published in the May 1, 2008, issue of *Business Week*.

## CONNECTING TO THE TOPIC

JuicyCampus.com is a website that promotes gossip and campus rumors from colleges in the United States. Readers can vote on which posts they find "juiciest." The gossip posted by unidentified users, much of it malicious, is sparking a new debate about free speech online. While freedom of speech is protected by the Constitution, slander and lies are not. However, the Communications Decency Act of 1996 shields web publishers from liability for libelous comments posted by third parties. The section states "no provider or user of an interactive computer service shall be treated as the publisher or speaker of any information provided by another information content provider." Is JuicyCampus going too far? And do those smeared online have any recourse?

## WORDS IN CONTEXT

defamatory (6)   damaging one's reputation (adj.)
slander (6)   false and malicious statements (n.)
unfettered (8)   free, unrestricted (adj.)
elicit (9)   draw out (v.)
proliferation (10)   rapid growth (n.)
subpoena (10)   command one to appear in court and give testimony (v.)
akin (14)   similar, alike (adj.)

1   **M**elissa heard the gossip about her Princeton University classmates on JuicyCampus.com even before she saw the Web site.

2   She's anorexic.

3   He's a closeted homosexual.

4   She's spreading sexual diseases.

5   Since it was set up last year, JuicyCampus has become a popular place for college kids around the country to share such gossip. Melissa ultimately found her own name connected with the malicious rumors. But the Princeton junior couldn't do anything about it. All the comments were anonymous and JuicyCampus won't remove posts based on students' objections. "The second someone's name appears on the site, it's a death sentence," she says.

6   She's not the only one who feels that way. Complaints about the site have poured into the office of New Jersey Attorney General Anne Milgram, and Milgram has opened an investigation into JuicyCampus. She

wants the site to provide a way to remove **defamatory** posts, but the problems go beyond **slander**. Milgram worries the Web site's guarantee of anonymity could lead to harassment, assault, or worse. One young woman said strange men started knocking on her door at night after comments were posted on the site detailing her alleged sexual activities and giving her home address. "There are public safety issues," says Milgram. Her effort has generated support among legal authorities from Connecticut to California.

7    JuicyCampus denies any wrongdoing. Founder and Chief Executive Matt Ivester says the site has no legal responsibility to police or remove comments based on claims of defamation. "We are confident that we haven't violated any laws," he says, "and we're disappointed that this is where [the attorney general] is focusing her time." The Web site doesn't charge its users any fees, instead generating revenue from advertising.

8    Ivester has plenty of support. Many tech executives and legal experts argue that anonymous, **unfettered** speech is essential on the Internet. It's not just the principle; it's the business. Web sites such as Amazon.com, YouTube, and MySpace depend on user participation to generate content. Monitoring or screening users could prove costly or impossible for some sites. "To shift the burden [of screening content] to Web site operators is precisely the opposite of what has led to a well-developed Internet," says Matt Zimmerman, senior staff attorney with the Electronic Frontier Foundation, a nonprofit civil liberties advocate.

9    Adeo Ressi has seen the controversy at first hand. He founded a Web site called TheFunded, which allows entrepreneurs to anonymously rate venture capital firms and provide comments on firm employees. He says cloaking participants' identities is essential to **elicit** candid assessments, and allows the Web site to provide valuable information about the venture industry. "Anonymity is necessary in order to get to the truth," he says.

10    The **proliferation** of such interactive Internet sites is what's given rise to the current debate. In the past, there were a relatively small number of sites that allowed user comments, players such as Yahoo! and America Online. If needed, prosecutors like Milgram could **subpoena** a site's host to discover a user's identity. But now there are thousands of Web sites that allow comments, and many wipe out or fail to store the records necessary to track down visitors to the site. "It used to be that if someone slammed you anonymously, you subpoenaed AOL and they got his home address and his full name," says Michael Fertik, chief executive of ReputationDefender, which tracks commentary for clients online. "But that's no longer the case."

11    Melissa understands the issues only too well. The confident 20-year-old welcomes a reporter to her dorm room dressed for the gym. She talks about JuicyCampus dismissively. She doesn't believe the site deserves any attention and is annoyed that it has gotten so much of hers. "It is just a mean concept and no one uses it for anything more than reporting mean things," she says.

12    The posts about her, with her full name, include attacks on her integrity, accusing her of backstabbing friends and social climbing. Normally, she would have shrugged it off. But because the posts could stay online for years, she frets about their effect on her reputation, perhaps even as she interviews for jobs. "It's not funny," she says. "I don't know if an employer would consider this a reliable source of anything, but if they went on and found a prospective employee's name, it's worrisome." She asked that her last name not be used for this story to avoid calling more attention to the posts.

13    Milgram believes JuicyCampus' own terms of service could require it to remove such material. The site asks users not to post content that is abusive, defamatory, or invasive of privacy, among other things. Not upholding those terms could violate New Jersey's Consumer Fraud Act, Milgram says.

14    There are few legal means to compel Web sites to police message boards. For more than a decade, section 230 of the Communications Decency Act of 1996 has protected sites from suits concerning user comments, defining such sites as **akin** to public parks rather than publications. Now some lawmakers are saying those protections are too broad. One member of California's state assembly has called for suggestions to change state law to address the problem.

15    The growing dangers of online speech have been illustrated by tragic cases, such as the suicide of 13-year-old Megan Meier in October. The young teen hanged herself a day after being insulted online by a person she believed to be Josh Evans, a 16-year-old boy with whom she had formed a friendship on MySpace. Evans didn't exist. He was later revealed to be a false profile allegedly created by a neighbor.

16    As the legal debate rages, Princeton students are trying another tactic to shut down anonymous gossip online: attacking the sites' business model. They're organizing boycotts of JuicyCampus and similar ventures, to cut off traffic and, by extension, ad revenue.

17    Behind the movement at Princeton is Connor Diemand-Yauman, 20-year-old president of the 2010 class. He created a new Web site,

OwnWhatYouThink.com, that asks students to pledge not to visit anonymous gossip sites and to stand behind their online statements. "This is about changing the way our generation and our culture look at the way we communicate with one another," he says. Since the campaign's launch on Apr. 1, 2008 nearly 1,000 students have signed the pledge. Ivester says the boycott won't have any damaging effect on the site.

18    One warm afternoon, Diemand-Yauman and dozens of other students held a rally to promote their cause. As an antidote to abusive content online, hundreds of positive statements about students from their classmates were projected onto a massive screen.

19    She gives the best hugs.

20    He is sweet and smart.

21    She is always around when I need a friend.

22    Some wore shirts, emblazoned with a retort to JuicyCampus and sites like it: "Anonymity = Cowardice."  ◆

## CONSIDERING THE ISSUES

1. In your opinion which of the following arguments has more validity: "Milgram worries the Web site's guarantee of anonymity could lead to harassment, assault, or worse" or "Many tech executives and legal experts argue that anonymous, unfettered speech is essential on the Internet"? Explain.

2. Who should be protected more by governmental policies: a person posting comments on the Internet or a person who is written about on the Internet? What types of governmental policies should be in place to protect this person?

## CRAFT AND CONTENT

1. Catherine Holahan opens and ends her essay with sample comments about students. Is this "full-circle" approach to her writing effective? Does it keep her reporting objective or does it strengthen one of the arguments about which she is reporting? Explain.

2. The author uses the suicide of Megan Meier to illustrate the "growing dangers of online speech." By using this example, is Holahan giving a fair representation of these dangers or an overly sensational one? Explain.

### CRITICAL THINKING

1. In this essay, Adeo Ressi asserts that "Anonymity is necessary in order to get to the truth." What "truth" is Ressi referring to? Is truth commonly viewed as objective or subjective? How is truth viewed when applied to websites such as Juicycampus.com?

2. The author tells us that Melissa "frets about" the comments posted about her on Juicy.com and "their effect on her reputation, perhaps even as she interviews for jobs." Do you believe that Melissa has anything to worry about? Do companies view Juicy-campus.com and other websites looking for information on their applicants, and if so, would they see this information as valid or important? Are there other ways that the comments on Juicy.com could potentially affect Melissa's reputation? Explain.

### WRITING ABOUT THE ISSUES

1. Go onto Juicycampus.com and read the comments posted. What is the ratio of negative to positive comments? What is the level of maliciousness of the comments? Do you think the site users would have written what they did if they were required to attach their names to their words? Explain other ways in which being given anonymity could possibly change our actions or behaviors.

2. Think back to a time when you were gossiped about or when you gossiped about someone else. Reflect on what was said, how you felt during that time, and what consequences, if any, were enacted. How do you feel about gossip now, and what consequences, if any, should be enacted on those who gossip regularly?

# Who's Undermining Freedom of Speech on Campus Now?

*David Beito, Robert "K.C." Johnson, and Ralph E. Luker*

David Beito is an associate professor of history at the University of Alabama and the founding member of George Mason University's History News Network (HNN) blog, "Liberty and Power." "K. C." Johnson is a professor of history at Brooklyn College and the CUNY Graduate Center. Ralph E. Luker is an associate professor of history at Antioch College and co-editor of the first two volumes of *The Papers of Martin Luther King* (1994). This essay appeared online on HNN on April 11, 2005.

## CONNECTING TO THE TOPIC

In an effort to curtail criticism of campus speech codes, some colleges and universities have adopted speech codes that define acceptable speech. Critics of such codes argue that they curtail campus discourse and erode the very foundation of a college education, posing a dangerous threat to ideals of free speech. Speech code advocates counter that certain types of language can create uncomfortable situations for some students, that this interferes with learning and the right to pursue an education without fear of intimidation. But who decides what is acceptable speech? Are campus speech codes going too far?

## WORDS IN CONTEXT

**abridge** (1)    curtail or limit (v.)
**Aggie** (3)    name often given to students or teams from mechanical and agricultural schools, especially Texas A&M (n.)
**Trojan Horse** (9)    something that appears to be legitimate but really has destructive effects (n.)

1    **F**reedom of speech is crucial both to a healthy democracy and the life of the mind. The First Amendment to the United States Constitution prohibits Congress from any act that would **abridge** it and the charters of most of our colleges and universities recognize that freedom of thought and speech are essential to a healthy academic community. Yet, freedom of speech has been a contested value since the birth of the Republic, most commonly in periods of war, from the Alien and Sedition Acts of 1798 through the USA PATRIOT Act.

2    It isn't surprising, then, that freedom of speech is now under siege. What is new in our academic communities is that it is threatened both from within and from outside them. The internal threat to free speech in academia is posed by "speech codes." They take many forms and vary from one college to the next university. After the 1960s, when American colleges and universities ceased to operate *in loco parentis*, campus

speech codes emerged on one campus after another as a means of securing a "safe space" for some students who were offended by certain kinds of speech. On one campus or another, speech that is discomforting, embarrassing, flirtatious, gender specific, inappropriate, inconsiderate, harassing, intimidating, offensive, ridiculing or threatens a loss of "self-esteem" is banned by speech codes. Too often, they target student critics of academic bureaucracy.

3    Taken literally, speech codes would ban healthy jeering at a visiting sports team. Wouldn't want to intimidate those **Aggies**! More importantly, teachers have to be able to urge students to consider perspectives that they had not previously considered, without fear of being accused of being "offensive." Ultimately, speech codes are problematic because they vest final authority in the subjectivity of the offended. Whether it is "intentional or unintentional," for example, Brown University bans all "verbal behavior" that may cause "feelings of impotence, anger, or disenfranchisement." The nation's Founders, who did not mind offending British authorities, would have been ill-educated by such constrictions on free speech.

4    The problem with speech codes is that speech that should be self-governed by good manners and humility is prescripted by inflexible legal codification. Fortunately, however, Philadelphia's Foundation for Individual Rights in Education has fought and won a series of legal battles that have curtailed the prevalence of speech codes in public higher education. In private colleges and universities, where First Amendment rights do not necessarily prevail, the struggle continues on an institution by institution basis.

5    Just when there is good news to report about the unconstitutionality of speech codes on public campuses, however, new threats to free speech arise from outside the academic community. They come from the Center for the Study of Popular Culture in Los Angeles. The Center and its legal arm, the Individual Rights Foundation, are led by David Horowitz. A militant activist on the left in the 1960s, Horowitz abandoned it 25 years ago to become a militant activist on the right. Most recently, he has campaigned for enactment of an "Academic Bill of Rights."

6    Like campus speech codes, Horowitz's Academic Bill of Rights appears well intentioned. Insisting that academic communities must be more responsive to outside criticism, it adopts a form of the American Association of University Professors' 1915 "General Report of the Committee on Academic Freedom and Tenure." It holds that political and religious beliefs should not influence the hiring and tenuring of faculty or the evaluation of students, that curricular and extra-curricular activities should expose students to the variety

of perspectives about academic matters and public issues, and that institutions must not tolerate obstructions to free debate nor, themselves, become vehicles of partisan advocacy. Who could oppose such commitments? They are already features of the professorate's assumed values.

7    Yet, the American Association of University Professors and the American Civil Liberties Union criticize Horowitz's "Academic Bill of Rights" as an effort to "proscribe and prescribe activities in classrooms and on college campuses." One has only to look at the legislative progress of Horowitz's political campaign to understand why. His Academic Bill of Rights has been introduced in Congress by Representative Jack Kingston (R-GA), but it's had greater promotion in the state legislatures of California, Colorado, Florida, Georgia, Indiana, Maine, Massachusetts, Ohio, Tennessee, and Washington.

8    Instead of being the even-handed vehicle it claims to be, everywhere it is a function of right-wing attacks on academic communities. In Florida, for example, Representative Dennis Baxley says that the bill he introduced will give students legal standing to sue professors who do not teach "intelligent design" as an acceptable alternate to the theory of evolution. His critics respond that it could give students who are holocaust deniers or who oppose birth control and modern medicine legal standing to sue their professors. Beyond the governing authority of Florida's public colleges and universities and in the name of free thought and free speech, it would encode in state law restrictions against those values.

9    The Founders, who recalled their own exercise of free speech and free thought when they challenged British governing authority, wrote guarantees protecting them from constricting government action. In academic communities, we need an alliance across ideological divides to support free speech by abolishing "speech codes" and to fight the "Academic Bill of Rights" in state legislatures and the Congress because it is a **Trojan Horse** that intends the opposite of what it claims on its face. ◆

## CONSIDERING THE ISSUES

1. Imagine that a condition of acceptance to your school involved your signing an agreement that you would refrain from using racist, sexist, or offensive language on campus or face suspension or expulsion. Weighing the social benefits against the restrictions of your freedom of expression, write a paper in which you explain why you would or would not sign such an agreement.

2. Have you ever felt uncomfortable in class or while participating in an online class newsgroup because of something a professor or student said? What were the circumstances, and how did you react? If this has never happened, can you think of any circumstances that might make you feel uncomfortable in class? Explain.

## CRAFT AND CONTENT

1. In paragraph 3, the authors assert that "Ultimately, speech codes are problematic because they vest final authority in the subjectivity of the offended." What does this statement mean? Do you agree with the authors' position? Why or why not?

## CRITICAL THINKING

1. The authors note that the Academic Bill of Rights could be used by students who oppose birth control or deny the Holocaust the grounds to sue professors. Review the Academic Bill of Rights (following this essay) and explain why you agree or disagree that this is a valid concern.
2. The authors argue that Horowitz's "Academic Bill of Rights" is "a Trojan Horse that intends the opposite of what it claims on its face." What is a Trojan Horse? How does the term apply to the point the authors are making in this essay? Explain.

## WRITING ABOUT THE ISSUES

1. Research the arguments for and against campus speech codes as expressed in university publications available online for at least four colleges or universities. How are the codes similar and how are they different? Are they open for interpretation? In your opinion, do they unfairly restrict freedom of speech on campus? Write a short essay on this issue. If your own campus has a speech code, include it in your discussion.
2. The authors begin their essay with historical references of challenges to the First Amendment (from the Alien and Sedition Acts of 1798 to the USA PATRIOT Act). Research these acts and write a short essay connecting these historical challenges to free speech and the current political and social climate.

# Academic Bill of Rights
*David Horowitz*

David Horowitz is president of the Center for the Study of Popular Culture and the author of *Left Illusions: An Intellectual Odyssey* (2003).

## WORDS IN CONTEXT

**faction** (2)   a small group within a larger group (n.)
**transcendent** (3)   encompassing all (adj.)
**orthodoxy** (5)   beliefs or practices (n.)
**admonished** (5)   criticized, rebuked (v.)
**indoctrinate** (5)   To instruct with a point of view or promote a body of beliefs (v.)
**substantive** (14)   considerable (adj.)

## I. The Mission of the University

1   The central purposes of a University are the pursuit of truth, the discovery of new knowledge through scholarship and research, the study and reasoned criticism of intellectual and cultural traditions, the teaching and general development of students to help them become creative individuals and productive citizens of a pluralistic democracy, and the transmission of knowledge and learning to a society at large. Free inquiry and free speech within the academic community are indispensable to the achievement of these goals. The freedom to teach and to learn depend upon the creation of appropriate conditions and opportunities on the campus as a whole as well as in the classrooms and lecture halls. These purposes reflect the values— pluralism, diversity, opportunity, critical intelligence, openness and fairness— that are the cornerstones of American society.

## II. Academic Freedom

2   *1. The Concept.* Academic freedom and intellectual diversity are values indispensable to the American university. From its first formulation in the General Report of the Committee on Academic Freedom and Tenure

of the American Association of University Professors, the concept of academic freedom has been premised on the idea that human knowledge is a never-ending pursuit of the truth, that there is no humanly accessible truth that is not in principle open to challenge, and that no party or intellectual **faction** has a monopoly on wisdom. Therefore, academic freedom is most likely to thrive in an environment of intellectual diversity that protects and fosters independence of thought and speech. In the words of the General Report, it is vital to protect "as the first condition of progress, [a] complete and unlimited freedom to pursue inquiry and publish its results."

3      Because free inquiry and its fruits are crucial to the democratic enterprise itself, academic freedom is a national value as well. In a historic 1967 decision (*Keyishian v. Board of Regents of the University of the State of New York*) the Supreme Court of the United States overturned a New York State loyalty provision for teachers with these words: "Our Nation is deeply committed to safeguarding academic freedom, [a] **transcendent** value to all of us and not merely to the teachers concerned." In *Sweezy v. New Hampshire* (1957) the Court observed that the "essentiality of freedom in the community of American universities [was] almost self-evident."

4      *2. The Practice.* Academic freedom consists in protecting the intellectual independence of professors, researchers and students in the pursuit of knowledge and the expression of ideas from interference by legislators or authorities within the institution itself. This means that no political, ideological or religious orthodoxy will be imposed on professors and researchers through the hiring or tenure or termination process, or through any other administrative means by the academic institution. Nor shall legislatures impose any such orthodoxy through their control of the university budget.

5      This protection includes students. From the first statement on academic freedom, it has been recognized that intellectual independence means the protection of students—as well as faculty—from the imposition of any **orthodoxy** of a political, religious or ideological nature. The 1915 General Report **admonished** faculty to avoid "taking unfair advantage of the student's immaturity by **indoctrinating** him with the teacher's own opinions before the student has had an opportunity fairly to examine other opinions upon the matters in question, and before he has sufficient knowledge and ripeness of judgment to be entitled to form any definitive opinion of his own." In 1967, the AAUP's Joint Statement on Rights and Freedoms of

Students reinforced and amplified this injunction by affirming the insepa-
rability of "the freedom to teach and freedom to learn." In the words of the
report, "Students should be free to take reasoned exception to the data or
views offered in any course of study and to reserve judgment about matters of opinion."

6      Therefore, to secure the intellectual independence of faculty and students and to protect the principle of intellectual diversity, the following principles and procedures shall be observed. These principles fully apply only to
public universities and to private universities that present themselves as
bound by the canons of academic freedom. Private institutions choosing to
restrict academic freedom on the basis of creed have an obligation to be as
explicit as is possible about the scope and nature of these restrictions.

7   1.  All faculty shall be hired, fired, promoted and granted tenure on the
        basis of their competence and appropriate knowledge in the field of
        their expertise and, in the humanities, the social sciences, and the
        arts, with a view toward fostering a plurality of methodologies and
        perspectives. No faculty shall be hired or fired or denied promotion
        or tenure on the basis of his or her political or religious beliefs.

8   2.  No faculty member will be excluded from tenure, search and hiring
        committees on the basis of their political or religious beliefs.

9   3.  Students will be graded solely on the basis of their reasoned answers
        and appropriate knowledge of the subjects and disciplines they study,
        not on the basis of their political or religious beliefs.

10  4.  Curricula and reading lists in the humanities and social sciences
        should reflect the uncertainty and unsettled character of all human
        knowledge in these areas by providing students with dissenting
        sources and viewpoints where appropriate. While teachers are and
        should be free to pursue their own findings and perspectives in pre-
        senting their views, they should consider and make their students
        aware of other viewpoints. Academic disciplines should welcome a
        diversity of approaches to unsettled questions.

11  5.  Exposing students to the spectrum of significant scholarly viewpoints
        on the subjects examined in their courses is a major responsibility of
        faculty. Faculty will not use their courses for the purpose of political,
        ideological, religious or anti-religious indoctrination.

12  6.  Selection of speakers, allocation of funds for speakers programs and
        other student activities will observe the principles of academic free-
        dom and promote intellectual pluralism.

13  7. An environment conducive to the civil exchange of ideas being an essential component of a free university, the obstruction of invited campus speakers, destruction of campus literature or other effort to obstruct this exchange will not be tolerated.

14  8. Knowledge advances when individual scholars are left free to reach their own conclusions about which methods, facts, and theories have been validated by research. Academic institutions and professional societies formed to advance knowledge within an area of research, maintain the integrity of the research process, and organize the professional lives of related researchers serve as indispensable venues within which scholars circulate research findings and debate their interpretation. To perform these functions adequately, academic institutions and professional societies should maintain a posture of organizational neutrality with respect to the **substantive** disagreements that divide researchers on questions within, or outside, their fields of inquiry. ◆

## CRITICAL THINKING

1. In the preceding essay, David Beito, Robert "K. C." Johnson, and Ralph E. Luker explain that Horowitz's Academic Bill of Rights has been the basis of great debate on college campuses and even Congress. Outline the arguments that both supporters and opponents might pose regarding this document.

2. The Academic Bill of Rights has been used as the basis of legislation in Congress and has been introduced on the state level to state governments. Write a letter to your state's representative explaining why you support or do not support the Academic Bill of Rights from the perspective of a college student.

3. Read Stanley Fish's response to the Academic Bill of Rights, "'Intellectual Diversity': The Trojan Horse of a Dark Design," printed in the *Chronicle of Higher Education* on February 13, 2004, at http://chronicle.com/free/v50/i23/23b01301.htm (if the link is broken, search for the article by its title online). Why does Fish object to the Academic Bill of Rights? What evidence does he provide that the bill is flawed? Explain.

# Policy Statement on Discriminatory Harassment

*Emory University*

## CONNECTING TO THE TOPIC

Do colleges and universities have a moral obligation to protect free speech or ensure a peaceful, respectful learning environment for all students? Many schools have opted for the latter and have come down hard on speech code offenders. One student at the University of Pennsylvania faced disciplinary action for calling a group of rowdy sorority sisters a bunch of "water buffalo." A student group at Gonzaga University had to fight against a letter going into its personal file for posting fliers that included "discriminatory" language announcing a book reading. The fliers used the word "hate"—part of the title of the speaker's book, *Why the Left Hates America*. Recently, the English department at Harvard University found itself in the awkward situation of having to postpone a poetry reading by an Irish poet because some faculty and students objected to his political views. The next item is a reprint of Emory University's policy statement on discriminatory harassment. In what ways is this statement, and others like it adopted by colleges and universities across the country, ambiguous? What does it protect? What does it censure?

## WORDS IN CONTEXT

**foreseeable** (2)   known beforehand (adj.)
**epithet** (2)   scornful, abusive, or condescending word or phrase (n.)
**explicitly** (3)   expressed clearly (adv.)
**implicitly** (3)   implied (adv.)
**pretextual** (5)   used as an excuse (adj.)

## Effective as of January 27, 2004

1   It is the policy of Emory University that all employees and students should be able to enjoy and work in an educational environment free from discriminatory harassment. Harassment of any person or group of persons on the basis of race, color, national origin, religion, sex, sexual orientation, age, disability, or veteran's status is a form of discrimination specifically

prohibited in the Emory University community. Any employee, student, student organization, or person privileged to work or study in the Emory University community who violates this policy will be subject to disciplinary action up to and including permanent exclusion from the University.

2    Discriminatory harassment includes conduct (oral, written, graphic, or physical) directed against any person or group of persons because of race, color, national origin, religion, sex, sexual orientation, age, disability or veteran's status and that has the purpose or reasonably **foreseeable** effect of creating an offensive, demeaning, intimidating, or hostile environment for that person or group of persons. Such conduct includes, but is not limited to, objectionable **epithets**, demeaning depictions or treatment, and threatened or actual abuse or harm.

3    In addition, sexual harassment includes unwelcome sexual advances, requests for sexual favors, and other verbal or physical conduct of a sexual nature when:

- submission to such conduct is made either **explicitly** or **implicitly** a term or condition of an individual's employment or a student's status in a course, program, or activity.
- submission to or rejection of such conduct by an employee or student is used as the basis for employment or academic decisions affecting that employee or student.
- such conduct has the purpose or effect of unreasonably interfering with an employee's work performance or a student's academic performance or creating an intimidating, hostile, or offensive employment, educational, or living environment.

4    All University Vice Presidents, Deans, and Division and Department Chairpersons should take appropriate steps to disseminate this policy statement and inform employees and students of procedures for lodging complaints. All members of the student body, faculty, and staff are expected to assist in implementing this policy.

5    The scholarly, educational, or artistic content of any written, oral, or other presentation or inquiry shall not be limited by this Policy. It is the intent of this paragraph that academic freedom be allowed to all members of the academic community. Accordingly, this provision shall be liberally construed but shall not be used as a **pretextual** basis for violation of this Policy.

6    Any student or employee with a complaint of discriminatory harassment should contact the Vice President of Equal Opportunity Programs to

obtain information on the procedure for handling such complaints. Any questions regarding either this policy statement or specific fact situation should be addressed to the Emory University Office of Equal Opportunity Programs. ◆

## CONSIDERING THE ISSUES

1. Does your college or university have a speech code? Locate your student handbook and look up your school's policies on harassment.
2. Do you think censure is an effective way to prevent offensive speech? Does it stop such speech? Does stopping the speech stop the attitudes and opinions behind it, or is that not the issue? Why or why not?

## CRAFT AND CONTENT

1. After reading this policy statement, do you understand it? Are there any areas that are confusing or difficult to read? If you were a student at Emory, would you know what language was considered unacceptable? Explain.
2. Who is bound by this policy statement? What would happen if someone violated it? Explain.

## CRITICAL THINKING

1. Do harassment codes such as this one violate students' First Amendment rights? Why or why not?
2. Do you think Emory's policy is a good one? Explain why you agree or disagree with it, and why.

## WRITING ABOUT THE ISSUES

1. Write a letter to the editor of your school newspaper advocating for restricted or unlimited speech on campus. In your letter, explain why you have adopted this position, and provide supporting material for your argument. How do you think your letter would be received by the student body at your school? Explain.

# VISUAL CONNECTIONS

## Silencing Free Speech

*The Counterweight* is a student-run, nonpartisan publication published by the Bucknell University Conservatives Club. It is "dedicated to promoting the free exchange of ideas in an environment where meaningful debate and ideological diversity are often lacking." It seeks to serve the Bucknell community by "infusing it with the ingredients necessary for a balanced educational experience . . . includ[ing] conservative, libertarian, and classical liberal thought." *The Counterweight* vowed to reprint Bucknell's speech code in every issue until "the administration does the right thing and eliminates it." As of the printing of this book, Bucknell's speech code is still in place.

### CONNECTING TO THE TOPIC

Student-run newspapers and campus magazines often serve as the voice of the student body, or at least a segment of it. Take a look at some of your own campus newspapers and magazines. On what issues do they report? Do they promote a particular agenda or embrace a particular point of view? Do you think they are free to "promote the free exchange of ideas," or are they hampered by campus speech codes?

## CONSIDERING THE ISSUES

1. Consider how this photograph relays a message to the viewer. What can you determine about campus speech codes based upon what you see in the photo? What "shape" is the tape on the young woman's mouth? What does this symbol mean? What if the woman were gagged? Explain.
2. If you saw this magazine cover on your own campus newsletter or magazine, would you be led to read the article? Why or why not?

## CRITICAL THINKING

1. How does this magazine cover make you feel, and why? Explore the implications of this photograph and the ways it is designed to elicit a response from the viewer.
2. Freedom of speech is a fundamental right that many Americans hold sacred. Does it surprise you that many college campuses restrict free speech? Explain.

# TOPICAL CONNECTIONS

## GROUP PROJECT

1. Imagine that you have been chosen to be members of a student committee asked to draft a speech code for your university or college. As a group, draft such a code. Consider students' rights to free speech, what constitutes hate speech, and what limits can be placed on hate speech. Write a prologue to your code explaining and supporting its tenets.

## WEB PROJECTS

2. Several authors in this chapter observe how some students are fighting speech codes on their campuses. Visit the Foundation for Individual Rights in Education, Inc. (FIRE) website at www.thefire.org/index.php and review the cases it is

currently fighting. Select one case that you find particularly compelling and state your own position on the issue. Research the issue as thoroughly as possible, reviewing student newspapers, any administrative commentary, and press received in local newspapers.

3. In a January 2003 article in *Boston* magazine, "The Thought Police," Harvey Silverglate states that the First Amendment should protect your right to say what you wish, but that you are not immune to what happens as a result of your speech. You may be subjected to anger, public shunning, and social pressure, but you should not be officially punished for your language. Write a response to Silverglate expressing your own opinion on this assessment of the First Amendment. You may review the article at *Boston* magazine's website at www.bostonmagazine.com.

## FOR FURTHER INQUIRY

1. In 1996, Robert B. Chatelle, cochair of the Political Issues Committee National Writers Union, wrote a letter to Wesleyan University President Douglas Bennet to express concern about a Wesleyan student who had been suspended by the university's student judicial board for violating the Wesleyan speech code. Read Chatelle's argument at http://users.rcn.com/kyp/schools/bennet2.html. After determining for yourself both sides of the conflict, write your own views in an essay. Support your position using information from the readings in this unit as well as from your own personal experience.

# 6 | What's the Big Deal About Immigration?

The United States of America is a union predicated on similar moral values, political and economic self-interest, a common legal system, and a democratic form of government. While we have much in common, we are also a nation of immigrants—people of different ethnic backgrounds, religions, traditions, languages, and cultures. We are a nation whose motto *e pluribus unum* ("one out of many") bespeaks a pride in its multicultural heritage. But we are also a nation divided by race and ethnicity. We may glorify the memory of our own immigrant ancestors, but do not always welcome new waves of immigrants. This unit explores current issues connected with immigration and immigration reform, especially with respect to immigrants coming from Mexico and South America.

Most of the arguments involving immigration focus on illegal aliens circumventing U.S. laws. Some critics argue that immigrants themselves have changed—that the current wave of newcomers is different from those of the past, that this group refuses to assimilate, threatens the American way of life, and expects free handouts. Immigration advocates counter that all immigrant groups resist integration to a certain extent at first and then are assimilated into mainstream culture. They also contend that immigrants promote diversity, revitalize the workforce, and are good for the economy. With such diverse perspectives and positions, the issue can be challenging to navigate. Should new immigrants be required to learn English? What happens when illegal immigrants have children in the United States? Are immigrants from Mexico changing American culture? If so, is that a bad thing? And what does the United States owe, if anything, to the thousands of people who seek a better life here?

222

## CRITICAL THINKING

1. What is happening in this cartoon? What is the man doing at the bottom of the image?
2. What does the cartoonist's caption, "The New Melting Pot" mean? What was the "old" melting pot? What does the cartoonist imply has changed?
3. What do you need to know about immigration—both past and present—in order to understand the point the cartoonist is trying to make?

THE NEW MELTING POT...

ILLEGAL IMMI- GRATION

Mike Lester — The Rome News-Tribune * Posted 05/29/2007

# Kidding Ourselves About Immigration

*Michael Kinsley*

Michael Kinsley is a political journalist and television commentator. For many years, he served as a co-host on the political news program *Crossfire*. He is frequently published both in traditional print media and on-line. He is a former editor of the *New Republic* and started the online news journal *Slate*. This article appeared in the December 6, 2007, issue of *TIME* magazine.

## CONNECTING TO THE TOPIC

Most of us can trace our roots to an ancestor who left his or her country and immigrated to the United States. In many cases, this relocation was legal—that is, the government legally allowed this person to enter the United States and live and work here. Today, the United States seems to be very selective about to whom they extend immigrant status. The thousands left in line must find another way across the border. In this next essay, Michael Kinsley at-tempts to force Americans to own up to what they really mean when they say they are against illegal immigration. And the truth isn't very nice.

## WORDS IN CONTEXT

**agin** (4)   (*Chiefly Upper Southern U.S.*) against; opposed to: *I'm agin him.* (prep.)
**queue** (7)   line (n.)

1   What you are supposed to say about immigration—what most of the political candidates say, what the radio talk jocks say—is that you are not against immigration. Not at all. You salute the hard work and noble aspira-tions of those who are lining up at American consulates around the world. But that is legal immigration. What you oppose is illegal immigration.

2   This formula is not very helpful. We all oppose breaking the law, or we ought to. Saying that you oppose illegal immigration is like saying you oppose illegal drug use or illegal speeding. Of course you do, or should. The question is whether you think the law draws the line in the right place. Should using marijuana be illegal? Should the speed limit be raised—or

lowered? The fact that you believe in obeying the law reveals nothing about what you think the law ought to be, or why.

3    Another question: Why are you so upset about this particular form of lawbreaking? After all, there are lots of laws, not all of them enforced with vigor. The suspicion naturally arises that the illegality is not what bothers you. What bothers you is the immigration. There is an easy way to test this. Reducing illegal immigration is hard, but increasing legal immigration would be easy. If your view is that legal immigration is good and illegal immigration is bad, how about increasing legal immigration? How about doubling it? Any takers? So in the end, this is not really a debate about illegal immigration. This is a debate about immigration.

4    And it's barely a debate at all. Immigration has long divided both parties, with advocates and opponents in each. Among Republicans, support for immigration was economic (corporations), while opposition was cultural (nativists). Among Democrats, it was the reverse: support for immigration was cultural (ethnic groups), while opposition was economic (unions). Now, for whatever reason, support for immigration is limited to an eccentric alliance of high-minded Council on Foreign Relations types, the mainstream media, high-tech entrepreneurs, Latinos, and the *Wall Street Journal* editorial page. Everyone else, it seems, is **agin**.

5    Maybe the aginners are right, and immigration is now damaging our country, stealing jobs and opportunity, ripping off taxpayers, fragmenting our culture. I doubt it, but maybe so. Certainly, it's true that we can't let in everyone who wants to come. There is some number of immigrants that is too many. I don't believe we're past that point, but maybe we are. In any event, a democracy has the right to decide that it has reached such a point. There is no obligation to be fair to foreigners.

6    But let's not kid ourselves that all we care about is obeying the law and all we are asking illegals to do is go home and get in line like everybody else. We know perfectly well that the line is too long, and we are basically telling people to go home and not come back.

7    Let's not kid ourselves, either, about who we are telling this to. To characterize illegal immigrants as **queue**-jumping, lawbreaking scum is seriously unjust. The motives of illegal immigrants—which can be summarized as "a better life"—are identical to those of legal immigrants. In fact, they are largely identical to the motives of our own parents, grandparents and great-grandparents when they immigrated. And not just that. Ask yourself, of these three groups—today's legal and illegal immigrants and the immigrants of generations ago—which one has proven most dramatically

its appreciation of our country? Which one has shown the most gumption, the most willingness to risk all to get to the U.S. and the most willingness to work hard once here? Well, everyone's story is unique. But who loves the U.S. most? On average, probably, the winners of this American-values contest would be the illegals, doing our dirty work under constant fear of eviction, getting thrown out and returning again and again.

8    And how about those of us lucky enough to have been born here? How would we do against the typical illegal alien in a "prove how much you love America" reality TV show? ◆

### CONSIDERING THE ISSUES

1. In his essay, Kinsley says, "To characterize illegal immigrants as queue-jumping, lawbreaking scum is seriously unjust." Do you agree or disagree with this assertion? How should we characterize illegal immigrants? How would the illegal immigrants probably characterize themselves?
2. What are American values? Kinsley states "the winners of this American-values contest would be the illegals." Does this statement express your view of American values? Explain.

### CRAFT AND CONTENT

1. The author makes many assumptions about his audience in this essay. First of all, explain who Kinsley believes his audience is and then find at least three examples in his writing in which he makes assumptions about his readers. What are those assumptions?
2. According to this article, how have illegal immigrants shown their appreciation for the United States? In what other ways do or could immigrants show their appreciation for their newly adopted nation?

### CRITICAL THINKING

1. Kinsley mentions that "support for immigration is limited to an eccentric alliance of high-minded Council on Foreign Relations types, the mainstream media, high-tech entrepreneurs, Latinos,

and the *Wall Street Journal* editorial page." Do you think this statement is accurate? Why do you think these groups would support immigration?

2. If the United States could decrease illegal immigration into our country by doubling legal immigration, should that be done? What would be other pros and cons of doubling legal immigration?

## WRITING ABOUT THE ISSUES

1. Kinsley ends his essay by asking his presumably American audience, "How would we do against the typical illegal alien in a 'prove how much you love America' reality TV show?" Develop this reality TV show idea by explaining how native-born Americans would compete with illegal immigrants in proving how much each group loves the United States. In other words, write a premise for this reality TV show.

2. This essay makes a bold statement: "There is no obligation to be fair to foreigners." Make a list of situations in which this statement would prove to be accurate and then make a list of situations in which this statement would not be accurate. If you were traveling to another country and were considered a "foreigner," how would you expect to be treated?

# A Quiz to Forge Americans
*Gregory Rodriguez*

Gregory Rodriguez is a senior fellow at the New America Foundation, a nonpartisan public policy institute "dedicated to bringing exceptionally promising new voices and ideas to the fore of the nation's public discourse." He is a contributing editor to the opinion section of the *Los Angeles Times* and a political analyst for MSNBC. His writing has appeared in the *Wall Street Journal,* the *Economist,* the *Washington Post,* and the *New York Times,* among others. He is the author of *Mongrels, Bastards, Orphans and Vagabonds: Mexican Immigration and the Future of Race in America* (2007). This article was published in the October 8, 2007, edition of the *Los Angeles Times.*

## CONNECTING TO THE TOPIC ————————————————

To become a U.S. citizen, an immigrant must take an exam. In 2007, a new U.S. citizenship exam was introduced and tested in 10 cities. The new exam, slated to be used across the country in October 2008, poses more questions about the meaning of democracy and fewer questions connected to historical facts. Instead of asking how many stripes are on the flag, for example, the test asks why there are 13 (one for each of the original 13 colonies). Advocates for the exam claim that the information is material that every citizen should know. Critics argue that the changes make the test even more daunting. What should every citizen know? How would you measure up if you had to take the exam?

## WORDS IN CONTEXT ————————————————

**exclusionary** (2)   discriminatory (adj.)
**gauge** (5)   measure (n.)
**rampant** (8)   out of control (adj.)
**obsolete** (8)   no longer useful (adj.)
**centrifugal** (10)   moving away from a center (adj.)
**coercive** (10)   ballying, forceful (adj.)
**assimilationist** (10)   blending in by hiding or giving up cultural identity (adj.)

1   **S**ome immigrant rights activists are afraid that the new citizenship test unveiled by the government two weeks ago will create a new and higher barrier for people who want to become Americans.

2   They're wrong. Far from being an **exclusionary** tool, the new test, which will be given to legal resident aliens who apply for citizenship after October 1, 2008, is actually a rare mechanism for immigrant inclusion, the kind our country needs more of.

3   It's true that, historically, whenever the government has introduced a new citizenship exam, it has been responding to shifting national attitudes toward immigration. And the winds today for immigrants—be they legal or illegal—are not so friendly. What's more, in July 2007, the government raised the citizenship application fee from $400 to $675. That wasn't exactly a welcome wagon.

4   Despite expectations to the contrary, the U.S. Citizenship and Immigration Services lived up to its promise to create a new test that would promote democratic values and civic integration—and wouldn't be any more

difficult than the old one. The new exam does more than simply measure one's ability to memorize facts. Instead of asking "What country did we fight during the Revolutionary War?" for example, the new exam is more likely to ask, "Why did the colonists fight the British?" It is more about concepts than facts, and it requires newcomers to learn about what it means to be American, not simply how many stripes are on the flag or who wrote "The Star-Spangled Banner."

5      A slew of man-on-the-street news stories over the last few weeks revealed that plenty of native-born Americans (who are citizens by accident of birth) wouldn't be able to answer the new questions off the top of their head. Quick: What are two rights only for United States citizens? (Voting, running for office, carrying a U.S. passport, holding a federal job.) But that's a meaningless **gauge** of the test's difficulty because prospective citizens will be able to study all 100 potential questions and acceptable answers before their oral exam, during which they must answer six out of 10 correctly. So far, of the 6,000 applicants who volunteered to take the new test, 92.4% have passed—higher than the overall 84% pass rate for the test we've been using since 1986.

6      Too easy, you say? Keep in mind that exclusionary tests were used in other eras to limit immigration and manipulate the ethnic composition of the population. In the early 20th century, for instance, a literacy test was implemented to impede arrivals from southern and eastern Europe. This new exam, however, is concerned with teaching the soon-to-be-naturalized immigrant how to be a good citizen. And that's a welcome shift in federal policy.

7      For most of our history, the government has done very little to help immigrants integrate into the mainstream. For all intents and purposes, federal immigration policy largely began and ended at the nation's borders. A small number of political refugees—who come here fleeing persecution—get government resettlement assistance. But most immigrants are left to their own devices. Indeed, foreign wars and international crises have fostered more loyalty to the U.S. among new arrivals than anything the federal government has done.

8      Some say that **rampant** globalization and the movement of millions of people across borders have rendered the concept of national citizenship **obsolete**. Nonsense. They have only made it more important. Citizenship is not just a legal status that confers rights and benefits. Particularly in a highly diverse nation like ours, it is an identity that should give us a sense of a shared fate and belonging. It is also a license to integrate oneself into American civic culture and to participate in a remarkable system of self-government.

9    For the last two generations, the government and schools have stressed the importance of respecting cultural pluralism. And that's fine and good. But in this new era of high immigration—12% of today's population is foreign-born, shy of the 15% highs in 1890 and 1910—it seems critical for the government to encourage new citizens to identify with our shared political culture.

10   **Centrifugal** forces always have seemed strongest in the United States; we push outward, toward new frontiers, far suburbs, away from one another. So it might seem quaint to institute a new civic rite that emphasizes belief in a common culture. But it's not. The new citizenship test is an important step in the right direction, and a far cry from the **coercive assimilationist** programs of the early 20th century.

11   With any luck, it'll be one of many new efforts that help Americans— new and old—balance our healthy regard for cultural pluralism with an equally strong respect for our shared political culture.  ◆

### CONSIDERING THE ISSUES

1. What is the purpose of giving immigrants an exam on American history in order for them to become citizens of the United States? Do you agree with having such a test? If not, why not? If so, what type of questions would you want the test to ask?

2. Rodriguez ends his article by expressing hope that the United States can "balance our healthy regard for cultural pluralism with an equally strong respect for our shared political culture." Explain what this means and then discuss how this balance could be achieved and if, indeed, it should be achieved.

### CRAFT AND CONTENT

1. Rodriguez gives his readers examples of why the U.S. government wanted to create "exclusionary" exams in the past. Which examples are given, and why do you think the government wanted to exclude certain types of immigrants? Do you know of any other examples of the U.S. government wanting to exclude certain types of immigrants?

2. Rodriguez begins his article discussing the new test for becoming a naturalized citizen. At what point does he switch to a different topic? What is this new topic? Find the transitional sentence(s)

linking the two topics and explain how these two topics are (or aren't) related.

## CRITICAL THINKING

1. Rodriguez opens his essay by saying, "Some immigrant rights activists are afraid that the new citizenship test unveiled by the government two weeks ago will create a new and higher barrier for people who want to become Americans." Why might immigrant rights activists be "afraid" of a "higher barrier" to becoming a U.S. citizen? At what level should the barrier be?
2. The author asserts that "the winds today for immigrants—be they legal or illegal—are not so friendly." Do you agree that there is an unfriendly climate toward immigrants at this time? Give examples that either support or refute his statement.

## WRITING ABOUT THE ISSUES

1. Research the steps for becoming a naturalized citizen by visiting websites such as http://immigration-law.freeadvice.com/citizenship/naturalization_requirements.htm. Do you agree with the steps that an immigrant must take in order to become a citizen? What would you keep the same? What would you change? Write an essay explaining your answer.
2. Below are sample questions the U.S. Citizenship and Immigration Services use for the oral portion of the test to become a U.S. citizen. Which type of questions do you find to be most justified for gaining citizenship? Try to answer the questions in both and then check your answers online at http://www.usimmigrationsupport.org/citizenship_test.html. Were you able to answer all of the questions correctly? Which ones did you have trouble with and why?

FORMER TEST: Sample U.S. Citizenship Test Questions
   1. How many stars are there in our flag?
   2. How many states are there in the Union?
   3. What color are the stars on our flag?
   4. What do the stars on the flag mean?
   5. How many stripes are there in the flag?

6. What date is the Day of Independence?
7. Independence from whom?
8. What country did we fight during the Revolutionary War?
9. Who was the first president of the United States?
10. What do we call a change in the constitution?

REDESIGNED TEST: Sample U.S. Citizenship Test Questions

1. Name one war fought by the United States in the 1900s.
2. What did Susan B. Anthony do?
3. What is one thing Benjamin Franklin is famous for?
4. There were 13 original states. Name three.
5. What is one responsibility that is only for United States citizens?
6. What does the judicial branch do?
7. Name your U.S. Representative.
8. Who makes federal laws?
9. What does the Constitution do?
10. What is the supreme law of the land?

# 300 Million and Counting

*Joel Garreau*

Joel Garreau is the author of several books on culture and values, most recently *Radical Evolution: The Promise and Peril of Enhancing Our Minds, Our Bodies, and What It Means to Be Human* (2005). He served as a senior fellow at George Mason University and the University of California at Berkeley. Garreau is also a reporter and editor at the *Washington Post*. This essay appeared in the October 2006 issue of *Smithsonian Magazine*.

## CONNECTING TO THE TOPIC

At the end of 2006, the United States reached the population milestone of approximately 300 million residents. This figure represents a body of people, who, at one time or another, arrived here from someplace else. With the exception of Native Americans, the people living in this country came with little more than a plan to succeed in a new land. Some came by ship and later, airplane;

and many arrived on foot, crossing borders from the north and south. In the next essay, author Joel Garreau explores what this milestone means to a nation of immigrants.

## WORDS IN CONTEXT

**demographics** (1)    the statistical study of populations and population trends (n.)
**tipping point** (2)    the moment or event where many small factors add up to create a significant event or change (n.)
**protracted** (11)    drawn-out (adj.)
**fortuitous** (13)    lucky, fortunate (adj.)
**formidable** (16)    significant (adj.)
**anomalous** (24)    unusual, unlikely, unexpected (adj.)

1    People in the **demographics** business like to think of themselves as the only futurists you can trust. They've got a point: if you want to know how many 21-year-olds there will be in 2027, just count the number of infants living today. Absent a catastrophe of biblical proportions, you'll come up with a pretty good prediction.

2    What demographers admit they're not so good at is anticipating change. (For example, they were terrible at projecting the impact of birth control.) At the height of the "population explosion" hysteria four decades ago, few believed that birthrates could fall so far and so fast that the population of a major country like Russia would actually start shrinking (as it did about 14 years ago). Germany's **tipping point** seems to have arrived in 2002, and Japan's in 2005.

3    So what are we to make of the moment, projected by the U.S. Census Bureau to arrive this month, when the population of the United States reaches 300 million, behind only that of China and India? Demographics are simply the arithmetic of culture and values—it only quantifies, it doesn't explain. Is 300 million a good thing? A bad thing? Thinking about that number provides an opportunity to talk about where we're headed and what makes us tick.

4    Readers who remember November 20, 1967, when the population of the United States passed 200 million, may recall the predictions of Paul R. Ehrlich. In *The Population Bomb*, in 1968, he foretold "certain" mass starvation by 1975 because of population growth. "The battle to feed all of humanity is over," Ehrlich's first sentence read. "In the 1970s and 1980s

hundreds of millions of people will starve to death in spite of any crash programs," he declared. At best, North America and Europe would have to undergo "mild" food rationing within the decade as starvation and riots swept across Asia, Latin America, Africa and the Arab countries; at worst, the turmoil in a foodless Third World would set off a series of international crises leading to thermonuclear war.

5    Of course, things didn't quite work out that way. The problem in the United States is obesity. Even in places like Somalia and Sudan, famines have been intractable not because of any global lack of food, but because the food has not gotten to the people who need it—too often because corrupt regimes have withheld it as a means of political control. Nonetheless, Ehrlich's misjudgment sold more than three million copies, and the phrase "population bomb" entered the vocabulary.

6    That's why some people find it hard to wrap their minds around the big news in demographic circles today. It's not catastrophic population growth. It's catastrophic population shrinkage.

7    Yes, shrinkage. True, the total global population has not yet finished increasing. But nearly half the world's population lives in countries where the native-born are not reproducing fast enough to replace themselves. This is true in Western Europe, Eastern Europe, Russia, Japan, Canada and the United States. It's also true in much of East Asia, pockets of Latin America and such Indian megacities as New Delhi, Mumbai (Bombay), Kolkata (Calcutta) and Chennai (Madras). Even China is reproducing at levels that fall short of replacement.

8    Typically, a couple has to produce about 2.1 children to replace themselves, allowing for death among the young. Even in traditionally Catholic countries in Europe, the birthrate has dropped to shockingly low levels in the last two generations: 1.3 in both Italy and Spain in 2005. In metropolitan Tokyo, the rate dropped to 0.98. In Hong Kong and Macau, it hit 0.96 and a hitherto unthinkable 0.84, respectively, the latter the lowest on record. Few demographers ever dreamed that in the absence of war, famine and pestilence—in fact, as a result of urbanization, development and education—birthrates would drop so dramatically. No one knows where the bottom is. Keep this up, and eventually your civilization will disappear.

9    The United States' population is growing at the rate of almost 1 percent per year, thanks in part to immigration and its secondary effects. Not only does the United States accept more legal immigrants as permanent residents than the rest of the world combined, but these recent arrivals tend

to have more children than established residents—until, as their descendants attain affluence and education, the birthrates of these Americans also drop below replacement levels. Overall—that is, counting both immigrants and the native-born—the United States has a replacement rate of 2.03.

10 Nearly half of the nation's children under 5 belong to a racial or ethnic minority. The face of the future is already in our schools: our kindergartens now prefigure the country as a whole, circa 2050—a place where non-Hispanic whites are a slight majority. High-achieving school systems are already adapting: in Fairfax County, Virginia, for example, where 93 percent of all high-school graduates go on to post-secondary education, programs that teach English as a second language accommodate more than 100 native tongues, including more than five flavors of Chinese.

11 Few Americans quarrel with the idea of legal immigration. Not only is it part of the national narrative, but we're especially delighted when these immigrants help create companies such as Intel, eBay and Google. Of course large numbers of people showing up without paperwork stirs passions, as attested to this year by the rise of the Minuteman Project of civilians patrolling the border with Mexico, the deployment of National Guard troops to do the same, the **protracted** debate over immigration bills in Congress and the stark demonstrations related to the legislation.

12 However that debate is resolved, it's probably worth noting a few historical assimilation practices in the United States. First, this country has a long and distinguished record of taking illiterate peasants from every desert, tundra and bog and turning them into overfed suburbanites in three generations or less. Second, new immigrants usually do not marry outside their ethnic group; their adult children do, with some controversy, and their adult grandchildren can't remember what the fuss was all about. Finally, the traditional deal America has offered immigrants is: work, pay taxes, learn English, send your kids to school and stay out of trouble with the law, and we'll pretty much leave you alone.

13 One **fortuitous** result of the enormous wave of immigrants coming to the United States is that the median age here is only a little over 35, one of the lowest among the world's more developed countries. This country also has the most productive population per person of any country on the planet—no matter how you measure it, and especially compared with Japan and the members of the European Union.

14 This is crucial to everyone who plans to retire, because once you do, you'll want a bunch of young, hardworking, tax-paying people supporting you, whether directly, through family contributions, or indirectly, through

Social Security or pension programs. Unless you're rich enough to live off your investments, there is no alternative. As it happens, retirement is on the minds of many, and not just in the United States.

15    Today, virtually every developed country's population is older, typically, than that of just about every human society before 1950.

16    Much has been written about how hard it's going to be for European countries and Japan to support their aging populations at the generous level of social services to which previous generations have become accustomed. But global graying offers an even more **formidable** challenge to less wealthy countries.

17    By 2025, according to the United Nations and the U.S. Census Bureau, China will account for less than a fifth of the world's population, but almost a fourth of the world's people over 65, many of them in China's poorest areas. That means that in less than 20 years, large parts of China will have to support very aged populations on very low average incomes.

18    This is a problem Americans should be grateful they don't have, for all sorts of reasons.

19    First, China's version of Social Security is a colossal mess, even by the standards of the American and European systems. It covers only about a sixth of all workers. Its unfunded liabilities appear to exceed the country's total gross national product—maybe by a lot.

20    Second, the ages-old Chinese practice of adult children supporting their parents is coming undone. Traditionally, that obligation has passed through males; daughters are supposed to help support their husbands' parents before seeing to their own. But there's a problem here: because of Chinese population control, a woman turning 60 in 2025 will likely have had fewer than two children in her lifetime, and the odds are about one in three that she will not have borne a son.

21    If you're old and poor and you can't rely on either your government or your grown children for support, you have to keep working. In China, this does not mean greeting customers at Wal-Mart, much less answering the technical support line at Dell. Many of China's elderly barely have a primary school education, live in rural areas and haven't had the food and health care that would allow them to be vigorous in their old age. Nonetheless, the only work available to them is farming, which without mechanized tools is a tough row to hoe.

22    It's not a pretty future. Even if China's economy continues to grow by 8 percent per year, every year, for two decades—a scenario that is difficult to construct—the older generation is in big trouble. "China's outlook for

population aging," political economist Nicholas Eberstadt writes, is "a slow-motion humanitarian tragedy already underway."

23    But not even China is as bad off as Russia. Americans talk about age 40 being the new 30 and 80 being the new 60, but in Russia, 30 is the new 40. Since the 1960s, just about each new generation of Russians has become more fragile than the one that preceded it. Every year, 700,000 more Russians die than are born.

24    "Pronounced long-term deterioration of public health in an industrialized society during peacetime is a highly **anomalous**, indeed counterintuitive proposition for the modern sensibility," Eberstadt writes. "Nevertheless, over the four decades between 1961–62 and 2003, life expectancy at birth in Russia fell by nearly five years for males." What's more, he notes, this increased mortality was concentrated among working-age men: "Between 1970–71 and 2003, for example, every female cohort between the ages of 25 and 59 suffered at least a 40 percent increase in death rates; for men between the ages of 30 and 64, the corresponding figures uniformly exceeded 50 percent, and some cases exceeded 80 percent."

25    Demographers and public health specialists are at a loss to explain these awful numbers, though such obvious factors as diet, smoking, drinking and sedentary lifestyles certainly enter in. One mystery in the "ongoing Russian health disaster," Eberstadt adds, "is that the problem looks to be worse than the sum of its parts: that is to say, death rates are significantly higher than one would predict on the basis of observed risk factors alone."

26    Whatever the answer, the future is grim: a Russian man has barely a fifty-fifty chance of making it to age 65 while, in the developed world, the over-80s make up the fastest-growing portion of the population.

27    Are you feeling any more comfortable with America's healthier, younger 300 million by now? Wait, there's more.

28    At the rate ethnic Germans are not reproducing, they will probably lose the equivalent of the entire population of the former East Germany by mid-century. Who will fill up the rest of the country? Immigrants from Muslim countries are the odds-on bet. But as last year's riots in France and subway bombings in England demonstrate, Europe is not having a lot of luck assimilating its immigrants. In the Netherlands, for example, where nationality is based on ancient ties to family or land, concepts that seem unremarkable in North America—such as "Moroccan-Americans" or "Moroccan-Canadians"—simply have no meaning. The Dutch language offers two words: *autochtonen* ("us") and *allochtonen* ("them"); the Dutch people are still working to find ways to incorporate the latter into the former.

29    And yet: just about the time you start feeling comparatively good about living in a nice, young, healthy, assimilationist United States, you get smacked upside the head by the mind-boggling and peculiarly American problems this country's growth creates.

30    One is that to accommodate our growth of almost 1 percent a year—about 2.8 million new Americans annually—we have to build the equivalent of one Chicago per year. That's not impossible. Lord knows we have enough developers eager to do the job. What's more, if you fly across this country and look down, you will see that it includes a lot of emptiness. If you are among those people stuck in endless traffic jams from Boston to Richmond and from San Diego to Santa Barbara, you may find this hard to believe, but only 4 percent of all the land in the contiguous United States is urbanized, and only 5.5 percent is developed.

31    The problem is that we want to build these new Chicagos in nice places—the Mediterranean climes of California, or the deserts of Phoenix and Las Vegas, or near the oceans or the Gulf of Mexico. (More than half the American population already lives within coastal counties of the Atlantic, Pacific, Gulf of Mexico or Great Lakes.) The mountains will also do, which is why you see explosive growth near Virginia's Blue Ridge, the Gold Country of the California Sierra and even the Big Sky Country of Montana.

32    Unfortunately, in our search for new utopias we don't merely pave over paradise; we massively annoy the planet. Natural disasters are getting more expensive not only because the weather is getting worse but also because we keep putting our new Chicagos in harm's way.

33    What are the morals of these recitations?

34    Two leap to mind.

35    The first is, whenever you start thinking that this country is screwed up beyond redemption, it pays to travel beyond our borders. It's amazing how often the not-so-wonderful realities that we think of as terrible problems constitute other people's dreams.

36    The second is, demographics may not be destiny. But the numerical study of who we are and how we got that way does have a refreshing habit of focusing our attention on what's important, long-term, about our culture and values—where we're headed, and what makes us tick. ◆

## CONSIDERING THE ISSUES

1. Do you think there are too many people living in the United States? Too few? Is your view of immigration laws and trends

influenced at all by your understanding of U.S. population numbers?

2. What problems does U.S. immigration create today? Where do people settle? What challenges do we face that our forebearers did not?

## CRAFT AND CONTENT

1. How does Garreau use history and demographic data to support his argument? Explain. What are the limits of demographic data? What can it tell us about U.S. population and culture?

2. Summarize Garreau's argument in this essay? What does he think should be done about U.S. immigration policies, and why?

## CRITICAL THINKING

1. Garreau notes that the "problems" of immigration—both legal and illegal—are minimal when you look at history. "This country has a long and distinguished record of taking illiterate peasants from every desert, tundra and bog and turning them into overfed suburbanites in three generations or less." How does he support this view?

2. What is happening to the world's population? What might current population trends mean for other countries?

## WRITING ABOUT THE ISSUES

1. Why is it important to the United States that immigration continues, largely at current levels? How is the United States dependent of immigration to remain a viable force in the global economy? Write an essay exploring the importance of immigration to the United States and its role in sustaining population growth and the financial stability of the country.

2. Garreau states that the next time you find yourself criticizing the United States, you should go abroad and see how difficult people in some other nations have it. Respond to this assertion with your own viewpoint. If you have been abroad, compare the issues facing those countries with those Garreau outlines in his article.

# Educating Illegal Immigrants

*Todd Rosenbaum*

The next essay is an editorial by student Todd Rosenbaum that was published in the March 14, 2006, issue of the *Cavalier Daily*, the student newspaper of the University of Virginia. Rosenbaum, a political philosophy and American studies major, wrote this article during his senior year.

## CONNECTING TO THE TOPIC

Many students take for granted their right to an education. Rosenbaum asks his fellow students to consider the immigration argument from a different perspective—that of students who are children of illegal aliens. Should the children of illegal immigrants be entitled to the same educational benefits as legal U.S. residents? And if not, who suffers more? By barring such children from the educations that may help make them productive members of society, are laws such as the one Rosenbaum challenges doing more harm than good?

## WORDS IN CONTEXT

**ubiquitous** (4)   very common, found everywhere (adj.)
**naturalization** (6)   the process of becoming a citizen (n.)
**viable** (6)   likely, plausible (adj.)

1   Imagine that you're a 20-year-old University student—this should be a relatively easy exercise for many of you. You've got the entire world at your feet, a wealth of opportunities which are not afforded to those without a college degree. Now imagine that you're suddenly forced to withdraw from school because you can no longer afford tuition. Suddenly, all of those opportunities you had a split-second ago vanish. If only you were granted in-state tuition, you could afford to stay. But you're not, and here's the clincher: You've lived in Virginia for the past 10 years.

2   Sadly, this is reality for many students who reside in the Commonwealth of Virginia. They are the sons and daughters of illegal immigrants, who came to the United States as children with no say in their destinies. And a few Virginia lawmakers are doing all they can to make it difficult for them

to enroll in Virginia's public colleges and universities. By not extending in-state tuition to these students, most of them are effectively barred from attending our public institutions of higher education because they cannot afford to. As non-U.S. citizens, they do not qualify for student loans or grants. Chances for them to improve their own situations are starkly limited.

3    It should not be our lawmakers' prerogative to discriminate against them because of their parents' decisions. Instead, they should focus on helping young illegal immigrants in Virginia to establish legal status. This also means affording them opportunities which will allow them to develop as productive and responsible members of our society.

4    Comforted by our **ubiquitous** diversity statements and anti-discrimination clauses, we are often fooled into thinking that discrimination like this no longer exists in the United States. But some Virginia lawmakers have tried unsuccessfully in the past to ban outright the enrollment of illegal immi-grants in Virginia's institutions of higher education. Now, they are seeking to keep most illegal immigrants out of our colleges and universities by en-suring that in-state tuition rates are never extended to them. Federal statute backs this discriminatory attitude: states are forbidden to extend higher-education benefits to students who reside here illegally, if the benefits are not extended to all non-U.S. citizens. Any state law that violates this statute would require a successful legal challenge in federal court in order to be upheld.

5    But why should we extend these benefits to those who have chosen to disregard our immigration laws? Again, young illegal immigrants rarely make the choice to immigrate on their own. More importantly, there is also federal constitutional precedent for affording illegal immigrants edu-cational benefits.

6    A 1982 Supreme Court case ensured that those residing in the United States are able to attend public primary and secondary schools regardless of their legal statuses. Many of the students who have benefited from that decision are now graduating from our nation's public high schools—fully capable of excelling in college, but unable to afford to do so. Many of them have taken steps towards **naturalization** and are awaiting approval, which can take years. Others are unable to afford the application costs which accompany the naturalization process. Returning to their countries of origin, after having made so much educational progress, is hardly a **viable** option.

7    At the same time, lawmakers must be sensitive to how a law which ex-tends in-state tuition to illegal immigrants residing in Virginia could impact

its general policy on who qualifies for in-state rates. Offering reduced tuition for undocumented residents of the state could legally bind Virginia to extend in-state rates to all out-of-state students, hardly a realistic option.

8    A compromise worthy of attention has been proposed which would not extend in-state tuition to illegal immigrants in general, but would make an exception for those who have a history in Virginia. For example, graduating from high school here, belonging to a family that pays taxes and actively seeking legal residency could together form acceptable criteria. According to the *Washington Post*, this could allow up to a few thousand illegal immigrants who reside in Virginia a chance to attend college here.

9    For those who worry about illegal immigrants' drain on our state and national resources, it seems counterintuitive to oppose such legislation. In the long term, allowing these immigrants improved access to higher education is likely to improve their contributions to our society and reduce the burdens they place on it. It will only aid us to help those who are willing and eager to improve their own situations to do so.  ◆

## CONSIDERING THE ISSUES

1. Rosenbaum states, "It should not be our lawmakers' prerogative to discriminate against them because of their parents' decisions." Should children of illegal immigrants be penalized for their parents' choices?
2. Should the children of illegal immigrants be granted the same rights as children of U.S. citizens? Is this a moral/ethical issue of extending opportunities to all children in this country? Or is it a legal one? Explain.

## CRAFT AND CONTENT

1. Rosenbaum encourages his readers to "imagine" they are university students. How does this introductory exercise help lead into his argument? Explain.
2. Summarize Rosenbaum's argument and outline his supporting points.

## CRITICAL THINKING

1. Rosenbaum asks, "Why should we extend benefits to those who have chosen to disregard our immigration laws?" What answer

does he give for this rhetorical question? Do you agree with his viewpoint?

2. What reasons does Rosenbaum give for extending state funding for education to the children of illegal immigrants?

## WRITING ABOUT THE ISSUES

1. Write a response to Rosenbaum's editorial in the form of a letter to the editor of the student newspaper, the *Cavalier Daily*.

2. Rosenbaum raises an important and interesting question—why should we, in effect, punish the children of illegal immigrants for decisions made by their parents? Imagine you were raised in the United States but not afforded citizenship because of your parents' status. What rights would you expect? How would you react if you were barred from the rights enjoyed by your peers?

# Blog Matters

A blog ("web log") is an online diary or commentary site that features regular entries that describe events, impressions, and viewpoints. Blogs may contain text, images, video, and often link to other websites, blogs, and online media. Most blogs allow readers to comment on the content of the post and to each other. As of 2007, the blog search engine estimated there were over 112 million blogs. While many blogs are maintained by individuals, some are run by journals, newspapers, and other media outlets. Remember that most blogs are not monitored for factual accuracy, and often express the opinion and views of the "blogger" writing the content.

The blog below is written by journalist Marc Cooper. Cooper serves on the faculty of the USC Annenberg School where he teaches reporting and writing in the graduate journalism program. He is also associate director of Annenberg's Institute for Justice and Journalism.

# What Dream?

*Marc Cooper*
*October 25, 2007*

1   I'm speaking on a panel about immigration on Friday so I've been thinking quite a bit about the issue. Mostly, I've been trying to find the words to express my sadness if not my revulsion over the latest chapter in Congressional fecklessness. Two days ago, the Senate killed off the last, agonizing chance of any immigration reform during the 2008 session when it refused to pass the so-called Dream Act.

2   Truth is, I can't find those words. Can't find them because there is, indeed, no rational reason to have opposed the legislation—except for good, old-fashioned xenophobic scapegoating.

3   In this case, then, I will cede the word to columnist Eugene Robinson, who pretty much sums up my disgust:

4   *Has America become a mean, ungenerous, cramped and crabby nation, a deeply insecure colossus—one that just might be taking all those Viagra and Cialis commercials a bit too personally? Is the country desperate to find scapegoats for a perceived decline in, um, vigor? Or is America still a confident land of hope and promise, a place still potent with possibility?*

5   *The Senate vote Wednesday in which Republicans, supported by a handful of red-state Democrats, narrowly scuttled the Dream Act, a bill that would have provided a path to citizenship for some young undocumented immigrants—but only those who did everything this country once found worthy and admirable in pursuit of the American dream.*

6   *Under the proposal, men and women who fulfilled several conditions—they had to be under 30, had to have been brought into the country illegally before they were 16, had to have been in the United States for at least five years and had to be graduates of U.S. high schools—would have been given conditional legal status. If they went on to complete two years of college or two years of military service, they would have been eligible for permanent residency . . .*

7   In case you didn't understand, this act was aimed at young people who were brought here by their parents, kids who had no choice, who have grown up here, and who would be given legal status only by entering college or the military.

8    Wouldn't want that, would we? Better that they remain in the shadows, unable in many cases to go to college. Better they dedicate themselves, then, to some black market activity rather than be "rewarded" for decent, civil behavior and their contributions to the greater society.

9    This episode gives new dimensions of meaning to the phrase The American Dream. More like, dream on.

### *Listener* Says:
### *October 26th, 2007 at 12:07 PM*

Yep, Marc. We're stuck between countervailing forces. Immobilized. Unable to go forwards or backwards. Our collective inability to act (pro or con on any level) pretty much means we get to watch what happens, as it happens over time. The 'ambulatory' among us (corporate, business or individual) have the ability to move with (or, against) the tides for as long as those resources allow. The rest of us will have to simply bob along and let this *force of nature* wash us ashore—somewhere— wherever those currents decide to drop us. Interesting times.

### *Madan Ahluwalia* Says:
### *October 26th, 2007 at 1:16 PM*

Without education, we are all dead. There is a saying "there is no difference between a man who cannot read and one who does not want to read." It simply emphasizes the importance of education.

More education is only good—especially educating the children and making them better citizens of the world, let alone America. I feel that candidates are too afraid to vote on sensitive immigration issues to lose their conservative electorate.

### *Bill Bradley* Says:
### *October 28th, 2007 at 9:54 AM*

You'll recall last year—when all these changes in immigration law were "inevitable"—I pointed out that there were many deep political flaws in that view.

So long as most voters don't feel that there is a serious effort to secure the borders, or that immigrants here are interested in being part of mainstream American society, none of these things will happen. ◆

### RESPOND TO THE BLOG:

What do you think? Was the Senate wrong to not pass the DREAM act? Are we perpetuating a cycle of poverty by not offering immigrant children educational opportunity?

# Immigration Quotas Versus Individual Rights: The Moral and Practical Case for Open Immigration

*Harry Binswanger*

Harry Binswanger is an American philosopher and writer and a board member of the Ayn Rand Institute. He is the author of *The Ayn Rand Lexicon* (1988) and *The Biological Basis of Teleological Concepts* (1990). This essay was published in *Capitalism Magazine,* April 2, 2006.

### CONNECTING TO THE TOPIC

When people raise the issue of immigration, they usually focus on illegal immigrants—people who enter the country without going through proper legal channels. As of 2007, the United States accepts more legal immigrants as permanent residents than any other country in the world. The United States grants legal immigrant status to over 700,000 people each year, not including refugee admissions. While it is difficult to determine exact numbers, another estimated 500,000 people come to the United States illegally. Estimates of the number of illegal immigrants currently residing in the United States range from 10 to 13 million. In the next essay, philosophy professor Harry Binswanger explains why he feels all people, regardless of immigration quotas, should be allowed to immigrate to the United States. No one, he explains should be considered illegal, and all people, with a few exceptions he outlines, should be granted residency rights. It is not an issue of law, but an issue of human rights.

### WORDS IN CONTEXT

**coercive** (5)   bullying, forceful (adj.)
**implicit** (9)   unstated but understood (adj.)
**dichotomy** (17)   a pair of opposing concepts (n.)

**qua** (18)   in the capacity of, as (prep.)
**jettisoning** (21)   tossing aside, abandoning (v.)
**fallacy** (27)   misleading belief, faulty idea (n.)
**protectionist** (27)   protecting domestic workers and industries from international competition (adj.)
**finite** (27)   limited (adj.)

1   This is a defense of phasing-in open immigration into the United States. Entry into the U.S. should ultimately be free for any foreigner, with the exception of criminals, would-be terrorists, and those carrying infectious diseases. (And note: I am defending freedom of entry and residency, not the automatic granting of U.S. citizenship).

2   An end to immigration quotas is demanded by the principle of individual rights. Every individual has rights as an individual, not as a member of this or that nation. One has rights not by virtue of being an American, but by virtue of being human.

3   One doesn't have to be a resident of any particular country to have a moral entitlement to be secure from governmental coercion against one's life, liberty, and property. In the words of the Declaration of Independence, government is instituted "to secure these rights"—to protect them against their violation by force or fraud.

4   A foreigner has rights just as much as an American. To be a foreigner is not to be a criminal. Yet our government treats as criminals those foreigners not lucky enough to win the green-card lottery. Seeking employment in this country is not a criminal act. It coerces no one and violates no one's rights (there is no "right" to be exempt from competition in the labor market, or in any other market).

5   It is not a criminal act to buy or rent a home here in which to reside. Paying for housing is not a **coercive** act—whether the buyer is an American or a foreigner. No one's rights are violated when a Mexican, or Canadian, or Senegalese rents an apartment from an American owner and moves into the housing he is paying for. And what about the rights of those American citizens who want to sell or rent their property to the highest bidders? Or the American businesses that want to hire the lowest-cost workers? It is morally indefensible for our government to violate their right to do so, just because the person is a foreigner.

6     Immigration quotas forcibly exclude foreigners who want not to seize but to purchase housing here, who want not to rob Americans but to engage in productive work, raising our standard of living. To forcibly exclude those who seek peacefully to trade value for value with us is a violation of the rights of both parties to such a trade: the rights of the American seller or employer and the rights of the foreign buyer or employee.

7     Thus, immigration quotas treat both Americans and foreigners as if they were criminals, as if the peaceful exchange of values to mutual benefit were an act of destruction.

8     To take an actual example, if I want to invite my Norwegian friend Klaus to live in my home, either as a guest or as a paying tenant, what right does our government have to stop Klaus and me? To be a Norwegian is not to be a criminal. And if some American business wants to hire Klaus, what right does our government have to interfere?

9     The **implicit** premise of barring foreigners is: "This is our country, we let in who we want." But who is "we"? The government does not own the country. Jurisdiction is not ownership. Only the owner of land or any item of property can decide the terms of its use or sale. Nor does the majority own the country. This is a country of private property, and housing is private property. So is a job.

10     American land is not the collective property of some entity called "the U.S. government." Nor is there such thing as collective, social ownership of the land. The claim, "We have the right to decide who is allowed in" means some individuals—those with the most votes–claim the right to prevent other citizens from exercising their rights. But there can be no right to violate the rights of others.

11     Our constitutional republic respects minority rights. Sixty percent of the population cannot vote to enslave the other 40%. Nor can a majority dictate to the owners of private property. Nor can a majority dictate on whom private employers spend their money. Not morally, not in a free society. In a free society, the rights of the individual are held sacrosanct, above any claim of even an overwhelming majority.

12     The rights of one man end where the rights of his neighbor begin. Only within the limits of his rights is a man free to act on his own judgment. The criminal is the man who deliberately steps outside his rights-protected domain and invades the domain of another, depriving his victim of his exclusive control over his property, or liberty, or life. The criminal, by his

own choice, has rejected rights in favor of brute violence. Thus, an immigration policy that excludes criminals is proper.

13    Likewise, a person with an infectious disease, such as smallpox, threatens with serious physical harm those with whom he comes into proximity. Unlike the criminal, he may not intend to do damage, but the threat of physical harm is clear, present, and objectively demonstrable. To protect the lives of Americans, he may be kept out or quarantined until he is no longer a threat.

14    But what about the millions of Mexicans, South Americans, Chinese, Canadians, etc. seeking entry who are not criminal and not bearing infectious diseases? By what moral principle can they be excluded? Not on the grounds of majority vote, not on the grounds of protecting any American's rights, not on the grounds of any legitimate authority of the state.

## The Moral and the Practical

15    That's the moral case for phasing out limits on immigration. But some ask: "Is it practical? Wouldn't unlimited immigration—even if phased in over a decade—be disastrous to our economic well-being and create overcrowding? Are we being told to just grit our teeth and surrender our interests in the name of morality?"

16    This question is invalid on its face. It shows a failure to understand the nature of rights, and of moral principles generally. Rational moral principles reflect recognition of the basic nature of man, his nature as a specific kind of living organism, having a specific means of survival. Questions of what is practical, what is to one's self-interest, can be answered only in that context. It is neither practical nor to one's interest to attempt to live and act in defiance of one's nature as a human being.

17    Yet that is the meaning of the moral-practical **dichotomy**. When one claims, "It is immoral but practical," one is maintaining, "It cripples my nature as a human being, but it is beneficial to me"—which is a contradiction.

18    Rights, in particular, are not something pulled from the sky or decreed by societal whim. Rights are moral principles, established by reference to the needs inherent in man's nature **qua** man.

19    Every organism has a basic means of survival; for man, that means is: reason. Man is the rational animal, homo sapiens. Rights are moral principles that spell out the terms of social interaction required for a rational being to survive and flourish. Since the reasoning mind cannot function under physical coercion, the basic social requirement of man's survival is: freedom. Rights prescribe freedom by proscribing coercion.

20    Rights reflect the fundamental alternative of voluntary consent or brute force. The reign of force is in no one's interest; the system of voluntary cooperation by mutual consent is the precondition of anyone achieving his actual interests.

21    To ignore the principle of rights means **jettisoning** the principled, moral resolution of conflicts, and substituting mere numbers (majority vote). That is not to anyone's interest. Tyranny is not to anyone's self-interest.

22    Rights establish the necessary framework within which one defines his legitimate self-interest. One cannot hold that one's self-interest requires that he be "free" to deprive others of their freedom, treating their interests as morally irrelevant. One cannot hold that recognizing the rights of others is moral but "impractical."

23    Since rights are based on the requirements of man's life as a rational being, there can be no conflict between the moral and the practical here: if respecting individual rights requires it, your interest requires it.

24    Freedom or force, reason or compulsion—that is the basic social alternative. Immigrants recognize the value of freedom—that's why they seek to come here.

25    The American Founders defined and implemented a system of rights because they recognized that man, as a rational being, must be free to act on his own judgment and to keep the products of his own effort. They did not intend to establish a system in which those who happen to be born here could use force to "protect" themselves from the peaceful competition of others.

## Economics

26  One major fear of open immigration is economic: the fear of losing one's job to immigrants. It is asked: "Won't the immigrants take our jobs?" The answer is: "Yes, so we can go on to better, higher-paying jobs."

27    The **fallacy** in this **protectionist** objection lies in the idea that there is only a **finite** amount of work to be done. The unstated assumption is: "If Americans don't get to do that work, if foreigners do it instead, we Americans will have nothing to do."

28    But work is the creation of wealth. A job is a role in the production of goods and services—the production of food, of cars, computers, the providing of internet content—all the items that go to make up our standard of living. A country cannot have too much wealth. The need for wealth is limitless, and the work that is to be done is limitless.

29      From a grand, historical perspective, we are only at the beginning of the wealth-creating age. The wealth Americans produce today is as nothing compared to what we'll have 200 years from now—just as the standard of living 200 years in the past, in 1806, was as nothing compared to ours today.

30      Unemployment is not caused by an absence of avenues for the creation of wealth. Unemployment is caused by government interference in the labor market. Even with that interference, the number of jobs goes relentlessly upward, decade after decade. This bears witness to the fact that there's no end to the creation of wealth and thus no end to the useful employment of human intelligence and the physical effort directed by that intelligence. There is always more productive work to be done. If you can give your job to an immigrant, you can get a more valuable job.

31      What is the effect of a bigger labor pool on wage rates? If the money supply is constant, nominal wage rates fall. But real wage rates rise, because total output has gone up. Economists have demonstrated that real wages have to rise as long as the immigrants are self-supporting. If immigrants earn their keep, if they don't consume more than they produce, then they add to total output, which means that prices fall (if the money supply is constant).

32      And, in fact, rising real wages was the history of our country in the nineteenth century. Before the 1920s, there were no limits on immigration, yet our standard of living rocketed upward. Self-supporting immigrants were an economic benefit, not an injury.

33      The protectionist objection that immigrants take away jobs and harm our standard of living is a solid economic fallacy.

## Welfare

34 A popular misconception is that immigrants come here to get welfare. To the extent that is true, immigrants do constitute a burden. But this issue is mooted by the passage, under the Clinton Administration, of the Personal Responsibility and Work Opportunity and Reconciliation Act (PRWORA), which makes legal permanent residents ineligible for most forms of welfare for 5 years. I support this kind of legislation.

35      Further, if the fear is of non-working immigrants, why is the pending legislation aimed at employers of immigrants?

## Overcrowding

36 America is a vastly underpopulated country. Our population density is less than one-third of France's.

37    Take an extreme example. Suppose a tidal wave of immigrants came here. Suppose that half of the people on the planet moved here. That would mean an unthinkable eleven-fold increase in our population—from 300 million to 3.3 billion people. That would make America almost as "densely" populated as today's England (360 people/sq. km. vs. 384 people/sq. km.). In fact, it would make us less densely populated than the state of New Jersey (453 per sq. km.). And these calculations exclude Alaska and Hawaii, and count only land area.

38    Contrary to widespread beliefs, high population density is a value, not a disvalue. High population density intensifies the division of labor, which makes possible a wider variety of jobs and specialized consumer products. For instance, in Manhattan, there is a "doll hospital"—a store specializing in the repair of children's dolls. Such a specialized, niche business re-quires a high population density in order to have a market. Try finding a doll hospital in Poughkeepsie. In Manhattan, one can find a job as a Pilates Method teacher or as a "Secret Shopper" (two jobs actually listed on Craig's List). Not in Paducah.

39    People want to live near other people, in cities. One-seventh of Eng-land's population lives in London. If population density is a bad thing, why are Manhattan real-estate prices so high?

## The Value of Immigrants

40 Immigrants are the kind of people who refresh the American spirit. They are ambitious, courageous, and value freedom. They come here, often with no money and not even speaking the language, to seek a better life for themselves and their children.

41    The vision of American freedom, with its opportunity to prosper by hard work, serves as a magnet drawing the best of the world's people. Im-migrants are self-selected for their virtues: their ambitiousness, daring, in-dependence, and pride. They are willing to cast aside the tradition-bound roles assigned to them in their native lands and to re-define themselves as Americans. These are the people America needs in order to keep alive the individualist, hard-working attitude that made America.

42    Open immigration: the benefits are great. The right is unquestionable.
So let them come.  ◆

## CONSIDERING THE ISSUES

1. Do you think that the United States should limit the number of immigrants allowed to enter the country? What about restrictions on the number of refugees who can enter the United States?
2. Binswanger observes that foreigners do not deserve to be treated as criminals, yet U.S. citizens often think of them in this light. Do you think of illegal aliens as criminals? Why or why not?

## CRAFT AND CONTENT

1. Binswanger, who taught philosophy at the Ayn Rand Institute, references Rand several times in this essay. How do these references support the position he takes in his essay?
2. Evaluate Binswanger's tone, style, and language in this essay. How does he try to persuade his readers to agree with his point of view? What appeals does he make? Does he explore both sides of the issue? Explain.

## CRITICAL THINKING

1. Why does Binswanger believe immigration should be open to everyone? Do you agree with his perspective that entrance to the United States is a human right? Why or why not?
2. What distinction does Binswanger make between free and open residency and U.S. citizenship? Explain.
3. Who, according to Binswanger, should be excluded from entry to the United States? Do his criteria for exclusion run counter to his reasons for allowing all people to emigrate? Why or why not?

## WRITING ABOUT THE ISSUES

1. What rights should be granted to everyone? Do human rights extend beyond national borders? Write an essay in which you outline your own definition of human rights and discuss how these rights extend to immigration. If you wish, you may reference

the declaration of human rights ratified by the United Nations in 1948 at http://www.un.org/rights.

2. Binswanger's argument hinges on his audience's agreement that he is stating obvious moral truths. Create a list of reasons why foreigners should, or should not, be allowed unlimited access to the United States. Give at least one reason why each item on your list is an obvious truth.

# VISUAL CONNECTIONS

## Two Views of U.S. Immigration

### CONNECTING TO THE TOPIC

In 2005, over 1.2 million illegal immigrants were apprehended by the Border Patrol along the 2,000 mile U.S.–Mexico border. The Border Patrol itself admits a certain impotence in the situation, estimating that they catch only about one out of every four illegal border crossers. Proposed solutions range from opening the borders and broadening immigration quotas to building walls and deporting entire families. Current debate centers on what should be done to prevent illegal immigration and what to do with the immigrants who are already here. Should children receive health care? Education? Does providing such services unfairly tax legal residents? Who decides? The cartoons below consider two different viewpoints on illegal immigration.

## Border Fence

*Daryl Cagle*

# The Enemy Within?

*John Cole*

## CONSIDERING THE ISSUES

1. Consider the point of view of an immigrant to the United States by imagining your own journey to another country. Focusing on your feelings and goals, would you seek to assimilate and integrate in your new country, or merely live there for a while with the intention of one day returning to the United States? Would you learn the language? What employment, if any, would you seek? How would you raise a family? What concerns and fears might you have?

## CRITICAL THINKING

1. What is happening in each of these cartoons? What position does each cartoonist take on the issue of illegal immigration? How do their cartoons reflect current debate over immigration today?
2. What was your reaction to each of these cartoons? Do you think they fairly depict the issues at hand? Why or why not?
3. What visual elements contribute to the impression of each cartoon? What clichés do they use, and how do they twist visual clichés to make a point? Explain.

# The Next Americans

*Tomás R. Jiménez*

Tomás Jiménez teaches sociology at the University of California, San Diego. His research and teaching focus on immigration, assimilation, social mobility, and identity. His writing has appeared in many scholarly journals. He is a Fellow at the New American Foundation, where he writes about the role of government in immigrant assimilation. This article was published in the *Los Angeles Times* on May 27, 2007.

## CONNECTING TO THE TOPIC

Critics of immigration often assert that an influx of foreigners threatens the American way of life and our national identity. By refusing to assimilate, and demanding multicultural acceptance in government and in the classroom, immigrants are forcing Americans to be more like them, instead of the other way around. A June 2006 *NBC/Wall Street Journal* poll found the public evenly divided on the fundamental question of whether immigration helps or hurts the country, with 44 percent saying it helps and 45 percent saying it hurts the U.S. Are immigrants changing America's identity? Are they likely to hurt or help America in the long run? In the next article, sociology professor Tomás Jiménez explains why he thinks immigrants don't destroy our national identity—but, rather, they renew it.

## WORDS IN CONTEXT

**anarchist** (4)    an advocate of the overthrow of compulsory government (n.)
**cohesive** (8)    well integrated, unified (adj.)
**polyglot** (9)    able to speak or write many languages, multilingual (adj.)
**ubiquitous** (10)    being everywhere at once, omnipresent (adj.)
**prodigal** (12)    wasteful, recklessly extravagant with money (adj.)
**palpable** (13)    plainly seen or perceived; evident; tangible (adj.)

1    Behind the outcry over the controversial immigration reform legislation making its way through the Senate lies an unsettling question for many Americans. Should the bill become a reality, an estimated 12 million unauthorized immigrants, the vast majority of whom are Latino, would become eligible for citizenship immediately, and opportunities for millions of others to follow them would be created. What effect will these permanently settled immigrants have on American identity?

2    Some critics of the legislation are already arguing that inviting millions of immigrants to stay permanently in the U.S. and become citizens will hasten the fading of a cohesive nation. They say that immigrants may become more interwoven into the fabric of the United States, but the ethnic patches to which they bind their identities will remain all too distinguishable from the rest of the American quilt.

3    How immigrants and their descendants see themselves will change over time, and they will simultaneously transform many aspects of what it means to be an American. This is undoubtedly an uncomfortable process,

fraught with tension between newcomers and established Americans that can occasionally become explosive. But the real issue is whether the United States can provide opportunities for upward mobility so that immigrants can, in turn, fortify what is most essential to our nation's identity.

4    History is instructive on whether immigrants will create a messy patchwork of ethnicities in the U.S. About a century ago, a tide of Southern and Eastern European immigrants arriving on our shores raised fears similar to those we hear today. Then, as now, Americans worried that the newcomers were destroying American identity. Many were certain that Catholic immigrants would help the pope rule the United States from Rome, and that immigrant **anarchists** would destroy American democracy. Some eugenicists thought that the dark-skinned immigrants from Southern Europe would contaminate the American gene pool.

5    None of this came to pass, of course. The pope has no political say in American affairs, the United States is still a capitalist democracy, and there is nothing wrong with the American gene pool. The fact that these fears never materialized is often cited as proof that European-origin immigrants and their descendants successfully assimilated into an American societal monolith.

6    However, as sociologists Richard Alba and Victor Nee point out, much of the American identity as we know it today was shaped by previous waves of immigrants. For instance, they note that the Christian tradition of the Christmas tree and the leisure Sunday made their way into the American mainstream because German immigrants and their descendants brought these traditions with them. Where religion was concerned, Protestantism was the clear marker of the nonsecular mainstream. But because of the assimilation of millions of Jews and Catholics, we today commonly refer to an American "Judeo-Christian tradition," a far more encompassing notion of American religious identity than the one envisioned in the past.

7    Immigrants are also redefining American identity today, though there are differences. For one, assimilation no longer exclusively means shedding all remnants of ethnicity and adopting a way of life largely identified with Anglo Protestants. For instance, it was not at all uncommon in the early 20th century for teachers to give young immigrant pupils a stern rap across their knuckles for speaking their parents' mother tongue in school. By contrast, multiculturalism and the value of diversity are now widely adopted.

8    Although some see this as undercutting a **cohesive** U.S., we nonetheless regularly celebrate, even if sometimes superficially, the various ethnic

strands in our multicultural nation. Education, business and political leaders tout the virtues of diversity, and the world of commerce affirms ethnic identity through ethnically oriented marketing aimed at selling everything from laundry detergent to quinceañera celebration packages at Disneyland.

9     These differences from the past have not—and are not—reversing the course of assimilation, even if they have given it a new tone. There are notable signs that immigrants and their children are already adopting features of American identity as their own. Consider, for instance, language, a central front in debates over assimilation. The growth of non-English-speaking immigrant populations, particularly those that speak Spanish, and the explosive rise in commercial services and media that cater to them have led commentators such as Pat Buchanan to pronounce the coming of a **polyglot** society. But nothing appears to be further from the truth.

10     Even in Los Angeles County, where 36% of the population is foreign-born and more than half speak a language other than English at home, English is not losing out in the long run. According to a recent study by social scientists Rubén Rumbaut, Douglas Massey and Frank Bean, published in the *Population and Development Review,* the use of non-English languages virtually disappears among nearly all U.S.-born children of immigrants in the county. Spanish shows more staying power among the U.S.-born children and grandchildren of Mexican immigrants, which is not surprising given that the size of the Spanish-speaking population provides near-**ubiquitous** access to the language. But the survival of Spanish among U.S.-born descendants of Mexican immigrants does not come at the expense of their ability to speak English and, more strikingly, English overwhelms Spanish-language use among the grandchildren of these immigrants.

11     An equally telling sign of how much immigrants and their children are becoming "American" is how different they have become from those in their ethnic homelands. Virtually all of today's immigrants stay connected to their countries of origin. They send money to family members who remain behind. Relatively inexpensive air, rail and bus travel and the availability of cheap telecommunication and e-mail enable them stay in constant contact, and dual citizenship allows their political voices to be heard from abroad. These enduring ties might lead to the conclusion that continuity between here and there threatens loyalty to the Stars and Stripes.

12     But ask any immigrant or their children about a recent visit to their country of origin, and they are likely to tell you how American they felt. The family and friends they visit quickly recognize the **prodigal** children's

tastes for American styles, their American accents and their declining cultural familiarity with life in the ethnic homeland — all telltale signs that they've Americanized. As sociologist David Fitzgerald puts it, their assimilation into American society entails a good deal of "dissimilation" from the countries the immigrants left behind.

13   American identity is absorbing something quite significant from immigrants and being changed by them. Language, food, entertainment and holiday traditions are **palpable** aspects of American culture on which immigrants today, as in the past, are leaving their mark. Our everyday lexicon is sprinkled with Spanish words. We are now just as likely to grab a burrito as a burger. Hip-hop is tinged with South Asian rhythms. And Chinese New Year and Cinco de Mayo are taking their places alongside St. Patrick's Day as widely celebrated American ethnic holidays.

14   But these are not the changes to American identity that matter most. At its core, American identity is a shared belief in the United States as a land of opportunity—a place where those who work hard and display individual effort realize their ambitions. Today's immigrants, including the estimated 12 million that may soon become authorized, have the potential to fortify the idea of the United States as a land of opportunity. Their willingness to risk their lives to come here and the backbreaking work many of them do attest to their ambition.

15   But their capacity to refresh what is essential to American identity depends a great deal on our ability to stay true to its essence—to be a land of opportunity. This means that we should be, above all, concerned that the rungs on the ladder of economic mobility are sturdy and closely spaced.

16   If we are going to take on the formidable challenge of further integrating 12 million mostly poor immigrants, we have to provide better public schools, a more affordable college education, healthcare and jobs that offer a decent wage and benefits so that they and their children are able to rejuvenate the American dream. The real threat is not that immigrants will fail to buy into what's essential to American identity, but that we will fall short in providing them the tools to do so.  ◆

### CONSIDERING THE ISSUES

1.  Why does the prospect of 12 million Latino immigrants becoming citizens make so many people nervous? Do you think racism is a factor? What if 12 million Danish immigrants or 12 million Italian immigrants were at issue? Do you think critics of

immigration would voice the same concerns? What if the 12 million immigrants were not poor? Explain.

2. What is "American identity"? When immigration critics refer to the "American identity" what do they mean?

## CRAFT AND CONTENT

1. At the end of his essay, Jiménez provides a list of things the United States must do if it is to successfully integrate its 12 million illegal, mostly poor immigrants. Review this list and evaluate how it would be implemented. What are the economic and social costs of implementing such a list? Is it easy to say, but hard to do? Is the list missing anything you think is important?

2. How does Jiménez apply history and statistics to support his viewpoint? Explain.

## CRITICAL THINKING

1. Jiménez notes that throughout American history, citizens have feared that the next wave of immigrants would change America for the worse. What really happened? Can history predict what we can expect in the future?

2. Some Americans fear that the close connections between today's immigrant populations and their countries of origin threaten their loyalty to the United States and their commitment to American culture and society. What response does Jiménez provide to this concern? Do you agree with his argument? Why or why not?

## WRITING ABOUT THE ISSUES

1. Jiménez observes that past waves of immigrants—from Germany, Ireland, and Italy, for example—subtly left their mark on American identity. Icons such as the Christmas tree, Italian food, and St. Patrick's Day celebrations have become part of the "American fabric." Using the data in the table below (based on data on *legal* immigration to the United States from the 2000 U.S. Census and *2004 Yearbook of Immigration Statistics*) and what you have read about immigration and national identity in the essays in this chapter, write an essay projecting the impact current groups of

**Top Ten Foreign Countries—Foreign Born Population Among U.S. Immigrants**

| Country | Number per year | 2004 | 2010 (projected) |
|---|---|---|---|
| Mexico | 175,900 | 8,544,600 | 9,600,000 |
| India | 59,300 | 1,244,200 | 1,600,000 |
| Philippines | 47,800 | 1,413,200 | 1,700,000 |
| El Salvador | 33,500 | 899,000 | 1,100,000 |
| Dominican Republic | 24,900 | 791,600 | 941,000 |
| Canada | 24,200 | 774,800 | 920,000 |
| Korea | 17,900 | 772,600 | 880,000 |
| Cuba | 14,800 | 1,011,200 | 1,100,000 |

immigrants will make on American identity. What will be considered "American" 100 years from now?

2. Visit PBS's website for the program *Independent Lens: The New Americans* at http://www.pbs.org/independentlens/newamericans/index.html. Read some of the immigrant stories and pick one to write about. Explain why you feel that story is particularly compelling. Connect the story to points Jiménez raises in his article.

# TOPICAL CONNECTIONS

## GROUP PROJECTS

1. Interview a number of people who either immigrated to the United States or are in the country as legal residents (on student visas, etc.). Ask them to discuss their experiences as foreigners coming to live in the United States. Were they welcomed? Did they find a community to support them?

2. Are there particular traditions, practices, and behaviors that we expect new immigrants to adopt when they arrive in the United States? If so, what are they? Write an essay describing the things you think new immigrants should be willing to do in order to live in the United States.

3. Listen to Richard Gonzales's radio commentary, "Mexican Immigrants Weigh Issues of Assimilation" which aired on NPR October 8, 2004 (you can access this broadcast at the NPR

website). Gonzales explains that Mexican immigrants, who make up 37 percent of all recent immigrants, differ substantially from other immigrants in many categories. After listening to the report, discuss your reactions as a group. Like several other authors in this section, Gonzales focuses on issues connected to assimilation. What questions would you have liked to ask if you were allowed to call in to his program? As a group, prepare three questions and share them with the class.

## WEB PROJECT

1. Explore how ethnic and racial characteristics divide and unite us as a nation. According to the report *Changing America* by the President's Initiative on Race, the gaps among races and ethnic groups in the areas of education, jobs, economic status, health, housing, and criminal justice are substantial. Access this report online. Choose one subject area from its table of contents, and read through that chapter and charts. Then, summarize the information you have learned about the differences among the different racial and ethnic groups and discuss how you think these disparities affect our chances of creating a society in which all Americans can participate equally.

## FOR FURTHER INQUIRY

1. Several authors in this unit observe that every immigrant population was met with prejudice and suspicion. Research this phenomenon in greater depth with a particular immigrant group. For example, you could research impressions of the Irish arriving on the east coast during the early nineteenth century, or Japanese and Chinese groups arriving on the west coast in the late nineteenth century. What challenges did these groups face? How were they viewed by then-current citizens? How can their experience inform the current debate over immigration reform?
2. Research the Immigration and Nationality Act of 1952. Why was this act implemented, and whom did it affect? How did the Act change after 2001 and why? Discuss the act and whether it is in need of reform again. Offer suggestions for change, or support its tenets as currently outlined.

# 7 Is Climate Change a Pressing Problem or Pumped-up Propaganda?

The issue of climate change, also known as global warming, is at the forefront of political and public policy debates. Natural disasters, human health, biodiversity, endangered species, water resources, international trade, financial services, transportation networks, agriculture—virtually any area of human experience is in some way affected by climate. Environmental models predict that the earth's temperature is likely to rise between 2 and 11 degrees Fahrenheit (1 to 6 C) by 2100. And while most scientists and politicians agree that the earth is indeed getting warmer, they disagree on why and what it means.

The debate focuses on the cause of climate change, what, if anything, should be done about it, and what it means for the environment in years to come. An increase in global temperatures may lead to other changes in our ecosystem, such as a rising sea level, altered weather patterns, and the extinction of species of animals. Agricultural yields and coastal communities are also at risk.

A majority of scientists postulate that climate change and global warming are caused by the human use of fossil fuels, including coal, oil, and natural gas, all of which release carbon into the atmosphere and increase the greenhouse effect. They warn that if humans do not make changes that reduce greenhouse emissions, we could face catastrophic environmental consequences. On the other hand, some scientists and politicians question whether humans and the fuel they use are even the cause of increased greenhouse gases and postulate that rising temperatures are simply a normal aspect of a dynamic earth.

Scientists Roger Pielke Jr. and Daniel Sarewitz describe the debate as the "Cassandras" vs. the "Dorothies." The Cassandras—named for the Greek heroine cursed to predict the future but never to be believed—

## CRITICAL THINKING

1. What is happening in this cartoon? Who is the creature in the middle of the "footprint"? What does he represent?
2. What does the footprint mean? What is a "carbon footprint"? Why does it matter to the creature in the drawing?
3. What is the meaning of the words the creature is saying? How do they connect to who he is and what he represents?
4. Calculate your "carbon footprint" at Nature Conservancy's website on climate change. Report your score.

foretell a doomed planet if we do not make radical policy changes immediately. The Dorothies—so named for the character in *The Wizard of Oz*—see themselves as the revealers of truth, who pull away the curtain to expose the wizards who manipulate scientific models for political gain. The reality, however, may lie somewhere in between. This unit explores the complexities of this very pressing issue.

Joe Heller – Green Bay Press-Gazette * Posted 04/21/2008

# Global Warming Heats Up

*Jeffrey Kluger*

Jeffrey Kluger is a senior writer for *TIME* magazine and the author of several books on science including *Splendid Solution: Jonas Salk and the Conquest of Polio* (2005) and *Simplexity: Why Simple Things Become Complex (and How Complex Things Can Be Made Simple)* (2008). His writing has appeared in many scientific journals and magazines, including *Discover* and *Science Digest*. This article, slightly abridged, with reporting by David Bjerklie, Andrea Dorfman, Dan Cray, Greg Fulton, Andrea Gerlin, Rita Healy, and Eric Roston, was published in *TIME* magazine on March 26, 2006.

## CONNECTING TO THE TOPIC

The climate is crashing, claims writer Jeffrey Kluger, and global warming is to blame. And unlike most natural processes, which take hundreds or thousands of years to evolve, the crisis could hit soon. In this next article, Kluger takes a look at our changing earth, what abrupt climate change might mean, and what we can do about it.

## WORDS IN CONTEXT

**calve:** (2)   breaking off of smaller pieces of a glacier (v.)
**sodden** (2)   soaking wet (adj.)
**palpable** (6)   easily sensed (adj.)
**deluge** (12)   flood (n.)
**cryonic** (15)   deep-frozen (adj.)
**inhibit** (20)   hinder; try to prevent (v.)
**flora and fauna** (21)   plants and animals (n.)
**switchgrass** (25)   a grass native to North America that is a potential source
   of ethanol (n.)

1   No one can say exactly what it looks like when a planet takes ill, but it probably looks a lot like Earth. Never mind what you've heard about global warming as a slow-motion emergency that would take decades to play out. Suddenly and unexpectedly, the crisis is upon us.

2    It certainly looked that way last week as the atmospheric bomb that was Cyclone Larry—a Category 4 storm with wind bursts that reached 125 m.p.h.—exploded through northeastern Australia. It certainly looked that way last year as curtains of fire and dust turned the skies of Indonesia orange, thanks to drought-fueled blazes sweeping the island nation. It certainly looks that way as sections of ice the size of small states **calve** from the disintegrating Arctic and Antarctic. And it certainly looks that way as the **sodden** wreckage of New Orleans continues to molder, while the waters of the Atlantic gather themselves for a new hurricane season just two months away. Disasters have always been with us and surely always will be. But when they hit this hard and come this fast—when the emergency becomes commonplace—something has gone grievously wrong. That something is global warming.

3    The image of Earth as organism—famously dubbed Gaia by environmentalist James Lovelock—has probably been overworked, but that's not to say the planet can't behave like a living thing, and these days, it's a living thing fighting a fever. From heat waves to storms to floods to fires to massive glacial melts, the global climate seems to be crashing around us. Scientists have been calling this shot for decades. This is precisely what they have been warning would happen if we continued pumping greenhouse gases into the atmosphere, trapping the heat that flows in from the sun and raising global temperatures.

4    Environmentalists and lawmakers spent years shouting at one another about whether the grim forecasts were true, but in the past five years or so, the serious debate has quietly ended. Global warming, even most skeptics have concluded, is the real deal, and human activity has been causing it. If there was any consolation, it was that the glacial pace of nature would give us decades or even centuries to sort out the problem.

5    But glaciers, it turns out, can move with surprising speed, and so can nature. What few people reckoned on was that global climate systems are booby-trapped with tipping points and feedback loops, thresholds past which the slow creep of environmental decay gives way to sudden and self-perpetuating collapse. Pump enough $CO_2$ into the sky, and that last part per million of greenhouse gas behaves like the 212th-degree Fahrenheit that turns a pot of hot water into a plume of billowing steam. Melt enough Greenland ice, and you reach the point at which you're not simply dripping meltwater into the sea but dumping whole glaciers. By one recent measure, several Greenland ice sheets have doubled their rate of slide, and just last week the journal *Science* published a study suggesting that by the end of the century, the world could be locked in to an eventual rise in sea levels of as much as 20 ft. Nature, it seems, has finally got a bellyful of us.

6    "Things are happening a lot faster than anyone predicted," says Bill Chameides, chief scientist for the advocacy group Environmental Defense and a former professor of atmospheric chemistry. "The last 12 months have been alarming." Adds Ruth Curry of the Woods Hole Oceanographic Institution in Massachusetts: "The ripple through the scientific community is **palpable**."

7    And it's not just scientists who are taking notice. Even as nature crosses its tipping points, the public seems to have reached its own. For years, popular skepticism about climatological science stood in the way of addressing the problem, but the naysayers—many of whom were on the payroll of energy companies—have become an increasingly marginalized breed. In a new TIME/ABC News/Stanford University poll, 85% of respondents agree that global warming probably is happening. Moreover, most respondents say they want some action taken. Of those polled, 87% believe the government should either encourage or require lowering of power-plant emissions, and 85% think something should be done to get cars to use less gasoline. Even Evangelical Christians, once one of the most reliable columns in the conservative base, are demanding action, most notably in February in 2006, when 86 Christian leaders formed the Evangelical Climate Initiative, demanding that Congress regulate greenhouse gases.

8    Such public stirrings are at last getting the attention of politicians and business leaders, who may not always respond to science but have a keen nose for where votes and profits lie. State and local lawmakers have started taking action to curb emissions, and major corporations are doing the same. Wal-Mart has begun installing wind turbines on its stores to generate electricity and is talking about putting solar reflectors over its parking lots. HSBC, the world's second-largest bank, has pledged to neutralize its carbon output by investing in wind farms and other green projects. Even President Bush, hardly a favorite of greens, now acknowledges climate change and boasts of the steps he is taking to fight it. Most of those steps, however, involve research and voluntary emissions controls, not exactly the laws with teeth scientists are calling for.

9    Is it too late to reverse the changes global warming has wrought? That's still not clear. Reducing our emissions output year to year is hard enough. Getting it low enough so that the atmosphere can heal is a multigenerational commitment. "Ecosystems are usually able to maintain themselves," says Terry Chapin, a biologist and professor of ecology at the University of Alaska, Fairbanks. "But eventually they get pushed to the limit of tolerance."

## CO₂ and the Poles

10  As a tiny component of our atmosphere, carbon dioxide helped warm Earth to comfort levels we are all used to. But too much of it does an awful lot of damage. The gas represents just a few hundred parts per million (p.p.m.) in the overall air blanket, but they're powerful parts because they allow sunlight to stream in but prevent much of the heat from radiating back out. During the last ice age, the atmosphere's $CO_2$ concentration was just 180 p.p.m., putting Earth into a deep freeze. After the glaciers retreated but before the dawn of the modern era, the total had risen to a comfortable 280 p.p.m. In just the past century and a half, we have pushed the level to 381 p.p.m., and we're feeling the effects. Of the 20 hottest years on record, 19 occurred in the 1980s or later. According to NASA scientists, 2005 was one of the hottest years in more than a century.

11      It's at the North and South poles that those steambath conditions are felt particularly acutely, with glaciers and ice caps crumbling to slush. Once the thaw begins, a number of mechanisms kick in to keep it going. Greenland is a vivid example. Late last year, glaciologist Eric Rignot of the Jet Propulsion Laboratory in Pasadena, Calif., and Pannir Kanagaratnam, a research assistant professor at the University of Kansas, analyzed data from Canadian and European satellites and found that Greenland ice is not just melting but doing so more than twice as fast, with 53 cu. mi. draining away into the sea last year alone, compared with 22 cu. mi. in 1996. A cubic mile of water is about five times the amount Los Angeles uses in a year.

12      Dumping that much water into the ocean is a very dangerous thing. Icebergs don't raise sea levels when they melt because they're floating, which means they have displaced all the water they're ever going to. But ice on land, like Greenland's, is a different matter. Pour that into oceans that are already rising (because warm water expands), and you **deluge** shorelines. By some estimates, the entire Greenland ice sheet would be enough to raise global sea levels 23 ft., swallowing up large parts of coastal Florida and most of Bangladesh. The Antarctic holds enough ice to raise sea levels more than 215 ft.

## Feedback Loops

13  One of the reasons the loss of the planet's ice cover is accelerating is that as the poles' bright white surface shrinks, it changes the relationship of Earth and the sun. Polar ice is so reflective that 90% of the sunlight that

strikes it simply bounces back into space, taking much of its energy with it. Ocean water does just the opposite, absorbing 90% of the energy it receives. The more energy it retains, the warmer it gets, with the result that each mile of ice that melts vanishes faster than the mile that preceded it.

14   That is what scientists call a feedback loop, and it's a nasty one, since once you uncap the Arctic Ocean, you unleash another beast: the comparatively warm layer of water about 600 ft. deep that circulates in and out of the Atlantic. "Remove the ice," says Woods Hole's Curry, "and the water starts talking to the atmosphere, releasing its heat. This is not a good thing."

15   A similar feedback loop is melting permafrost, usually defined as land that has been continuously frozen for two years or more. There's a lot of earthly real estate that qualifies, and much of it has been frozen much longer than two years—since the end of the last ice age, or at least 8,000 years ago. Sealed inside that **cryonic** time capsule are layers of partially decayed organic matter, rich in carbon. In high-altitude regions of Alaska, Canada and Siberia, the soil is warming and decomposing, releasing gases that will turn into methane and $CO_2$. That, in turn, could lead to more warming and permafrost thaw, says research scientist David Lawrence of the National Center for Atmospheric Research (NCAR) in Boulder, Colo. And how much carbon is socked away in Arctic soils? Lawrence puts the figure at 200 gigatons to 800 gigatons. The total human carbon output is only 7 gigatons a year.

16   One result of all that is warmer oceans, and a result of warmer oceans can be, paradoxically, colder continents within a hotter globe. Ocean currents running between warm and cold regions serve as natural thermoregulators, distributing heat from the equator toward the poles. The Gulf Stream, carrying warmth up from the tropics, is what keeps Europe's climate relatively mild. Whenever Europe is cut off from the Gulf Stream, temperatures plummet. At the end of the last ice age, the warm current was temporarily blocked, and temperatures in Europe fell as much as 10°F, locking the continent in glaciers.

17   What usually keeps the Gulf Stream running is that warm water is lighter than cold water, so it floats on the surface. As it reaches Europe and releases its heat, the current grows denser and sinks, flowing back to the south and crossing under the northbound Gulf Stream until it reaches the tropics and starts to warm again. The cycle works splendidly, provided the water remains salty enough. But if it becomes diluted by freshwater, the salt concentration drops, and the water gets lighter, idling on top and stalling the current. Last December, researchers associated with Britain's

National Oceanography Center reported that one component of the system that drives the Gulf Stream has slowed about 30% since 1957. It's the increased release of Arctic and Greenland meltwater that appears to be causing the problem, introducing a gush of freshwater that's overwhelming the natural cycle. In a global-warming world, it's unlikely that any amount of cooling that resulted from this would be sufficient to support glaciers, but it could make things awfully uncomfortable.

18   "The big worry is that the whole climate of Europe will change," says Adrian Luckman, senior lecturer in geography at the University of Wales, Swansea. "We in the U.K. are on the same latitude as Alaska. The reason we can live here is the Gulf Stream."

## Drought

19  As fast as global warming is transforming the oceans and the ice caps, it's having an even more immediate effect on land. People, animals and plants living in dry, mountainous regions like the western U.S. make it through summer thanks to snowpack that collects on peaks all winter and slowly melts off in warm months. Lately the early arrival of spring and the unusually blistering summers have caused the snowpack to melt too early, so that by the time it's needed, it's largely gone. Climatologist Philip Mote of the University of Washington has compared decades of snowpack levels in Washington, Oregon and California and found that they are a fraction of what they were in the 1940s, and some snowpacks have vanished entirely.

20   Global warming is tipping other regions of the world into drought in different ways. Higher temperatures bake moisture out of soil faster, causing dry regions that live at the margins to cross the line into full-blown crisis. Meanwhile, El Niño events—the warm pooling of Pacific waters that periodically drives worldwide climate patterns and has been occurring more frequently in global-warming years—further **inhibit** precipitation in dry areas of Africa and East Asia. According to a recent study by NCAR, the percentage of Earth's surface suffering drought has more than doubled since the 1970s.

## Flora and Fauna

21  Hot, dry land can be murder on **flora and fauna**, and both are taking a bad hit. Wildfires in such regions as Indonesia, the western U.S. and even inland Alaska have been increasing as timberlands and forest floors grow

more parched. The blazes create a feedback loop of their own, pouring more carbon into the atmosphere and reducing the number of trees, which inhale $CO_2$ and release oxygen.

22     Those forests that don't succumb to fire die in other, slower ways. Connie Millar, a paleoecologist for the U.S. Forest Service, studies the history of vegetation in the Sierra Nevada. Over the past 100 years, she has found, the forests have shifted their tree lines as much as 100 ft. upslope, trying to escape the heat and drought of the lowlands. Such slow-motion evacuation may seem like a sensible strategy, but when you're on a mountain, you can go only so far before you run out of room. "Sometimes we say the trees are going to heaven because they're walking off the mountaintops," Millar says.

23     Across North America, warming-related changes are mowing down other flora too. Manzanita bushes in the West are dying back; some prickly pear cacti have lost their signature green and are instead a sickly pink; pine beetles in western Canada and the U.S. are chewing their way through tens of millions of acres of forest, thanks to warmer winters. The beetles may even breach the once insurmountable Rocky Mountain divide, opening up a path into the rich timbering lands of the American Southeast.

24     In Alaska, salmon populations are at risk as melting permafrost pours mud into rivers, burying the gravel the fish need for spawning. Small animals such as bushy-tailed wood rats, alpine chipmunks and piñon mice are being chased upslope by rising temperatures, following the path of the fleeing trees. And with sea ice vanishing, polar bears—prodigious swimmers but not inexhaustible ones—are starting to turn up drowned. "There will be no polar ice by 2060," says Larry Schweiger, president of the National Wildlife Federation. "Somewhere along that path, the polar bear drops out."

## What We Can Do

25     So much environmental collapse happening in so many places at once has at last awakened much of the world, particularly the 141 nations that have ratified the Kyoto treaty to reduce emissions—an imperfect accord, to be sure, but an accord all the same. The U.S., however, which is home to less than 5% of Earth's population but produces 25% of $CO_2$ emissions, remains intransigent. Many environmentalists declared the Bush Administration hopeless from the start, and while that may have been premature, it's undeniable that the White House's environmental record—from the abandonment of Kyoto to the President's broken campaign pledge to

control carbon output to the relaxation of emission standards—has been dismal. George W. Bush's rhetorical nods to America's oil addiction and his praise of such alternative fuel sources as **switchgrass** have yet to be followed by real initiatives.

26    The anger surrounding all that exploded recently when NASA researcher Jim Hansen, director of the Goddard Institute for Space Studies and a longtime leader in climate-change research, complained that he had been harassed by White House appointees as he tried to sound the global-warming alarm. "The way democracy is supposed to work, the presumption is that the public is well informed. They're trying to deny the science." Up against such resistance, many environmental groups have resolved simply to wait and hope for something better in 2009.

27    Increasingly, state and local governments are filling the void. The mayors of more than 200 cities have signed the U.S. Mayors Climate Protection Agreement, pledging, among other things, that they will meet the Kyoto goal of reducing greenhouse-gas emissions in their cities to 1990 levels by 2012. Nine eastern states have established the Regional Greenhouse Gas Initiative for the purpose of developing a cap-and-trade program that would set ceilings on industrial emissions and allow companies that overperform to sell pollution credits to those that underperform—the same smart, incentive-based strategy that got sulfur dioxide under control and reduced acid rain. And California passed the nation's toughest automobile-emissions law last summer.

28    "There are a whole series of things that demonstrate that people want to act and want their government to act," says Fred Krupp, president of Environmental Defense. Krupp and others believe that we should probably accept that it's too late to prevent $CO_2$ concentrations from climbing to 450 p.p.m. (or 70 p.p.m. higher than where they are now). From there, however, we should be able to stabilize them and start to dial them back down.

29    That goal should be attainable. Curbing global warming may be an order of magnitude harder than, say, eradicating smallpox or putting a man on the moon. But is it moral not to try? We did not so much march toward the environmental precipice as drunkenly reel there, snapping at the scientific scolds who told us we had a problem.

30    The scolds, however, knew what they were talking about. In a solar system crowded with sister worlds that either emerged stillborn like Mercury and Venus or died in infancy like Mars, we're finally coming to appreciate the knife-blade margins within which life can thrive. For more than a century we've been monkeying with those margins. It's long past time we set them right. ◆

## CONSIDERING THE ISSUES

1. What do you know about global warming and climate change? Do you think it is a pressing issue in need of immediate correction? Or are we making a big deal over nothing? Explain.
2. Kluger notes that some areas of the world could radically change due to global warming. If the world warmed 10 degrees in the next 100 years, and the ocean level rose as a result, what would that mean for the area of the world you come from? For example, if you grew up in Florida, would your hometown be underwater? How might the world change as a result?

## CRAFT AND CONTENT

1. What proof does Kluger provide that global warming is indeed happening? How might critics respond to his assertion that global warming must be the reason behind so many recent weather-related tragedies? Explain.
2. Can you determine the position of the author on the issue of global warming from this article? What assumptions do this *TIME* magazine writer and his team make about their audience and its political/social leanings?

## CRITICAL THINKING

1. Kluger notes in paragraph 7 that "even Evangelical Christians . . . are demanding action." Why does he highlight this group of people? Do you think the fact that they support action on the issue of greenhouse gases buttresses Kluger's points? Does being religiously conservative mean that one holds a conservative viewpoint on issues related to the environment? Why or why not?
2. What is a feedback loop? Why is the feedback loop connected to polar ice of particular concern to environmental scientists?
3. What changes, according to the author, are likely to come about as a result of global warming?

## WRITING ABOUT THE ISSUES

1. What should the role of the U.S. government be in addressing the issue of global warming? Is it an issue for state government or our federal government? Write an essay in which you explore

the role of government as it connects to global warming today and in the future.

2. Severe weather is often attributed to global warming—cyclones, tsunamis, hurricanes. Write about a time when the weather had a significant impact on your own life. It could be a memory of a blizzard that occurred while you were a child, or a personal experience with a recent catastrophe such as Hurricane Katrina (2005) or Hurricane Ike (2008).

# VISUAL CONNECTIONS

## An Inconvenient Truth

### CONNECTING TO THE TOPIC

The 2006 movie *An Inconvenient Truth*, directed by Davis Guggenheim and featuring Al Gore, presents the issue of global warming and Gore's efforts to educate the American public on this issue. The film's website, explains that the movie "offers a passionate and inspirational look at [Gore's] fervent crusade to halt global warming's deadly progress in its tracks by exposing the myths and misconceptions that surround it. In the wake of defeat in the 2000 election, [Gore] re-set the course of his life to focus on a last-ditch, all-out effort to help save the planet from irrevocable change." The information that follows also appears on the site.

1    **C**arbon dioxide and other gases warm the surface of the planet naturally by trapping solar heat in the atmosphere. This is a good thing because it keeps our planet habitable. However, by burning fossil fuels such as coal, gas and oil and clearing forests we have dramatically increased the amount of carbon dioxide in the Earth's atmosphere and temperatures are rising.

2    The vast majority of scientists agree that global warming is real, it's already happening and that it is the result of our activities and not a natural occurrence.[1] The evidence is overwhelming and undeniable.

3    We're already seeing changes. Glaciers are melting, plants and animals are being forced from their habitat, and the number of severe storms and droughts is increasing. There is no doubt we can solve this problem. In fact, we have a moral obligation to do so. Small changes to your daily routine can add up to big differences in helping to stop global warming. The time to come together to solve this problem is now.

- The number of Category 4 and 5 hurricanes has almost doubled in the last 30 years.[2]
- Malaria has spread to higher altitudes in places like the Colombian Andes, 7,000 feet above sea level.[3]
- The flow of ice from glaciers in Greenland has more than doubled over the past decade.[4]
- At least 279 species of plants and animals are already responding to global warming, moving closer to the poles.[5]

4    If the warming continues, we can expect catastrophic consequences.

- Deaths from global warming will double in just 25 years—to 300,000 people a year.[6]

---

[1] According to the Intergovernmental Panel on Climate Change (IPCC), this era of global warming "is unlikely to be entirely natural in origin" and "the balance of evidence suggests a discernible human influence of the global climate."

[2] Emanuel, K. 2005. Increasing destructiveness of tropical cyclones over the past 30 years. *Nature* 436: 686–688.

[3] World Health Organization.

[4] Krabill, W., E. Hanna, P. Huybrechts, W. Abdalati, J. Cappelen, B. Csatho, E. Frefick, S. Manizade, C. Martin, J. Sonntag, R. Swift, R. Thomas, and J. Yungel, 2004. Greenland Ice Sheet: Increased coastal thinning. *Geophysical Research Letters* 31.

[5] *Nature.*

[6] World Health Organization.

- Global sea levels could rise by more than 20 feet with the loss of shelf ice in Greenland and Antarctica, devastating coastal areas worldwide.[7]
- Heat waves will be more frequent and more intense.
- Droughts and wildfires will occur more often.
- The Arctic Ocean could be ice-free in summer by 2050.[8]
- More than a million species worldwide could be driven to extinction by 2050.[9] ◆

### CRITICAL THINKING

1. How does this information sheet present the issue of global warming? What language does it use, and how does this language persuade the reader? Explain.
2. Watch the movie and write a review. What are the movie's strengths and weaknesses? What struck you as compelling? Questionable? Is the movie balanced? Biased? Slanted? Fair? Does it offer solutions?
3. Examine the movie poster promoting the film. How does the poster use imagery, symbolism, and nuances of light and dark to convey a feeling? If you saw this poster and knew nothing about the movie or its subject matter, what might you surmise from the poster alone?

## A Convenient Untruth

*Andrew Potter*

Andrew Potter is a former member of the editorial board of the Canadian political journal *This Magazine*. He is currently a visiting scholar with the Educational Policy Institute in Toronto and is a columnist on culture and politics for

---

[7]*Washington Post*, "Debate on climate shifts to issue of irreparable change," Juliet Eilperin, January 29, 2006.

[8]*Arctic climate impact assessment, 2004: Impacts of a warming Arctic.* Cambridge, UK: Cambridge University Press. Also quoted in *TIME* magazine, Vicious Cycles, Missy Adams, March 26, 2006.

[9]*TIME* magazine, "Feeling the Heat," David Bjerklie, March 26, 2006.

*Maclean's,* a Canadian weekly current affairs magazine. He is the co-author, with Andrew Potter, of *Rebel Sell: Why the Culture Can't Be Jammed* (2004). This article was published in the April/May 2008 issue of *This Magazine.*

## CONNECTING TO THE TOPIC ────────────

In 2007, journalist Alan Weisman published *The World Without Us,* a non-fiction book about what would happen to the natural and built environment if humans suddenly disappeared. One of the most disturbing aspects of the book is that this scenario is so plausible in a world where nuclear war, biological weapons of mass destruction, and even global warming threaten life as we know it. The book became a best seller. In the next essay, journalist Andrew Potter wonders why some people seem eager to see the human race fail. We should be concerned about climate change, he agrees, but should environmental watchdogs be acting so smug?

## WORDS IN CONTEXT ────────────────

**Left** (1)   politically liberal parties, individuals, or movements (n.)
**animating** (2)   inspiring to action (adj.)
**pessimistic** (2)   doubting, negative (adj.)
**aesthetic** (3)   concerned with beauty and appearances (adj.)

1    **O**ne of the most disturbing aspects of the growing concern over climate change is the giddy delight with which some members of the **Left** await the coming global catastrophe. Of course they don't admit to being delighted. Instead, they claim to be extremely upset about the prospect of melting ice caps, rising sea levels, drought, flooding, crop failure, species extinction and so on. But let's be honest, listening to a global warming hysteric rhyme off the terrible and inevitable consequences of driving to work or buying a Big Mac is to hear someone in the rapture of a geo-pornographic fantasy.

2    Let us call these people "declinists," and their **animating** philosophy "declinism." What motivates declinism is an attitude so **pessimistic** that it is almost theological: not only are things worse than they used to be, but they're getting worse with every passing year. Furthermore, the declinist believes that the various strategies that are usually proposed for making things better—the promotion of liberal democracy, technological development and economic growth—cannot be the solution to our problems, since

they are actually the cause. That is, it is the principles that underwrite modernity itself that are the problem. As the declinist sees it, the rights-based politics of liberal individualism, combined with the free-market economy, have served to undermine local attachments and communitarian feelings, leading us to seek meaning in shallow consumerism and mindless entertainments.

3    That is why climate change is the ultimate declinist wet dream. Sure, there is a long tradition of declinist hobby horses, including overpopulation, the exhaustion of natural resources and the industrial poisoning of the land and the sea, but climate change is the rug that pulls the whole room together. From cars and consumerism to mass travel, fast food and inexpensive lighting, declinism gathers up everything the left dislikes about contemporary society and puts it all in the dock facing the same charge: it is causing the planet to heat up. Thanks, then, to the imagined horrors of climate change, declinism transforms what is essentially an **aesthetic** preference for live entertainment over television, locally grown produce over fast food and the ability to walk to work instead of commuting in a car into a lifestyle choice of world-historical importance.

4    The way the logic of it works out, the declinist wins no matter what happens. We either adopt more energy-efficient, low-impact, "human scale" lifestyles, or the atmosphere will heat up, the economy will collapse and we'll be forcibly thrown back into a subsistence economy. Fate, as the great Canadian pessimist George Grant once wrote, leads the willing and drives the unwilling, and we're headed for a 12th-century economy whether we like it or not. It's a future that the high priest of declinism, James Howard Kunstler (author of *The Geography of Nowhere* and *The Long Emergency*), can hardly wait for. While he spent his entire career fighting a losing intellectual battle against the car culture of suburbia, global warming has given him renewed faith in the ability of humanity to destroy itself through consumption. As he wrote recently, "let the gloating begin."

5    There is no point in arguing with declinism, because it is not a set of empirical propositions but an ideology. Over the past hundred years, life got steadily better by almost any conceivable measure. Life expectancy rose while infant mortality dropped; the air quality of our cities improved, our food got cheaper and more nutritious, and the workplace became safer as wages steadily climbed. If you have any question as to the arrow of progress, ask yourself one question: Given a choice, when would you rather have been born, 1900 or 2000?

6    Declinism is both a sin and a betrayal. It is a sin because it displays an utter lack of faith in humanity, believing that we will inevitably abuse the

gifts of freedom, knowledge and power and become the agents of our own destruction. It is a betrayal of modernity and of the liberal ideals that have breathed life and hope into human progress for the past four hundred years. In its resentment of modernity, the declinist left finds itself in agreement with a broad spectrum of Islamofascists, evangelical nuts and tinfoil-hat anarchists, who equally fear the globalized future and pray for a return to a glorious but thoroughly imaginary past. If it takes a global catastrophe to get us there, so much the better.

7    They say that politics makes for strange bedfellows. But when it comes to the politics of declinism, the sleeping arrangements are positively perverted.  ◆

### CONSIDERING THE ISSUES

1. According to the author, environmentalists are eager to "let the gloating begin" when they hear of the possible downfall of modern society due to climate change. What are these environmentalists hoping for?
2. Potter states, "It is the principles that underwrite modernity itself that are the problem." Do you agree or disagree that modernity has caused a potential for global catastrophe? Explain.

### CRAFT AND CONTENT

1. Define the term "declinism" and explain how this philosophy, according to Potter, "is both a sin and a betrayal." Explain whether you agree or disagree with Potter's viewpoint and why.
2. The author ends his essay by asserting, "When it comes to the politics of declinism, the sleeping arrangements are positively perverted." Who does Potter suggest that declinists are "sleeping with," and why is it "perverted"?
3. Identify places in Potter's essay in which he makes sexual references. Why do you think he makes these sexual innuendos? Do they contribute to his essay?

### CRITICAL THINKING

1. In his essay, Potter is concerned with how environmentalists tell of "melting ice caps, rising sea levels, drought, flooding, crop

failure, species extinction and so on." His concern is not so much with the actual climate change but with the way it is being discussed by environmentalists. What is his point? Why does he highlight this issue?

2. Do you believe, as Potter suggests, that choosing "live entertainment over television, locally grown produce over fast food and the ability to walk to work instead of commuting in a car" is essentially an aesthetic preference? Explain.

## WRITING ABOUT THE ISSUES

1. Write a short essay answering the question that Potter proposes to his audience: "Given a choice, when would you rather have been born, 1900 or 2000?"

2. Brainstorm a list of as many lifestyle choices as you can think of that could potentially become "of world-historical importance." Which of these lifestyle choices are you most likely to adopt?

# Global Warming Delusions
*Daniel B. Botkin*

Daniel Botkin is president of the Center for the Study of the Environment and professor emeritus in the Department of Ecology, Evolution, and Marine Biology at the University of California, Santa Barbara. He is the author of *Discordant Harmonies: A New Ecology for the Twenty-First Century* (2001). This editorial appeared in the October 21, 2007, edition of the *Wall Street Journal*.

## CONNECTING TO THE TOPIC

Despite claims made by global warming activists such as Al Gore that the "debate is over" on the issue of global warming, some researchers argue that we are still only guessing about the future impact of global warming on our ecosystem. Professor Daniel Botkin asserts in this next essay that the debate over climate change is far from over. Instead, he explains, our popular imagination has been captured by hype that has little scientific basis. There's no "consensus" on global warming, he argues, and he offers proof.

## WORDS IN CONTEXT

**megafauna** (2)   large or fairly large animals considered as a group within a
   particular region or era (n.)
**malaria and encephalitis** (3)   two deadly infectious diseases transmitted to
   humans by mosquitoes (n.)
**naysayers** (5)   people who take a negative view; those who oppose or deny (n.)
**eloquently** (6)   described vividly and persuasively, with force (adv.)
**inclement** (11)   stormy (adj.)
**charismatic** (15)   particularly charming and engaging (adj.)

1   **G**lobal warming doesn't matter except to the extent that it will affect
life—ours and that of all living things on Earth. And contrary to the latest
news, the evidence that global warming will have serious effects on life is
thin. Most evidence suggests the contrary.

2   Case in point: This year's United Nations report on climate change
and other documents say that 20% to 30% of plant and animal species
will be threatened with extinction in this century due to global warming—
a truly terrifying thought. Yet, during the past 2.5 million years, a period
that scientists now know experienced climatic changes as rapid and as
warm as modern climatological models suggest will happen to us, almost
none of the millions of species on Earth went extinct. The exceptions
were about 20 species of large mammals (the famous **megafauna** of the
last ice age—saber-tooth tigers, hairy mammoths and the like), which
went extinct about 10,000 to 5,000 years ago at the end of the last ice age,
and many dominant trees and shrubs of northwestern Europe. But elsewhere, including North America, few plant species went extinct, and few
mammals.

3   3 We're also warned that tropical diseases are going to spread, and
that we can expect **malaria and encephalitis** epidemics. But scientific papers by Prof. Sarah Randolph of Oxford University show that temperature
changes do not correlate well with changes in the distribution or frequency
of these diseases; warming has not broadened their distribution and is
highly unlikely to do so in the future, global warming or not.

4   The key point here is that living things respond to many factors in addition to temperature and rainfall. In most cases, however, climate-modeling-
based forecasts look primarily at temperature alone, or temperature and

precipitation only. You might ask, "Isn't this enough to forecast changes in the distribution of species?" Ask a mockingbird. The *New York Times* recently published an answer to a query about why mockingbirds were becoming common in Manhattan. The expert answer was: food—an exotic plant species that mockingbirds like to eat had spread to New York City. It was this, not temperature or rainfall, the expert said, that caused the change in mockingbird geography.

5    You might think I must be one of those know-nothing **naysayers** who believes global warming is a liberal plot. On the contrary, I am a biologist and ecologist who has worked on global warming, and been concerned about its effects, since 1968. I've developed the computer model of forest growth that has been used widely to forecast possible effects of global warming on life—I've used the model for that purpose myself, and to forecast likely effects on specific endangered species.

6    I'm not a naysayer. I'm a scientist who believes in the scientific method and in what facts tell us. I have worked for 40 years to try to improve our environment and improve human life as well. I believe we can do this only from a basis in reality, and that is not what I see happening now. Instead, like fashions that took hold in the past and are **eloquently** analyzed in the classic 19th century book *Extraordinary Popular Delusions and the Madness of Crowds,* the popular imagination today appears to have been captured by beliefs that have little scientific basis.

7    Some colleagues who share some of my doubts argue that the only way to get our society to change is to frighten people with the possibility of a catastrophe, and that therefore it is all right and even necessary for scientists to exaggerate. They tell me that my belief in open and honest assessment is naïve. "Wolves deceive their prey, don't they?" one said to me recently. Therefore, biologically, he said, we are justified in exaggerating to get society to change.

8    The climate modelers who developed the computer programs that are being used to forecast climate change used to readily admit that the models were crude and not very realistic, but were the best that could be done with available computers and programming methods. They said our options were to either believe those crude models or believe the opinions of experienced, data-focused scientists. Having done a great deal of computer modeling myself, I appreciated their acknowledgment of the limits of their methods. But I hear no such statements today. Oddly, the forecasts of computer models have become our new reality, while facts such as the

few extinctions of the past 2.5 million years are pushed aside, as if they were not our reality.

9    A recent article in the well-respected journal *American Scientist* explained why the glacier on Mt. Kilimanjaro could not be melting from global warming. Simply from an intellectual point of view it was fascinating—especially the author's Sherlock Holmes approach to figuring out what was causing the glacier to melt. That it couldn't be global warming directly (i.e., the result of air around the glacier warming) was made clear by the fact that the air temperature at the altitude of the glacier is below freezing. This means that only direct radiant heat from sunlight could be warming and melting the glacier. The author also studied the shape of the glacier and deduced that its melting pattern was consistent with radiant heat but not air temperature. Although acknowledged by many scientists, the paper is scorned by the true believers in global warming.

10    We are told that the melting of the arctic ice will be a disaster. But during the famous medieval warming period—A.D. 750 to 1230 or so—the Vikings found the warmer northern climate to their advantage. Emmanuel Le Roy Ladurie addressed this in his book *Times of Feast, Times of Famine: A History of Climate Since the Year 1000,* perhaps the greatest book about climate change before the onset of modern concerns with global warming. He wrote that Erik the Red "took advantage of a sea relatively free of ice to sail due west from Iceland to reach Greenland. . . . Two and a half centuries later, at the height of the climatic and demographic fortunes of the northern settlers, a bishopric of Greenland was founded at Gardar in 1126."

11    Ladurie pointed out that "it is reasonable to think of the Vikings as unconsciously taking advantage of this [referring to the warming of the Middle Ages] to colonize the most northern and **inclement** of their conquests, Iceland and Greenland." Good thing that Erik the Red didn't have Al Gore or his climatologists as his advisers.

12    Should we therefore dismiss global warming? Of course not. But we should make a realistic assessment, as rationally as possible, about its cultural, economic and environmental effects. As Erik the Red might have told you, not everything due to a climatic warming is bad, nor is everything that is bad due to a climatic warming.

13    We should approach the problem the way we decide whether to buy insurance and take precautions against other catastrophes—wildfires, hurricanes, earthquakes. And as I have written elsewhere, many of the actions we would take to reduce greenhouse-gas production and mitigate

global-warming effects are beneficial anyway, most particularly a movement away from fossil fuels to alternative solar and wind energy.

14    My concern is that we may be moving away from an irrational lack of
concern about climate change to an equally irrational panic about it. Many of
my colleagues ask, "What's the problem? Hasn't it been a good thing to raise
public concern?" The problem is that in this panic we are going to spend our
money unwisely, we will take actions that are counterproductive, and we will
fail to do many of those things that will benefit the environment and ourselves.

15    For example, right now the clearest threat to many species is habitat
destruction. Take the orangutans, for instance, one of those **charismatic**
species that people are often fascinated by and concerned about. They are
endangered because of deforestation. In our fear of global warming, it
would be sad if we fail to find funds to purchase those forests before they
are destroyed, and thus let this species go extinct.

16    At the heart of the matter is how much faith we decide to put in science—even how much faith scientists put in science. Our times have benefited from clear-thinking, science-based rationality. I hope this prevails
as we try to deal with our changing climate.  ◆

### CONSIDERING THE ISSUES

1. In this editorial, Daniel Botkin states, "As Erik the Red might
   have told you, not everything due to a climatic warming is bad,
   nor is everything that is bad due to a climatic warming." What
   does he mean? In what ways could global warming be positive?
2. Do you think the scientific community is in agreement that
   global warming is an immediate crisis? On what do you base
   your assessment? Has the media promoted one view over others? Do you think that the "case is still open," as Botkin suggests? Why or why not?

### CRAFT AND CONTENT

1. Botkin notes in several places that he is "not a naysayer." What
   is a naysayer? Why does he make a point of stating to his audience that he is not one? Do you agree?
2. This editorial was first printed in the *Wall Street Journal*. Based
   on what you know about this publication, how is its audience
   likely to interpret this editorial?

## CRITICAL THINKING

1. How does Botkin refer to Al Gore and his role in the global warming debate? What can a reader infer about how Botkin feels about Gore? Explain.
2. As an academic and an ecologist, does Botkin's professional pedigree make him a more credible authority than other commentators on the issue of global warming? Why or why not?

## WRITING ABOUT THE ISSUES

1. Make a list of all the authorities and critics on global warming Botkin cites in his essay. Research the positions of the people or organizations he cites and summarize each person's stance in a single paragraph. After preparing your research, review Botkin's essay and determine whether his criticisms are on target or misplaced.
2. Write an editorial for the newspaper of your choice presenting, briefly, your position on the issue of global warming. Include the name of the newspaper at the top of your editorial for your instructor's reference. Consider the political bent of the newspaper for which you are writing and its typical readership as you write.

# Blog Matters

A blog ("web log") is an online diary or commentary site that features regular entries that describe events, impressions, and viewpoints. Blogs may contain text, images, video, and often link to other websites, blogs, and online media. Most blogs allow readers to comment on the content of the post and to each other. As of 2007, the blog search engine estimated there were over 112 million blogs. While many blogs are maintained by individuals, some are run by journals, newspapers, and other media outlets. Remember that most blogs are not monitored for factual accuracy, and often express the opinion and views of the "blogger" writing the content.

The blog below is hosted by "The Daily Galaxy—News from Planet Earth & Beyond," a blog site syndicated by Reuters News and created and produced by Galaxy Media, LLC.

# Please Stop Talking About the Global Warming Consensus

*George Musser for Scientific American Magazine*
*March 15, 2007*

1    Last year, I started a thread on this blog to discuss doubts about global warming and humanity's role in it. I tried to catalog the misgivings in as evenhanded as way as possible and conducted a simple poll to see which broad category of doubts people found most persuasive.

2    The top two results were:

   1. The present warming could be a natural uptick.

   2. People who argue that human activity causes global warming cannot be trusted.

3    I offered a partial reply to the first of these last year. To summarize: different influences on the climate produce distinct patterns—for example, of spatial variation in temperature—and the observed patterns match what greenhouse gases should produce. They do not match what intrinsic climate variability or other natural causes would bring about.

4    But the climate debate that my colleague Dave Biello and I went to last night reminded me that the second of these concerns is still very much alive. Most of the arguments raised by the debaters and by audience members seemed to stem from the feeling that climate scientists and activists are haughty, sanctimonious, and hypocritical.

5    Like the climate itself, this is a very complex issue, having to do with attitudes toward intellectuals in our society and the way scientific findings can enter a meatgrinder of politics and ideology. Let me bite off just one piece: what I see as overuse of the term "scientific consensus."

6    When scientists use this term, they mean it to say that certain scientific questions have been settled to most people's satisfaction and that it's time to move on to other questions. But when non-scientists see this term, it sounds like a case of groupthink.

7    There's no doubt that the term is useful. A consensus view in any field of science represents humanity's best guess as to what's going on. The guess might well be wrong, but what else is there to go on? It's not as though there are answers in the back of the book to look at. People often say that science isn't a democracy; scientific questions aren't decided by

majority rule. Well, then, what are they decided by? Experiments and observations, surely. But who runs the experiments and makes the observations? Who interprets the outcome? Who double-checks them? It is a social process.

8      If as a scientist I disagree with the consensus, I have to be very sure of myself to put my own judgment up against the collective wisdom. And if there's one thing scientists learn very early in their careers, it is that such supreme self-confidence is usually misplaced. Nearly all scientists have painful memories of being pounced on in an oral exam for giving a sketchy answer, or presenting a paper before hundreds of people that turned out to be dead wrong. Most experts in a field realize that the more you know, the more you realize you don't know. They learn to doubt their own judgment. If I get one answer and everyone else gets a different one, my first inclination should be that I'm wrong, not that everyone else is.

9      Sometimes, the individual is right and the community is wrong. It happens in times of scientific revolution, which by definition involve the overturning of a consensus view. But such revolutions are rare. We remember Einstein because he was unusual. Climate science shows no signs of being in a revolutionary phase. Evidence for anthropogenic warming is getting stronger with time. Discrepancies are diminishing rather than increasing. Technically, scientists are correct to assert that their field has reached consensus.

10      So the invocations of consensus are seen, by scientists, as expressions of humility. Yet the general public sees them as expressions of arrogance. To the man in the street, all the talk about scientific consensus sounds like: "Trust us, folks. Don't worry your pretty little heads about it. Just think what we tell you to think."

11      That rubs Americans, in particular, the wrong way. America wouldn't be America without its suspicion of establishments of every kind. Hollywood valorizes the lone outsider fighting the powers that be. I think this romantic view is a healthy part of our country's culture—it's a safeguard against tyranny and an incentive for individuals to get involved in public life. But scientists can find themselves on the wrong side of the stick. They may see themselves as lone outsiders, but much of the rest of the country sees them as part of the machine. The British, for their part, really get off on puncturing pretentiousness—god help you if you walk into a pub and act full of yourself, as many climate scientists do.

12      The term "scientific consensus" is counterproductive in other ways, too. It sounds like asking people to take things on faith, which is contrary

to the whole point of science. It also lets skeptical scientists claim they are being muzzled. They can argue that they are estranged from mainstream science for what they say, when in fact the problem is how they say it—their incomplete arguments or their unwillingness to apply the same skepticism to their own results that they apply to others'. Talking about consensus shifts the responsibility for their estrangement from them to the faceless wall of the powers that be.

13      So while I think there's a role for mentioning scientific consensus, it should be used very sparingly. Telling people that there is a consensus cannot substitute for explaining why there is a consensus. As much as climate scientists may be wearying of debate, they need to press onward and treat each question as though it was the first time they had ever heard it. ◆

**RESPOND TO THE BLOG:**

What do you think? At what point can "consensus" be defined? With your group, discuss the meaning of the word "consensus." Is it when everyone agrees? A majority? How much influence should a consensus carry in a democratic society? For example, if a majority of people—especially experts on an issue—assume a particular position, does it follow that laws and policies should be based on their opinion? Why or why not?

# On the Climate Change Beat, Doubt Gives Way to Certainty
*William K. Stevens*

William K. Stevens was a science reporter for the *New York Times*. He is the author of *Miracle Under the Oaks: The Revival of Nature in America* (1995) and *The Change in the Weather* (2001). This article was published in the February 6, 2007, issue of the *New York Times*.

## CONNECTING TO THE TOPIC

The debate on global warming has gone from the question of whether it is actually happening, to what is causing it, to what will be the outcome in the near future. Now that no one is disputing the existence of global warming, the argument turns to what we should do and why we should care. Stevens, in this article, challenges anyone who still doesn't believe in the causes of global warming and suggests that we should start to care—and quickly.

## WORDS IN CONTEXT

**quaint** (2)   old-fashioned (adj.)
**preponderant** (5)   greater in amount or influence (adj.)
**stringent** (5)   strict (adj.)
**maverick** (8)   nonconformist (n.)
**discerned** (9)   recognized (adj.)
**parlance** (10)   debate (n.)
**contrarians** (14)   opponents (n.)
**unabated** (22)   unstopped (adj.)

1   In the decade when I was the lead reporter on climate change for this newspaper, nearly every blizzard or cold wave that hit the Northeast would bring the same conversation at work.

2   Somebody in the newsroom would eye me and say something like, "So much for global warming." This would often, but not always, be accompanied by teasing or malicious expressions, and depending on my mood the person would get either a joking or snappish or explanatory response. Such an exchange might still happen, but now it seems **quaint**. It would be out of date in light of a potentially historic sea change that appears to have taken place in the state and the status of the global warming issue since I retired from the *New York Times* in 2000.

3   Back then I wrote that one day, if mainstream scientists were right about what was going on with the earth's climate, it would become so obvious that human activity was responsible for a continuing rise in average global temperature that no other explanation would be plausible.

4   That day may have arrived.

5   Similarly, it was said in the 1990s that while the available evidence of a serious human impact on the earth's climate might be **preponderant** enough to meet the legal test for liability in a civil suit, it fell short of the more **stringent** "beyond a reasonable doubt" test of guilt in a criminal case.

6   Now it seems that the steadily strengthening body of evidence about the human connection with global warming is at least approaching the higher standard and may already have satisfied it.

7     The second element of the sea change, if such it is, consists of a demonstrably heightened awareness and concern among Americans about global warming. The awakening has been energized largely by dramatic reports on the melting Arctic and by fear—generated by the spectacular horror of Hurricane Katrina—that a warmer ocean is making hurricanes more intense.

8     Politicians are weighing in on the subject as never before, especially with the advent of a Democratic-led Congress. It appears likely, if not certain, that whoever is elected president in 2008 will treat the issue seriously and act accordingly, thereby bringing the United States into concert with most of the rest of the world. Just last week, Senator John McCain of Arizona, a presidential aspirant and the co-author of a bill mandating stronger action, asserted that the argument about global warming "is over." Back in the day, such words from a conservative Republican would have been unimaginable, even if he were something of a **maverick**.

9     I've been avidly watching from the sideline as the strengthening evidence of climate change has accumulated, not least the discovery that the Greenland ice cap is melting faster than had been thought. The implications of that are enormous, though the speed with which the melting may catastrophically raise sea levels is uncertain—as are many aspects of what a still hazily **discerned** climatic future may hold.

10     Last week, in its first major report since 2001, the world's most authoritative group of climate scientists issued its strongest statement yet on the relationship between global warming and human activity. The Intergovernmental Panel on Climate Change said the likelihood was 90 percent to 99 percent that emissions of heat-trapping greenhouse gases like carbon dioxide, spewed from tailpipes and smokestacks, were the dominant cause of the observed warming of the last 50 years. In the panel's **parlance**, this level of certainty is labeled "very likely."

11     Only rarely does scientific odds-making provide a more definite answer than that, at least in this branch of science, and it describes the endpoint, so far, of a progression:

- In 1990, in its first report, the panel found evidence of global warming but said its cause could be natural as easily as human.
- In a landmark 1995 report, the panel altered its judgment, saying that "the balance of evidence suggests a discernible human influence on global climate."
- In 2001, it placed the probability that human activity caused most of the warming of the previous half century at 66 percent to 90 percent—a "likely" rating.

12 And now it has supplied an even higher, more compelling seal of numerical certainty, which is also one measure of global warming's risk to humanity.

13 To say that reasonable doubt is vanishing does not mean there is no doubt at all. Many gaps remain in knowledge about the climate system. Scientists do make mistakes, and in any case science continually evolves and changes. That is why the panel's findings, synthesized from a vast body of scientific studies, are generally couched in terms of probabilities and sometimes substantial margins of error. So in the recesses of the mind, there remains a little worm of caution that says all may not be as it seems, or that the situation may somehow miraculously turn around—or, for that matter, that it may turn out worse than projected.

14 In several respects, the panel's conclusions have gotten progressively stronger in one direction over almost two decades, even as many of its hundreds of key members have left the group and new ones have joined. Many if not most of the major objections of contrarians have evaporated as science works its will, although the **contrarians** still make themselves heard.

15 The panel said last week that the fact of global warming itself could now be considered "unequivocal," and certified that 11 of the last 12 years were among the 12 warmest on record worldwide. (The fact of the warming is one thing contrarians no longer deny.)

16 But perhaps the most striking aspect of the 2007 report is the sheer number and variety of directly observed ways in which global warming is already having a "likely" or "very likely" impact on the earth.

17 In temperate zones, the frequency of cold days, cold nights and frosts has diminished, while the frequency of hot days, hot nights and heat waves has increased. Droughts in some parts of the world have become longer and more intense. Precipitation has decreased over the subtropics and most of the tropics, but increased elsewhere in the Northern and Southern Hemispheres.

18 There have been widespread increases in the frequency of "heavy precipitation events," even in areas where overall precipitation has gone down. What this means is that in many places, it rains and snows less often but harder—well-documented characteristics of a warming atmosphere. Remember this in the future, when the news media report heavy, sometimes catastrophic one-day rainfalls—four, six, eight inches—as has often happened in the United States in recent years. Each one is a data point in an trend toward more extreme downpours and the floods that result.

19 All of these trends are rated 90 percent to 99 percent likely to continue.

20    The list goes on.

21    And for the first time, in the wake of Hurricane Katrina, the panel reported evidence of a trend toward more intense hurricanes since 1970, and
said it was likely that this trend, too, would continue.

22    Some of the panel's main conclusions have remained fairly stable
over the years. One is that if greenhouse gas emissions continue
**unabated**, they will most likely warm the earth by about 3 to 7 degrees
Fahrenheit by the end of this century, with a wider range of about 2 to 12
degrees possible. The warming over the Northern Hemisphere is projected
to be higher than the global average, as is the case for the modest one-
degree warming observed in the last century.

23    The projected warming is about the same as what the panel estimates
would be produced by a doubling of atmospheric concentrations of greenhouse gases, compared with the immediate preindustrial age. It would also
be almost as much warming as has occurred since the depths of the last ice
age, 20,000 years ago.

24    Some experts believe that no matter what humans do to try to rein in
greenhouse gas emissions, a doubling is all but inevitable by 2100. In this
view, the urgent task ahead is to keep them from rising even higher.

25    If the concentrations were to triple, and even if they just double, there
is no telling at this point what the world will really be like as a result, except to speculate that on balance, most of its inhabitants probably won't
like it much. If James E. Hansen, one of the bolder climate scientists of the
last two decades, is right, they will be living on a different planet.

26    It has been pointed out many times, including by me, that we are engaged in a titanic global experiment. The further it proceeds, the clearer
the picture should become. At age 71, I'm unlikely to be around when it
resolves to everyone's satisfaction—or dissatisfaction. Many of you may
be, and a lot of your descendants undoubtedly will be.

27    Good luck to you and to them. ◆

## CONSIDERING THE ISSUES

1. We have heard from the media that global warming is pretty
   much accepted as a fact. If it is indeed a fact, what accounts for
   the ongoing debate? Explain.
2. Based on what you have read and heard, how will the earth be
   affected by global warming? What do you presume is happening? On what do you base your understanding of the issue?

## CRAFT AND CONTENT

1. Stevens gives us "proof" of the impact of global warming on the earth. What is this proof, and why should we view it as credible?

2. Stevens titles his essay, "On the Climate Change Beat, Doubt Gives Way to Certainty," yet he still chooses to use conditional and uncertain language such as "may," "it seems," and "if such it is" throughout his essay. Go through the essay and underline all of the uses of language of doubt and then explain why the author might have chosen to use this language instead of a more direct and authoritative language. Try changing the sentences to more direct statements and see if the meaning or tone changes.

3. Which metaphor does the author use in describing the impact of global warming? Describe how he uses this metaphor and explain whether it is effective.

## CRITICAL THINKING

1. According to the article, scientists project that the trend would be "almost as much warming as has occurred since the depths of the last ice age, 20,000 years ago." Discuss what would happen to the earth were it 'to heat up now as much as it did when coming out of an ice age. In what ways could humans adapt to this new environment?

2. Stevens speculates that many of his readers and undoubtedly their descendants will be around when global warming comes to a head, but he won't. Why do you think Stevens cares about the effects of global warming when he won't be around to see them?

## WRITING ABOUT THE ISSUES

1. Stevens asserts that even though most agree that the debate about global warming is over, "contrarians still make themselves heard." Go online and see if you can find any articles written within the last year arguing that there is no such thing as global warming or that global warming is natural and not manmade or will not have a devastating impact on the environment. Who is writing these articles? Would you consider the writers to

be credible sources? Read at least one of the articles and then briefly evaluate the believability of the argument.

2. Write an essay in which you describe what life might be like in the year 2100 due to global warming. Do you agree with the climate scientist James E. Hansen that "people "will be living on a different planet"?

# VISUAL CONNECTIONS

## Snap! Freezing Bears

### CONNECTING TO THE TOPIC

In February 2007, a photograph of two polar bears on an ice floe became the most popular photo on yahoo.com. The image ran with a story in the Australian newspaper the *Sunday Telegraph*, with the words, "They cling precariously to the top of what is left of the ice floe, their fragile grip the perfect symbol of the tragedy of global warming. Captured on film by Canadian environmentalists, the pair of polar bears look stranded on chunks of broken ice." The article went on to postulate that the plight of the bears was just one more example of the effects of global warming. But it soon emerged that the photo wasn't all it appeared to be. While attributed to Canadian environmentalists, it was taken by an Australian marine biology student Amanda Byrd in the summertime. The following transcript, which describes the controversy and how the photo was taken out of context, aired on *Media Watch* on February 4, 2007.

1      *T*hey cling precariously to the top of what is left of the ice floe, their fragile grip the perfect symbol of the tragedy of global warming. Captured on film by Canadian environmentalists, the pair of polar bears look stranded on chunks of broken ice.—The Sunday Telegraph, "A Planet on the Edge," February 4, 2007

2    Those stranded polar bears on the shrinking Arctic ice—victims of global warming—certainly tugged at the heart-strings.

3    That photo was published not only in the *Sunday Telegraph*.

4    It made it onto the front page of the *New York Times*.

5    And the *International Herald Tribune*.

6    It also ran in London's *Daily Mail*, *The Times* of London and Canada's *Ottawa Citizen*—and that's just to name a few.

7    All used it as evidence of global warming and the imminent demise of the polar bear. But the photo wasn't current. It was two and a half years old. And it wasn't snapped by Canadian environmentalists. It was taken by an Australian marine biology student on a field trip.

8    And in what month did she take it?

9    The time of year was August, summer.

10    Summer, when every year the fringes of the Arctic ice cap melt regardless of the wider effects of global warming.

11    So were the polar bears stranded?

12    They did not appear to be in danger . . . I did not see the bears get on the ice, and I did not see them get off. I cannot say either way if they were stranded or not.

*—Email from Amanda Byrd to Media Watch*

13    And they didn't appear stranded to Denis Simard of Environment Canada. He told Canada's *National Post*:

14      You have to keep in mind that the bears are not in danger at all. This is a perfect picture for climate change . . . you have the impression they are in the middle of the ocean and they are going to die . . . But they were not that far from the coast, and it was possible for them to swim . . . They are still alive and having fun.

*—The National Post (Canada) March 23, 2007*

15    Polar bears are good swimmers. So how did all this come about?

16    Photographer Amanda Byrd gave her photo to fellow cruiser, Dan Crosbie—to have a look. Crosbie gave the image to the Canadian Ice Service, who gave the image to Environment Canada, who distributed the image to 7 media agencies, including AP.

17     The Associated Press released the photo two and a half years after it was taken, on the day the United Nations released its major global warming report.

18     That's where Sydney's *Sunday Telegraph* got the photo, running it with a story taken from the [London's] *Daily Mail* as Neil Breen explains:

> . . .the photograph represents polar bears standing on ice that's melting. Now obviously there's a disputed account of when that was taken now, and maybe it was taken in the Alaskan Summer when you would naturally expect ice to melt but at the time it was sent to us, Associated Press in their caption to us told us that the picture was taken of melting ice caps and to do with global warming and that it was sent to them by a Canadian ice authority and we had no reason to question it.
>
>     *—Statement from Neil Breen (Editor of the Sunday Telegraph)*
> *to Media Watch*

19     But Amanda Byrd didn't think her photo necessarily described whether global warming is occurring. "I take neither stand, I simply took the photos . . . If I released the image myself, it would have been as a striking image. Nothing more," said Byrd in an email to Media Watch.

20     That's not how Al Gore saw it. He used it in a presentation on man-made global warming.

> "Their habitat is melting . . . beautiful animals, literally being forced off the planet," Mr. Gore said, with the photo on the screen behind him. "They're in trouble, got nowhere else to go." (Audience members let out gasps of sympathy . . .)
>
>     *—The National Post (Canada), Gore pays for photo after*
> *Canada didn't, 23rd March, 2007*

21     Well, that's because they're bears . . . and at a distance, they're rather cute. ◆

## CRITICAL THINKING

1. How much does knowing the context of this photo influence our interpretation of it?
2. Some environmental advocates countered that while the photo may have been cited out of context, the issue it raises is very real. Is it ever justifiable to skew information, such as

occurred with this photo, if it is arguably used to forward a good cause? Why or why not?

3. Could the photo have run with the global warming articles with the correct information? Would it have been as effective? Why or why not?

4. This photo stirred a great deal of controversy. Write a letter to your congressional representative in which you make an appeal for action on the issue of global warming. You may take any position on this issue you wish, but support your viewpoint with some data gathered from the essays and visuals in this casebook.

# TOPICAL CONNECTIONS

## GROUP PROJECT

1. What do college students think about the most pressing issues facing them today? Access the survey online at the Pew Research Center website. Each member of your group should poll at least 20 students. Compile the data and compare it to the results reported by the Pew Research Center. How are the concerns of college students similar to and different from those of the general public? Do you think age is a factor in how people respond to these concerns? Does political affiliation have any influence on the responses of college students? Does your survey reveal any strong disparities between groups? Explain.

## WEB PROJECT

1. Visit the Woods Hole Oceanographic Institution website and read its position on climate change and the environment at http://www.whoi.edu/institutes/occi, especially its research on abrupt climate change and global warming. Select a recent WHOI "Feature Story" (posted on the website under the "Related Topics" heading) and prepare a summary of the article for class discussion.

## FOR FURTHER INQUIRY

1. Several essays in this unit refer to the Kyoto Treaty, also known as the Kyoto Protocol. The United States is one of the few nations that did not ratify the treaty. Go online to look up the details on

the Kyoto Protocol. After learning more about it, write a one-page response expressing whether you believe the United States should or should not ratify it. In addition to the treaty itself, you may reference the reasons other nations have cited for ratifying (or not ratifying, as in the case of Australia) the treaty. Share your response as part of an in-class debate on whether the United States should have ratified the Kyoto Protocol.

# 8 | Is Fast Food Responsible for a Crisis in Public Health?

In 2008, the Centers for Disease Control reported that Americans were becoming more obese, faster, than when last measured only a few years before. Over 65 percent of U.S. adults, reports the Trust for America's Health, are considered either overweight or obese as defined by U.S. body mass index guidelines. And the future looks grim. According to projections, 73 percent of U.S. adults could be overweight or obese by 2010. And it is not just adults getting bigger. Childhood obesity is reaching an all-time high, with adult diseases such as type 2 diabetes presenting in children as young as six.

American physicians describe the situation as "epidemic." Perhaps even more distressing is the fact that despite the proliferation of health clubs and new exercise equipment, Americans are getting fatter and the effects of all the excess weight are apparent. An estimated 300,000 Americans die of obesity-related causes each year, and the direct medical costs of obesity are over $100 billion annually.

In addition to the proliferation of fast food restaurants, America has become more sedentary—physical education programs have been cut from many schools, we spend more time in front of computers and television screens than we do engaging in activities outdoors, and time constraints often require that we grab a bite at the local fast food chain rather than go home and fix a nutritious meal. The result of this combination of factors is visible—America has a weight problem on its hands.

But who is responsible for this crisis in public health? Is it the junk food companies advertising to young kids? Is it the fast food industry with its high-caloric offerings and encouragement to increase the portion size for a

## CRITICAL THINKING

1. Who are the people in the drawing? How are they depicted? What do you need to know in order to identify these people and understand what is happening? Explain.
2. Summarize your overall feelings regarding this editorial cartoon. Is the message funny? Disturbing? Explain.
3. Would this cartoon have worked well 20 years ago? Explain.

few more cents? Should we consider suing the fast food companies? This unit examines the continuing controversy over the connection between the expanding American waistline and the perceived crisis in public health.

Brian Fairrington – Cagle Cartoons – Posted 08/30/2005

# What's to Blame for the Surge in Super-Size Americans?

*Tori DeAngelis*

> Tori DeAngelis is a freelance writer who has written for *Psychology Today, Common Boundary,* the *APA Monitor,* and other publications. This article appeared in the January 2004 issue of *Monitor on Psychology,* a publication of the American Psychological Association.

## CONNECTING TO THE TOPIC

Are Americans relentlessly marching toward their own doom? Researchers are increasingly connecting today's fast-food culture and human biology to an epidemic of obesity. Human biology seems to have hard-wired us to store fat—just in case food runs out, our bodies like to store fat when food is plentiful. That might have made sense when humans were out hunting for their next meal, but we no longer live in caves, and getting food often requires only a short walk to the kitchen. What is to blame for the obesity explosion, and can we do anything about it?

## WORDS IN CONTEXT

**debilitating** (4)   detrimental to heath and vitality (adj.)

**vigor** (4)   energy and intensity (n.)

**virulent** (6)   toxic or poisonous (adj.)

**facet** (7)   aspect (n.)

**lauded** (13)   praised (v.)

**subcutaneous** (14)   just beneath the skin (adj.)

**propensity** (15)   tendency, inclination (n.)

**endocrine** (16)   relating to endocrine glands or the hormones they secrete (adj.)

**hypothalamus** (17)   a part of the brain located beneath the thalamus that regulates body temperature and certain metabolic processes (n.)

**countervailing** (18)   counteracting, compensating for (adj.)

**premise** (21)   the idea on which an argument is based or from which a conclusion is drawn (n.)

**disseminated** (22)   distributed, widely spread (v.)

1 It's a little hard to grasp, but the majority of us—about 65 percent, according to current government estimates—are obese or overweight. Compare that with 1960, when only 45 percent of Americans fell into those categories and proportionally far fewer were obese.

2 What's happened? Is it overindulgence—too much Ben & Jerry's and too little exercise? Maybe. But science is finding it's not so simple. In a special section of the Feb. 7, 2003, issue of *Science* (Vol. 299. No. 5608), some of the nation's top obesity experts agreed that multiple, complex factors—environmental, biological and genetic—make losing and even maintaining weight in today's environment an uphill battle.

3 "When you look at the big picture, there is really a mismatch between our physiology and our environment," says physiological psychologist and obesity expert James O. Hill, PhD, of the University of Colorado Health Sciences Center, who wrote one of the articles featured in *Science*. "We have an environment that provides food everywhere—it's inexpensive, good-tasting and served in large portions—and we have a physiology that says, 'Eat whenever food's available,'" Hill says.

4 Other environmental factors related to a lack of physical activity, such as sit-down jobs with ever-longer hours, further increase the odds we'll put on pounds, he says. Those extra pounds, as amply noted by the media, can lead to diabetes, stroke, heart attacks and other **debilitating** conditions, and such problems associated with obesity now cost the health-care system an estimated $117 billion per year. While solutions to the problem differ and much remains to be proven, there's already enough information to tackle the problem with **vigor**, psychologists concur.

## Environmental Causes?

5 Scientists of all stripes now agree that environmental factors such as easy access to junk food, sedentary jobs and high stress rates—once considered a radical and even ridiculous proposition by some—play a major role in the obesity epidemic.

6 "I think we can make the case that the epidemic is environmental in origin," says nutritional biochemist and pediatric expert William H. Dietz, MD, PhD, director of the Division of Nutrition and Physical Activity at the U.S. Centers for Disease Control and Prevention (CDC). "What we can't be very specific about is which of those environmental factors is

most **virulent.**" Data on direct cause and effect are still pretty scarce, he notes, and besides, many factors, are probably at play.

7      Indeed, says Yale University psychologist Kelly Brownell, PhD, an internationally known obesity expert who was the first to finger environmental causes for the epidemic, you could take almost any **facet** of modern life and find a possible culprit. His villain of choice is the food industry. In his new book, *Food Fight: The Inside Story of the Food Industry, America's Obesity Crisis and What We Can Do About It* (McGraw-Hill, 2003), Brownell cites several factors he thinks give the convenience-food industry an edge in the fight for consumers' taste buds. Unhealthy foods, he argues, are accessible, convenient, engineered with fat and sugar to be tasty, heavily promoted and cheap. By contrast, healthy foods are less accessible, less convenient, less tasty, not promoted and more expensive. "If you came down from Mars and didn't know anything about our country but those factors, you'd predict an epidemic of obesity," as he puts it.

8      Other features of the food business promote weight gain, too, Brownell maintains. More people are eating out than ever, and restaurant food tends to be higher in fat and calories and served in bigger portions than meals made at home. In addition, while research shows that people tend to eat the amount put in front of them, food manufacturers compete with one another to offer ever-larger sizes of low-cost, calorie-laden foods like French fries and soft drinks.

9      Other researchers are looking at how unhealthy eating may pair with other modern habits, such as television-viewing. CDC's Dietz began looking at the association in children 15 years ago, and others have since picked up the ball, finding what Dietz calls "a clear and significant association between TV-viewing and obesity in kids," and, in some cases, adults. What's not clear, Dietz says—and is an example of the cause-and-effect conundrum—is whether the relationship exists because TV-viewing promotes greater food intake, or because it represents sedentary time that children would otherwise spend being active.

10     Stanford University pediatric specialist Thomas N. Robinson, MD, is testing these variables, and in a still-unpublished study, shows that youngsters consume about 25 percent of their daily food in front of the television. When they decrease their viewing time, he posits, they eat less.

## Enter the Beer Belly

11  Researchers also are looking at eating habits and obesity in relation to another modern ill: stress. In the November issue of *Health Psychology*

(Vol. 22, No. 6), Debbie Ng, then a graduate student at the University of Minnesota and now at the Fred Hutchinson Cancer Research Center in Seattle, and University of Minnesota psychology professor Robert Jeffery, PhD, examined self-report data from 12,110 mostly white, middle-aged workers employed in a range of settings who took part in an earlier smoking-cessation program at 26 work sites in the Minneapolis and St. Paul, Minn., area.

12    Those reporting higher levels of stress—measured on a four-item scale asking how often in the past month they'd felt difficulties piling up and getting out of control, for example—also said they ate less healthy, fattier diets and exercised less often than those reporting less stress, the team found. (Stressed workers also reported smoking more.) The study is one of the largest to date to show these associations, Jeffery notes, and adds to research demonstrating that stress and poor health outcomes are often mediated by other factors, such as unhealthy eating habits.

13    Another new study—**lauded** as groundbreaking by many scientists—provides a possible biological explanation and working model for why people may eat fattier foods when under chronic stress. The study, by neuroscientist Mary Dallman, PhD, of the University of California, San Francisco, and colleagues, also suggests why stress eaters may initially gain weight in the abdomen. The research, reported in the *Proceedings of the National Academy of Sciences* (Vol. 100, No. 20), compared rats placed under chronic stress by physical restraint or exposure to cold with rats under acute stress and those not stressed at all. Chronically stressed rats chose fattier, more sugary diets, gained weight in their bellies and became calmer as a result. It also paints to likely hormonal underpinnings of those behaviors—essentially, that chronic stress activates a particular negative hormonal feedback system in rats' brains that's aborted when the animals eat high-fat food and gain belly fat.

14    "The research strongly suggests that eating high-carbohydrate and high-fat diets increased abdominal fat in these rats," says Dallman. "That, in, turn, reduced the brain's drive to activate the chronic stress response system." The reason weight goes to the belly rather than elsewhere, Dallman posits, is that belly-fat cells host more steroid receptors than **subcutaneous** fat cells, allowing fat in move quickly to the liver and be converted to energy. "The belly is a wonderful depot, as long as you don't overdo it," Dallman says. "If you do overdo it, it gets you into all kinds of trouble—the kinds of problems doctors worry about when they see patients who have a 'gut,'" she notes.

## The Gene Factor

15 Others are examining genetic reasons why some of us may be more prone to weight gain than others, given the same environmental influences. Neurobiologist Sarah Leibowitz, PhD, of Rockefeller University, has been studying strains of rats that are prone or resistant to obesity. Some of the rats are genetically engineered, or inbred, while others represent natural variation, called outbred. While she studies obesity-proneness in both strains, Leibowitz says she is "particularly eager to detect predictive markers in the outbred animals because they mimic the human population." About 30 percent show a strong **propensity** toward obesity, she says.

16 Obesity-prone rats of both types, she is finding, have different **endocrine** responses to eating than resistant rats. These responses are associated with disturbances in gene expression in the brain, she is finding, and also predict long-term weight gain. Over time, Leibowitz says, she'd like to define markers of gene expression in obesity-prone rats while they're still of normal weight, to help predict future weight gain and to design interventions accordingly. "The understanding of such markers could eventually help us target these kinds of systems in people at an early age," she explains.

17 Related to these findings, a November study reported in the new online journal *PLoS Biology* by French researcher Philippe Froguel and colleagues shows that obese people harbor a different form of a chromosome 10 gene, GAD2, than their non-obese relatives. The researchers hypothesize that having the gene variant may increase the amount of the neurotransmitter GABA—known to stimulate appetite—in the **hypothalamus** of the obese subjects. The two findings square with general scientific wisdom on the topic, which holds that genes may influence different people's susceptibility to obesity and overweight, says CDC's Dietz. Some studies, in fact, suggest that as much as 50 percent of the population may be so prone, he says.

## What to Do?

18 Given the apparent difficulty of knocking weight off, especially for some of us, what's to be done? Individual and group interventions are one solution, and a number boast intriguing success. Other proposed fixes include wide-scale public health and policy interventions. State legislatures introduced about 150 bills last year related to the topic, and federal legislators are

jumping on the bandwagon as well. In November, Rep. Rosa L. DeLauro (D-Conn.) and Sen. Tom Harkin (D-Iowa) introduced companion bills in the House and Senate that would extend nutrition labeling beyond packaged foods to include foods at fast-food and other chain restaurants. (Groups like the Center for Consumer Freedom are proposing **countervailing** legislation that would ban obesity-related lawsuits against restaurants.)

19   Brownell says such legislative hardball is a good solution: Food companies that create unhealthy food products and use aggressive or underhanded means to promote their products should be challenged, he says, much in the manner that the tobacco industry has been challenged. Likewise, he writes in *Food Fight,* political leaders should be encouraged to be innovative and to remove political barriers that prevent good national policy on the matter, he says.

20   Brownell acknowledges, however, that answers may end up coming not from the political arena, but from the grassroots. He cites recent moves by the cities of Los Angeles and New York to ban soft drink machines in schools as examples. He also believes in framing the argument around protecting children. "If we feel that children are victimized by this environment and that they are a group we need to protect, then many things will fall into place," he explains.

21   Hill is involved in an innovative public intervention that starts with a simple **premise:** energy in = energy out. Called "America on the Move," the program is based on calculations showing that the average American—who has been gaining an extra pound or two a year—has to burn off about 100 extra calories a day to "break even" at the end of the year. Hill deliberately touts the program as one to help people prevent weight gain rather than lose weight—an aim he says is the product of 25 years of seeing how difficult permanent weight loss can be, especially for some. Using the energy-balance formula, "it doesn't matter what your genetic pattern is, you won't gain weight," he explains.

22   Eight states are currently signed up for the program and 20 more are interested, Hill says. It's being **disseminated** through a number of vehicles including a Web site (www.americanonthemove.org), organizations including the YMCA, AARP and American College of Sport Medicine, and soon, health-care professionals. Hill notes that while people can achieve the 100-calories-a-day goal by eating less or exercising more, he emphasizes physical activity because of how difficult it is to restrict eating. Among his simple suggestions is using a step counter to log an extra

2,000 steps a day—the distance, roughly a mile—that it takes to burn 100 calories.

23   He admits that given the complexity of the problem, it's a pretty basic plan. "It's a simple idea, and that's what we were worried about—that people would say, that's just too simple to work," he notes. "But, in fact, it's simple enough that it works." ◆

## CONSIDERING THE ISSUES

1. What environmental factors often kept people from gaining too much weight in the past? Which of these environmental factors does society now lack? What has changed and why?
2. Consider the kinds of food you purchase. What do you buy? Do you buy fast food? How often? Are your choices driven by necessity—that is, do you pick foods that can be eaten on the go or are easy to prepare? Do you try to find "healthy" items, or is it difficult to tell what is good for you and what is not? Explain.

## CRAFT AND CONTENT

1. DeAngelis uses subtitles throughout her essay. Do these subtitles help organize her main points and keep her article on target? Do they lead the reader to make certain conclusions regarding her content?
2. Outline this essay using the organizing techniques described in the introduction of this textbook. Remember to include thesis statement, subtitles, and primary and secondary points.

## CRITICAL THINKING

1. The author refers to a cause-and-effect conundrum regarding television viewing and eating. In your opinion, does TV-viewing promote greater food intake or are children gaining weight watching television because they are being too sedentary?
2. As part of her conclusion, DeAngelis gives several suggestions to stop the rise of obesity. Evaluate her suggestions, and explain which ones you think are the most effective or appropriate for Americans to follow. Explain.

## WRITING ABOUT THE ISSUES

1. Think about the food served in the cafeterias at your college. What variety of food is offered? Is the claim made by Yale University psychologist Kelly Brownell that "healthy foods are less accessible, less convenient, less tasty, not promoted and more expensive" true in your cafeteria? What responsibility, if any, do colleges and other institutions have to provide and promote healthy dietary options? Explain.
2. Write a cause-and-effect essay in which you show how factors such as "easy access to fast food and junk food, sedentary jobs and high stress rates" can lead to obesity, or why they do not.

# You Want Fries with That?

*Richard Daynard*

Richard Daynard is a professor in the School of Law at Northeastern University. He is well-known for his work to establish the legal responsibility of the tobacco industry for tobacco-induced death, disease, and disability, and currently serves as chair of the Tobacco Products Liability Project and editor-in-chief of the *Tobacco Products Litigation Reporter*. This essay was published in the May 2003 issue of *Northeastern University Magazine*.

## CONNECTING TO THE TOPIC

Many people have heard about the lawsuits against big tobacco companies for deceptive practices. One comment made during the height of the cigarette litigation was that if tobacco could be sued, fast food and other "non-healthy" products would soon follow. In 2002, two teenage girls did just that—they sued McDonald's for making them fat. While their case was thrown out, it opened the door for similar, more targeted lawsuits. In the next piece, law professor Richard Daynard discusses why he feels the fast food industry is ripe for a lawsuit. Is the fast food industry responsible for widespread obesity? Should they pay? Should they change?

## WORDS IN CONTEXT

**libertarian** (2)   one who advocates maximizing individual rights and minimizing the role of the state (n.)
**purveyor** (2)   one that offers provisions, especially food (n.)
**aesthetic** (8)   concerning the appreciation of beauty (adj.)
**inundation** (12)   flood (n.)
**hedonism** (13)   pursuit of pleasure, especially the pleasures of the senses (n).
**epidemiological** (17)   concerning the branch of medicine that deals with the study of the causes, distribution, and control of disease in populations (adj.)

1   **W**hen I was organizing lawsuits against the tobacco industry in the 1980s and 1990s, the tobacco companies' favorite spin became like a mantra: "First, they go after cigarettes. Next, it'll be red meat and dairy products!"

2   Recently, a writer for a **libertarian** magazine caustically reminded me my response had always been "No way." Yet here I am, a decade or two later, urging litigation against **purveyors** of meat and dairy (and sugar) products—fast-food and packaged-food companies, in particular.

3   What gives? Well, I had a conversion. It began in April 2002, after New York University nutritionist Marion Nestle wrote a book entitled *Food Politics*, and I was asked to comment on whether her thesis opened the door to obesity litigation.

4   Nestle argues that Americans are getting dangerously fat because we're consuming more food than we did twenty years ago, largely because food companies maximize their profits by maximizing the amount of food their customers eat.

5   The companies accomplish this through a variety of misleading marketing ploys, and by buying off or manipulating those who are supposed to protect us—politicians, dietitians' organizations, and school boards, for instance.

6   I found Nestle's argument plausible and disturbing. What really shocked me was the scope and seriousness of the obesity crisis. In 1978, 15 percent of Americans were obese (meaning, more than thirty pounds above a healthy weight). This was a modest uptick from 13 percent twenty years earlier.

7   But by 2000, the obesity percentage had more than doubled, to 31 percent. An additional 34 percent of the population was overweight (ten to thirty pounds above a healthy weight). In other words, 65 percent of Americans were too heavy. The statistics for children, though lower than those for adults, were escalating even more dramatically.

8    And the problem isn't just an **aesthetic** one: Overweight and obese people are developing diabetes, heart disease, cancer, and other medical conditions in huge numbers. Indeed, in 2000, annual premature deaths related to obesity were estimated at roughly 300,000, approaching the figure for tobacco-related deaths. Perhaps most striking is the epidemic of type 2 diabetes among children and adolescents; until recently, this disease was known as adult-onset diabetes.

9    But questionable behavior that contributes to a public-health crisis doesn't by itself add up to a viable lawsuit. The obvious differences between Big Macs and Marlboros made me question whether my experience with tobacco litigation was applicable to the food industry.

10   There's no such thing as "moderate" smoking, for example. Even a little is bad for you (though a lot is obviously worse). Eating, on the other hand, is a biological requirement; too little food for a sustained period is as bad as too much.

11   And there are other important distinctions. People who eat too much get immediate feedback, in the form of an expanding waistline; smokers can harbor lung cancer or heart disease for years without symptoms. Nicotine is strongly addictive, which explains why people continue to smoke even when they know the dangers. Finally, though cigarettes can injure or kill nonsmokers, there's no such thing as "passive eating."

12   Nonetheless, the more I learned about the food industry's operations—the massive marketing budgets; the deceptive health and low-fat claims; the rush to supersize everything; the **inundation** of soft-drink promotions and machines in schools; the extra sugars and fats added to seemingly healthy potato, chicken, and fish dishes at fast-food restaurants—the more I became convinced that changing the industry's behavior is the key to stopping the obesity epidemic.

13   True, the food industry isn't responsible for many factors that contribute to obesity: "bad" genes, inactivity, conflicting advice from nutrition experts, **hedonism**, lack of willpower.

14   But these factors don't account for our bigger belt sizes. The genetic makeup of a population doesn't change much over a few decades. Weakness of will and hedonistic desires are pretty much what they've always been. Average physical activity may have declined since the late 1970s, but it wasn't very impressive then. What's making us fat has to do with changes in the way we're eating. And the food industry is obviously responsible for a lot of these changes.

15   But where does litigation fit in? Back in 1988, I wrote an article for the *Journal of the National Cancer Institute* in which I described five possible public-health benefits of tobacco-industry litigation.

16    First, that holding tobacco companies financially responsible for even a fraction of the cost of tobacco-related medical care and lost productivity—more than $100 billion annually—would force them to raise prices, thereby discouraging consumption, particularly among children and adolescents. This has in fact happened: Dramatic price increases prompted by the industry's settlement of lawsuits brought by the states were followed by equally dramatic reductions in smoking among minors.

17    Second, that lawsuits would have an important educational effect, translating **epidemiological** statistics into easily understood cases of real people. This too has happened. Even the industry's "personal responsibility" defense—anyone stupid enough to smoke shouldn't complain about getting lung cancer—helps discourage smoking by underlining a causal link the tobacco companies otherwise used to deny.

18    Third, that the ability of plaintiffs' lawyers to obtain and publicize internal industry records documenting misbehavior would serve to delegitimize the industry, making legislative and regulatory remedies politically practicable. More than thirty million pages of such documents are now available. The shocking behavior they reveal has made "tobacco executive" a term of opprobrium and tobacco money a dangerous commodity for politicians.

19    Fourth, that health insurers would be able to seek industry reimbursement for money spent caring for tobacco victims. To date, tens of billions of reimbursement dollars have been paid to the states.

20    And fifth, that if the tobacco industry responded like other industries confronted with product-liability claims, it would change its behavior: make its products less deadly, for example, or its marketing less deceptive. This alone has not happened, the tobacco industry having apparently concluded that its only future lies on the "dark side."

21    Similar benefits can be anticipated from food litigation, whether it takes the form of product-liability suits on behalf of obese citizens or, more likely, consumer-protection suits on behalf of classes of customers ripped off by unfair or deceptive marketing practices.

22    For instance, there's no reason why the cheapest foods should be the least nutritious. Foods made with added sugars and fats are especially "obesigenic." If, as a result of litigation costs, the most obesigenic foods carry a higher price tag than simpler, more nutritious foods—the kind your parents or grandparents used to cook at home—that would make a big difference to the American waistline.

23    Food litigation has already produced an explosion of media coverage, which has spotlighted the obesity epidemic. Food-industry trade groups

have responded—to the current suit against McDonald's, in particular—by insisting that everyone knows you shouldn't eat a steady diet of fast foods, despite the fact that most fast-food business comes from customers who do precisely that.

24 Unearthing documents that show how food companies manipulate and mislead consumers into buying their obesigenic products is likely to anger the public and complicate the benign image of food executives. And if health authorities can establish a causal connection between, for example, soft-drink concessions in schools, obesity, and the resulting health effects and costs, suits to recover these costs might be possible. Finally, if McDonald's has to pay for the harm caused by its Chicken McNuggets (which a court recently described as "Chicken McFrankenstein") or Filet-O-Fish, maybe it'll figure out how to formulate them without all the added fats and starches.

25 After all, food companies don't have to walk on the dark side. ◆

## CONSIDERING THE ISSUES

1. Have you ever been on a diet? If so, what motivated you to go on one in the first place? Do you think the media influences how attractive we believe ourselves to be? If you have never considered your weight to be an issue, write about why it has not been a concern for you.

2. Consider the meaning behind Daynard's comment that the problem of obesity isn't simply an "aesthetic" one. Why does he use this word? What does it imply about obese and overweight individuals? Another way of looking at this question is to think about our common perceptions of beauty. What is a beautiful body? Is the obesity problem more connected to beauty or health? What do you think?

## CRAFT AND CONTENT

1. Daynard cites five benefits of tobacco-industry litigation. What is the relevance of this list to his argument supporting lawsuits against the fast food industry? Explain.

2. Daynard has been teaching law since the 1960s. In what ways could this essay serve as a lecture? Identify areas of his argument that make it seem you are in a classroom listening to Daynard teaching. What questions would you ask him based on his lecture, and why?

3. In his conclusion, Daynard notes that a "court recently described" Chicken McNuggets as "Chicken McFrankenstein." What does this statement imply? Does it lead the reader to make a particular assumption about the opinion of the court? The judge who made this comment also threw out the lawsuit against McDonald's. If you did not know this, would you think that the judge was in favor of a lawsuit against McDonald's? Explain.

## CRITICAL THINKING

1. Daynard proposes in paragraph 22 that the price of nutritious food be made cheaper so that people with lower incomes can afford it. What does food cost? Consider the differences in price for "junk food" versus "healthy food." Do you think Daynard makes a good point? Explain.
2. Following Daynard's example, create a similar list of five reasons why suing fast food companies is a good idea.

## WRITING ABOUT THE ISSUES

1. Have the lawsuits filed in 2003 had any impact on fast food menu items? Take a look at some menu offerings on the websites of several large fast food chains such as McDonald's, Burger King, and Taco Bell. Do you think healthy additions to fast food menus will help alleviate the obesity epidemic? Why or why not?
2. Track your calorie intake over a two- or three-day period, noting everything you eat. Don't change the way you normally eat so that the test can accurately measure your eating habits. Tabulate your total intake for each day and average the number. Note your serving sizes (for example, a "serving" of macaroni and cheese is about 260 calories, but a whole box is about 780 calories). Did you consume more or less than you thought you would? What about serving size—is a serving an accurate way to measure how much you should eat of a particular item? Write a short essay about your experience and what it indicates about your eating habits.

# Blog Matters

A blog ("web log") is an online diary or commentary site that features regular entries that describe events, impressions, and viewpoints. Blogs may contain text, images, video, and often link to other websites, blogs, and online media. Most blogs allow readers to comment on the content of the post and to each other. As of 2007, the blog search engine estimated there were over 112 million blogs. While many blogs are maintained by individuals, some are run by journals, newspapers, and other media outlets. Remember that most blogs are not monitored for factual accuracy, and often express the opinion and views of the "blogger" writing the content.

The commentary blog below is hosted by AdBusters Magazine, "a global network of artists, activists, writers, students, educators and entrepreneurs who wish to advance a social activist movement of the information age," maintained by Adbusters Media Foundation.

# Bare Bones

*Emily Wierenga*
*March 25, 2008*

1　have a friend named Carolyn who lives in the hospital. Carolyn is 12 years old. She prefers the white-walled rooms to her home, because there she doesn't have to go hungry.

2　At home, she doesn't let herself eat. Food is a sweet-talking demon that haunts her mind and threatens her life. Her stomach rumbles 24 hours a day, a comforting lullaby to her starved brain. She sees World Vision commercials and remarks, "Those children are so lucky. They don't have to eat."

3　How twisted have we become? Jealous over bloated African children who would do anything for a crust of bread, while we're regurgitating entire loaves? Something has to change.

4　CosmoGIRL!, Teen Vogue, YM, Seventeen . . . piles of wasted trees trashing up the perspectives of today's North American Children. Skinny models decorate the pages, bare bones jagged and useless, faces gaunt with disillusionment and hunger, ribs exposed for the world to count.

5　We've been suckered into a disgusting cycle: we pile on the pounds from chocolate bars and potato chips, drive through McDonald's for a greasy heart-stopper, and top it all off with a Slurpee from 7-Eleven. Later, we race the treadmill for an hour, chasing away our guilt, only to plop in front of the television to gorge on celebratory ice cream and commercials.

6　Then there are those who veer to the other side of the health-highway: organic fruits and vegetable, extra lean beef, lite cheese, no-fat yogurt, no-calorie sodas, anti-oxidant tomatoes, polyunsaturated margarines, green teas, flourless bread and high doses of Omega 3, topped off with some salty Styrofoam snacks known as Rice Cakes.

7　What are we teaching our children? To choose between one of two extremes? Whatever happened to good old-fashioned balance?

8　Cut the cable cord, spend the summer on a farm, and work up an appetite growing your own food. Fill your offspring with nutrients and values that will strengthen their bones and nurture their minds.

9　Then maybe instead of being jealous of starving children overseas, this generation will weep in compassion for the unnecessary wealth we regurgitate every day.

*Posted by: LOL*
*March 19, 2008*

I don't know anymore. This is like saying its bad to be fat or healthy. I guess everything is bad. I agree that the food we eat is crap but that's what we are given because a lot of people are to dumb or busy writing articles that just repeat the same thing over and over. Action is our only hope now. I have different friends and some are fat some are skinny and I like them each for what they are. Some of them have medical conditions others don't. What I'm trying to say is we shouldn't pass judgment on people. Just because you see a skinny person it doesn't mean they have anorexia. Just talk to people and be happy.

*Posted by: Ian B*
*March 19, 2008*

Nicely done. I first found it a little shocking that this was a 12 year old talking . . . but I do recall girls in grade 5 reading *Seventeen* magazine . . . they were not 17. I agree, the idea that we can binge and purge lacks sustainability in all respects.

*Posted by: College Girl*
*March 19, 2008*

I totally agree with your 5th paragraph. I am guilty of it.

*Posted by: G*
*March 19, 2008*

I think it has a lot to do with how women are treated in this culture. They are supposed to be pretty, obedient dolls just so they can get each other's approval. They are not supposed to be strong, independent, free thinkers.

*Posted by: Stephanie*
*March 19, 2008*

Yes, the CosmoGirls and Teen Vogues of our time teach children that being skinny is beautiful. But then Dove comes out with a campaign showing women with different body shapes, and many people said crude things. It's no surprise why children as young as 12 have these feeling about thinness. Living on a farm and growing your own vegetables won't solve this culture's REAL problem: the perception of beauty.

## RESPOND TO THE BLOG:

What do you think? Are we caught up in a culture that is making kids fat and then making them feel bad about it? What can be done to fix the problem?

# Fast Food Isn't to Blame

*R. A. Ames*

R. A. Ames is a part-time student at a college in Massachusetts. He wrote this essay for a critical writing course in the fall semester of 2003.

## CONNECTING TO THE TOPIC

In the next essay, writing student R. A. Ames asserts that the source of weight difficulties lies with people themselves, and not with the fast food industry. He acknowledges that his essay may seem harsh, but he believes that until people assume responsibility for their actions, the obesity problem will only get worse. How responsible are we for choosing the things we eat? Is body size simply a matter of the will? Are fast food lawsuits just another way Americans can absolve themselves of personal culpability for their actions?

## WORDS IN CONTEXT

**metabolism** (2)   the process by which substances are broken down in the body (n.)

**euphemism** (11)   the substitution of a mild, indirect, or vague term for a term considered harsh, blunt, or offensive (n.)

1    It seems like America has an obesity problem and it is getting worse. Frankly, I am a little sick of it. I have a part-time job as a clerk at a department store at the local mall, and I see many different types of people. More and more of the store's patrons are shopping in the large size section. Later, I see them eating at the food court, putting thousands of calories into their mouths in a single sitting.

2    Now I don't mean to be insensitive here, as I am sure many overweight people are already thinking of a hundred angry retorts to my first paragraph. The fact is, I have been overweight myself and I know that it is no picnic (pardon the pun). I read those articles on "loving yourself" and tried to buy into the whole "fat is beautiful" propaganda. The truth is that it is a whole lot easier to get fat than to stay thin. And because of this, it is much more appealing to try and make yourself believe that cultural attitudes against obesity are the fault of advertisers, the fashion industry, society, you name it. And if you aren't blaming external forces, you cite internal ones—your **metabolism** or your genes. The only one you don't want to blame is yourself.

3    This essay is not about my "success story." The fact of the matter is, I was fat, I knew I needed to change, and I did. One day at a time. And over the course of two years, I got down to a healthy weight. But just as slimming down was an act of my will, so was getting fat. And this is the point that most overweight people seem to want to avoid. They are fat because they got themselves that way.

4    If you are fat, with the very rare exception of those suffering from specific diseases affecting metabolism (and such people are rather rare), the only finger to point is right at yourself. The food that you put in your mouth got in there because your hands lifted it there, plain and simple. No one tied you down and stuffed food into your mouth. You willingly ate yourself into the state that you are in. And the problem is that it is very, very easy to do. We live in a land of plenty—literally. The very luxury of choice makes it very hard—if we didn't have access to such temptation, we would probably be better off. But that doesn't mean that it is the restaurant's fault. Maybe you have no willpower to tell yourself "no," but it is still your responsibility. Overweight people need to own up to this unpleasant fact.

5    In my opinion, I have no right to tell anyone else what to do, as long as they aren't hurting me. I won't tell someone that they shouldn't smoke, even though the harmful effects of smoking are well-documented.

Likewise, I won't tell someone not to eat himself or herself into a size XXL, as long as I don't need to sit next to them on a train on my way to school. (And this isn't because I think large people are unpleasant—it is just uncomfortable to be squished in between two overweight people with six stops left to go.)

6     I compare obesity to smoking because they are essentially very similar. The deadly health hazards of smoking—lung cancer, emphysema, bronchial infection, mouth cancer, etc., have been clearly established. The health hazards of obesity—diabetes, heart disease, and certain cancers, have also been well publicized. Both smoking and eating are something that you consciously do, perhaps addictively, but you still have to put a cigarette in your mouth the same way you put a candy bar. And now the two have one more thing in common—smokers and overeaters are blaming corporate industries for their acts of free will. To quote a famous news-journalist, "give me a break."

7     Now, instead of taking responsibility for their weight problem, fat people, like smokers (and what about the obese people who also smoke . . . I would love to be their HMO), are blaming the fast food industry. They are even suing corporations such as McDonald's for financial restitution. (Hey, you didn't think that they would sue for a health club membership?)

8     Let's think this through. You are hungry, and you want to eat. What do you do? Do you drive to a supermarket and pick up some turkey breast from the deli and some whole wheat bread? No, you drive to Burger King and order a Double Whopper with Cheese with a King size fries (hey, it is just a few cents more). You eat the 1070-calorie Whopper sandwich and the 600 calorie fries, ingesting 100 grams of fat in the process. You wash it down with a 300-calorie large soda.

9     Lo and behold, you get fat. Amazing. How did this happen? Oh, that's right, the fast food companies. They made you fat with their tasty and tempting fattening foods and their sly way of offering super-sized versions of their already caloric offerings. You had better sue them.

10     Am I the only one who sees just how absurd this is? Why are overweight people even arguing about this? America is suffering—2/3 of its population is overweight. It is high time that the population wakes up and takes responsibility for its actions. There is a frightening trend going on in America—we are becoming a nation of whiners who refuse to accept responsibility for anything. We sue at the drop of a hat. We smoke ourselves into hospital beds, and yes, we are eating ourselves to death. The "land of the free" means that we are free to make our own decisions, but part of this

freedom is the responsibility to own up to our choices. It doesn't mean free to do what we want and then blame someone else when we don't like the final results.

11    Unless we send a message as a society that this behavior is simply unacceptable, the problem is going to get worse. People respond to social and financial pressure. Maybe one solution would be to demand higher health insurance premiums for obese people–their condition is something they can change, unlike a disease condition like cancer or Alzheimer's. And I say that we stop being so sensitive in how we discuss obesity. We don't want to offend anyone. We use **euphemisms**—overweight women wear "women's sizes" (how about calling them "overweight sizes"?) and obese men are called "portly." They are already deceiving themselves; we shouldn't help.

12    I know my view may be unpopular. I know it may sound mean. But I think that the very reason it may be unpopular is because it holds more than a kernel of truth. Obesity hits the very core of us—it has deeply emotional and psychological components. To admit that you are obese is hard. To admit that you got yourself in such a condition is even harder. I know that. But until we do—as individuals and as a nation—we are going to get worse. And that is a future I really don't want to think about, because our present is grim enough.  ◆

## CONSIDERING THE ISSUES

1. In your opinion, how personally responsible are we for our body size and shape? What factors can we control, and what factors are beyond our power? Do you hold yourself responsible for your physique? Explain.
2. What is the social view of obese people? Are they subjected to harsher social scrutiny? Are they treated differently? What about on television? How are overweight men and women portrayed on television? Explain.

## CRAFT AND CONTENT

1. Why does Ames tell his audience that he has struggled with his own weight? Does this admission make his essay seem more valid? Do you think he feels that it does? Explain.

2. What is Ames's tone in this essay? What is your reaction to this tone? Explain.

3. In paragraph 5, Ames notes that he feels that he has "no right to tell anyone else what to do." Does he stick to this claim throughout the rest of his essay? Explain.

### CRITICAL THINKING

1. At the end of his essay, Ames provides some possible solutions to America's obesity problem. Evaluate these solutions. Are they likely to work? Why or why not?

2. Evaluate Ames's comparison of smoking to eating. In what ways are the two similar, and in what ways are they different? How would Richard Daynard likely respond to this comparison? Explain.

### WRITING ABOUT THE ISSUES

1. Write a response to Ames in which you either agree or disagree, in whole or in part, with his argument. Cite specific areas of his essay that you find of particular interest. Support your response with as much factual evidence as you can find.

2. Write an essay in which you express your own opinion on the McDonald's obesity lawsuits. Do you think McDonald's should be held accountable, even in part, for America's obesity crisis? Do you think that the issue is one of personal or corporate responsibility? Explain.

# Body Mass Index
*National Institutes of Health*

### CONNECTING TO THE TOPIC

Body mass index (BMI) is a measure of body fat based on height and weight that applies to both adult men and women. According to the National Institutes of Health, BMI is a reliable indicator of total body fat, which has been found to increase your risk of disease and death. While the score is usually

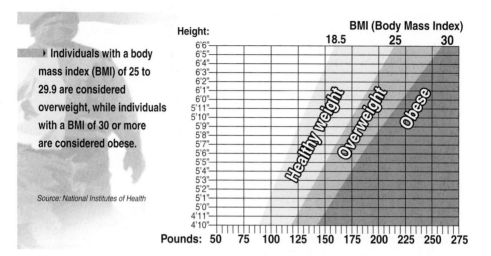

▸ Individuals with a body mass index (BMI) of 25 to 29.9 are considered overweight, while individuals with a BMI of 30 or more are considered obese.

*Source: National Institutes of Health*

valid, BMI isn't perfect. It may overestimate body fat in athletes and others who have a muscular build, and underestimate body fat in older persons and others who have lost muscle mass.

# Indiana Jones and the Kingdom of Fat Kids
*Rahul K. Parikh*

Rahul K. Parikh, M.D., a fellow of the American Academy of Pediatrics, is a pediatrician in the San Francisco Bay area. He has written for the *Chronicle,* the *Contra Costa Times,* and *New America Media* and is regularly published on Salon.com where he writes on medical issues. Parikh also serves as chief of patient education at Kaiser Permanente Medical Center in California.

## CONNECTING TO THE TOPIC

One particularly lucrative merchandising technique is having fast food restaurants place movie-related toys in their kids' meals. There movie tie-ins are extremely popular with children and promote both the movie and the fast food restaurant; however, with childhood obesity at alarming rates, movie tie-ins to fast food are irresponsible, says this pediatrician. In this open letter to George Lucas and Steven Spielberg, posted on Salon.com on May 21, 2008, Dr. Parikh appeals to the famous directors to stop cutting deals with fast food companies and promoting unhealthy lifestyles to America's most impressionable population—its children.

## WORDS IN CONTEXT

**cardiovascular** (5)  pertaining to the heart (adj.)
**epidemic** (5)  wide-spread, affecting many people or populations (n.)
**correlated** (9)  connected, associated (adj.)
**conglomerate** (11)  describing corporations made up of several companies (adj.)

1  Dear Mr. Lucas and Mr. Spielberg,

2  When I was a kid, your movies were a big part of my summers. So were all the goodies that came with them—"Star Wars" action figures, Indiana Jones trading cards, Reese's Pieces (E.T.'s favorite candy). Somewhere in my parents' house, I think I've still got a box of treasures with all of those memories. Among them are souvenirs I picked up at Taco Bell and Burger King, like a "Return of the Jedi" soda glass with a portrait of the menacing Darth Vader painted on it.

3  A generation later, I still eagerly anticipate your movies. My friends and I lined up hours in advance to see "The Phantom Menace" in 1999, and I weaseled my way out of a family obligation with the in-laws so I could catch "Attack of the Clones" in 2002. A couple of weeks ago, I hopped online to check out the trailer for the new Indiana Jones movie, "Indiana Jones and the Kingdom of the Crystal Skull," and I'm looking forward to buying the first three films of DVD.

4  In the 30 years since you've started making movies, one thing that hasn't changed is a kid's (or in my case, a grown man's) imagination and wonder. And who sparks that better than you?

5  But a lot of other things about kids have changed. Their health is one of them. Today, almost one in four kids is obese, putting them at risk for, among other things, diabetes and **cardiovascular** disease. The **epidemic** of obesity is serious enough that we're predicting that this current generation won't live as long their parents and grandparents. That's incredible if you think about it.

6    Which brings me to why I wrote this letter. I'm a pediatrician, and every day I see overweight kids coming into my office. Getting families and kids to change how they eat is an uphill battle, and it doesn't get easier when big studios like yours wheel and deal with companies that peddle junk food and fast food.

7    You tied "Star Wars" to Pepsi and Frito-Lay, plastering Yoda and Obi-Wan over 2-liter bottles and Doritos bags. Recently I was watching CNBC and saw the chief marketing officer of Burger King unveil the Indy Whopper, a mammoth, juicy burger with pepper jack cheese and jalapeño sauce (to give it "adventure," the CMO pointed out), a tie-in to "Indiana Jones and the Kingdom of the Crystal Skull." I see you also got Mars to manufacture a Snicker's Adventure Bar with coconut and chai that has Dr. Jones' face on the wrapper.

8    Besides the fact that none of these foods is healthy, one has to ask if they're what your characters would eat. Would Lord Vader chug down a

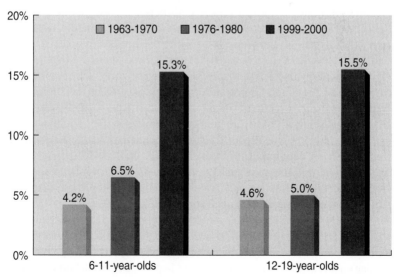

**Proportion of Overweight
Children in the United States**

Source: Centers for Disease Control and Prevention, National Center for Health Statistics, Health, United States, 2003, Table 69.

Pepsi before he wielded his light saber? (If he did, would he drink it with a straw or take off his entire mask?) Wouldn't Indy, now a senior citizen, have more than just a little bump in his cholesterol if he had scarfed down his namesake burger with fries and a soda? How could he be fit enough to chase down ancient relics while dodging boulders and outwitting Nazis?

9　　You may think I'm playing the blame-the-media-and-Hollywood game. But an increasing body of medical evidence shows that child advertising and obesity are **correlated**. Take a look at a study by the Kaiser Family Foundation. According to the report, each week American kids spend a full-time job's worth of time in front of the TV, on the Web and playing video games. They will see about 40,000 ads per year, and two-thirds of those ads are for junk food and fast food. Studies show that what kids see on TV is what they tell their parents they want for supper. No doubt the Indy Double Whopper—with bacon!—will be flying off the greasy grill in short order.

10　　It's not all the media's fault. Parents need to take charge of what foods they're buying and how they're preparing those foods. Many families, especially poor ones, get a whole lot for their hard-to-earn dollars when they buy cheap, processed and calorie-dense foods. Fresh fruits and vegetables are more expensive, don't last as long and take time to prepare—time that's hard to find if both parents work full time to pay the bills. This gap between the waistlines of the rich, middle class and poor is only going to get worse with rising food prices. It's also a crime that many hospitals, like shopping malls, now contain a McDonald's, where patients with Type 2 diabetes, cancer and other serious illnesses can gorge on fast food before and after they get treated for those very diseases.

11　　So I'm asking you: Why do you still tie in your movies with junk food and fast food? I know that you and your corporate partners make millions from deals with **conglomerate** food companies and fast-food chains. But do you really need the extra cash at this point? Wouldn't it be better, in a corporate crusader kind of way, to change course? Stop these deals, or partner with somebody who thinks a little healthier?

12　　I don't want to single out just movies. There's a ton of companies that use characters and celebrities to peddle junk food. Check out this summary from the Center for Science in the Public Interest. Being a sports fan, my favorite is the one about Jason Giambi, who endorsed Pepsi by saying that drinking several a day really "lifts him up." (Actually, I think it's safe to say that it was more than Pepsi that lifted Jason's batting average during the 1990s.)

13    On the other hand, you are two of the most powerful and influential people in the media today. Mr. Lucas, you've even been called the forefather of the movie tie-in. So if you change, and do so publicly, others may well follow suit. About two years ago, Disney backed out of its long-term partnership with McDonald's in part because of the issue of childhood obesity. Would you both be willing to do the same?

14    If not, then perhaps a little truth in advertising, or in cinema, is in order. You should show us how your characters would look if they ate the food that you helped peddle. In that vein, you got Jabba the Hutt right. But Princess Leia in her skimpy steel bikini with cellulite? Indiana Jones having to hit the brakes during a car chase and find a glass of water so he can take his Lipitor? Now that I think about it, wouldn't Viagra have been the best tie-in for the new movie?

15    Humor aside, I ask you to consider the reality of childhood obesity. It's a serious problem; it needs serious solutions. Doing your part would help more than you might imagine.

16    Sincerely, Rahul K. Parikh, M.D. ◆

### CONSIDERING THE ISSUES

1. In your opinion, who is responsible for addressing the issue of childhood obesity—parents, schools, the government, restaurants, the media, others? Explain.
2. Both as a child and as an adult, have you ever wanted or purchased a food product because it had a famous movie character or person on it? Was the food healthy or "junk food"? What made you want to purchase the product?

### CRAFT AND CONTENT

1. This argument against movie tie-ins was written as an "open" letter to two famous movie directors. Why do you think that Dr. Parikh chose to write his argument this way, and what do you think was the reaction of Mr. Lucas and Mr. Spielberg upon learning of this "letter"?
2. Find the thesis statement to Dr. Parikh's argument (when the author states his purpose for writing the letter). Where is it located? What is he writing about before he gets to his thesis

statement? Why do you think he chooses to begin his letter in this way?

## CRITICAL THINKING

1. The author asks for "a little truth in advertising, or in cinema." If movie makers use tie-ins to products, should the movie then be compelled to portray its characters using these products in a realistic way? How would this affect the movie-going experience?
2. Parikh states, "Humor aside, I ask you to consider the reality of childhood obesity." In what ways is Parikh being humorous, and does Parikh's use of humor add to or detract from the effectiveness of his argument? Is using humor a good technique for persuasion? Explain.

## WRITING ABOUT THE ISSUES

1. Craft a letter back to Dr. Rahul K. Parikh in which you pretend to be either Mr. George Lucas or Mr. Steven Spielberg. Think of how Lucas or Spielberg would realistically respond to Parikh's argument.
2. Dr. Parikh asks for Mr. Lucas and Mr. Spielberg to "Check out this summary from the Center for Science in the Public Interest." Go to the Center for Science in the Public Interest website at http://www.cspinet.org/new/200311101.html and view the CSPI report, which "identifies a plethora of ways that companies target kids in their homes, in their schools, on the web, and wherever else kids go." Then brainstorm a list of other ways that companies target children.

# When America Relaxes, 'Food Police' Should Keep Quiet
*Paul King*

Paul King is senior editor of *Nation's Restaurant News,* in which this article was first published in the August 25, 2003, issue.

## CONNECTING TO THE TOPIC ─────────────────

Americans love fast food. But if we try to blame the fast food industry for America's obesity problem, could we end up with "banned" foods? Could fast food companies deem some foods just too high a liability? What could happen to our freedom of choice? Could the "food police" ruin fast food?

1   The Walt Kelly cartoon character Pogo once uttered the now-famous line. "We have met the enemy, and they is us!"

2   In the quickly heating debate over obesity in America, nowhere was the inescapable truth of Pogo's statement more evident for me than during my recent vacation in Pittsburgh.

3   The scene was on The Boardwalk, the collection of eateries found at a water park called Sandcastle. It was a great place for people-watching, especially if you wanted to view out-of-shape adults in ill-advised swimwear.

4   It was also the first place I actually had encountered the fried Twinkie. I had heard and read about the fat-laden, cream-filled sponge cake, but I never had seen one. There it was, on the menu at one of the snack stands, alongside the funnel cakes and—believe it or not—fried Oreos.

5   I just had to taste the fried Twinkie—for research only, of course— and so while my children took one more slide down the Tornado water ride, I got on line to place my order, two Twinkies for $2.50.

6   For the uninitiated, making a fried Twinkie is simple. You take a chilled Twinkie—you have to chill it so the cream filling doesn't liquefy in the fryer—dip it in funnel cake batter and then quickly deep-fry it. The chilling-and-frying method gives you a hot-cold combination when you bite into it.

7   "Do you get many orders for these?" I asked the blonde teenager behind the counter while I waited for my made-to-order treat.

8   "Yeah, we get some," the girl answered. "But more people order the Oreos."

9   "Do you like them?" I asked.

10  "Nope," she said. "I think they're nasty. I just eat the funnel cakes."

11  As I waited, I noticed the heavy-set couple directly to my right, who were waiting for their order, the Funnel Cake Supreme. Sandcastle, which operates its own foodservice, makes that colossally caloric confection by taking its already artery-clogging fried dough and topping it with a thick ribbon of vanilla or chocolate soft-serve ice cream. Then, to gild the lily, your server pours a generous helping of syrupy strawberries on the ice cream.

12    For $4 the dessert is a real bargain in that it easily could feed four people. But the couple had ordered one apiece. I stared, slack-jawed, as they walked away to the seating area. I was so mesmerized by the sight that I didn't immediately hear my order being called.

13    As my family gathered around the table to taste our dessert, I mentally recalled all the stories I'd been reading over the past few months about lawsuits being filed against fast-food chains and about activists railing against soda and chips being sold to our nation's school-children.

14    In all truthfulness I think that the "food police" have a very valid point: Most Americans, given several nutritional paths, will choose the tastiest road. That way leads to madness, but many people gladly are willing to go crazy in that manner.

15    They also are right to be concerned about the message most food advertising sends to our young people and to try to counter that with nutrition education and some modicum of control over what foods our kids can buy while they are in the hands of our educators.

16    But do we really need crusading attorneys who blame the fast-food industry for the nation's obesity woes, and their ilk, to save us from ourselves? Does our already litigious society need to clog the courts with nutrition lawsuits faster than our eating habits can harden our blood vessels? I don't think so.

17    I'll never eat a Funnel Cake Supreme. But when I'm treating my family to a day out, whether at an amusement park or a sports event, I expect to have the opportunity to have that choice. The enemy may be us, but I'll accept that. It's sweeter than the alternative. ◆

## CONSIDERING THE ISSUES

1. In his essay, King watches with great interest an obese couple eating an excessively caloric dessert. Do you notice what other people eat around you? Do you make judgments about those people based on what they eat and how they look? Do you consider your own menu choices when you know others may see what you are eating? Explain.

2. Could lawsuits influence what kinds of foods we are offered at fast food chains in the future? How have lawsuits already affected menu offerings? Do you think Big Macs and Whoppers could face extinction? Why or why not?

## CRAFT AND CONTENT

1. What is the purpose of the Walt Kelly quote at the beginning of King's narrative? How does this quote connect to his essay? Explain.

2. How does King describe lawyers in paragraph 16? What words does he choose? What does his word choice reveal about how King feels about fast food litigators?

## CRITICAL THINKING

1. How does King feel about the large couple's choice of dessert? Does he feel that they should have ordered two Funnel Cake Supremes? Do you think he would have had the same opinion if the couple was more physically fit?

2. Who are the "food police"? What impact could they have on our fast food choices? Explain.

## WRITING ABOUT THE ISSUES

1. Write a personal narrative mirroring King's experience. Go to a fast food outlet and order something on the menu. Note the people around you, and what they are eating. Write about your impressions of the experience.

# We Eat; Therefore, They Are

*Rosie Mestel*

Rosie Mestel is a medical writer at the *Los Angeles Times*. In addition to the *LA Times*, her articles have appeared in many publications, including *New Scientist*, *Health* magazine, and *Discover*.

## CONNECTING TO THE TOPIC

While many people assume that board-certified physicians help develop and approve the government's dietary recommendations, few are aware of the intense political lobbying that goes on behind the scenes influencing these recommendations. Food is big business in the United States. Companies that sell foods that are high in fat or sugar have a great deal riding on what dietary recommendations the government officially supports. As this article published in the August 10, 2004, edition of the *LA Times* explains, official recommendations may not be free of political influence.

## WORDS IN CONTEXT

**regally** (1)　as if holding court; with a kingly air (adv.)

**haggard** (6)　appearing worn or tired (adj.)

**castigated** (12)　severely criticized (adj.)

**tepid** (22)　lacking enthusiasm; literally, lukewarm (adj.)

**ire** (24)　with anger; intense anger (n.)

**strenuous** (24)　requiring great effort or energy (adj.)

**blight** (26)　something that prevents or impairs growth; lacking in hope or ambition (n.)

**rollicking** (28)　high-spirited and enthusiastic (adj.)


1　Inside a packed ballroom at the local Holiday Inn, 13 government-appointed scientists sat **regally** around a table, debating servings of fish.

2　"What do we want to recommend for children? Fish twice a week?" asked chairwoman Janet King.

3　"Small fish," another panel member said.

4　"Children are advised to eat smaller portions of fish than adults?"

5　"Can we defer a vote on that?" pleaded another.

6　The august panel of nutrition researchers had been talking this way for 45 minutes. The ballroom was filled with silent listeners scribbling away on notepads. Some of the listeners were looking a little **haggard**. They had already witnessed exhaustive discussions on protein, sugar, fat, grains, breakfast, exercise and a record-breaking 2 1/2-hour standoff on vitamin D. "Mind-numbing isn't the half of it," said a woman in line for the restroom. "I want to strangle them."

7　After a year's work, the Dietary Guidelines Advisory Committee is in the final stages of overhauling the Dietary Guidelines for Americans, which will be formally adopted next year. Since 1980, the guidelines—consisting of seven to 10 short statements and an accompanying booklet—have been issued every five years by the departments of Agriculture and Health and Human Services.

8    School menus must comply with the guidelines; so must the Women, Infants and Children program, which provides food to low-income mothers. The food pyramid, currently receiving its own overhaul, is also based on the guidelines. America now waits hungrily for the latest update.

9    Do these scholars think we should still "choose a variety of fruits and vegetables daily" as the guidelines currently decree? Should we continue to "choose and prepare food with less salt," and "aim for a healthy weight"? Would it remain wise to "choose beverages and foods to moderate your intake of sugars"?

---

### Dietary Advice Through the Ages

1917: The Department of Agriculture releases a 14-page pamphlet, 'How to Select Foods, encouraging Americans to eat from five food groups: milk and meat; cereals; vegetables and fruits; fats and fat foods; sugars and sugary foods.

1941: First recommended daily allowances released by the National Academy of Sciences.

1959: Nutrition researcher Ancel Keys and wife Margaret publish guidelines for avoiding heart disease, including 'do not get fat; if you are fat, reduce'; 'restrict saturated fats'; and 'be sensible about cigarettes, alcohol, excitement, business strain.'

1977: Dietary Goals for the United States—a report from the Senate Select Committee on Nutrition and Human Needs—recommends cutting back on salt, saturated fat, sugar and cholesterol. Food industry groups protest, as do some scientists and doctors.

1980: First edition of the Dietary Guidelines for Americans. People are told to avoid too much sugar, sodium, fat, saturated fat and cholesterol; to maintain an ideal weight; eat a variety of foods; and drink alcohol only in moderation.

1991: The Food Guide Pyramid is completed, sparking food industry protest. Agriculture Secretary Edward R. Madigan withdraws the pyramid, claiming it is confusing to children.

1992: The Food Guide Pyramid is released to the public.

*Sources: 'Food Politics' by Marion Nestle, 2002; U.S. Department of Agriculture; Department of Health and Human Services. Researched by Times staff writer Rosie Mestel*

10    To reach their conclusions, committee members—unpaid volunteers generally drawn from academia—have waded through thousands of pages of studies on fat, heart disease, television watching, obesity and the effect of fiber on stool weight. They have investigated the best way to wash broccoli and argued bitterly on the matter of sugar. They have been aided by testimony and letters from hundreds of groups and individuals, including the Sugar Association, the Grocery Manufacturers of America, the American Heart Association, People for the Ethical Treatment of Animals, the Bible-based Hallelujah Diet and scads of disciples of Dr. Joseph Mercola, author of "The No-Grain Diet."

11    The job is "enormous—probably one of the most difficult jobs I ever had," said Dr. Cutberto Garza, director of the division of nutritional sciences at Cornell University and chairman of the 2000 Dietary Guidelines Advisory Committee.

12    He didn't get paid, but he had some exciting times. Before the job was done, his committee sparked a lawsuit by an advocacy group claiming the panel had a pro-milk bias, was challenged by one senator for being too positive about alcohol and **castigated** by 30 other senators for being too negative about sugar.

13    Writing the dietary guidelines is honor, toil, aggravation and tedium— in unequal measure. The results of the group's work are bland and seemingly obvious bits of advice that most Americans have never read.

14    "It is interesting to see how they put it all together," whispers one audience member. "It is a little bit boring, of course." [ . . .]

15    Complaints surfaced from the moment the committee was appointed last year. The Center for Science in the Public Interest pointed fingers at seven of the 13 selected committee members for having financial relationships with industry groups, including the Sugar Association, the Campbell Soup Company and the American Cocoa Research Institute.

16    How, asked the consumer group, could Americans be sure the scientists were unbiased?

17    Richard Hanneman, president of the Salt Institute, was pretty ticked too. He has peppered the committee with letters complaining about the unfair and unscientific treatment given to salt in the 2000 guidelines, which told Americans to "choose and prepare foods with less salt."

18    "We could not accept that," said Hanneman, who hasn't missed a dietary guideline meeting since 1990. "We don't think there's evidence that the public should consume less salt."

19    The Sugar Association and the Grocery Manufacturers of America both wrote to say that the guidelines don't focus enough on physical activity—just on what people eat. The grocery manufacturers have suggested that the name of the guidelines be changed to the Dietary and Physical Activity Guidelines.

20    Such intensity about eating advice did not exist a century ago when the government began issuing guidelines, said Marion Nestle, a professor of nutrition, food studies and public health at New York University and author of the 2002 book, *Food Politics: How the Food Industry Influences Nutrition and Health.*

21    In the early days, the Department of Agriculture advised people to eat widely and plentifully, in keeping with its role promoting American agriculture. The advice has changed through the years—there were five food groups in 1917, 12 in 1933, eight in 1942 and either seven or 11 in 1943, depending on which pamphlet you consulted.

22    The tips were at times on the **tepid** side: The 1979 "Hassle-Free Guide to a Better Diet" told readers that many scientists felt diet contributed to chronic disease, but others did not, "so the choice is yours."

23    The trouble began when the government started advising people to start eating less of certain foods, Nestle said. One flap erupted in 1977 after a Senate committee report suggested Americans cut back on saturated fats, sugar, cholesterol and salt. The cattle, dairy, egg and sugar industries protested—and the report was revised, easing up on salt and cholesterol and dumping the phrase "reduce consumption of meat" for a friendlier "choose meats, poultry and fish which will reduce saturated fat intake."

24    The food pyramid also drew **ire** upon its completion in 1991 because its pointed shape indicated that some foods should be eaten less than others. **Strenuous** objections from the National Cattlemen's Association and National Milk Producers Federation—both of whose products were nearer the top of the pyramid—caused a one-year delay in the pyramid's release.

25    Creating the guidelines is still "political—from start to finish," said Nestle, who was on the 1995 Dietary Guidelines Committee. "It's science politics. It's politics politics. It's corporate politics." She recalled tensely standing her ground to ensure that a phrase she hated—"there is no such thing as a good or bad food; all foods are part of a healthy diet"—was not included in the 1995 guidelines.

26    Nestle bemoaned the fact that even as Americans fatten up, no one is ever told to eat less of any specifically identified food—not even a candy

bar or soft drinks. And she snorted at the guideline about sugar, which as far as she's concerned has been infected by a creeping **blight** of wishy-washiness.

27 In 1980, people were flatly told to "avoid too much sugar." By 2000, the committee was going to tell Americans to "choose beverages and foods to limit your intake of sugar"—but the word "limit" was tossed out at the last minute by the government (after industry protests) and replaced with the weaker word "moderate." This time, people are holding their breath to see if there will be a sugar guideline at all. [. . .]

28 [The May] meeting of the committee was supposed to be the last, but a **rollicking** debate about vitamin D threw everything off schedule. No one was certain when the meeting would end. "I'm figuring midnight," said a USDA employee, placidly stitching away on a patchwork quilt to pass the time. Fresh science, it seemed, had emerged since 2000, revealing that many people are deficient in the vitamin. But some committee members were nervous about recommending a big jump in intake.

29 Brisk progress was made on some subjects: Eight draft guidelines were crafted advising Americans to "keep food safe to eat," "monitor your body weight to achieve health," "choose and prepare foods with less salt" and "be physically active every day."

30 For the first time, the committee planned to recommend Americans slash their intake of trans fats, those hardened, partially hydrogenated vegetable oils found in stick margarines and many baked goods.

31 But sugar was a sticky mess. As the committee took up the issue again, an excited rustle went through the audience like so many candy bars being unwrapped. Dr. Carlos Camargo, assistant professor of medicine and epidemiology at Harvard University, cited three recent studies reporting that kids drinking the greatest number of sugary soft drinks ended up plumper later on.

32 Nutrition researchers Teresa Nicklas, professor of pediatrics at Baylor College of Medicine, and Joanne Lupton, professor of nutrition at Texas A&M University, lobbed back other types of studies that didn't find that link.

33 Camargo, noting his position as president of the American College of Epidemiology, said that the other types of studies were inferior in design.

34 Well, Lupton said, if we're going to ignore them for sugar, we have to ignore those kinds of studies for other issues too.

35 "We're here to make a difference," Camargo said.

36     "I don't think we are here to make a difference," Lupton said. "I think we are here to evaluate the science."

37     The mood began to lighten when sugar was put off again and matters drifted on, past cholesterol and fish to a discussion of alcohol, in which nothing, as usual, was left unquestioned. The panel debated a recommendation that alcohol be avoided by children and those operating heavy machinery. One committee member asked for the pertinent data.

38     They forged ahead, moving on to fiber's impact on heart disease and bowel motion. Lupton explained that there had been more than 100 studies on the effect of fiber on stool weight and its consequent speedier passage through the bowel. "So there is a very strong . . . are you laughing at me for talking about this?" she said.

39     Some committee members were giggling.

40     "It is interesting where we, as a society, have placed our research efforts . . . 100 trials on stool," Camargo said. Lupton tried to explain that constipation is one of the most common disorders in Western countries, affecting up to 10% of children and maybe 20% of people aged 65 and older. A blond woman five rows back was laughing so hard she was crying.

41     Some people in the audience took advantage of the uproar and sneaked out for an evening snack. ◆

## CONNECTING TO THE TOPIC

1. Does the U.S. government, with its "official" food pyramid, have a responsibility for the overall public health? Why or why not?

2. Do you follow the Dietary Guidelines for Americans? For example, do you look at the nutritional information on the sides of food products? Does the information on the panel influence what you eat? Explain.

## CRAFT AND CONTENT

1. In paragraph 27, Mestel describes how the very words used to caution Americans on sugar intake became a subject of great debate. The recommendation changed from "avoid" to "limit" to "moderate." What do these words mean to the average consumer? Would you be influenced to eat less sugar if you were told to "limit" your intake as opposed to "moderate" it? Explain.

2. In paragraph 36, in response to Dr. Carlos Camargo's charge that the committee was there "to make a difference," professor Joanne Lupton replied, "I don't think we are here to make a difference. I think we are here to evaluate the science." What does she mean? Do you agree with Camargo's position or Lupton's position, and why?

## CRITICAL THINKING

1. Before reading this article, were you aware of how the Dietary Guidelines for Americans were determined? What assumptions regarding government recommendations did you have? After reading this article, are you more or less confident in the government's strategy for developing the new guidelines? Explain.
2. Marion Nestle expresses frustration that while Americans are obviously dealing with health problems related to expanding waistlines, "no one is ever told to eat less of any specifically identified food—not even a candy bar or soft drinks." Should certain foods carry warnings? Is it up to the individual to know which foods are healthy and which ones are not? Is it the government's responsibility to guide the public? Explain.

## WRITING ABOUT THE ISSUES

1. Write an essay exploring your own eating habits as they are influenced—or not influenced—by the guidelines set forth by the government or on the sides of prepared-food packages. Include in your response the nutritional information cited online by fast food companies such as McDonald's. Is this information helpful? Why or why not?
2. Mestel provides a glimpse into the inner workings of a government panel responsible for developing the Dietary Guidelines for Americans. Based on what you have read, explain how you feel about this panel and its effectiveness. If you wish, make recommendations of your own about how the Dietary Guidelines for Americans should be drafted.

# VISUAL CONNECTIONS

## Now What Do We Eat?

### CONNECTING TO THE TOPIC

Over the last two decades, thousands of schoolchildren were taught the "food pyramid" approved by the United States Department of Agriculture. Many Americans believed that they understood what healthy eating habits included, even if they didn't actually have such habits themselves. But the food pyramid has come under fire as Americans begin to rec-

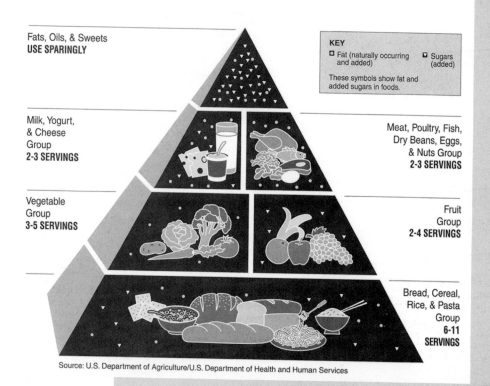

# Food Guide Pyramid
## A Guide to Daily Food Choices

Fats, Oils, & Sweets
**USE SPARINGLY**

**KEY**
□ Fat (naturally occurring and added)  ▪ Sugars (added)
These symbols show fat and added sugars in foods.

Milk, Yogurt, & Cheese Group
**2-3 SERVINGS**

Meat, Poultry, Fish, Dry Beans, Eggs, & Nuts Group
**2-3 SERVINGS**

Vegetable Group
**3-5 SERVINGS**

Fruit Group
**2-4 SERVINGS**

Bread, Cereal, Rice, & Pasta Group
**6-11 SERVINGS**

Source: U.S. Department of Agriculture/U.S. Department of Health and Human Services

ognize a growing obesity crisis nationwide. Is it time to revise the food pyramid? Walter Willett of the Harvard School of Public Health thinks it is. He has created a new food pyramid and has published a book, *Eat, Drink, and Be Healthy*, encouraging all Americans to change their eating habits in order to enjoy more healthy lives. A graphic of the traditional food pyramid, familiar to most people from their days in health class, appears on the preceding page, and Willett's revised pyramid can be seen below.

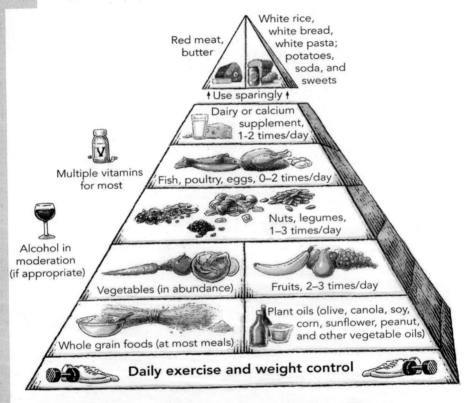

## CONSIDERING THE ISSUES

1. Do you try to follow the recommendations of the USDA food pyramid? How much food, based on servings, do you think you would eat if you followed the traditional pyramid? Explain.
2. What information do you need to know in order to understand what is happening in this picture? Explain.

## CRITICAL THINKING

1. Review the recommendations of each pyramid carefully. Consider how your dietary habits compare to each graph. What pyramid seems more healthy, and why? How does your diet compare to the recommendations in each graph? Explain.
2. The pyramid on the facing page was designed by a professor of health and has not yet been approved by the USDA. Based on what you read in Mestel's article, do you think it is likely that Willett's pyramid will be approved for the general public? Why or why not?

# TOPICAL CONNECTIONS

## GROUP PROJECTS

1. Discuss in your group the following question: If you could be either very beautiful or very wealthy, what would you choose? Explain the motivation behind your choice. Based on your group's multiple responses, can you make any conclusions about the influence of body size, beauty, and social acceptance in today's society?
2. Together with your group, develop a lawsuit against a popular fast food chain. Identify the reason behind the suit, the people on whose behalf you are suing, and the expected restitution. Refer to specific points made in the essays in this chapter.

## WEB PROJECTS

1. One of the issues explored in this chapter is whether the fast food industry should assume some financial responsibility for health issues connected to obesity in this country. In Colorado, laws protect certain industries and workers, such as dude ranches and ski-lift operators, from "frivolous lawsuits." In January 2004, the Colorado legislature submitted a bill to protect fast food industries against obesity lawsuits. Research this issue in greater depth on the Internet (try newspapers such as http://www.denverpost.com). Should states pass such bills? Are they a good idea? Why or why not?

2. In April of 2005, the U.S. Department of Agriculture revised the traditional food pyramid. View the new pyramid at http://www.pyramid.gov and compare it to the two other pyramids featured on pages 345 and 346. Which pyramid do you prefer, and why? Do we need a visual to explain how we should eat? If you were in charge of the USDA, how would you approach the issue of explaining dietary recommendations to children and adults? To support your project, research additional information on nutrition online at http://www.nal.usda.gov/fnic and http://www.nutrition.org.

## FOR FURTHER INQUIRY

1. The obesity crisis is not just an adult problem—childhood obesity rates have tripled over the last 20 years. Disease conditions such as type 2 diabetes, more commonly called "adult onset" diabetes, and heart disease are striking children at an alarming rate. Research the issue of childhood obesity. Why are children getting heavier? What can be done to stop this disturbing trend? And what could happen if we don't? Visit the Kid Source website addressing childhood obesity at http://www.kidsource.com/kidsource/content2/obesity.html for more information. The National Institutes of Health also provides information on this issue at http://www.nih.gov/news/WordonHealth/jun2002/childhoodobesity.htm.

# 9 | Can Religion and Science Coexist?

**M**any of us are familiar with the concept of the separation of church and state. Beyond the immediate legality of the doctrine, as defined by the First Amendment, is the issue that expressions of religious belief are unacceptable in any state or public arena—such as at political events, on public greens, and in schools. While many expressions of faith have been banned from public schools—such as Christmas pageants, public prayers, and convocations—the issue of religion has arisen in the biology classroom with renewed fervor.

The debate over the teaching of evolution verses "intelligent design" in the classroom is certainly not new. In 1925, the Scopes "monkey trial" brought the debate into public discourse, and the courthouse, with legendary trial lawyer Clarence Darrow challenging William Jennings Bryan, a fundamentalist Christian and staunch opponent of evolution. Darrow contested a Tennessee law that forbade the teaching, in any state-funded educational establishment in Tennessee, of "any theory that denies the story of the Divine Creation of man as taught in the Bible, and to teach instead that man has descended from a lower order of animals." The trial highlighted what happens when religion and science collide in public schoolrooms.

Almost 60 years later, the U.S. Supreme Court ruled that creationism should not be taught in public schools directly in the 1987 case of *Edwards v. Aguillard*. The most recent debate concerns the teaching of "intelligent design"—which many critics claim is just a reshaping of creationism. Also at issue is the idea of promoting evolution as "another theory" on how life began, one that should have equal weight with other theories, including religious ones.

350

## CRITICAL THINKING

1. What is happening in this cartoon? Who are the people in the cartoon, and what are they discussing? Explain.
2. What is the meaning of the boy's reason for not answering the math question? What point is the cartoon making through the boy's explanation?
3. Based on this cartoon, what can you determine about the cartoonist's position on intelligent design in the classroom?

Debate often centers on how evolution fits into religious explanations of human life, and its lack of compatibility with the literal interpretation of the creation stories of the Bible and the Qur'an. In the United States, the tension between the scientific community and religious teachings focuses

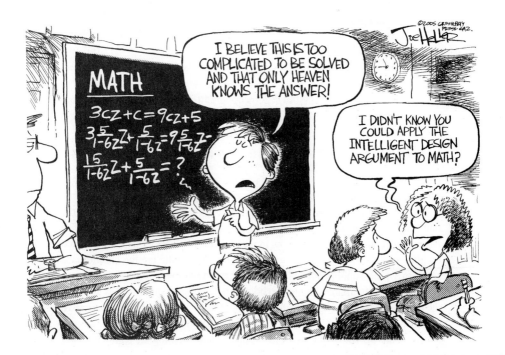

on public education and the separation of church and state. Beyond the issue of religion in the classroom is the broader question of whether science itself runs counter to religious teaching. Should evolution be taught to children whose parents oppose the science on religious grounds? Should alternative theories to evolution be taught as well, even if they are based on religious texts? Can you be religious and still believe in evolution and other science-based explanations for life? This unit explores the current debate over religion and science, evolution and intelligent design, and the political and social nuances connected with these issues.

# Say It Ain't So

*Karl Giberson*

Karl Giberson is on the faculty of Eastern Nazarene College, where he teaches interdisciplinary honors seminars and the history of science. He also serves as director of the Forum on Faith and Science. He has written for various publications, including *Discover, Perspectives on Science & Faith, Books & Culture*, and *Christianity Today*. He is the author of several books, most recently *Oracles of Science: Celebrity Scientists Versus God and Religion* (2007 with Mariano Artigas) and *Saving Darwin: How to Be a Christian and Believe in Evolution* (2008). His next book, *The Anointed: America's Evangelical Experts*, is expected to be published in 2009 by Harvard University Press. This essay appeared in volume 10 of *Applied Developmental Science* in 2006.

## CONNECTING TO THE TOPIC

Controversy over whether scientific or biblical explanations of life's origins should be taught in our public schools emerged more than 80 years ago. Today, evolutionists and creationists are engaged in a nationwide legal battle. On the one hand, evolutionists maintain that the principles put forth by Charles Darwin, including natural selection, make up a scientific theory that is supported by abundant data and visible evidence. On the other hand are the creationists, some of whom support not only the belief that God made the world—a concept embraced by many scientists who also believe in evolution—but also that the earth is only as old as the Bible states—about 10,000 years. Do alternative theories—especially religiously based ones—belong in the nation's schoolbooks? Can we find some middle ground? Here, theologian Karl Giberson outlines the controversy and its history.

## WORDS IN CONTEXT

**cavorting** (2)  dancing around happily (v.)

**Gomorrah** (5)  in the Bible, a corrupt and sinful city (n.)

**referendum** (7)  legislative measure voted on by the public (n.)

**ambivalence** (8)  hesitation (n.)

**manifest** (8)  evident, obvious (adj.)

**mitigating** (12)  watering down, moderating (adj.)

**grist to the mill** (17)  more evidence, ideas, etc., added to an argument; literally, grain brought to a mill to be ground into flour (n.)

**pedagogy** (18)  teaching method or practice (n.)

**canon** (18)  official, accepted body of texts (n.)

**pernicious** (22)  wicked, harmful (adj.)

**benign** (23)  harmless (adj.)

**oxymoron** (27)  contradiction, especially in a figure of speech (n.)

**dichotomy** (31)  division in two (n.)

1    "**S**ay it ain't so, Joe" is the saddest phrase in the long drama that is America's national pastime. This enduring lament, uttered by a small boy tugging on the sleeve of his hero, the great Shoeless Joe Jackson, captured the anguish of fans of the 1919 Chicago White Sox. Shoeless Joe was coming out of a Chicago courthouse in 1920, having testified of his role in accepting a bribe to throw the World Series. A great darkness had settled on America's pastime as fans across the country wished that somehow, it just wasn't so, that the sun would rise on a new morning, and it would turn out that one of the greatest teams in baseball was not populated by crooks.

2    "Say it ain't so" has also been the response of ordinary Americans to Darwin's theory of evolution, which has been in America almost as long as baseball. Just as we can't accept that the heroes of our national pastime are crooks, we can't accept that we descended from a lower order of animals, that we are related to the chimpanzee and the baboon, that we were not specially created by God. Surely we are not the product of random chance stirring in the mud to make life, **cavorting** in the forest to make intelligence, dropping from the trees to walk on two legs. Say it ain't so.

3    America has never made peace with Darwin's theory of evolution, now well over a century old. Outlawed in many states around the time of the infamous Scopes Monkey Trial, soft-pedaled in biology textbooks for decades, challenged in court during the 1980s in Arkansas and Louisiana,

Darwin's controversial theory is still under assault; its current attacker is called Intelligent Design.

4    "Under assault" is a strong but appropriate metaphor for this conflict. America's ongoing confrontation with Darwinism is nothing less than a culture war, fought on many fronts, with many weapons, with an odd assortment of allies. At stake, if the heated rhetoric is to be believed, is America's future.

5    Shall we continue, asks one side, to follow Darwin and his materialistic philosophy down that long decadent road to **Gomorrah**, and allow America to descend into moral anarchy? Or shall we reject Darwin, recover our glorious Christian past, restore the founding values that have made this country great, and once again place America in the prosperous light of God's favor?

6    Or, asks the other side, shall we reject science in favor of superstition? Shall we halt the clock of progress and wander back into a blinkered past, leaving the rest of the world to move forward without us? Shall we embrace false stories and teach them to our children simply because we like them? Shall we abandon scientific truth to the rest of the world and content ourselves with a medieval worldview?

7    The above paragraphs, despite their rhetorical extremes, do not caricature America's controversy over evolution. How in the world did a debate about a biological theory acquire such an apocalyptic tone? How did Darwin's theory become a **referendum** on America's morality trajectory?

## Evolution Versus Intelligent Design

8 Science in the United States, while revered for its contributions to our modern way of life and our understanding of the world, is viewed by many Americans with **ambivalence**. Religious conservatives, firmly planted within a tradition of attributing natural phenomena to God and reading God's purposes in nature, are uneasy about the *naturalism* of "natural science." This naturalism, which they call *materialism*, is and always has been corrosive of traditional religious beliefs. In its extreme form naturalism can be cast in an aggressively atheistic mode and has often been used in this way by those eager to discredit religion. Conservative religious opposition to a purely naturalistic science that rules out the supernatural has been a perennial feature of the cultural response to scientific progress. In America this concern has been **manifest** in a persistent opposition to evolution in particular, but also cosmology, geology, and even psychology.

The debate over intelligent design dominating today's headlines is simply the current manifestation of this long-standing controversy and is energized by the same concerns as its predecessors.

9    Twentieth-century America witnessed several celebrated legal confrontations aimed at weakening the teaching of evolution in public schools. The Scopes Monkey Trial in 1925 in Dayton, Tennessee, was the most famous of these and has taken up an enduring, if misleading, residence in our culture in the form of the play and movie *Inherit the Wind*.

10    The Scopes Trial followed expansions in public education that saw more students staying in school past the 8th grade and thus encountering science at the high school level. This science included evolution, which many parents, especially in the conservative South, found offensive. As a result Tennessee passed a law sponsored by John Washington Butler, a farmer, making it illegal to teach that "man has descended from a lower order of animals." The rest, as they say, is history, or in this case Hollywood.

11    Hollywood's version of the Scopes Monkey Trial is deeply memorable and seared into America's national psyche, largely because the play and the movie introduced many powerful fictional elements. [. . .] William Jennings Bryan was a great and nationally beloved politician, of the sort we no longer see in Washington. What did he care about the details of a scientific theory? Why would he launch himself into a controversy for which he was woefully unprepared? Bryan campaigned against evolution, not as a scientific theory, but as a dangerous and misguided social program. Bryan was convinced that evolution provided a rationale for disastrous social mischief, calling it a "merciless law by which the strong crowd out and kill off the weak." This survival-of-the-fittest mentality had led Germany into World War I and was eroding faith among educated Americans, a charge that echoed across the 20th century and is still being heard.

12    Bryan's nemesis in the Scopes Trial, the infamous agnostic Clarence Darrow, also came to Dayton with troubling views of evolution. Shortly before he signed on with the ACLU to defend Scopes, Darrow argued the controversial Leopold and Loeb case, which made national headlines. Americans read daily of Darrow's spirited defense of two wealthy and privileged Chicago teenagers who, apparently for fun, had murdered 14-year-old Bobby Franks with a chisel. The disturbing story had the nation clamoring for the death penalty. Darrow rescued the boys from death row, **mitigating** the horror of their crime with an eloquent argument based partly on Darwin's theory of evolution. Human beings, said Darrow, can never fully escape their animal natures.

13    The social baggage that both Bryan and Darrow associated with evolution was not just populist confusion, the sort of error typically committed by the scientifically uninformed. It was, quite literally, *textbook* Darwinism and could be found in, for example, in the bestselling biology text of the day, Hunter's *A Civic Biology*.

14    When placed in its social context, the controversy in Dayton was no more an argument about the merits of a biological theory than the controversy over nuclear weapons is an argument about a physics theory. Right or wrong, scientific theories often come laden with social baggage. Only in ivory towers where detached academics ply their trade is scientific knowledge ever "pure" and unadulterated. In the real world, where people vote, pay taxes, attend church, and send their children to public schools, scientific ideas are embedded in social agendas that dominate the response to those ideas. Whether Bryan and Darrow understood evolution correctly is not the point. Evolution still carries a lot of social baggage and it is this baggage, not the explanatory power of natural selection, that rallies America around Intelligent Design.

## Design's Assault on Evolution

15  The fallout from Scopes was complex. Both sides claimed victory but nothing was resolved. Bryan and his followers were held up to ridicule in much of the country, but other states passed anti-evolution laws and textbook publishers downplayed evolution to be on the safe side.

16    This changed in 1959 when the Russian launch of Sputnik startled America's scientific community, convincing them that American science needed reform. The result was a curriculum in which evolution dominated biology, consistent with the role it had come to play in that discipline. Once again American teenagers were learning evolution in high school and their parents were getting alarmed. Descended from monkeys? Say it ain't so. . . .

17    The new curriculum spawned the movement that came to be known as Scientific Creationism. Led by a Southern Baptist named Henry Morris, the creationists captured the religious hearts and troubled minds of grassroots America with their simple message that evolution and its materialistic baggage did not need to be embraced. It was a flawed theory promoted, not because the evidence supported it, but because of its resonance with atheistic naturalism. Populist arguments that evolution was incompatible with Christianity moved millions of evangelicals firmly into the creationist camp.

Public debates in which polished creationists defeated unprepared evolutionists added **grist to the mill**. Polls revealed that most Americans were creationists and wanted the theory taught in their public schools.

18     The goals were modest. Rather than outlawing evolution, the demand was simply for "equal time." In 1982 in Little Rock, Arkansas, a formal legal challenge was launched, mandating an "American-sounding" equal time high school **pedagogy**, requiring that creationism be taught alongside evolution. Dubbed "Scopes II" the Arkansas encounter captured headlines and generated a substantial literature. Ultimately, however, the Judge ruled that there was no basis for teaching creationism alongside evolution in Arkansas' public schools. Creationism, wrote Judge Overton, "fails to follow the **canons** defining scientific theory."

19     Legal challenges to the teaching of evolution worked their way to America's Supreme Court where, presumably once and for all, creationism was declared unscientific, religious, and inappropriate for America's high school biology classes.

20     The same grassroots opposition to evolution that carried Bryan to Dayton to prosecute John Scopes endures undiminished into the 21st century. This anti-science populism gave birth to the Intelligent Design (ID) movement just over a decade ago.

## Creationism Evolves into Intelligent Design

21 The defeats suffered by creationism in the years since Scopes culminated in the Supreme Court's 1987 rejection of a Louisiana law that forbid the teaching of evolution unless creation science was also taught. The court ruled, simply and definitively, that creationism could not be taught in America's public schools. Evolution had apparently won, and creationism retreated to a substantial but largely fundamentalist comfort zone, where it continues to flourish, out of sight of mainstream science.

22     Conservative intellectuals found this disturbing. If evolution won the academy, they reasoned, its **pernicious** naturalism would soon pervade the intellectual foundations of all aspects of American life. No one was more disturbed about all this than the brilliant, colorful, theologically conservative Berkeley law professor Phillip Johnson. If creationism was too religious for America's public schools, as the misguided and liberal courts had ruled, he would provide an anti-evolutionary alternative that was not so obviously religious. He would give the courts, which he understood very well, having clerked for Earl Warren, something they could not

summarily reject as a breach of the battered-but still-standing wall between church and state.

23    Thus was born the intelligent design movement, or ID2. Conceived as
a nominally secular assault on evolution and the naturalism of science, ID
has evolved into a well-funded and politically savvy assortment of
lawyers, philanthropists, scientists, polemicists, philosophers, and bandwagon jumpers. With considerable financial support from the Seattle-
based Discovery Institute, ID is challenging high school science teaching,
working through local school boards instead of the courts. The top-down
approach of the creationists had required taking on a relatively sophisticated class of educators, something the creationists were simply not prepared to do. The new ID strategy was much simpler—fight a lot of small
battles rather than a large war. A relatively modest investment could em-
power a campaign to elect sympathetic members to a local school board,
who would then pass a resolution undermining the teaching of evolution.
And, by crafting these resolutions to sound both **benign** and secular, they
often passed with minimal fanfare.

24    Following Johnson's don't-sound-religious-in-public strategy, the ID
movement, with secular sounding rhetoric, asks only that high school students be alerted, for example, to the "problems" with evolutionary theory and
that "alternative explanations" be provided. What could be more reasonable?

25    The strategy of ID is to portray the conflict between their position and
evolution as being between rival scientific theories, something that is not
uncommon. There are, in fact, poorly understood natural phenomena that
have rival scientific hypotheses competing as explanations. Astronomy,
for example, has long tolerated competing explanations for dark matter, or
the origin of the moon, or the peculiar tilt of Uranus. In such cases textbooks present multiple explanations, not so students can make up their
own minds about which is correct, but because the different explanations
have substantial support within the scientific community and science *does
not yet have a definitive understanding.*

26    ID would like their explanation placed alongside evolution as a viable
alternative and, in the name of fair play and open-mindedness, taught to
America's high school students. This sounds generous and appeals, like
the "equal time" argument advanced at the Arkansas trial, to America's
sense of fair play. But it is a false claim. Unlike the alternative explanations for the origin of the moon, there are no alternatives to evolution. One
looks in vain in the scientific literature for alternatives to evolution. To be
sure, there are many controversies, but they are all located *within* evolution,

and are about the details of how evolution works. There simply is no scientific theory of Intelligent Design within science. But there is also no theory of Intelligent Design outside science either.

## The Bogeyman of Naturalism

27 Science, as understood by most of its practitioners, is no more incompatible with religion than plumbing. Science does not **oxymoronically** seek *supernatural* explanations for *natural* phenomena, any more than plumbers invoke the supernatural to explain leaky faucets or running toilets. Many scientists—and presumably plumbers as well—have no objection to supernatural explanations outside of science (and plumbing). But science *qua science* is, and always has been, *natural* science. The problem, however, as we have noted repeatedly, is that science invariably comes with baggage.

28 The leading spokespersons for science—Richard Dawkins, Stephen Hawking, Edward O. Wilson, Carl Sagan, Stephen Jay Gould, and Steven Weinberg, to name the six who are most responsible for current cultural perceptions of science—paint a rather different picture of science than the innocent search for natural explanations for natural phenomena. They all argue that there is nothing beyond the natural phenomena studied by science. If we define and measure science—and knowledge in general—by the standards of its leading public figures, it certainly appears that science validates an all-encompassing naturalism that leaves no room for the religions so near the hearts of most Americans. In fact, all six of the above scientists are actually hostile to traditional religion and use science, especially evolution, to argue against it.

29 ID draws its considerable public support from this very concern. If you are convinced, perhaps by reading the many books of the scientists mentioned in the preceding paragraph, that science is incompatible with your religion, you are faced with a choice: If your primary loyalty, in concert with most Americans, is to your religion, then you must reject science, or at least accept that there is something deeply wrong with it. ID offers an eloquent explanation of exactly what that might be, with the added bonus of an alternative science to replace the flawed one.

30 Johnson and his foot soldiers in the ID movement have challenged the big guns of science in what amounts to a culture war that goes way beyond any scientific controversy over evolution. Lost in this culture war is the fact that the majority of scientists are not hostile to religion and many of them are actually quite religious.

31     So, while Intelligent Design might be poor science, its supporters are entirely justified in calling attention to those who would enlarge the naturalism of science into an all-encompassing worldview. The philosophical debate over ID starts with a false **dichotomy** embraced by protagonists on both sides: the world must be explained by either God or the natural causes of science, but they are mutually exclusive. ID chooses God, concluding that there is something faulty in science that must be changed. The leading public voices for science choose natural causes, concluding that there is no room for God.

32     America is a deeply religious nation, with a long history of near universal religiosity. When confronted with scientific theories that appear to undermine their religion, their response has always been the same: Say it ain't so. ◆

## CONSIDERING THE ISSUES

1. Should public schools be forced to teach both evolution and creationism, or Intelligent Design? Is this contradictory to the mandate separating church and state or a way to find a compromise on a controversial subject?
2. How does Giberson's essay trace the "evolution" of creationism and Intelligent Design in public schools? Explain.

## CRAFT AND CONTENT

1. How is the title, "Say it Ain't So," significant to the essay's main point? How does the title reflect the controversy over Darwin, evolution, and creationism? How does Giberson connect the title and the story behind it to the controversy he illustrates in his essay?
2. Outline the "evolution debate" timeline as described by Giberson in this essay. What conclusions can you draw about what might happen next in this timeline based on the history of the debate Giberson provides?

## CRITICAL THINKING

1. Giberson describes how the debate over evolution has a long history that extends over 80 years. Do you think it is likely that

Americans will ever reach a compromise on this subject that satisfies the majority? Why or why not?

2. According to Giberson, what accounts for the increasing popularity of Intelligent Design? Why does it appeal to so many people?

## WRITING ABOUT THE ISSUES

1. What is Intelligent Design (ID)? Write an essay in which you agree or disagree with the theory. In your essay, address the broader question "Are science and religion mutually exclusive?"

2. Why are Americans so frustrated by the evolution-versus-creation debate? What is at stake intellectually, socially, and religiously?

3. Giberson references the movie, *Inherit the Wind.* Research this movie online. Based on his essay, why do you think he objects to the premise of the movie? Explain.

# A New Theology of Celebration
*Francis S. Collins*

Collins is a physician-geneticist who is most widely known for his leadership of the Human Genome Project that identified the genetic blueprint of Homo sapiens. Collins's commitment to providing free access to genomic information made the data immediately available to the scientific community, propelling research in many areas of science and medicine. He is the author of *The Language of God: A Scientist Presents Evidence for Belief* (2006) in which he explains why he considers scientific discoveries an "opportunity to worship." This editorial appeared in the September/October 2007 issue of *Science and Spirit* magazine.

## CONNECTING TO THE TOPIC

In this editorial, a renowned biologist reflects on the current battle between atheists and fundamentalist Christians. On the one hand, many atheists claim that intelligent people must reject religion as unreasonable and illogical. On the other hand, fundamentalist religious groups are forcing believers to agree that the world is 10,000 years old and any other interpretation is a rejection of their religious faith. Collins, himself a religious convert, describes his vision for a new theology in which faith and science cooperate and happily coexist. Is his vision nothing more than wishful thinking?

## WORDS IN CONTEXT

**audacious** (1)    bold (adj.)
**theologians** (8)    scholars of sacred texts (n.)
**Pollyanna** (9)    naively optimistic person; based on a character in a series of early-twentieth-century children's books (n.)

1    I have often been accused of being optimistic. In the early days of the Human Genome Project, some very wise people predicted that this **audacious** project would end in failure. But as the leader of the effort from 1993 until its conclusion in 2003 (ahead of schedule and under budget, no less), I never doubted that the best and brightest minds that were recruited to work on this historic project would prevail. And they did.

2    So my faith in the ability of science to answer questions about nature paid off. But that is not the most important area where faith is part of my life. After spending my young years as an atheist, I became convinced through reading the logical arguments of C. S. Lewis and the words of the Bible that belief in God was more plausible than atheism. After two years of struggle, I became a Christian at age twenty-seven. Since then, my faith in God has been the rock on which I stand, a means to answer critical questions on which science remains silent: What is the meaning of life? Is there a God? Do our concepts of right and wrong have any real foundation? What happens after we die?

3    As one of a large number of scientists who believe in God, I find it deeply troubling to watch the escalating culture wars between science and faith, especially in America. A spate of angry books by atheists, many of them using the compelling evidence of Darwin's theory of evolution as a rhetorical club over the heads of believers, argues that atheism is the only rational choice for a thinking person. Some go so far as to label religious faith as the root of all evil and insinuate that parents who teach their children about religion are committing child abuse.

4    Partially in response to these attacks, believers, especially evangelical Christians, have targeted evolution as godless and incompatible with the

truths of the Bible. Many Americans see Earth as less than 10,000 years old, a "young Earth" belief that clashes with mountains of data from cosmology, physics, chemistry, geology, paleontology, anthropology, biology, and genetics. Intelligent Design, which proposes that evolution is insufficient to account for complexity, enjoys wide support in the church despite rejection in the scientific community.

5       What a sad situation. Are we not all seeking the truth? That is what God calls us to. It seems unlikely that God, the author of all creation, is threatened by what science is teaching us about the awesome complexity and grandeur of His creation. Can God be well served by lies about nature, no matter how noble the intentions of those who spread them?

6       The current circumstance is not tenable over the long run. Despite their claims to hard-nosed objectivity, atheists have gone wildly outside the evidence by declaring God imaginary. They are proposing an impoverished perspective that will not satisfy most of their intended converts. For their part, fundamentalists who demand acceptance of a unilateral interpretation of Genesis are making that a litmus test for true faith, which wise theologians over the centuries have not found necessary.

7       Could we not step back from the unloving rhetoric of these entrenched positions and seek a path towards truth? If science is a way of uncovering the details of God's creation, then it may actually be a form of worship. Did not God, in giving us the intelligence to ask and answer questions about nature, expect us to use it? We should be able to learn about God in the laboratory as well as in the cathedral.

8       The shrill voices at the extremes of this debate have had the microphone for too long. Although they will no doubt continue to rail against each other, the rest of us should find ways to bring together scientists who are open to spiritual truths, **theologians** who are ready to embrace scientific findings about the universe, and pastors who know the real concerns and needs of their flocks. Together, in a loving and worshipful attitude, we could formulate a new and wondrous natural theology. This kind of theology celebrates God as the creator, embraces His majestic universe from the far-flung galaxies to the "fearfully and wonderfully made" nature of humanity, and accepts and incorporates the marvelous things that God has given us the chance to discover through science.

9       If we make a serious and prayerful attempt to do this together, perhaps in a few years this new "celebration theology" could eliminate the conflict between science and faith. God didn't start the conflict. We did. I may sound unrealistic, even a bit of a **Pollyanna**, by proposing that we

could draw this unnecessary battle to a close. But, I remind you, I have often been accused of being optimistic. ◆

## CONSIDERING THE ISSUES

1. In your opinion, are religious faith and the acceptance of science—especially evolutionary biology—compatible? Why or why not?
2. If you were a parent, would you want your child to be taught evolution in school? Intelligent Design? Would you want other theories or ideas, including religious ones, taught as well? Why or why not?

## CRAFT AND CONTENT

1. Consider how Collins frames his argument. How does he define and identify the issue and controversy? How does he persuade readers to understand his point of view?
2. Why does Collins open his editorial with a reference to his leadership of the Human Genome Project? Does this detailing of his background help his argument? Why or why not?
3. Collins writes this editorial from the perspective of a believing Christian. Identify areas of his essay that reveal his religious stance.

## CRITICAL THINKING

1. Collins explains that the current debate over evolution has become so polarized that meaningful debate has become impossible. What problems does he identify, and what solutions does he offer?
2. Collins identifies himself as a convert to Christianity, but could his argument and his points appeal to people of other religious faiths? to atheists? to fundamentalists? Why or why not?

## WRITING ABOUT THE ISSUES

1. Write a short response to Collins in which you agree or disagree, in whole or in part, with his position that science and religion can coexist in harmony with one another.

2. Collins observes that the debate over evolution has, because of the nature of the arguments, become an "all-or-nothing" argument. Either you are completely in favor of evolution, or you are against it. And some people who are religious are finding they must "pick a side" or risk going against the faithful. Have you faced the situation Collins describes? If so, describe your position and the experience. If not, write a short essay exploring this dilemma.

# Remove Stickers, Open Minds
*Kenneth Miller*

> Kenneth Miller is a professor of biology at Brown University and coauthor of *Biology* (2002). He is particularly known for his opposition to creationism, including the Intelligent Design movement, and has written a book on the subject, *Finding Darwin's God: A Scientist's Search for Common Ground Between God and Evolution* (2000), in which he furthers the argument that beliefs in God and evolution are not mutually exclusive. This editorial appeared in the *Boston Globe* on January 22, 2005.

## CONNECTING TO THE TOPIC

In the academic school year of 2004–2005, Georgia's Cobb County Board of Education required stickers to be pasted into biology textbooks, stating that "Evolution is a theory, not a fact, regarding the origin of living things. The material should be approached with an open mind, studied carefully, and critically considered." After complaints from parents and teachers, a federal judge ordered the school system to remove stickers from the textbooks, saying that such disclaimers were an unconstitutional endorsement of religion. "By denigrating evolution, the school board appears to be endorsing the well-known prevailing alternative theory, creationism or variations thereof, even though the sticker does not specifically reference any alternative theories." The next piece is an editorial by biology professor Kenneth Miller discussing the argument and the verdict.

## WORDS IN CONTEXT

**denigrating** (5)    insulting, mocking (v.)
**genome** (12)    the complete genetic information of an organism's DNA (n.)

1    Isn't evolution a theory? Of course it is. So why did a federal district court judge last week [January 2005] order a board of education in Georgia to remove stickers from biology textbooks that seemed to tell students that evolution was just a theory?

2    Is this a case of censorship? Is a closed-minded scientific establishment trying to keep evidence against evolution out of the classroom? Is a federal court telling educators that evolution is now federally protected dogma?

3    The answer is far simpler. The judge simply read the sticker and saw that it served no scientific or educational purpose. Once that was clear, he looked to the reasons for slapping it in the textbooks of thousands of students, and here the record was equally clear. The sticker was inserted to advance a particular set of religious beliefs—exactly the argument advanced by the parents of six students in the district who sued the Cobb County Board of Education to get the stickers removed.

4    So what's wrong with telling students that evolution is a theory? Nothing. But the textbook they were using already described evolution as a theory, and I ought to know. Joseph Levine and I wrote the biology book Cobb County's high school students are using. Chapter 15 is titled "Darwin's Theory of Evolution."

5    Hard to be clearer than that. So why did the Cobb County Board of Education slap a warning label inside a book that already refers to evolution as a theory? Cooper hit correctly when he wrote that "by **denigrating** evolution, the school board appears to be endorsing the well-known prevailing alternative theory, creationism or variations thereof, even though the sticker does not specifically reference any alternative theories."

6    Exactly. What the sticker said was that "Evolution is a theory, not a fact, regarding the origin of living things." The problem with that wording is that evolution is both a theory and a fact. It is a fact that living things in the past were different from living things today and that the life of the past changed, or evolved, to produce the life of the present. Recent news reports the discovery of a new mammalian fossil in China that has a small dinosaur in its stomach. This fossil is a fact—clear evidence that some early mammals were able to prey upon dinosaurs, at least little ones.

7     And it is just one of millions of fossils that support the fact that life has changed over time, the fact of evolution. How did that change take place? That's exactly the question that evolutionary theory attempts to answer. Theories in science don't become facts—rather, theories explain facts. Evolutionary theory is a comprehensive explanation of change supported by the facts of natural history, genetics, and molecular biology.

8     Is evolution beyond dispute? Of course not. In fact, the most misleading part of the sticker was its concluding sentence: "This material should be approached with an open mind, studied carefully, and critically considered." Think about that. The sticker told students that there was just one subject in their textbooks that had to be approached with an open mind and critically considered. Apparently, we are certain of everything in biology except evolution. That is nonsense. What that sticker should have told students is what our textbook makes clear: *Everything* in science should be approached with critical thinking and an open mind.

9     The forces of anti-evolution will pretend that the sticker case is an example of censorship and that the sinister forces of science have converged on classrooms to prevent honest and open examination of a controversial idea.

10    There is great irony in such charges. As conservative icon Alan Bloom pointed out in his landmark book *The Closing of the American Mind,* one of the worst forms of intellectual intolerance is to promote a false equivalence between competing ideas. Acting as though all ideas (or all theories) have equal standing actually deprives students of a realistic view of how critical analysis is done. That's as true in science as it is in the cultural conflicts.

11    Judge Cooper saw this point clearly: "While evolution is subject to criticism, particularly with respect to the mechanism by which it occurred, the sticker misleads students regarding the significance and value of evolution in the scientific community."

12    Does it ever. In reality, evolution is a powerful and hard-working theory used at the cutting edge of scientific inquiry in developmental biology, **genome** analysis, drug discovery, and scientific medicine. To pretend otherwise is to shield students from the reality of how science is done.

13    What the removal of the sticker will do is not to close a window but to open one that will let students see a science of biology in which all theories, not just one, are the result of constant, vigorous, critical analysis. A science in which evolution is at the centerpiece of a 21st-century revolution in our understanding of the grandeur and majesty of life.

14    So, what should be done with those stickers, now pasted into thousands of textbooks? I'd pass along a suggestion I received from a science teacher in Cobb County itself: Glue an American flag on top of each and every one of them.  ◆

### CONSIDERING THE ISSUES

1. If you took biology in high school, how much time, if any, did you spend on the theory of evolution? Were you taught any other views, such as Intelligent Design? Explain.
2. Miller explains, "Evolution is both a theory and a fact." How can it be both? How does he support this statement?

### CRAFT AND CONTENT

1. What credentials does Miller bring to his argument? Does he adequately describe the opposing viewpoint?
2. Review paragraph 10, in which Miller paraphrases Alan Bloom. How does Bloom's comment support Miller's argument?

### CRITICAL THINKING

1. In this article, the author describes how a conservative school board challenged evolution by putting a sticker in biology textbooks. How much control should school boards have over what is taught in the classroom? Who should decide what is taught in public schools? What if a majority of parents, for example, object to evolution?
2. Miller explains that, despite the reasoned wording, the stickers placed in the Cobb County biology textbooks were really challenging evolution and supporting a religious viewpoint. Do you agree with his assessment? Explain.

### WRITING ABOUT THE ISSUES

1. In this essay, Judge Cooper ruled that the stickers placed in biology textbooks were misleading to students. If you had been the

judge ruling on this case, what decision would you have made? Defend your decision with a reasoned explanation, drawing from this essay and any others in this section.

# The Flying Spaghetti Monster
*Steve Paulson*

Steven Paulson is the executive producer and an interviewer for *To the Best of Our Knowledge,* a radio program syndicated nationally by Public Radio International and Sirius Satellite Radio. He has written for the *Independent, Milwaukee Journal Sentinel,* and many other newspapers. His radio reports have also been broadcast on NPR's *Morning Edition, All Things Considered,* and *Weekend Edition Sunday.* This interview, slightly abridged for space, was conducted on October 13, 2006, and appeared in *Atoms and Eden: Conversations about Science and Faith,* a column in Salon.com magazine.

## CONNECTING TO THE TOPIC

No balanced discussion addressing issues connected to science and religion should exclude the opinions of Richard Dawkins. Dawkins is the Charles Simonyi Professor of the Public Understanding of Science at Oxford University. He is a Fellow of the Royal Society and the author of nine books, including *The Blind Watchmaker* and *The God Delusion* (2006). He is the founder of the Foundation for Reason and Science and is considered by many the world's most famous atheist. Always controversial, Dawkins is one of the most outspoken anti-religious voices in the scientific arena. In his most recent book, *The God Delusion,* Dawkins argues that the existence of God is itself a scientific conjecture, one that doesn't hold up to evidence.

## WORDS IN CONTEXT

**agnostic** (8) skeptic, unbeliever (n.)
**apostates** (16) heretics, dissidents (n.)
**madrasahs** (18) Islamic theology schools (n.)
**mullahs** (18) teachers of Islamic law (n.)

**magisterium** (26)   religious power and authority (n.)
**parsimonious** (35)   economical, thrifty (adj.)
**facile** (40)   simplistic, easy (adj.)

1   In the roiling debate between science and religion, it would be hard to exaggerate the enormous influence of Richard Dawkins. The British scientist is religion's chief prosecutor—"Darwin's rottweiler," as one magazine called him—and quite likely the world's most famous atheist. Speaking to the American Humanist Association, Dawkins once said, "I think a case can be made that faith is one of the world's great evils, comparable to the smallpox virus but harder to eradicate."

2   Dawkins' outspoken atheism is a relatively recent turn in his public career. He first made his name 30 years ago with his groundbreaking book "The Selfish Gene," which reshaped the field of evolutionary biology by arguing that evolution played out at the level of the gene itself, not the individual animal. Dawkins now holds a chair in the Public Understanding of Science at Oxford University. Thanks to his tremendous talent for clear and graceful writing, he's done more to popularize evolutionary biology than any other scientist, with the possible exception of Stephen Jay Gould. Dawkins has a gift for explaining science through brilliant metaphors. Phrases like "the selfish gene" and "the blind watchmaker" didn't only crystallize certain scientific ideas; they entered the English vernacular. And his concept of "memes"—ideas themselves evolving like genes—spawned a new way of thinking about cultural evolution. I spoke with Dawkins by phone in Oxford shortly before he launched his American book tour. We talked about the dangers of unquestioned faith, the politics of the evolution debate, and why atheists are among the most intelligent people in the world.

3   **You've written about going to church as a boy. When did you become an atheist?**

4   I started getting doubts when I was about 9 and realized that there are lots of different religions and they can't all be right. And which one I happened to be brought up in was an arbitrary accident. I then sort of went back to religion around the age of 12, and then finally left it at the age of 15 or 16.

5   **Did God and religion just not make sense intellectually? Is that why you turned against religion?**

6    Yes, purely intellectually. I was never much bothered about moral questions like, how could there be a good God when there's so much evil in the world? For me, it was always an intellectual thing. I wanted to know the explanation for the existence of all things. I was particularly fascinated by living things. And when I discovered the Darwinian explanation, which is so stunningly elegant and powerful, I realized that you really don't need any kind of supernatural force to explain it.

7    **Why do you call yourself an atheist? Why not an agnostic?**

8    Well, technically, you cannot be any more than an **agnostic**. But I am as agnostic about God as I am about fairies and the Flying Spaghetti Monster. You cannot actually disprove the existence of God. Therefore, to be a positive atheist is not technically possible. But you can be as atheist about God as you can be atheist about Thor or Apollo. Everybody nowadays is an atheist about Thor and Apollo. Some of us just go one god further.

9    **When you're talking about God, are you really talking about the God of the Bible—Yahweh of the Old Testament?**

10    Well, as it happens, I am because I have an eye to the audience who's likely to be reading my book. Nobody believes in Thor and Apollo anymore so I don't bother to address the book to them. So, in practice, it's addressed to believers in the Abrahamic God.

11    **You are quite upfront about your goal with your new book *The God Delusion.* You are hoping that "religious readers who open it will be atheists by the time they put it down." Do you really think that will happen?**

12    No, I describe that as presumptuous. It's an ambition. I was hoping, in the best of all possible worlds, that would be the consequence of reading my book. I'm too realistic to think that it's going to happen in very many cases.

13    **What is so bad about religion?**

14    Well, it encourages you to believe falsehoods, to be satisfied with inadequate explanations which really aren't explanations at all. And this is particularly bad because the real explanations, the scientific explanations, are so beautiful and so elegant. Plenty of people never get exposed to the beauties of the scientific explanation for the world and for life. And that's very sad. But it's even sadder if they are actively discouraged from understanding by a systematic attempt in the opposite direction, which is what many religions actually are. But that's only the first of my many reasons for being hostile to religion.

15    **My sense is that you don't just think religion is dishonest. There's something evil about it as well.**

16    Well, yes. I think there's something very evil about faith, where faith means believing in something in the absence of evidence, and actually taking pride in believing in something in the absence of evidence. And the reason that's dangerous is that it justifies essentially anything. If you're taught in your holy book or by your priest that blasphemers should die or **apostates** should die—anybody who once believed in the religion and no longer does needs to be killed—that clearly is evil. And people don't have to justify it because it's their faith. They don't have to say, "Well, here's a very good reason for this." All they need to say is, "That's what my faith says." And we're all expected to back off and respect that. Whether or not we're actually faithful ourselves, we've been brought up to respect faith and to regard it as something that should not be challenged. And that can have extremely evil consequences. The consequences it's had historically—the Crusades, the Inquisition, right up to the present time where you have suicide bombers and people flying planes into skyscrapers in New York—all in the name of faith.

17    **But don't you need to distinguish between religious extremists who kill people and moderate, peaceful religious believers?**

18    You certainly need to distinguish them. They are very different. However, the moderate, sensible religious people you've cited make the world safe for the extremists by bringing up children—sometimes even indoctrinating children—to believe that faith trumps everything and by influencing society to respect faith. Now, the faith of these moderate people is in itself harmless. But the idea that faith needs to be respected is instilled into children sitting in rows in their **madrasahs** in the Muslim world. And they are told these things not by extremists but by decent, moderate teachers and **mullahs**. But when they grow up, a small minority of them remember what they were told. They remember reading their holy book, and they take it literally. They really do believe it. Now, the moderate ones don't really believe it, but they have taught children that faith is a virtue. And it only takes a minority to believe what it says in the holy book—the Old Testament, the New Testament, the Quran, whatever it is. If you believe it's literally true, then there's scarcely any limit to the evil things you might do.

19    **And yet most moderate religious people are appalled by the apocalyptic thinking of religious extremists.**

20    Of course they're appalled. They're very decent, nice people. But they have no right to be appalled because, in a sense, they brought it on the world by teaching people, especially children, the virtues of unquestioned faith.

21    **Are you saying if parents belong to a particular church, they should not teach their children about that religion?**

22    I would say that parents should teach their children anything that's known to be factually true—like "that's a bluebird" or "that's a bald eagle." Or they could teach children that there are such things as religious beliefs. But to teach children that it is a fact that there is one god or that God created the world in six days, that is child abuse.

23    **But isn't much of parenting about teaching values to children? Just as a family of vegetarians will teach their children about the evils of killing animals and eating meat, can't parents who believe in God teach their children the values of a religious upbringing?**

24    Children ask questions. And when a child says, "Why is it wrong to do so and so?" you can perfectly well answer that by saying, "Well, how would you like it if somebody else did that to you?" That's a way of imparting to a child the Golden Rule: "Do as you would be done by." The world would fall apart if everybody stole things from everybody else, so it's a bad thing to steal. If a child says, "Why can't I eat meat?" then you can say, "Your mother and I believe that it's wrong to eat meat for this, that and the other reason. We are vegetarians. You can decide when you're older whether you want to be a vegetarian or not. But for the moment, you're living in this house, so the food we give you is not meat." That I could see. I think it's child abuse not to let the child have the free choice of knowing there are other people who believe something quite different and the child could make its own choice.

25    **Once you get past the biblical literalists, I think most people assume that science and religion are actually quite compatible. Stephen Jay Gould famously argued that they were "non-overlapping magisteria": Science covers the empirical realm of facts and theories about the observable universe, and religion deals with ultimate meaning and moral value. But you're very critical of this argument, right?**

26    Yes, I think religious belief is a scientific belief, in the sense that it makes claims about the universe which are essentially scientific claims. If you believe the universe was created and inhabited by a supreme being, that would be a very different kind of universe from the sort of universe that wasn't created and does not house a creative intelligence. That is a scientific difference. Miracles. If you believe in miracles, that is clearly a scientific claim, and scientific methods would be used to evaluate any miracle that somebody claimed evidence for. Suppose, hypothetically, that forensic archaeologists, in an unlikely series of events, gained evidence—

perhaps from some discovered DNA—which showed that Jesus did not really have an earthly father, that he really was born of a virgin. Can you imagine any theologian taking refuge behind Stephen Jay Gould's non-overlapping **magisteria** and saying, "Nope, DNA evidence is completely irrelevant. Wrong magisterium. Science and religion have nothing to do with each other. They just peacefully coexist." Of course they wouldn't say that. If any such evidence were discovered, the DNA evidence would be trumpeted to the skies.

27 **What about the old adage that science deals with the "how" questions and religion deals with the "why" questions?**

28 I think that's remarkably stupid, if I may say so. What on earth is a "why" question? There are "why" questions that mean something in a Darwinian world. We say, why do birds have wings? To fly with. And that's a Darwinian translation of the evolutionary process whereby the birds that had wings survived better than the birds without. They don't mean that, though. They mean "why" in a deliberate, purposeful sense. So when you say religion deals with "why" questions, that begs the entire question that we're arguing about. Those of us who don't believe in religion—supernatural religion—would say there is no such thing as a "why" question in that sense. Now, the mere fact that you can frame an English sentence beginning with the word "why" does not mean that English sentence should receive an answer. I could say, why are unicorns hollow? That appears to mean something, but it doesn't deserve an answer.

29 **At one point in your book, you say you don't like confrontation. That will surprise a lot of people because you have become the lightning rod in the science and religion wars. Why do you think you evoke such powerful reactions?**

30 Well, I don't relish confrontation for its own sake. I don't spoil for a fight. I'd much rather have an amicable discussion. But I am a professional academic, and professional academics are used to arguing about all sorts of things. And we argue in a robust way, bringing forth evidence where we can and using our skills of argument to use that evidence. So I may come across as passionate. But that doesn't mean I go out of my way to have confrontations in an aggressive way. I don't.

31 **A lot of these scientists really do accept Stephen Jay Gould's idea of non-overlapping magisteria. These are hardcore evolutionists, but they say religion is an entirely different realm. So you, with your inflammatory rhetoric, just muddy the waters and make life more difficult for them.**

32　　　That is exactly what they say. And I believe that actually is the political reason for Steve Gould to put forward the non-overlapping magisteria in the first place. I think it's nonsense. And I'll continue to say that I think it's nonsense. But I can easily see, politically, why he said that and why other scientists follow it. The politics is very straightforward. The science lobby, which is very important in the United States, wants those sensible religious people—the theologians, the bishops, the clergymen who believe in evolution—on their side. And the way to get those sensible religious people on your side is to say there is no conflict between science and religion. We all believe in evolution, whether we're religious or not. Therefore, because we need to get the mainstream orthodox religious people on our side, we've got to concede to them their fundamental belief in God, thereby—in my view—losing the war in order to win the battle for evolution. If you're prepared to compromise the war for the sake of the battle, then it's a sensible political strategy.

33　　　Throughout the ages, one has resorted to that kind of political compromise. And maybe it would be a good thing for me to do as well. But as it happens, I think the war is more important. I actually do care about the existence of a supreme being. And therefore, I don't think I should say something which I believe to be false, which is that the question of whether God exists is a non-scientific question, and science and religion have no contact with each other, so we can all get along cozily and keep out those lunatic creationists.

34　　　**Let's stay with the battle over evolution for a moment. Why do you think Darwinian evolution leads logically to atheism?**

35　　　Well, I'm not sure it's a logical thing. I call it consciousness raising. I think the most powerful reason for believing in a supreme being is the argument for design. Living things in particular look complicated, look beautiful, look elegant, look as though they've been designed. We are all accustomed to thinking that if something looks designed, it is designed. Therefore, it's really no wonder that before Darwin came along, just about everybody was a theist. Darwin blew that argument out of the water. We now have a much more elegant and **parsimonious** explanation for the existence of life.

36　　　So the big reason for believing in God used to be the argument for biological design. Darwin destroyed that argument. He didn't destroy the parallel argument from cosmology: Where did the universe come from? Where did the laws of physics come from? But he raised our consciousness to the power of science to explain things. And he made it unsafe for anyone in the future to resort automatically and uncritically to a designer just because they don't immediately have an explanation for something. So when people say, "I can't see how the universe could have come into being without God," be very careful because you've had your fingers burned before over biology. That's the consciousness-raising sense in which, I think, Darwinism leads to atheism.

37 **I want to turn to what you would call "the real war"—the war be-tween supernaturalism and naturalism. A lot of religious people call you a reductionist and a materialist. They say you want to boil every-thing down to what can be measured and experimentally tested. "If you can't measure it, if you can't test it, it's not real."**

38 The words "reductionist" and "materialist" are loaded. They have a negative connotation to many people. I'm a reductionist and a materialist in a much grander sense. When we try to explain the workings of some-thing really complicated, like a human brain, we can be reductionist in the sense that we believe that the brain's behavior is to be explained by neu-rons and the behavior of neurons is to be explained by molecules within the neurons, etc. Similarly, computers. They're made of integrated cir-cuits. They're nothing but a whole lot of ones and naughts shuffling about. That's reductive in the sense that it seems to leave a lot unexplained. There is nothing else in computers apart from integrated circuits and resis-tors and transistors. Nevertheless, it's a highly sophisticated explanation for understanding how the computer does the remarkably complicated things it does. So don't use the word "reductive" in a sort of reducing sense. And ditto with "materialist."

39 **It seems to me this is actually one of the key questions in the whole religion and science debate. What do you do with conscious-ness? I mean, do you really think the mind is totally reducible to neural networks and the electro-chemical surges in the brain? Or might there be something else that goes beyond the physical mechan-ics of the brain?**

40 Well, once again, let's not use the word "reducible" in a negative way. The sheer number of neurons in the brain, and the complication of the connections between the neurons, is such that one doesn't want to use the word "reducible" in any kind of negative way. Consciousness is the biggest puzzle facing biology, neurobiology, computational studies and evolutionary biology. It is a very, very big problem. I don't know the an-swer. Nobody knows the answer. I think one day they probably will know the answer. But even if science doesn't know the answer, I return to the

question, what on earth makes you think that religion will? Just because science so far has failed to explain something, such as consciousness, to say it follows that the **facile**, pathetic explanations which religion has produced somehow by default must win the argument is really quite ridiculous. Nobody has an explanation for consciousness. That should be a spur to work harder and try to understand it. Not to give up and just say, "Oh well, it must be a soul." That doesn't mean anything. It doesn't explain anything. You've said absolutely nothing when you've said that.

41   **A lot of what we're talking about comes down to whether science has certain limits. The basic religious critique of your position is that science can only explain so much. And that's where mystery comes in. That's where consciousness comes in.**

42   There are two ways of responding to mystery. The scientist's way is to see it as a challenge, something they've got to work on, we're really going to try to crack it. But there are others who revel in mystery, who think we were not meant to understand. There's something sacred about mystery that positively should not be tackled. Now, suppose science does have limits. What is the value in giving the label "religion" to those limits? If you simply want to define religion as the bits outside of what science can explain, then we're not really arguing. We're simply using a word, "God," for that which science can't explain. I don't have a problem with that. I do have a problem with saying God is a supernatural, creative, intelligent being. It's simple confusion to say science can't explain certain things; therefore, we have to be religious. To equate that kind of religiousness with belief in a personal, intelligent being, that's confusion. And it's pernicious confusion. ◆

### CONSIDERING THE ISSUES

1. Dawkins asserts that religion "encourages you to believe falsehoods, to be satisfied with inadequate explanations which really aren't explanations at all. And this is particularly bad because the real explanations, the scientific explanations, are so beautiful and so elegant." Do you find science to be more beautiful and elegant than religion? Explain your answer and try to come up with examples of when this might be true and when you find it to be false.

2. Can human beings behold an objective morality without the constructs of religious belief? Can you live by a code of ethics that exists outside of religious principles? Why or why not?

## CRAFT AND CONTENT

1. Language is a powerful tool and can change how we think. Review the interview and find where Dawkins says that he doesn't have a problem using the word "God." Paraphrase his explanation on why the word "God" isn't the problem but that the meaning behind the word "God" will lead to "pernicious confusion."
2. Steve Paulson asks Dawkins why he considers himself an atheist instead of an agnostic. Look both words up in a dictionary, break down their meanings, and then see if you agree with Dawkins's argument explaining why he is more an atheist than an agnostic. Is one of these words more powerful or loaded than the other, and if so, why is this important to Dawkins's view of himself?

## CRITICAL THINKING

1. Dawkins equates teaching of creationism with child abuse. Explain Dawkins's argument and then discuss ways in which this argument is valid or invalid.
2. Many scientists have conceded that religion and evolution can coexist as "non-overlapping magisteria." Dawkins, however, calls this nonsense and says that these scientists are politically motivated. Explain how politics plays a part in the creationism versus evolution debate, both according to Dawkins's interview and in your own experience.

## WRITING ABOUT THE ISSUES

1. Write an essay in which you describe your own beliefs in religion and science. Which one wins out in your experience, or are they perfectly balanced?
2. Summarize Dawkins's answer to the question, "What do you do with consciousness?" Be sure to include how Dawkins's views on both science and religion play a part in answering (or not answering) this question.

# Blog Matters

A blog ("web log") is an online diary or commentary site that features regular entries that describe events, impressions, and viewpoints. Blogs may contain text, images, video, and often link to other websites, blogs, and online media. Most blogs allow readers to comment on the content of the post and to each other. As of 2007, the blog search engine estimated there were over 112 million blogs. While many blogs are maintained by individuals, some are run by journals, newspapers, and other media outlets. Remember that most blogs are not monitored for factual accuracy, and often express the opinion and views of the "blogger" writing the content.

The blog below is by Brandon Keim on *Wired* magazine's blog pages. Keim describes the controversy over evolution and Intelligent Design and discusses recent decisions made by Florida courts on the issue.

# Evolution Beats Intelligent Design in Florida

*Brandon Keim*
*December 27, 2007*

1    Members of a Florida county school board who last month wanted a classroom balance between evolution with intelligent design have quietly reversed their positions. Shortly before Thanksgiving, four members of the Polk County School Board said they didn't support Florida's proposed science education guidelines, which designate evolution as a fundamental concept that every student should understand. *Wired Science* covered the controversy, which came hot on the heels of a Texas education official's firing for telling people about a lecture critical of intelligent design.

2    A new battle appeared to have broken out between proponents of evolution—the scientifically observed and accepted explanation for the development of life on Earth—and intelligent design, a religiously-inspired account of life's origins as being too complicated and coincidental to be explained by anything but divine intervention.

3    Barely a month later, reports the *Tampa Tribune*, "the controversy is dying with a whimper," with school board officials insisting that their personal belief in intelligent design shouldn't be taught to kids as science.

4    What happened? You can start with the Church of the Flying Spaghetti Monster. The satirical religious Web site asserts that an omnipotent, airborne clump of spaghetti intelligently designed all life with the deft touch of its "noodly appendage." Adherents call themselves Pastafarians. They deluged Polk school board members with e-mail demanding equal time for Flying Spaghetti Monsterism's version of intelligent design.

5    "They've made us the laughingstock of the world," said Margaret Lofton, a school board member who supports intelligent design. She dismissed the e-mail as ridiculous and insulting. The *Tribune* also credits attention generated by science bloggers, who took a locally reported story and made it national. And make no mistake—this was, and is, a national story. If evolution and intelligent design were forced to share classroom credibility in Florida, it would be that much easier for a similarly diluted curriculum to pass in Texas, which is embarking on its own curricula revisions.

6    If Texas wanted scientifically bankrupt textbooks, then textbook manufacturers should provide them—and other states would buy them, too. So chalk one up for science, and remember: just because you believe in God doesn't mean you can't believe in evolution. ◆

### RESPOND TO THE BLOG:

What do you think? You may wish to review the letter mentioned in Keim's posting at http://www.venganza.org.

---

# Darwin and the Nazis
*Richard Weikart*

Richard Weikart teaches history at California State University. He is the author of *From Darwin to Hitler: Evolutionary Ethics, Eugenics and Racism in Germany* (2004). His essay was published in the April 16, 2008, issue of the *American Prospect*.

## CONNECTING TO THE TOPIC

In the next essay, Richard Weikart discusses the controversy surrounding the 2008 film, *Expelled: No Intelligence Allowed*, starring Ben Stein, about scientists who have been ridiculed or even denied tenure for supporting Intelligent Design. As Weikart points out in the editorial below, Darwinism has been used by some intellectuals, politicians, and even students to question objective morality and justify abortion, euthanasia, infanticide, and genocide. Can one hold the principles of Darwin as valid and still value human life?

## WORDS IN CONTEXT

**mete** (1)   carefully measure and distribute (v.)
**anti-Semitism** (2)   vicious prejudice against Jewish people (n.)
**meticulous** (4)   very careful (adj.)
**aesthetics** (4)   the philosophy of beauty (n.)
**ineluctable** (4)   inevitable (adj.)
**underpinning** (5)   foundation, basis (n.)

**fobbed** (7)  given to or passed along deceitfully (adj.)
**staunch** (8)  loyal, steadfast (adj.)

1  Richard Dawkins, PZ Myers, and some other Darwinists are horrified that the forthcoming documentary, *Expelled: No Intelligence Allowed*, will promote Intelligent Design to a large audience when it opens at over a thousand theaters nationwide on April 18, 2008. Ironically, their campaign to discredit Ben Stein and the film confirms its main point, which is to expose the persecution **meted** out by Darwinists to those daring to criticize Darwinian theory.

2  One aspect of *Expelled* that troubles Dawkins and some of his colleagues is its treatment of the ethical implications of Darwinism, especially its discussion of the historical connections between Darwinism and Nazism. Isn't this a bit over-the-top, suggesting that Darwinism has something to do with Nazism? After all, Darwinists today are not Nazis, and Darwinism has nothing to do with **anti-Semitism.**

3  However, what is most objectionable about the Nazis' worldview? Isn't it that they had no respect for human life? Their rejection of the sanctity of human life led the Nazi regime to murder millions of Jews, hundreds of thousands of Gypsies, and about 200,000 disabled Germans. Where did the Nazis get the idea that some human beings were "lives unworthy of life"?

4  As I show in **meticulous** detail in my book, *From Darwin to Hitler: Evolutionary Ethics, Eugenics, and Racism in Germany*, the Nazis' devaluing of human life derived from Darwinian ideology (this does not mean that all Nazi ideology came from Darwinism). There were six features of Darwinian theory that have contributed to the devaluing of human life (then and now):

1. Darwin argued that humans were not qualitatively different from animals. The leading Darwinist in Germany, Ernst Haeckel, attacked the "anthropocentric" view that humans are unique and special.
2. Darwin denied that humans had an immaterial soul. He and other Darwinists believed that all aspects of the human psyche, including reason, morality, **aesthetics**, and even religion, originated through completely natural processes.
3. Darwin and other Darwinists recognized that if morality was the product of mindless evolution, then there is no objective, fixed morality and thus no objective human rights. Darwin stated in his *Autobiography* that one "can have for his rule of life, as far as I can

see, only to follow those impulses and instincts which are the strongest or which seem to him the best ones."

4. Since evolution requires variation, Darwin and other early Darwinists believed in human inequality. Haeckel emphasized inequality to such as extent that he even classified human races as twelve distinct species and claimed that the lowest humans were closer to primates than to the highest humans.

5. Darwin and most Darwinists believe that humans are locked in an **ineluctable** struggle for existence. Darwin claimed in *The Descent of Man* that because of this struggle, "[a]t some future period, not very distant as measured by centuries, the civilised races of man will almost certainly exterminate and replace throughout the world the savage races."

6. Darwinism overturned the Judeo-Christian view of death as an enemy, construing it instead as a beneficial engine of progress. Darwin remarked in *The Origin of Species*, "Thus, from the war of nature, from famine and death, the most exalted object which we are capable of conceiving, namely, the production of the higher animals, directly follows."

5  These six ideas were promoted by many prominent Darwinian biologists and Darwinian-inspired social thinkers in the late 19th and early 20th centuries. All six were enthusiastically embraced by Hitler and many other leading Nazis. Hitler thought that killing "inferior" humans would bring about evolutionary progress. Most historians who specialize in the Nazi era recognize the Darwinian **underpinnings** of many aspects of Hitler's ideology.

6  But what does this have to do with the present? Darwinists today are not Nazis.

7  If you look back at the six points outlined above, however, you will find that many Darwinists today are advancing the same or similar ideas. Many leading Darwinists today teach that morality is nothing but a natural product of evolution, thus undermining human rights. E. O. Wilson, one of the most prominent Darwinian biologists in the world, and Michael Ruse, a leading philosopher of science (the latter is in *Expelled*) famously stated that ethics is "an illusion **fobbed** off on us by our genes."

8  Many leading Darwinists today also claim that Darwinism undermines the Judeo-Christian conception of the sanctity of human life. Dawkins wrote in 2001 that we should try to genetically engineer an evolutionary ancestor to the human species to demolish the "speciesist" illusion that humans are special or sacred. In the same article he expressed support for involuntary euthanasia. Another critic of "speciesism," Peter

Singer, one of the leading bioethicists in the world, argues that Darwinism destroyed the Judeo-Christian sanctity-of-life ethic, so infanticide and euthanasia are permissible. James Watson, one of the world's most famous geneticists and a **staunch** Darwinist, has railed at the idea that humans are sacred and special.

9     Today's Darwinists are not Nazis and not all Darwinists agree with Dawkins, Wilson, Ruse, Singer, or Watson. However, some of the ideas being promoted today by prominent Darwinists in the name of Darwinism have an eerily similar ring to the ideologies that eroded respect for human life in the pre-Nazi era. ◆

### CONSIDERING THE ISSUES

1. When scientists refer to Darwinism, what do they mean? Define the term in your own words. After you finish reading this essay, review your definition and compare it with the one put forth by the author.

### CRAFT AND CONTENT

1. Review Weikart's six points. How does this format support his argument? Explain.
2. In this editorial, Weikart writes to explain the similarities between Nazism and Darwinism. Why does he wish to correlate the two? How might this comparison advance his argument? Do you think he does a good job comparing the two? Explain.

### CRITICAL THINKING

1. According to Weikart in what ways does Darwinism devalue human life? How is this devaluing of life connected to principles put forth by the Nazis?
2. Does Weikart's comparison of Nazism and Darwinism support the argument that Intelligent Design should be taught in the classroom? Why or why not?

### WRITING ABOUT THE ISSUES

1. Weikart's editorial refers to the 2008 documentary, *Expelled: No Intelligence Allowed*. Search online for the film's website

and trailer. What does the movie promote? Does it make a compelling argument for Intelligent Design? Explain.

2. Following the format he uses in his six points, write a response to Weikart's list in which you agree or disagree, either in whole or in part, with his view that Darwinian theory devalues human life.

## TOPICAL CONNECTIONS

### GROUP PROJECTS

1. Before reading this unit, did you already have an opinion on the theories of evolution and creationism, and a position on the controversy concerning both topics? Did any of the essays in this section influence your current point of view, or help you to form one? Why or why not? As a group, discuss your own opinions about this issue. What positions did you hold before reading the unit? Do you think your group represents a good cross-section of opinion?

2. Much of the debate over evolution versus creationism is that one cannot accept one theory without rejecting the other. Conduct a poll with students from your school. What are their positions? (Include individuals who harbor no opinion.) Based on the responses you gather, formulate a short assessment of popular opinion on your campus.

### WEB PROJECT

1. Several critics mention the "flying spaghetti monster" in their comments. Visit the website to which they are referring at http://www.venganza.org. What argument is the site making? How is it connected with the controversy outlined in this unit? Explain.

### FOR FUTHER INQUIRY

1. Giberson notes in his essay some of the leading spokespersons for science: Richard Dawkins, Stephen Hawking, Edward O. Wilson, Carl Sagan, Stephen Jay Gould, and Steven Weinberg. Research the positions on science and religion of these individuals. How are their positions similar, and how are they different?

# 10 | Why Do We Work?

**W**hile the answer to the question of why we work may seem obvious on the surface—to support ourselves and our loved ones—there are many reasons why we work. Some reasons, such as ambition, a drive to succeed and excel, and the desire to make the world a better place are considered noble reasons to work. They can help determine the career paths we take and how we will ultimately measure our success. But there are some reasons we might be less willing to admit, such as the ability to buy more expensive luxuries, drive better cars, support a particular lifestyle, or even to get away from our chaotic home lives.

Most college students enter their two- or four-year training programs in order to develop skills that will allow them to compete more successfully in the working world. But what are our expectations of the working world? What do we hope to get out of a job besides a regular paycheck? What satisfaction do you expect from a job? What defines a career? What is your idea of "making it"—of achieving success? An early retirement? Fame? Respect? This chapter explores some of the issues connected with why we work.

## CRITICAL THINKING

1. What is happening in this cartoon? Can you tell who the people are in the cartoon? What are they discussing? Explain.
2. Do you think this cartoon presents a stereotype of the American employment landscape? What issue does it intend to hold up for public scrutiny? Explain.
3. Have you ever had a "quitting fantasy"? Was it like the cartoonist describes here, or something else? Why do we harbor such fantasies? Do we dislike work or the powerlessness that accompanies so many jobs? Explain.

Andy Singer – Politicalcartoons.com – Posted 08/23/2007

# Why We Work
*Andrew Curry*

Andrew Curry is a general editor of *Smithsonian* magazine. His articles have appeared in many publications, including the *Washington Post*, the *Christian Science Monitor*, the *Miami Herald*, and the *Guardian*. This article appeared in the February 24, 2003, issue of *U.S. News and World Report* when Curry was an associate editor for that publication.

## CONNECTING TO THE TOPIC

Although most of us work because we have to, we also assume that this work will ultimately improve our lives. But is the pursuit of the American dream becoming just that—a dream? It seems as if Americans are working harder than ever before, with less leisure time. Today, American society is dominated by work. But there was a time when people could have followed a different path, when we could have opted as a nation to actually work *less*. When did the American workforce make the choice to have more stuff but less time? And was it the right choice?

## WORDS IN CONTEXT

**eccentric** (3)   behaving differently from the norm, as an oddball (adj.)
**starkly** (5)   bluntly (adv.)
**precarious** (6)   lacking in stability (adj.)
**affluent** (7)   wealthy (adj.)
**smelter** (10)   an iron works (n.)
**ample** (10)   in large number or quantity (adj.)
**apex** (13)   highest point (n.)
**propaganda** (14)   methodical and persistent distribution of a message advocating a particular cause or idea (n.)
**persistence** (16)   refusal to give up (n.)
**autonomy**(19)   ability to make one's own decisions; independence (n.)

1   Some do it for love. Others do it for money. But most of us do it because we have no other choice.

2     In 1930, W. K. Kellogg made what he thought was a sensible decision, grounded in the best economic, social, and management theories of the time. Workers at his cereal plant in Battle Creek, Michigan, were told to go home two hours early. Every day. For good.

3     The Depression-era move was hailed in *Factory and Industrial Management* magazine as the "biggest piece of industrial news since [Henry] Ford announced his five-dollar-a-day policy." President Herbert Hoover summoned the **eccentric** cereal magnate to the White House and said the plan was "very worthwhile." The belief: Industry and machines would lead to a workers' paradise where all would have less work, more free time, and yet still produce enough to meet their needs.

4     So what happened? Today, work dominates Americans' lives as never before, as workers pile on hours at a rate not seen since the Industrial Revolution. Technology has offered increasing productivity and a higher standard of living while bank tellers and typists are replaced by machines. The mismatch between available work and those available to do it continues, as jobs go begging while people beg for jobs. Though Kellogg's six-hour day lasted until 1985, Battle Creek's grand industrial experiment has been nearly forgotten. Instead of working less, our hours have stayed steady or risen—and today many more women work so that families can afford the trappings of suburbia. In effect, workers chose the path of consumption over leisure.

5     But as today's job market shows so **starkly**, that road is full of potholes. With unemployment at a nine-year high and many workers worried about losing their jobs—or forced to accept cutbacks in pay and benefits—work is hardly the paradise economists once envisioned.

6     Instead, the job market is as **precarious** today as it was in the early 1980s, when business began a wave of restructurings and layoffs to maintain its competitiveness. Many workers are left feeling insecure, unfulfilled, and under-appreciated. It's no wonder surveys of today's workers show a steady decline in job satisfaction. "People are very emotional about work, and they're very negative about it," says David Rhodes, a principal at human resource consultants Towers Perrin. "The biggest issue is clearly workload. People are feeling crushed."

7     The backlash comes after years of people boasting about how hard they work and tying their identities to how indispensable they are. Ringing cell phones, whirring faxes, and ever-present E-mail have blurred the lines between work and home. The job penetrates every aspect of life. Americans don't exercise, they work out. We manage our time and work on our

relationships. "In reaching the **affluent** society, we're working longer and harder than anyone could have imagined," says Rutgers University historian John Gillis. "The work ethic and identifying ourselves with work and through work is not only alive and well but more present now than at any time in history."

8    It's all beginning to take a toll. Fully one third of American workers—who work longer hours than their counterparts in any industrialized country—felt overwhelmed by the amount of work they had to do, according to a 2001 Families and Work Institute survey. "Both men and women wish they were working about 11 hours [a week] less," says Ellen Galinsky, the institute's president. "A lot of people believe if they do work less they'll be seen as less committed, and in a shaky economy no one wants that."

9    The modern environment would seem alien to pre-industrial laborers. For centuries, the household—from farms to "cottage" craftsmen—was the unit of production. The whole family was part of the enterprise, be it farming, blacksmithing, or baking. "In pre-industrial society, work and family were practically the same thing," says Gillis.

10    The Industrial Revolution changed all that. Mills and massive iron **smelters** required **ample** labor and constant attendance. "The factory took men, women and children out of the workshops and homes and put them under one roof and timed their movements to machines," writes Sebastian de Grazia in *Of Time, Work and Leisure*. For the first time, work and family were split. Instead of selling what they produced, workers sold their time. With more people leaving farms to move to cities and factories, labor became a commodity, placed on the market like any other.

11    Innovation gave rise to an industrial process based on machinery and mass production. This new age called for a new worker. "The only safeguard of order and discipline in the modern world is a standardized worker with interchangeable parts," mused one turn-of-the-century writer.

12    Business couldn't have that, so instead it came up with the science of management. The theories of Frederick Taylor, a Philadelphia factory foreman with deep Puritan roots, led to work being broken down into component parts, with each step timed to coldly quantify jobs that skilled craftsmen had worked a lifetime to learn. Workers resented Taylor and his stopwatch, complaining that his focus on process stripped their jobs of creativity and pride, making them irritable. Long before anyone knew what "stress" was, Taylor brought it to the workplace—and without sympathy. "I have you for your strength and mechanical ability, and we have other men paid for thinking," he told workers.

13    The division of work into components that could be measured and easily taught reached its **apex** in Ford's River Rouge plant in Dearborn, Michigan, where the assembly line came of age. "It was this combination of a simplification of tasks . . . with moving assembly that created a manufacturing revolution while at the same time laying waste human potential on a massive scale," author Richard Donkin writes in *Blood, Sweat and Tears.*

14    To maximize the production lines, businesses needed long hours from their workers. But it was no easy sell. "Convincing people to work 9 to 5 took a tremendous amount of **propaganda** and discipline," says the University of Richmond's Joanne Ciulla, author of *The Working Life: The Promise and Betrayal of Modern Work.* Entrepreneurs, religious leaders, and writers like Horatio Alger created whole bodies of literature to glorify the work ethic.

15    The first labor unions were organized in response to the threat of technology, as skilled workers sought to protect their jobs from mechanization. Later, semi- and unskilled workers began to organize as well, agitating successfully for reduced hours, higher wages, and better work conditions. Unions enjoyed great influence in the early 20th century, and at their height in the 1950s, 35 percent of U.S. workers belonged to one.

16    Union **persistence** and the mechanization of factories gradually made shorter hours more realistic. Between 1830 and 1930, work hours were cut nearly in half, with economist John Maynard Keynes famously predicting in 1930 that by 2030 a 15-hour workweek would be standard. The Great Depression pressed the issue, with job sharing proposed as a serious solution to widespread unemployment. Despite business and religious opposition over worries of an idle populace, the Senate passed a bill that would have mandated a 30-hour week in 1933; it was narrowly defeated in the House.

17    Franklin Delano Roosevelt struck back with a new gospel that lives to this very day: consumption. "The aim . . . is to restore our rich domestic market by raising its vast consuming capacity," he said. "Our first purpose is to create employment as fast as we can." And so began the modern work world. "Instead of accepting work's continuing decline and imminent fall from its dominant social position, businessmen, economists, advertisers, and politicians preached that there would never be 'enough,'" says University of Iowa Professor Benjamin Hunnicutt, author of *Work Without End: Abandoning Shorter Hours for the Right to Work.* "The entrepreneur and industry could invent new things for advertising to sell and for people to want and work for indefinitely."

18     The New Deal dumped government money into job creation, in turn encouraging consumption. World War II fueled the fire, and American workers soon found themselves in a "golden age"—40-hour workweeks, plenty of jobs, and plenty to buy. Leisure was the road not taken, a path quickly forgotten in the postwar boom of the 1950s and 1960s.

19     Decades of abundance, however, did not bring satisfaction. "A significant number of Americans are dissatisfied with the quality of their working lives," said the 1973 report "Work in America" from the Department of Health, Education and Welfare. "Dull, repetitive, seemingly meaningless tasks, offering little challenge or **autonomy**, are causing discontent among workers at all occupational levels." Underlying the dissatisfaction was a very gradual change in what the "Protestant work ethic" meant. Always a source of pride, the idea that hard work was a calling from God dated to the Reformation and the teachings of Martin Luther. While work had once been a means to serve God, two centuries of choices and industrialization had turned work into an end in itself, stripped of the spiritual meaning that sustained the Puritans who came ready to tame the wilderness.

20     By the end of the '70s, companies were reaching out to spiritually drained workers by offering more engagement while withdrawing the promise of a job for life, as the American economy faced a stiff challenge from cheaper workers abroad. "Employees were given more control over their work and schedules, and "human relations" consultants and motivational speakers did a booming business. By the 1990s, technology made working from home possible for a growing number of people. Seen as a boon at first, telecommuting and the rapidly proliferating "electronic leash" of cellphones made work inescapable, as employees found themselves on call 24/7. Today, almost half of American workers use computers, cellphones, E-mail, and faxes for work during what is supposed to be non-work time, according to the Families and Work Institute. Home is no longer a refuge but a cozier extension of the office.

21     The shift coincided with a shortage of highly skilled and educated workers, some of whom were induced with such benefits as stock options in exchange for their putting the company first all the time. But some see a different explanation for the rise in the amount of time devoted to work. "Hours have crept up partly as a consequence of the declining power of the trade-union movement," says Cornell University labor historian Clete Daniel. "Many employers find it more economical to require mandatory overtime than hire new workers and pay their benefits." Indeed, the trend

has coincided with the steady decline in the percentage of workers represented by unions, as the labor movement failed to keep pace with the increasing rise of white-collar jobs in the economy. Today fewer than 15 percent of American workers belong to unions.

22      In a study of Silicon Valley culture over the past decade, San Jose State University anthropologist Jan English-Lueck found that skills learned on the job were often brought home. Researchers talked to families with mission statements, mothers used conflict-resolution buzzwords with their squabbling kids, and engineers used flowcharts to organize Thanksgiving dinner. Said one participant: "I don't live life; I manage it."

23      In some ways, we have come full circle. "Now we're seeing the return of work to the home in terms of telecommuting," says Gillis. "We may be seeing the return of households where work is the central element again."

24      But there's still the question of fulfillment. In a recent study, human resources consultants Towers Perrin tried to measure workers' emotions about their jobs. More than half of the emotion was negative, with the biggest single factor being workload but also a sense that work doesn't satisfy their deeper needs. "We expect more and more out of our jobs," says Hunnicutt. "We expect to find wonderful people and experiences all around us. What we find is Dilbert." ◆

## CONSIDERING THE ISSUES

1. Curry begins his essay with the statement "Some do it for love. Others do it for money. But most of us do it because we have no other choice." Respond to this statement. What motivates you to work? Do you do it for the love of the job? For the money? Because you must? A little of each? Explain.

2. In this essay, Curry traces the historical origins of the American workforce and observes that there was a time before World War II when Americans made a choice to have more material things instead of having more leisure time. Which would you rather have? More money or more time? Explain.

3. Curry observes that e-mail, voice mail, cell phones, faxes, and computers have created "electronic leashes" that blur the boundaries between home and work. How much do you rely on this equipment? Would your quality of life be less if you did not have access to a cell phone? To e-mail? Do such devices keep us "on" 24/7? Why or why not?

## CRAFT AND CONTENT

1. Curry quotes several authors and professors who have researched transformations in the American workforce and work ethic. How do these authors, and the quotes he cites, support his overall point that American workers have "chosen a path of consumption over leisure"? Explain.

2. In paragraph 14, professor Joanne Ciulla observes that it "took a tremendous amount of propaganda" to convince people to work 9 to 5. What is propaganda? What do we associate with the word *propaganda*? What does it imply? Does it seem to fit this context? Why or why not?

3. What is the author's opinion of the state of the American worker? Identify specific statements in this essay that reveal his viewpoint.

## CRITICAL THINKING

1. Who was Frederick Taylor? How do his theories, and the science of management, relate to the state of the modern worker?

2. Participants in a study on Silicon Valley culture noted how they brought work-culture home in the form of "family mission statements," conflict resolution "buzzwords," and even flowcharts to organize Thanksgiving gatherings. Is work intruding on family life?

## WRITING ABOUT THE ISSUES

1. What is your definition of "the American Dream"? How important is money in your version of the dream? What priorities do you give to leisure time? Write an essay in which you compare the points Curry makes in his essay on the nature of the modern American workforce and your own lifestyle choices, now and in the future.

2. At the end of his article, Curry quotes consultants Towers Perrin, who found Americans in general to be deeply dissatisfied with work. Today's Americans expect more and get less out of their jobs. Write an essay about your expectations of job satisfaction now and in the future. Have you ever held a job that you truly loved? Do you expect to find one that provides you with a sense of achievement and satisfaction? How has your experience in the workforce thus far measured up to your expectations? Explain.

# VISUAL CONNECTIONS

## Major Occupational Groups and Annual Median Wages

| Occupation (SOC code) | Employment[1] | Annual median wage[2] |
|---|---|---|
| Management | 6,003,930 | $84,440 |
| Business and Financial Operations | 6,015,500 | $55,880 |
| Computer and Mathematical | 3,191,360 | $69,070 |
| Architecture and Engineering | 2,486,020 | $64,780 |
| Life, Physical, and Social Science | 1,255,670 | $55,300 |
| Community and Social Services | 1,793,040 | $37,170 |
| Legal | 998,590 | $69,760 |
| Education, Training, and Library | 8,316,360 | $42,580 |
| Arts, Design, Entertainment, Sports, and Media | 1,761,270 | $40,100 |
| Healthcare Practitioner and Technical | 6,877,680 | $54,440 |
| Healthcare Support | 3,625,240 | $23,820 |
| Protective Service | 3,087,650 | $33,510 |
| Food Preparation and Serving Related | 11,273,850 | $17,150 |
| Building and Grounds Cleaning and Maintenance | 4,403,900 | $21,170 |
| Personal Care and Service | 3,339,510 | $19,760 |
| Sales and Related | 14,332,020 | $23,740 |
| Office and Administrative Support | 23,270,810 | $28,920 |
| Farming, Fishing, and Forestry | 448,000 | $18,590 |
| Construction and Extraction | 6,708,200 | $36,540 |
| Installation, Maintenance, and Repair | 5,390,090 | $37,520 |

*Continued*

*continued*

| Occupation (SOC code) | Employment[1] | Annual median wage[2] *continued* |
|---|---|---|
| Production | 10,146,560 | $28,130 |
| Transportation and Material Moving | 9,629,030 | $26,320 |

Footnotes:

(1) Estimates for detailed occupations do not sum to the totals because the totals include occupations not shown separately. Estimates do not include self-employed workers.

(2) Annual wages have been calculated by multiplying the hourly mean wage by 2,080 hours; where an hourly mean wage is not published, the annual wage has been directly calculated from the reported survey data.

Period: May 2007 / SOC code: Standard Occupational Classification code—see http://www.bls.gov/soc/home.htm. Data extracted on July 5, 2008.

## CONSIDERING THE ISSUES

1. Do you have a full- or part-time job? If so, how much time do you spend working? Do you work more than you would like to? Less?
1. Think of the aspects that define you as a person. Describe how these characteristics help create your personal identity. Does work or career factor into your self-definition? Why or why not?
3. This chart outlines employment in the United States based on occupational groups. Visit the U.S. Department of Labor's website at http://www.bls.gov/ and read more about what people earn. Research your own future occupation. Based on what you read online and already know, explain why you think you will go into a particular industry or occupation, and what you expect in the future for this career.

# Measuring Success
*Renee Loth*

Renée Loth has been editor of the *Boston Globe*'s editorial page since 2000. She has served on the *Globe*'s staff for over 15 years. She previously wrote for *New England Monthly* magazine and worked as a political reporter for the *Boston Phoenix*. Loth is a frequent political commentator on local and national radio and TV programs, and has been an undergraduate study group leader at Harvard's Kennedy School of Government. This essay was first published in the *Boston Globe* on March 14, 1999. Although her essay is about 10 years old, the observations she makes are as true today as they were then.

## CONNECTING TO THE TOPIC

The Declaration of Independence describes our inalienable right to "life, liberty, and the pursuit of happiness." But what, exactly, is "the pursuit of happiness"? As the document has been interpreted, it often means the right to financial independence and success. Many college students enter the workforce with just such a sense of idealism. Time and experience often test this optimism, forcing many to redefine "the pursuit of happiness" along more realistic and mature lines. What is success? Does our definition change with time? What could college students learn about success from their more experienced friends and family?

## WORDS IN CONTEXT

**callow** (1)   young; lacking in experience and maturity (adj.)
**approbation** (2)   expressions of approval or appreciation (n.)
**mutable** (3)   changeable (adj.)
**superfluous** (5)   more than is necessary or than what is required (adj.)
**optimist** (8)   one who sees the positive side of things, who expects a favorable outcome (n.)
**fickle** (9)   highly changeable or unstable (adj.)
**chagrined** (11)   embarrassed (adj.)

1    **B**ack when I was a **callow** college student, I devised a neat grid system for what I hoped would be my life's achievements. I could count my life a good one, I thought, if I could attain both success and happiness. So I set about analyzing the component parts of each: Happiness I subdivided into sections labeled health and love; success, I determined, was composed of wealth and fame.

2    Once I actually entered the world of work, however, I learned that success is not so easy to define. For one thing, when I made my simple calculation, I never took into account the joy of creation; the **approbation** of one's peers; the energy of collaboration; or the sheer satisfaction of a job well done. These are real qualities of success that live outside of wealth or fame.

3    Also, I found that definitions of success are **mutable**, shifting along with our changing values. If we stick with our chosen fields long enough, we sometimes have an opportunity to meet our heroes, people we thought wildly successful when we were young. A musician friend told me that he spent most of his youth wanting to play like the greats, until he started getting to know some of them. To his surprise, many turned out to be embittered, dulled by drink or boredom, unable to hold together a marriage, or wantonly jealous of others. That's when he realized he wanted to play like himself.

4    Success is defined differently by different people. For some, it is symbolized by the number of buttons on the office phone. For others, it is

having only one button—and a secretary to field the calls. Some think the more nights and weekends they spend at the office, the more successful they must be. For others, success is directly proportional to time off.

5    And what about those qualities I did include in my handy grid system? Wealth—beyond what is needed to provide for oneself and one's family, with a little left over for airfare to someplace subtropical in January—turned out to be **superfluous**. And the little experience I had with fame turned out to be downright scary.

6    Several years ago, I had occasion to appear on a dull but respected national evening television news show. My performance lasted exactly six minutes, and my name flashed only twice. But when I got home from the live broadcast, my answering machine had maxed-out on messages.

7    I heard from a woman I had last seen in Brownie Scouts. I heard from former boyfriends, conspiracy theorists, and celebrity agents. I even got an obscene phone call—what kind of pervert watches PBS?— from someone who might have been an old friend pulling my leg. At least, I hope so.

8    For weeks afterward, I received tons of what an **optimist** might call fan mail. One fellow insisted that if I froze a particular frame of a political campaign ad I had been discussing, I could see the face of Bill Clinton in the American flag. Somebody sent me a chapter of a novel in progress with a main character disturbingly like me. Several people sent me chain letters.

9    I was relieved when the **fickle** finger of fame moved on to someone else.

10    When I was young and romanticizing about success, I liked a particular Joni Mitchell lyric: "My struggle for higher achievement and my search for love don't seem to cease." Ah, but the trouble with struggling and searching is that it keeps us in a permanent state of wanting—always reaching for more. The drive to succeed keeps us focused on the future, to the detriment of life in the moment. And the moment is all we ever really have.

11    When I look back at my simplistic little value system, I am a bit **chagrined** at how absolute I thought life was. But I am also happy to report that the achievements that have come my way are the ones that count. After 20 years of supercharged ambition, I have stumbled upon this bit of wisdom. Who needs wealth and fame? Two out of four ain't bad.  ◆

## CONSIDERING THE ISSUES

1.  Loth begins her essay by explaining how, as a college student, she developed a grid system that she felt would define her life's achievements. Following Loth's example, create your own list or grid in which you define what you think your life's

achievements might be. How do you define *happiness*? How do you define *success*?

2. What is your definition of wealth? To what extent is it connected to your definition of success? How important is it to your definition of success? Explain.

### CRAFT AND CONTENT

1. In paragraph 1, Loth recalls the days when she was "a callow college student." How does this word choice help establish both the tone and the theme of this essay? Explain.
2. In paragraph 10, Loth says in reference to the Joni Mitchell lyric she quotes, "The trouble with struggling and searching is that it keeps us in a permanent state of wanting." What does she mean by this statement? How does it relate to the point of this essay overall?

### CRITICAL THINKING

1. How did Loth redefine her early notion of success? Why do you think this happened?
2. Loth also changed her definition of fame and abandoned it as a goal of success. Why did she do this? Why do you think she wanted fame? Do you? Why or why not? Explain.

### WRITING ABOUT THE ISSUES

1. Write your own essay defining happiness and/or success. Be sure to employ the same strategies Loth does: think of your own experience, the things that make you feel happy and successful, and ask friends and family for their insights.
2. Since you too might be described as "a callow college student" at this point in your life, create a series of questions that you will ask older and more experienced friends, family, and acquaintances about happiness and success. Ask all sorts of people your questions, regardless of your own opinions of their happiness or success. Review your notes and write an essay in which you argue what success and happiness really mean based upon your interviews.

# Homeward Bound

## *Linda Hirshman*

Hirshman is a lawyer and well-known feminist. A retired professor of philosophy and Women's Studies at Brandeis University, she has written for a variety of periodicals, including *Glamour, Tikkun, Ms.*, and the *Boston Globe*. She is the author of several books, including *The Woman's Guide to Law School'* (1999), *Hard Bargains: The Politics of Sex* (1999), and *Get to Work: A Manifesto for Women of the World* (2006), in which she expands the argument that follows. Hirshman's essay, here abridged for space, appeared in the *American Prospect* on November 21, 2005.

## CONNECTING TO THE TOPIC

The next essay addresses the "mommy-wars debate" focusing on women who "opt-out" of work in favor of staying at home to care for their children. Prompted to write after reading a story in the *New York Times* describing the trend, Women's Studies Professor Linda Hirshman argues against what she believes to be the fallacies of "choice feminism" in which women can choose to stay at home or work outside of it. Hirshman fears that the progress made by the "second wave" of feminists in the 1970s will be lost as this new generation of women voluntarily give up economic and intellectual power in favor of staying at home. They are wasting their lives and their talents, because stay-at-home motherhood prevents women from truly "flourishing." She contends that this is no choice at all, because it removes women from positions of power and spheres of political and social influence. Her article set off a firestorm of controversy. In a follow-up article, Hirshman said, "even though I knew the Greeks made Socrates drink poison, the reaction to my judgment took me by surprise." Are young women making a mistake when they leave work for at-home motherhood? Or is this choice an example of how far women have come?

## WORDS IN CONTEXT

**ballistic** (1)   very agitated, behaving irrationally (adj.)
**albeit** (4)   although (conjunction)
**anomaly** (7)   deviation, exception (n.)
**anecdote** (9)   brief story used as an example (n.)

**utopian** (17)   hypothetically ideal (adj.)
**incalculably** (21)   beyond measure (adv.)
**ideological** (24)   theoretical, abstract (adj.)
**vaunted** (28)   highly praised (adj.)

1     **H**alf the wealthiest, most-privileged, best-educated females in the country stay home with their babies rather than work in the market economy. When in September the *New York Times* featured an article exploring a piece of this story, "Many Women at Elite Colleges Set Career Path to Motherhood," the blogosphere went **ballistic**, countering with anecdotes and sarcasm. Slate's Jack Shafer accused the *Times* of "weasel-words" and of publishing the same story—essentially, "The Opt-Out Revolution"—every few years, and, recently, every few weeks. A month after the flap, the *Times'* only female columnist, Maureen Dowd, invoked the elite-college article in her contribution to the *Times'* running soap, "What's a Modern Girl to Do?" about how women must forgo feminism even to get laid. The colleges article provoked such fury that the *Times* had to post an explanation of the then–student journalist's methodology on its Web site.

2     There's only one problem: There is important truth in the dropout story.

3     I stumbled across the news three years ago when researching a book on marriage after feminism. I found that among the educated elite, who are the logical heirs of the agenda of empowering women, feminism has largely failed in its goals. There are few women in the corridors of power, and marriage is essentially unchanged. The number of women at universities exceeds the number of men. But, more than a generation after feminism, the number of women in elite jobs doesn't come close.

4     Why did this happen? The answer I discovered—an answer neither feminist leaders nor women themselves want to face—is that while the public world has changed, **albeit** imperfectly, to accommodate women among the elite, private lives have hardly budged. The real glass ceiling is at home.

5     Looking back, it seems obvious that the unreconstructed family was destined to re-emerge after the passage of feminism's storm of social change. Following the original impulse to address everything in the lives of women, feminism turned its focus to cracking open the doors of the public power structure. This was no small task. At the beginning, there were male juries and male Ivy League schools, sex-segregated want ads, discriminatory employers, harassing colleagues. As a result of feminist

efforts—and larger economic trends—the percentage of women, even of mothers, in full- or part-time employment rose robustly through the 1980s and early '90s.

6    But then the pace slowed. The census numbers for all working mothers leveled off around 1990 and have fallen modestly since 1998. In interviews, women with enough money to quit work say they are "choosing" to opt out. Their words conceal a crucial reality: the belief that women are responsible for child-rearing and homemaking was largely untouched by decades of workplace feminism. Add to this the good evidence that the upper-class workplace has become more demanding and then mix in the successful conservative cultural campaign to reinforce traditional gender roles and you've got a perfect recipe for feminism's stall.

7    I, a 1970s member of the National Organization for Women (NOW) and a professor of women's studies, did not set out to find this. I stumbled across the story when, while planning a book, I happened to watch Sex and the City's Charlotte agonize about getting her wedding announcement in the "Sunday Styles" section of the *New York Times*. What better sample, I thought, than the brilliantly educated and accomplished brides of the "Sunday Styles," circa 1996? At marriage, they included a vice president of client communication, a gastroenterologist, a lawyer, an editor, and a marketing executive. In 2003 and 2004, I tracked them down and called them. I interviewed about 80 percent of the 41 women who announced their weddings over three Sundays in 1996. Around 40 years old, college graduates with careers: Who was more likely than they to be reaping feminism's promise of opportunity? Imagine my shock when I found almost all the brides from the first Sunday at home with their children. Statistical **anomaly**? Nope. Same result for the next Sunday. And the one after that.

8    Ninety percent of the brides I found had had babies. Of the 30 with babies, five were still working full time. Twenty-five, or 85 percent, were not working full time. Of those not working full time, 10 were working part time but often a long way from their prior career paths. And half the married women with children were not working at all.

9    How many **anecdotes** to become data? The 2000 census showed a decline in the percentage of mothers of infants working full time, part time, or seeking employment. Starting at 31 percent in 1976, the percentage had gone up almost every year to 1992, hit a high of 58.7 percent in 1998, and then began to drop—to 55.2 percent in 2000, to 54.6 percent in 2002, to 53.7 percent in 2003. Statistics just released showed further decline to 52.9 percent in 2004. Even the percentage of working mothers with children

who were not infants declined between 2000 and 2003, from 62.8 percent to 59.8 percent.

10      Although college-educated women work more than others, the 2002 census shows that graduate or professional degrees do not increase work-force participation much more than even one year of college. When their children are infants (under a year), 54 percent of females with graduate or professional degrees are not working full time (18 percent are working part time and 36 percent are not working at all). Even among those who have children who are not infants, 41 percent are not working full time (18 percent are working part time and 23 percent are not working at all).

11      Economists argue about the meaning of the data, even going so far as to contend that more mothers are working. They explain that the bureau changed the definition of "work" slightly in 2000, the economy went into recession, and the falloff in women without children was similar. How-ever, even if there wasn't a falloff but just a leveling off, this represents not a loss of present value but a loss of hope for the future—a loss of hope that the role of women in society will continue to increase.

12      The arguments still do not explain the absence of women in elite workplaces. If these women were sticking it out in the business, law, and academic worlds, now, 30 years after feminism started filling the selective schools with women, the elite workplaces should be proportionately female. They are not. Law schools have been graduating classes around 40-percent female for decades—decades during which both schools and firms experienced enormous growth. And, although the legal population will not be 40-percent female until 2010, in 2003, the major law firms had only 16-percent female partners, according to the American Bar Associa-tion. It's important to note that elite workplaces like law firms grew in size during the very years that the percentage of female graduates was grow-ing, leading you to expect a higher female employment than the pure grad-uation rate would indicate. The Harvard Business School has produced classes around 30-percent female. Yet only 10.6 percent of Wall Street's corporate officers are women, and a mere nine are Fortune 500 CEOs. Harvard Business School's dean, who extolled the virtues of interrupted careers on *60 Minutes*, has a 20-percent female academic faculty.

13      It is possible that the workplace is discriminatory and hostile to fam-ily life. If firms had hired every childless woman lawyer available, that alone would have been enough to raise the percentage of female law part-ners above 16 percent in 30 years. It is also possible that women are vol-untarily taking themselves out of the elite job competition for lower status

and lower-paying jobs. Women must take responsibility for the consequences of their decisions. It defies reason to claim that the falloff from
40 percent of the class at law school to 16 percent of the partners at all the
big law firms is unrelated to half the mothers with graduate and professional degrees leaving full-time work at childbirth and staying away for
several years after that, or possibly bidding down.

14    This isn't only about day care. Half my *Times* brides quit before the
first baby came. In interviews, at least half of them expressed a hope
never to work again. None had realistic plans to work. More importantly,
when they quit, they were already alienated from their work or at least not
committed to a life of work. One, a female MBA, said she could never
figure out why the men at her workplace, which fired her, were so excited
about making deals. "It's only money," she mused. Not surprisingly, even
where employers offered them part-time work, they were not interested in
taking it.

## What is to be done?

15    Here's the feminist moral analysis that choice avoided: The family—with
its repetitious, socially invisible, physical tasks—is a necessary part of
life, but it allows fewer opportunities for full human flourishing than public spheres like the market or the government. This less-flourishing sphere
is not the natural or moral responsibility only of women. Therefore, assigning it to women is unjust. Women assigning it to themselves is equally
unjust. To paraphrase, as Mark Twain said, "A man who chooses not to
read is just as ignorant as a man who cannot read."

16    The critics are right about one thing: Dopey *New York Times* stories
do nothing to change the situation. Dowd, who is many things but not a
political philosopher, concludes by wondering if the situation will change
by 2030. Lefties keep hoping the Republicans will enact child-care legislation, which probably puts us well beyond 2030. In either case, we can't
wait that long. If women's flourishing does matter, feminists must acknowledge that the family is to 2005 what the workplace was to 1964 and
the vote to 1920. Like the right to work and the right to vote, the right to
have a flourishing life that includes but is not limited to family cannot be
addressed with language of choice.

17    Women who want to have sex and children with men as well as good
work in interesting jobs where they may occasionally wield real social
power need guidance, and they need it early. Step one is simply to begin

talking about flourishing. In so doing, feminism will be returning to its early, judgmental roots. This may anger some, but it should sound the alarm before the next generation winds up in the same situation. Next, feminists will have to start offering young women not choices and not **utopian** dreams but solutions they can enact on their own. Prying women out of their traditional roles is not going to be easy. It will require rules—rules like those in the widely derided book *The Rules*, which was never about dating but about behavior modification.

18    There are three rules: Prepare yourself to qualify for good work, treat work seriously, and don't put yourself in a position of unequal resources when you marry.

19    The preparation stage begins with college. It is shocking to think that girls cut off their options for a public life of work as early as college. But they do. The first pitfall is the liberal-arts curriculum, which women are good at, graduating in higher numbers than men. Although many really successful people start out studying liberal arts, the purpose of a liberal education is not, with the exception of a minuscule number of academic positions, job preparation.

20    So the first rule is to use your college education with an eye to career goals. Feminist organizations should produce each year a survey of the most common job opportunities for people with college degrees, along with the average lifetime earnings from each job category and the characteristics such jobs require. The point here is to help women see that yes, you can study art history, but only with the realistic understanding that one day soon you will need to use your arts education to support yourself and your family. The survey would ask young women to select what they are best suited for and give guidance on the appropriate course of study. Like the rule about accepting no dates for Saturday after Wednesday night, the survey would set realistic courses for women, helping would-be curators who are not artistic geniuses avoid career frustration and avoid solving their job problems with marriage.

21    After college comes on-the-job training or further education. Many of my *Times* brides—and grooms—did work when they finished their educations. Here's an anecdote about the difference: One couple, both lawyers, met at a firm. After a few years, the man moved from international business law into international business. The woman quit working altogether. "They told me law school could train you for anything," she told me. "But it doesn't prepare you to go into business. I should have gone to business school." Or rolled over and watched her husband the lawyer using his first

few years of work to prepare to go into a related business. Every *Times* groom assumed he had to succeed in business, and was really trying. By contrast, a common thread among the women I interviewed was a self-important idealism about the kinds of intellectual, prestigious, socially meaningful, politics-free jobs worth their **incalculably** valuable presence. So the second rule is that women must treat the first few years after college as an opportunity to lose their capitalism virginity and prepare for good work, which they will then treat seriously.

22    The best way to treat work seriously is to find the money. Money is the marker of success in a market economy; it usually accompanies power, and it enables the bearer to wield power, including within the family. Almost without exception, the brides who opted out graduated with roughly the same degrees as their husbands. Yet somewhere along the way the women made decisions in the direction of less money. Part of the problem was idealism; idealism on the career trail usually leads to volunteer work, or indentured servitude in social-service jobs, which is nice but doesn't get you to money. Another big mistake involved changing jobs excessively. Without exception, the brides who eventually went home had much more job turnover than the grooms did. There's no such thing as a perfect job. Condoleezza Rice actually wanted to be a pianist, and Gary Graffman didn't want to give concerts.

23    If you are good at work you are in a position to address the third undertaking: the reproductive household. The rule here is to avoid taking on more than a fair share of the second shift. If this seems coldhearted, consider the survey by the Center for Work-Life Policy. Fully 40 percent of highly qualified women with spouses felt that their husbands create more work around the house than they perform. According to Phyllis Moen and Patricia Roehling's *Career Mystique*, "When couples marry, the amount of time that a woman spends doing housework increases by approximately 17 percent, while a man's decreases by 33 percent." Not a single *Times* groom was a stay-at-home dad. Several of them could hardly wait for Monday morning to come. None of my *Times* grooms took even brief paternity leave when his children were born.

24    How to avoid this kind of rut? You can either find a spouse with less social power than you or find one with an **ideological** commitment to gender equality. Taking the easier path first, marry down. Don't think of this as brutally strategic. If you are devoted to your career goals and would like a man who will support that, you're just doing what men throughout the ages have done: placing a safe bet.

25      In her 1995 book, *Kidding Ourselves: Babies, Breadwinning and Bargaining Power,* Rhona Mahoney recommended finding a sharing spouse by marrying younger or poorer, or someone in a dependent status, like a starving artist. Because money is such a marker of status and power, it's hard to persuade women to marry poorer. So here's an easier rule: Marry young or marry much older. Younger men are potential high-status companions. Much older men are sufficiently established so that they don't have to work so hard, and they often have enough money to provide unlimited household help. By contrast, slightly older men with bigger incomes are the most dangerous, but even a pure counterpart is risky. If you both are going through the elite-job hazing rituals simultaneously while having children, someone is going to have to give. Even the most devoted lawyers with the hardest-working nannies are going to have weeks when no one can get home other than to sleep. The odds are that when this happens, the woman is going to give up her ambitions and professional potential.

26      It is possible that marrying a liberal might be the better course. After all, conservatives justified the unequal family in two modes: "God ordained it" and "biology is destiny." Most men (and most women), including the liberals, think women are responsible for the home. But at least the liberal men should feel squeamish about it.

27      If you have carefully positioned yourself either by marrying down or finding someone untainted by gender ideology, you will be in a position to resist bearing an unfair share of the family. Even then you must be vigilant. Bad deals come in two forms: economics and home economics. The economic temptation is to assign the cost of child care to the woman's income. If a woman making $50,000 per year whose husband makes $100,000 decides to have a baby, and the cost of a full-time nanny is $30,000, the couple reason that, after paying 40 percent in taxes, she makes $30,000, just enough to pay the nanny. So she might as well stay home. This totally ignores that both adults are in the enterprise together and the demonstrable future loss of income, power, and security for the woman who quits. Instead, calculate that all parents make a total of $150,000 and take home $90,000. After paying a full-time nanny, they have $60,000 left to live on.

28      If these prescriptions sound less than family-friendly, here's the last rule: Have a baby. Just don't have two. Mothers' Movement Online's Judith Statdman Tucker reports that women who opt out for child-care reasons act only after the second child arrives. A second kid pressures the mother's organizational skills, doubles the demands for appointments,

wildly raises the cost of education and housing, and drives the family to the suburbs. But cities, with their Chinese carryouts and all, are better for working mothers. It is true that if you follow this rule, your society will not reproduce itself. But if things get bad enough, who knows what social consequences will ensue? After all, the **vaunted** French child-care regime was actually only a response to the superior German birth rate.

## Why do we care?

29 The privileged brides of the *Times*—and their husbands—seem happy. Why do we care what they do? After all, most people aren't rich and white and heterosexual, and they couldn't quit working if they wanted to.

30 We care because what they do is bad for them, is certainly bad for society, and is widely imitated, even by people who never get their weddings in the *Times*. This last is called the "regime effect," and it means that even if women don't quit their jobs for their families, they think they should and feel guilty about not doing it. That regime effect created the mystique around "The Feminine Mystique," too.

31 As for society, elites supply the labor for the decision-making classes—the senators, the newspaper editors, the research scientists, the entrepreneurs, the policy-makers, and the policy wonks. If the ruling class is overwhelmingly male, the rulers will make mistakes that benefit males, whether from ignorance or from indifference. Media surveys reveal that if only one member of a television show's creative staff is female, the percentage of women on-screen goes up from 36 percent to 42 percent. A world of 84-percent male lawyers and 84-percent female assistants is a different place than one with women in positions of social authority. Think of a big American city with an 86-percent white police force. If role models don't matter, why care about Sandra Day O'Connor? Even if the falloff from peak numbers is small, the leveling off of women in power is a loss of hope for more change. Will there never again be more than one woman on the Supreme Court?

32 Worse, the behavior tarnishes every female with the knowledge that she is almost never going to be a ruler. Princeton President Shirley Tilghman described the elite colleges' self-image perfectly when she told her freshmen last year that they would be the nation's leaders, and she clearly did not have trophy wives in mind. Why should society spend resources educating women with only a 50-percent return rate on their stated goals? The American Conservative Union carried a column in 2004 recommending that employers stay away from such women or risk going out of

business. Good psychological data show that the more women are treated with respect, the more ambition they have. And vice versa. The opt-out revolution is really a downward spiral.

33  Finally, these choices are bad for women individually. A good life for humans includes the classical standard of using one's capacities for speech and reason in a prudent way, the liberal requirement of having enough autonomy to direct one's own life, and the utilitarian test of doing more good than harm in the world. Measured against these time-tested standards, the expensively educated upper-class moms will be leading lesser lives.

34  When she sounded the blast that revived the feminist movement 40 years after women received the vote, Betty Friedan spoke of lives of purpose and meaning, better lives and worse lives, and feminism went a long way toward shattering the glass ceilings that limited their prospects outside the home. Now the glass ceiling begins at home. Although it is harder to shatter a ceiling that is also the roof over your head, there is no other choice.  ◆

### CONSIDERING THE ISSUES

1.  In your opinion and experience, are women socially pressured to stay at home? Do men want them to stay home once children enter the picture?
2.  What does Hirshman mean by saying that the "real glass ceiling is at home"? What is the "glass ceiling"? Explain.

### CRAFT AND CONTENT

1.  Summarize Hirshman's study of the *New York Times* brides. What did she discover? What conclusions did she draw from the data? Do her conclusions have merit? Does this group of women accurately represent the female body-politic of the United States? Explain.
2.  Evaluate Hirshman's recommendation (three rules) for young women. Do you agree with her plan? Do you think young women will view her plan differently from young men?

### CRITICAL THINKING

1.  Hirshman argues that when women leave the workforce, they not only put their own careers at risk, but jeopardize the economic

and political power of all women who seek to achieve in high-status jobs. Do you agree or disagree with her argument? Does the "conundrum" of "opting out" put all women at risk? Why or why not?

2. One reason Hirshman's article elicited such an angry response was the negative reaction of women who had elected to stay at home to her assertion that one could not "flourish" taking care of a home and children. Respond to her argument with your own viewpoint.

3. Hirshman points out that when women leave the workforce, they willingly give up their power and influence, both to their detriment and to that of generations to follow. What could happen if too many "elite" women "opt out"? Conversely, what does Hirshman imply could happen if enough women "opt in" and work hard at their professional careers?

## WRITING ABOUT THE ISSUES

1. Write an essay exploring the effects of the perception of women as homemakers and mothers in the media. Some of the areas of your exploration might draw from television, film, art, advertising, newspapers, music, and other popular media. How do media representations of women enforce (or refute) the perception of women as mothers and homemakers rather than professionals?

2. Hirshman's essay elicited angry responses from "across the blogosphere." Read a few entries from various blogs addressing the controversy. Write an essay summarizing the controversy and referring to blog entries reacting to Hirshman's article.

# Blog Matters

A blog ("web log") is an online diary or commentary site that features regular entries that describe events, impressions, and viewpoints. Blogs may contain text, images, video, and often link to other websites, blogs, and online media. Most blogs allow readers to comment on the content of the post and to each other. As of 2007, the blog search engine estimated there were over 112 million blogs. While many blogs are maintained by individuals, some are run by journals, newspapers, and other media outlets. Remember that most blogs are not monitored for factual accuracy, and often express the opinion and views of the "blogger" writing the content.

The blog below was written by Jason Lee Miller, a *WebProNews* editor and writer covering business and technology, on April 4, 2007. He explains what the data collected by Yahoo's HotJobs might mean. Are Americans really working too much?

# Yahoo Says Americans Work Too Much

*Jason Lee Miller*
*April 6, 2007*

1   **U**sually, when I go home for the day, I unplug. Unplugging means not even jacked in wirelessly: cell phone is off; computer (if I can help it) is off; laptop is off. The same goes for the weekend; if you want to get a hold of me, it can wait until Monday. Home is home, work is work, and I'm quite strict about their separation.

2   One day, I imagine I'll have to violate my own rules. I've already caved in regard to using a cell phone at all. I have an answering machine. Sometimes I'm not home. Deal with it, I'll call you back. Unfortunately, that plan didn't completely stick. My cell number is the only number some people have. Ho hum.

3   Yahoo HotJobs just released new data showing that around a quarter of survey respondents felt that wireless devices kept them "on a permanent corporate leash" and that they were easily distracted by work-related email and calls during personal time.

4   That's not as many as I thought would feel that way, especially since two-thirds of American respondents said they jack into work even while on vacation. Now, vacation is where I really draw the line. Work doesn't exist on vacation. Period.

5   It turns out most people seem to like the flexibility—but Yahoo worries we might be overdoing it.

6   "Wireless devices have become a professional reality," said vice president of marketing for Yahoo! HotJobs Susan Vobejda, "so it's important for people to set limits on when and how to disengage in order to maintain work-life balance.

7   "With 67 percent of respondents admitting to having used a wireless device to connect with work while on vacation, signs indicate that the American workforce may be facing burnout."

8   Vobejda says all that connectivity has changed the physical parameters of the workplace, and has extended the workday. And she be right about burn out.

9   An American in the 21st Century has to work 25 years to get the same number of paid vacation days that are mandatory minimums in Europe. In

all, American workers put in almost 400 more hours per year than their European counterparts. That's TEN weeks. Well, eight weeks, if we're talking Stateside hours.

10    Wireless connectivity is only increasing the work-a-holism. Twenty-seven percent of respondents admitted being so attached to their wireless device that the only time they're not texting, talking, emailing, or monitoring work is when they're sleeping.

11    Bet the missus doesn't like that much, either. A third said they found it more difficult to get their point across through electronic means than conversation. So next time you tell her you love her and want her, it may be a good idea to use your voice box instead of your inbox.

12    Despite the reservations of the admitted few, most respondents to Yahoo! HotJobs' survey appreciated the flexibility wireless connectivity offered them. Almost half reported they volunteered for virtual work access. Eighty-one percent stay connected with work via mobile phone; 65 percent via laptop; and 19 percent use smartphones.

13    Interestingly, they say the always-on lifestyle they've adopted "enhances" the work-life balance—something I'll take their words for and continue to turn off when I get home:

14    The rest of Yahoo! HotJobs findings:

> The majority (61 percent) agree that wireless devices make them feel like they have more freedom;
>
> Sixty-five percent say wireless devices allow them to work remotely and have a more flexible schedule;
>
> Almost half (48 percent) report that wireless devices allow them to spend more time with family and friends; and
>
> An overwhelming 70 percent agree that they are more productive thanks to a wireless device. ◆

## RESPOND TO THE BLOG

What do you think? Is your work your life? Do we work because we have to, or because we want to? Are we indeed working too hard, as Yahoo suggests, or are we doing what we want? Explain.

# The Most-Praised Generation Goes to Work

*Jeffrey Zaslow*

Jeffrey Zaslow is a senior writer and columnist for the *Wall Street Journal* in which his column, "Moving On," appears in the Personal Journal section. In 2000, he received the Will Rogers Humanitarian Award, given to a newspaper columnist who exemplifies the ideals and public service work of the noted humorist and columnist. He was honored for using his column to run programs that benefited 47,000 disadvantaged Chicago children, and for raising millions of dollars for Chicago charities. Zaslow's writing has appeared in many other newspapers and journals, including *TIME*, and *USA Today*, and he has appeared on *The Tonight Show*, *The Oprah Winfrey Show*, *Larry King Live*, and *The Today Show*. This editorial appeared in the April 20, 2007 edition of the *Wall Street Journal*.

## CONNECTING TO THE TOPIC

Über-stroked kids are reaching adulthood—and now their bosses (and spouses) have to deal with them. As Jeffrey Zaslow explains, the newest generation to enter the workforce is used to praise and encouragement. Older managers, ones who believed in sucking it up and doing your time in order to climb the corporate ladder, are befuddled by this group of twentysomethings who demand more attention and approval. Is it time for this coddled group to realize the world isn't all "Good job!" written on an essay, or should employers realize that in order to attract new talent, they are going to have to bring out the smiley stickers?

## WORDS IN CONTEXT

**calibrating** (22)   measuring (v.)
**moratorium** (27)   ban on; end to proceedings (n.)

1   You, You, You—you really are special, you are! You've got everything going for you. You're attractive, witty, brilliant. "Gifted" is the word that comes to mind.

2    Childhood in recent decades has been defined by such stroking—by parents who see their job as building self-esteem, by soccer coaches who give every player a trophy, by schools that used to name one "student of the month" and these days name 40. Now, as this greatest generation grows up, the culture of praise is reaching deeply into the adult world. Bosses, professors and mates are feeling the need to lavish praise on young adults, particularly twentysomethings, or else see them wither under an unfamiliar compliment deficit.

3    Employers are dishing out kudos to workers for little more than showing up. Corporations including Lands' End and Bank of America are hiring consultants to teach managers how to compliment employees using email, prize packages and public displays of appreciation. The 1,000-employee Scooter Store Inc., a power-wheelchair and scooter firm in New Braunfels, Texas, has a staff "celebrations assistant" whose job it is to throw confetti—25 pounds a week—at employees. She also passes out 100 to 500 celebratory helium balloons a week. The Container Store Inc. estimates that one of its 4,000 employees receives praise every 20 seconds, through such efforts as its "Celebration Voice Mailboxes."

4    Certainly, there are benefits to building confidence and showing attention. But some researchers suggest that inappropriate kudos are turning too many adults into narcissistic praise-junkies. The upshot: A lot of today's young adults feel insecure if they're not regularly complimented.

5    America's praise fixation has economic, labor and social ramifications. Adults who were overpraised as children are apt to be narcissistic at work and in personal relationships, says Jean Twenge, a psychology professor at San Diego State University. Narcissists aren't good at basking in other people's glory, which makes for problematic marriages and work relationships, she says.

6    Her research suggests that young adults today are more self-centered than previous generations. For a multiuniversity study released this year, 16,475 college students took the standardized narcissistic personality inventory, responding to such statements as "I think I am a special person." Students' scores have risen steadily since the test was first offered in 1982. The average college student in 2006 was 30% more narcissistic than the average student in 1982.

## Praise Inflation

7    Employers say the praise culture can help them with job retention, and marriage counselors say couples often benefit by keeping praise a constant part of their interactions. But in the process, people's positive traits can be

exaggerated until the words feel meaningless. "There's a runaway inflation of everyday speech," warns Linda Sapadin, a psychologist in Valley Stream, N.Y. These days, she says, it's an insult unless you describe a pretty girl as "drop-dead gorgeous" or a smart person as "a genius." "And no one wants to be told they live in a nice house," says Dr. Sapadin. "'Nice' was once sufficient. That was a good word. Now it's a put-down." The Gottman Institute, a relationship-research and training firm in Seattle, tells clients that a key to marital happiness is if couples make at least five times as many positive statements to and about each other as negative ones. Meanwhile, products are being marketed to help families make praise a part of their daily routines. For $32.95, families can buy the "You Are Special Today Red Plate," and then select one worthy person each meal to eat off the dish.

8    But many young married people today, who grew up being told regularly that they were special, can end up distrusting compliments from their spouses. Judy Neary, a relationship therapist in Alexandria, Va., says it's common for her clients to say things like: "I tell her she's beautiful all the time, and she doesn't believe it." Ms. Neary suspects: "There's a lot of insecurity, with people wondering, 'Is it really true?'"

9    "Young married people who've been very praised in their childhoods, particularly, need praise to both their child side and their adult side," adds Dolores Walker, a psychotherapist and attorney specializing in divorce mediation in New York.

10    Employers are finding ways to adjust. Sure, there are still plenty of surly managers who offer little or no positive feedback, but many withholders are now joining America's praise parade to hold on to young workers. They're being taught by employee-retention consultants such as Mark Holmes, who encourages employers to give away baseball bats with engravings ("Thanks for a home-run job") or to write notes to employees' kids ("Thanks for letting dad work here. He's terrific!")

11    Bob Nelson, billed as "the Guru of Thank You," counsels 80 to 100 companies a year on praise issues. He has done presentations for managers of companies such as Walt Disney Co. and Hallmark Cards Inc., explaining how different generations have different expectations. As he sees it, those over age 60 tend to like formal awards, presented publicly. But they're more laid back about needing praise, and more apt to say: "Yes, I get recognition every week. It's called a paycheck." Baby boomers, Mr. Nelson finds, often prefer being praised with more self-indulgent treats such as free massages for women and high-tech gadgets for men.

12    Workers under 40, he says, require far more stroking. They often like "trendy, name-brand merchandise" as rewards, but they also want

near-constant feedback. "It's not enough to give praise only when they're exceptional, because for years they've been getting praise just for showing up," he says.

13    Mr. Nelson advises bosses: If a young worker has been chronically late for work and then starts arriving on time, commend him. "You need to recognize improvement. That might seem silly to older generations, but today, you have to do these things to get the performances you want," he says. Casey Priest, marketing vice president for Container Store, agrees. "When you set an expectation and an employee starts to meet it, absolutely praise them for it," she says.

14    Sixty-year-old David Foster, a partner at Washington, D.C., law firm Miller & Chevalier, is making greater efforts to compliment young associates—to tell them they're talented, hard-working and valued. It's not a natural impulse for him. When he was a young lawyer, he says, "If you weren't getting yelled at, you felt like that was praise."

15    But at a retreat a couple of years ago, the firm's 120 lawyers reached an understanding. Younger associates complained that they were frustrated; after working hard on a brief and handing it in, they'd receive no praise. The partners promised to improve "intergenerational communication." Mr. Foster says he feels for younger associates, given their upbringings. "When they're not getting feedback, it makes them very nervous."

## Modern Pressures

16    Some younger lawyers are able to articulate the dynamics behind this. "When we were young, we were motivated by being told we could do anything if we believed in ourselves. So we respond well to positive feedback," explains 34-year-old Karin Crump, president of the 25,000-member Texas Young Lawyers Association.

17    Scott Atwood, president-elect of the Young Lawyers Division of the Florida Bar, argues that the yearning for positive input from superiors is more likely due to heightened pressure to perform in today's demanding firms. "It has created a culture where you have to have instant feedback or you'll fail," he says.

18    In fact, throughout history, younger generations have wanted praise from their elders. As Napoleon said: "A soldier will fight long and hard for a bit of colored ribbon." But when it comes to praise today, "Gen Xers and Gen Yers don't just say they want it. They are also saying they require

it," says Chip Toth, an executive coach based in Denver. How do young workers say they're not getting enough? "They leave," says Mr. Toth.

19    Many companies are proud of their creative praise programs. Since 2004, the 4,100-employee Bronson Healthcare Group in Kalamazoo, Mich., has required all of its managers to write at least 48 thank-you or praise notes to underlings every year.

20    Universal Studios Orlando, with 13,000 employees, has a program in which managers give out "Applause Notes," praising employees for work well done. Universal workers can also give each other peer-to-peer "S.A.Y. It!" cards, which stand for "Someone Appreciates You!" The notes are redeemed for free movie tickets or other gifts.

21    Bank of America has several formal rewards programs for its 200,000 employees, allowing those who receive praise to select from 2,000 gifts. "We also encourage managers to start every meeting with informal recognition," says Kevin Cronin, senior vice president of recognition and rewards. The company strives to be sensitive. When new employees are hired, managers are instructed to get a sense of how they like to be praised. "Some prefer it in public, some like it one-on-one in an office," says Mr. Cronin.

## No More Red Pens

22 Some young adults are consciously **calibrating** their dependence on praise. In New York, Web developer Mia Eaton, 32, admits that she loves being complimented. But she feels like she's living on the border between a twentysomething generation that requires overpraise and a thirtysomething generation that is less addicted to it. She recalls the pre-Paris Hilton, pre-reality-TV era, when people were famous—and applauded—for their achievements, she says. When she tries to explain this to younger colleagues, "they don't get it. I feel like I'm hurting their feelings because they don't understand the difference."

23    Young adults aren't always eager for clear-eyed feedback after getting mostly "atta-boys" and "atta-girls" all their lives, says John Sloop, a professor of rhetorical and cultural studies at Vanderbilt University. Another issue: To win tenure, professors often need to receive positive evaluations from students. So if professors want students to like them, "to a large extent, critical comments [toward students] have to be couched in praise," Prof. Sloop says. He has attended seminars designed to help professors learn techniques of supportive criticism. "We were told to throw away our red pens so we don't intimidate students."

24    At the Wharton School of the University of Pennsylvania, marketing consultant Steve Smolinsky teaches students in their late 20s who've left the corporate world to get M.B.A. degrees. He and his colleagues feel hand-cuffed by the language of self-esteem, he says. "You have to tell students, 'It's not as good as you can do. You're really smart, and can do better.'"

25    Mr. Smolinsky enjoys giving praise when it's warranted, he says, "but there needs to be a flip side. When people are lousy, they need to be told that." He notices that his students often disregard his harsher comments. "They'll say, 'Yeah, well...' I don't believe they really hear it."

26    In the end, ego-stroking may feel good, but it doesn't lead to happiness, says Prof. Twenge, the narcissism researcher, who has written a book titled *Generation Me: Why Today's Young Americans Are More Confident, Assertive, Entitled—and More Miserable than Ever Before.*

27    She would like to declare a **moratorium** on "meaningless, baseless praise," which often starts in nursery school. She is unimpressed with self-esteem preschool ditties, such as the one set to the tune of "Frère Jacques": "I am special/ I am special/ Look at me . . ."

28    For now, companies like the Scooter Store continue handing out the helium balloons. Katie Lynch, 22, is the firm's "celebrations assistant," charged with throwing confetti, filling balloons and showing up at employees' desks to offer high-fives. "They all love it," she says, especially younger workers who "seem to need that pat on the back. They don't want to go unnoticed."

29    Ms. Lynch also has an urge to be praised. At the end of a long, hard day of celebrating others, she says she appreciates when her manager, Burton De La Garza, gives her a high-five or compliments her with a cell-phone text message.

30    "I'll just text her a quick note—'you were phenomenal today,'" says Mr. De La Garza. "She thrives on that. We wanted to find what works for her, because she's completely averse to confetti." ◆

## CONSIDERING THE ISSUES

1. In your opinion, what is the culprit of "the Most-Praised Generation"? In other words, why did parents, schools, and communities of the last few decades decide that they needed to start praising their children more than earlier generations?

2. Who do you agree more with: author Twenge who asserts that there should be a moratorium on "meaningless, baseless praise"

or businesswoman Casey Priest who states, "When you set an expectation and an employee starts to meet it, absolutely praise them for it"?

### CRAFT AND CONTENT

1. Throughout this essay, Zaslow cites more than 20 examples of giving praise. Locate at least 10 ways to show appreciation, according to this article, and state which ones would and would not work best for you.
2. What attention-getting strategy does Zaslow use in his introduction? Did this make you interested in reading this article? Explain. How does the conclusion mirror the introduction?

### CRITICAL THINKING

1. Compare earlier generations with the later generations on how praise is required and received. Be sure to refer to the examples given in Zaslow's article as well as your own experiences.
2. In your opinion, will companies continue to pander to the new generation's need for praise or will the rise of a narcissistic culture cause a backlash?

### WRITING ABOUT THE ISSUES

1. Would you consider yourself narcissistic? Research which traits make up a narcissistic person and write a brief essay showing how your own personality compares or contrasts with that of a typical narcissist.
2. Zaslow states, "A lot of today's young adults feel insecure if they're not regularly complimented." Do you agree or disagree? Make a brainstorming list of other reasons for young adults to feel insecure.

# VISUAL CONNECTIONS

## The Office

### CONNECTING TO THE TOPIC

*The Office* is a television sitcom airing on NBC developed by Greg Daniels. *The Office* is shot in a single-camera setup, without a studio audience or a laugh track, and airs like a documentary. Set in Scranton, Pennsylvania, it portrays the everyday lives of office employees of a fictional paper company, Dunder Mifflin. The humor in *The Office* resonates with many viewers, as the cast represents the different archetypal personalities found in many offices across the country. Since first airing in 2005, the program has won several Golden Globe and Emmy awards.

### CONSIDERING THE ISSUES

1. What are our expectations of work? What sort of place do we hope to work in? What consideration, if any, do we give to our future work environment when choosing a major?
2. Have you watched *The Office?* View the program's website for a description of the program. What accounts for its popularity? What drives the humor in the program? Explain.

### CRITICAL THINKING

1. Who is the man in the photo? What is he doing? How does the picture demonstrate a moment in office life? Explain.
2. How does this photo tap into office clichés? Explain.
3. Watch an episode of *The Office* and summarize its plot. As you view the program, try to identify moments in which it holds up the office/work/life dynamic for ridicule.

# TOPICAL CONNECTIONS

## GROUP PROJECTS

1. Interview friends, family members, and acquaintances who work in corporations and industry about the reasons they work. As a group, develop a list of questions and interview at least five to eight people each about why they work outside the home. Make sure your questions are likely to elicit truthful responses. Prepare a short report on your findings.
2. Thirty years ago, men were expected to earn more than women. Do we still hold such beliefs? Poll your classmates to find out their opinions regarding income status. Do males feel that they should earn more? Would they feel less masculine if their girlfriends or wives earned more than they did? Do females look for higher incomes when they consider a partner? Analyze your results and write an argument that

draws conclusions from your survey and connects the results to feminism in the twenty-first century.

## WEB PROJECTS

1. In his essay, Andrew Curry mentions author Horatio Alger and his works that "glorified the work ethic." Who was Horatio Alger? Look up more information on this nineteenth-century author and the genre that became synonymous with his name. For Alger's heroes, what was the defining principle of work? Explain.

2. Visit the Work to Live Web site (http://www.worktolive.info) and read more about the state of the American workweek. Visit the "World Desk" and view information on the number of vacation days many nations afford workers. Write an essay in which you explore the concept of vacation time and its importance—or nonimportance—to the average American worker.

## FOR FURTHER INQUIRY

1. Watch a movie that explores different aspects of the American dream—*Death of a Salesman*, *The Great Gatsby*, *Wall Street*, *Field of Dreams*, etc. What arguments does the movie put forth about why we work and the connection between work and happiness?

2. Few teenagers have escaped the question "What are you going to do with your life?" from a curious, perhaps even concerned, relative. What they are really asking is what sort of work do you intend to do as an adult. Many people never find the answer. Author Po Bronson has written a book asking this very question, interviewing hundreds of successful and struggling people for their perspective on life, work, and happiness. Visit his website and read some of the testimonials at http://www.pobronson.com under the link "What Should I Do with My Life?" After reading a few excerpts and other material on his web page, write your own essay exploring this question.

# Credits

## Image Credits

Page 57C: 2002 Jeff Parker, Florida Today, and PoliticalCartoons.com; 86: Aram Boghosian; 97: Steve Greenberg, Seattle Post-Intelligencer 1996; 124: The Advertising Archives; 126: The Advertising Archives; 128: The Advertising Archives; 130: The Advertising Archives; 132: Art Director: Raibyn Cabiling, Photographer: Keren Freeman, Athlete: Dustin Dollin, Photo Courtesy Vans; 133: Courtesy www.adbusters.org; 143C: 2005 Larry Wright, The Detroit News, and PoliticalCartoons.com; 151: Melissa Gerr; 169: King Features Syndicate; 179: Frank Micelotta/Getty Images; 183C: 2007 Brian Fairrington and PoliticalCartoons.com; 223: Mike Lester, Rome News Tribune; 256C: 2006 Daryl Cagle, MSNBC, and PoliticalCartoons.com; 257C: 2007 John Cole, The Scranton Times-Tribune, and PoliticalCartoons.com; 267C: 2008 Joe Heller, Green Bay Press Gazette, and PoliticalCartoons.com; 279: Paramount Classics/Courtesy Everett Collection; 301: © 2008 Amanda Byrd/AlaskaStock.com; 307C: 2005 Brian Fairrington and PoliticalCartoons.com; 351C: 2005 Joe Heller, Green Bay Press Gazette, and PoliticalCartoons.com; 387C: 2007 Andy Singer and PoliticalCartoons.com; 422: Chris Haston/© NBC/Courtesy Everett Collection

## Text Credits

Douglas Rushkoff, "A Brand by Any Other Name." The *London Times,* April 30, 2000. Reprinted with permission of the author.

Benjamin Barber, "Black Friday. . . Gray Thursday." Huffingtonpost.com, November 26, 2007. Reprinted by permission.

Damien Cave, "On Sale at Old Navy: Cool Clothes for Identical Zombies!" *Salon,* November 22, 2000. Reprinted by permission.

William Lutz, "With These Words I Can Sell You Anything." *Doublespeak,* HarperCollins, 1989. Reprinted by permission of the author.

Rebecca Sato, "Scientists Find That Low Self-Esteem and Materialism Go Hand in Hand." Dailygalaxy.com, November 13, 2007. Reprinted by permission.

# Index of Authors and Titles